Classic Cult Fiction

CLASSIC CULT FICTION

A Companion to Popular Cult Literature

THOMAS REED WHISSEN

GREENWOOD PRESS
New York • Westport, Connecticut • London

Library of Congress Cataloging-in-Publication Data

Whissen, Thomas R.
Classic cult fiction: a companion to popular cult literature / Thomas Reed Whissen.
p. cm.
Includes bibliographical references and index.
ISBN 0-313-26550-X (alk. paper)
1. Fiction—History and criticism. 2. Romanticism. 3. Popular literature—History and criticism. 4. Authors and readers. 5. Reader-response criticism. I. Title.
PN3340.W48 1992
809.3—dc20 91-25723

British Library Cataloguing in Publication Data is available.

Library of Congress Catalog Card Number: 91-25723
ISBN: 0-313-26550-X

First published in 1992

Greenwood Press, 88 Post Road West, Westport, CT 06881
An imprint of Greenwood Publishing Group, Inc.

Printed in the United States of America

The paper used in this book complies with the Permanent Paper Standard issued by the National Information Standards Organization (Z39.48-1984).

10 9 8 7 6 5 4 3 2 1

Contents

Preface

In his unofficial biography of J. D. Salinger, Ian Hamilton says that *The Catcher in the Rye* is a book that spoke not only *to* him but *for* him. When a book has this kind of effect on a sizable number of readers, then we can say it deserves to be called a "cult book." Although enthusiasm for such books almost never culminates in any sort of formally organized following (like a fan club), it does create a sort of unofficial secret network of readers who, like the admirers of cult films and the followers of cult figures, do everything short of paying dues and wearing badges.

Cult books have been around ever since the novel became a genre in the eighteenth century. In fact, not long before the first cult book was published (*The Sorrows of Young Werther* by Johann Wolfgang von Goethe), cults had already formed around two of the eighteenth century's most intriguing literary frauds, James Macpherson and Thomas Chatterton. Both were first-class forgers whose "works" continued to influence the age long after they were exposed as forgeries.

Macpherson claimed to have discovered in a cave in Scotland some ancient Gaelic poetry, which he ascribed to a poet named Ossian. Before it was discovered that Macpherson had written the poetry himself, the epic poems of Ossian had already had their effect on the undercurrent of Romanticism that was to overwhelm the literary scene at the turn of the century. Actually, the poetry was pretty good, as Goethe himself admitted, and that was reason enough for him not to apologize for its influence on his own early writing. If he regretted anything, it was the youthful excesses he exhibited in *The Sorrows of Young Werther*, published in 1774 when he was only twenty-five. Later in life, the author of the ponderous *Faust* seemed to find *Werther* something of an embarrassment, although this never stopped him from revising it for new editions.

Thomas Chatterton's literary hoax was more in the nature of a prank. He took his own verse and simply altered the spelling to look "lyke thysse"—what he thought Old English looked like—and then palmed the poems off as the works of a fifteenth-century antiquarian by the name of Thomas Rowley. When he was found out, Chatterton committed suicide. Because he was only seventeen, it was his youth rather than his poetry that endeared him to future generations, particularly the Romantics of the next century who called him "that marvellous boy" and considered him a martyr to poetry.

But it is Goethe's *Werther* that is the first real cult book. It has all the elements that have since come to characterize cult literature, and it has them in generous amounts. In fact, it set the standard for judging what constitutes a cult book; most cult books since then can be easily measured against its contents. As time passed, of course, other cult books arose that spoke to new audiences about new concerns, and in the process some components of cult literature became subdued while others became exaggerated, but the common denominator that connects all cult literature is its debt to Romanticism.

Regardless of plot or setting, characters or time periods, symbols or themes, all cult books have elements of romantic hope and longing as well as romantic disillusion and melancholy. They dream of a different, usually better, world—or they warn against the direction they see the world heading. Entertainment, amusement, diversion, distraction—these are not their goals. They expect, they invite, they demand response. For this reason, they usually have few neutral readers. One either rejects them as trivial or boring or falls under their spell and becomes a cult follower.

Ever since *Werther*, the Western world has seen the cult book phenomenon occur at regular intervals. Although many of the books are forgotten or neglected today, many have outlasted their cult status to become mainstream classics. And some, like J. D. Salinger's *The Catcher in the Rye*, continue to work their same old magic on new generations of readers. Others, like François-René de Chateaubriand's *René* and Villiers de l'Isle-Adam's *Axel*, are mostly of interest today to literary scholars or aficionados of literary curiosities—*René* for its exotic picture of an America that never was and *Axel* for its outrageous decadence.

Although cult books first appeared in Europe and cult literature continues to be an international phenomenon, its center in this century is clearly located in the United States where, in the first few decades following World War II, the growing number of books that became underground or campus favorites turned the phenomenon of the cult book into a discernible movement. Although this study of cult literature offers a survey of cult classics since Goethe's *Werther*, its emphasis will be on the "golden age" of cult literature, those decades immediately following World War II, especially the prolific sixties.

Between 1945 and 1975, a number of cult books appeared in the United States in rapid succession. Their readers were usually college students who felt that these books had, in some mysterious way, been written exclusively with them in mind. They would become wildly enthusiastic about a current favorite, reading and rereading it, borrowing and lending it, broadcasting their enthusiasm to others, discussing it eagerly among themselves, carrying copies around with them, adopting the attitudes expressed in the book, speaking its language, affecting its pose, proselytizing its message. Gradually the book would catch on—to the surprise of everyone, including the publisher—and become a bestseller. Printing after printing would be exhausted as the word spread and curiosity grew.

People who ordinarily did not read were reading the book. People who told themselves they ought to be reading something else were reading the book. Critics could denounce or ignore the book, and curiosity would only mount. And if, as sometimes happened, the book was condemned—or, better yet, banned—excitement would intensify. Eventually the fever would break and interest decline, until the next cult book came along. These books, books of such intense and immediate appeal, inspired their generation, and to read them today is to gain tremendous insight into an era that continues to intrigue, baffle, even exasperate not only cultural historians but those who were cult followers themselves—not to mention those who merely lived through it and were never quite sure just what was going on.

Separately these books might have no assured place in literary history. Only time will tell. But together they constitute a genre as distinct as the Gothic novel or trench poetry or the theater of the absurd. To label this genre "cult fiction" is to risk confusion with the seamier connotation of "cult" (as well as"occult"), but properly understood, it comes about as close to identifying this rogue species as any label can.

What distinguishes cult literature from other literary genres is primarily that a book acquires cult status on the basis of reader response rather than the author's intention. Whereas an author can deliberately intend to write a novel of mystery or romance or fantasy, no one can set out to write a cult book intentionally. Whether or not the book becomes a cult favorite depends entirely on factors no author can control. The reading public will make what it wants of the book, and if it chooses to ignore a book, there is no way that book can inspire a cult.

By the same token, readers may take to a book that, at first glance, seems an unlikely candidate for cult status, and become so influenced by it that the book gathers the sort of worshipful following that can only be described as a cult. William Goldman, author of numerous bestsellers, including *Soldier in the Rain*, *Marathon Man*, and *Magic*, and award-winning author of the screenplays for these novels as well as the screenplays for *Butch Cassidy and the Sundance Kid* and *All the President's Men*, once remarked that nine-tenths of all the fan mail he receives and most of the questions he gets from strangers are about *The Princess Bride*, the offbeat fairytale he tossed off for his children but which he now calls, to his own surprise, his only cult book.

A cult book first appears within the framework of a conventional genre. Only later does it acquire the label of cult literature. *Stranger in a Strange Land* is a case in point. What started out as merely another title in the overcrowded science-fiction category became so enormously popular in the sixties that it stirred up large numbers of people who clung to its word as gospel and rearranged their lives according to its dictates. Apparently, there was something in this particular work of science fiction that was not in other works of that genre, even works similar in theme and superior in execution. Whatever this something was, it went beyond the routine conventions of the genre to speak to its readers in a voice different enough to convert them to its vision of reality. It is this mysterious difference that a study of cult literature must isolate and analyze if it is to account for this phenomenon.

What the critic must look into first is the climate of the times in which the book appeared and caught on, and that look must take into account not only the sociological, political, and economic environment but especially the cultural environment—the aesthetic, emotional, and intellectual milieu—in short, the *Zeitgeist*, in order to figure out what factors contributed to the ease with which so many minds became spontaneously receptive to particular influences at that particular time. Therefore, an examination of cult literature is much more than an exercise in literary analysis. In fact, the literary insights it provides, probing as they may be, are often incidental to the cultural ones.

Understanding the appeal of a cult book is the most effective way to understand the mentality and behavior of its disciples. In this sense, a cult book becomes a cult book not because of what it really says but because of what its enthusiasts think it says. While to some extent this is true of all fiction, in the case of a cult book the degree of reader involvement is much higher, so high in fact that readers and critics are usually in violent disagreement over the book's message, not to mention its literary merit. Cult readers do an awful lot of "reading into" the books they revere, finding in them whatever they want to find and simply ignoring anything that contradicts their expectations.

Cult books have a mesmerizing effect on their readers, holding them in thrall with a passionate intensity that has much in common with obsessive love. Occasionally this passion escalates into a fatal attraction from which the follower is never entirely able to break away, but in most cases it is more like a fever that raises temperatures for awhile but soon breaks. Since cult literature is largely defined by reader response, much of this study will be devoted to identifying elements in the literature in relation to the responses they stimulate. Varied as the literary qualities of cult books are, they all share certain stock ingredients that trigger stock responses. Regardless of how they are mixed, these ingredients must be present before readers take the books to heart and are prepared to swear by them. Nowhere in literature is the interaction between text and reader so flagrantly symbiotic.

A cult book owes both its immediate appeal and its transiency to the way in which it touches the nerve of its times with uncanny accuracy. As an example, consider a book like Joseph Heller's *Catch–22*, an antiwar novel that spoke to those who felt trapped in an authoritarian culture devoted to war, committed to conquest, where reality was military victory, manhood was tested by battle, and only deeds of heroism were proper accounts of the time. This was the way Heller's readers chose to view American society at that time, and *Catch–22* played this perception against a counterculture steeped in the myths of individuality and passive resistance and the belief that warmongers had seized control and were leading us down the path of destruction. Likewise, Kurt Vonnegut's *Slaughterhouse-Five* was anathema to any who had fought the Germans in World War II, but to the generation of the sixties, Americans, too, had been war criminals, and the firebombing of Dresden was as heinous as the ovens of Auschwitz.

We call such a reaction countercultural because it flies in the face of contemporary cultural practices. In a curious way, however, such a reaction is also reactionary in that it rejects contemporary cultural practices as a violation of the tradition from which they have strayed. The common heritage once shared by all is now ignored by most. Therefore, any book that honors this heritage, that offers hope for spiritual renewal at a time when other lights have failed, is the book that is truly relevant, the one that is likely to attract a passionate following and achieve cult status.

The foundations of cult fiction as well as its components will be discussed in general terms in the introductory essay that follows. The purpose of the essay is to establish the context within which cult books flourish in order to understand and appreciate a phenomenon that from a distance might seem merely freakish. The explanations of the common components of cult literature will provide a yardstick by which cult fiction can be approached and analyzed on its own terms. The rest of the study is devoted to individual essays on fifty separate cult books arranged alphabetically by title and covering the history of cult fiction since Goethe's *Werther*. Since many of these works have recognized literary and social significance beyond their currency as cult favorites, their interpretations within this special context are not meant either to challenge or reinforce existing criticism. However, looking at them from the perspective of their special status as cult favorites can add significantly to one's appreciation of them both as cultural-historical documents and as privileged works of literature.

This book would not fulfill its purpose if it did not inspire controversy. While some readers will groan at the inclusion of some title or other, other readers are bound to descry the omission of other titles that they feel have been inexcusably omitted. Much to my regret, I had to draw the line somewhere or never finish the book. This means I had to make choices; if there is sufficient hue and cry, there can always be a sequel. Isaac Asimov, Stephen Donaldson, Thomas Disch, and many other excellent science-fiction writers have been omitted partly because they have been so admirably discussed in works devoted exclusively to that genre, a genre that honestly deserves the special attention it has been receiving of late.

Another category that has been virtually neglected is that of mystery fiction. Devotees of Tony Hillerman, P. D. James, Ruth Rendell, and their like must look for them in works devoted largely to that impressive genre. The same must be said about spy novels and thrillers by people like Robert Ludlum, Jack Higgins, Ken Follett, and Richard Forsythe. They have their loyal readers, and there are titles these readers might sincerely designate as cult books. But the truth is that while most of these authors have books that have achieved astonishing commercial success, few of the titles can actually be said to speak both to and for their readers. This is also true of historical fiction or romance fiction or western fiction. Louis L'Amour has an enormous following, but I know of no single title that has become a reader's virtual bible.

However, I *do* include examples of most of these genres in this collection of commentaries on cult fiction. Oakley Hall's *Warlock*, for example, is a classic example of western cult fiction, while Jim Thompson's *The Killer Inside Me* is now recognized as a classic example of detective cult fiction.

There is, of course, also a vast adolescent literature featuring names like Robert Cormier (*The Chocolate War*) and Paula Danziger (*The Cat Ate My Gymsuit*). I have included S. E. Hinton's *The Outsiders* not only because it was a genuine cult book in its own right but also because her other books (*That Was Then, This Is Now; Rumblefish*) have acquired a strong following and because *The Outsiders* is wonderfully representative of the genre: teenagers at odds with the world and themselves, alienated, falsely tough, good but misguided, at the mercy of the adult world but ready to brave all difficulties and assert their independence.

There are undoubtedly many international favorites that some will think I have unjustly neglected, works by such authors as Yukio Mishima, V. S. Naipul, Patrick White, Salman Rushdie, Umberto Eco, Octavio

Paz, or Gabriel García Márquez. But while these writers have world-class reputations and a very respectable following, I have found no evidence of the obsession that characterizes the relationship between a cult reader and a cult book. On the contrary, what I have detected all too often is not obsession but affectation on the part of marginal intellectuals who would sooner display than actually read whichever book the literary establishment has decreed shall grace the cocktail tables this season. At the other end are those multivolume chronicles that avid readers buy and devour hot off the press, such as the V. C. Andrews series about children confined in an attic for years and years, or the Jean Auel series about life during the ice age. Although elements of cult fiction do find their way into these stories, the whole appeal seems to lie almost exclusively in the realm of what we traditionally call "escape literature."

A cult book, then, does not necessarily have to be a bestseller. In fact, many cult books have small but special audiences and are relatively unknown outside a narrow circle for either cultural or linguistic reasons. For example, a book such as Roch Carrier's French-Canadian antiwar novel *La Guerre, Yes Sir!* speaks primarily to the French-Canadians of rural Quebec from whose perspective even World War II seems remote and ridiculous, even though the novel's pacifist sentiments have universal appeal. And Peter Seeberg's Danish existentialist novel *The Imposter,* while its themes are modern and universal, had to await translation into other languages before its cult status in Denmark could be properly appreciated. While both novels were cult favorites within their narrow circles, neither has yet achieved wide enough recognition to warrant inclusion in this study.

The word "cult" is used quite freely these days to identify anything that is offbeat and kind of quirky, usually something that is not commercially successful but has a devoted following. Sometimes it appears as an advertising buzzword, as in the book jacket blurb that boasted "sure to be a cult classic"—which sounds more like wishful thinking than the self-fulfilling prophecy the promoters were hoping for. I have tried not to be taken in by this casual usage, although at times I have found it difficult to resist, as in the case of offbeat titles like *Warlock* or *The Killer Inside Me.*

The "top fifty" books that finally did find their way into this study include titles that are likely to amuse, amaze, even anger some readers. And the treatment of some of them is likely to have a similar effect. I cannot imagine it otherwise, for a cult book would not be a cult book if it did not stir the emotions. However, I would hope that readers of this book might venture beyond their particular cult favorites to explore titles they have either overlooked or avoided.

Meanwhile, I am looking forward to books yet unwritten that will speak not just *to* new readers but *for* them.

Acknowledgments

Lest I seem a wretched ingrate, let me state up front my indebtedness to a few very special people who have helped me produce this book. Above all, I must acknowledge the truly generous, truly selfless, truly gifted assistance of my wife, Anni, who painstakingly edited, critiqued, and proofread the manuscript of this book in all its many drafts. I wish also to thank Margaret Roach, Wright State University research librarian *extraordinaire,* not only for her immense help on this particular project but for twenty-five years of invaluable assistance tackling every kind of research problem. I would also like to thank Greenwood editor Marilyn Brownstein for her moral support. She is the editor I always hoped for. With these three ladies as my muses, how much luckier could I get?

Introduction

In 1873 Walter Pater, a self-effacing Oxford don, published a treatise on fifteenth-century Italy titled *Studies in the History of the Renaissance.* To his surprise and eventual chagrin, the conclusion to this book became something of a cult favorite primarily because it encouraged its readers to cultivate experience for its own sake, to live life as a series of sensations. "To burn always with this hard, gemlike flame, to maintain this ecstasy, is success in life," Pater said, and soon his devoted readers were in hot pursuit of thrills—or *frissons,* as they preferred to call them. "I would go to the stake for a sensation," said Oscar Wilde, the most celebrated of the book's admirers.

Such hysterical response prompted Pater to delete the entire conclusion from later editions of the book. However, the preface remained untouched, and it is here that Pater comments on intellectual alienation in a way that is peculiarly appropriate to a study not only of cults but of literary cults in particular. "There come . . . from time to time, eras of more favorable conditions, in which the thoughts of men draw nearer together than is their wont, and the many interests of the intellectual world combine in one complete type of general culture. . . . Here, artists and philosophers and those whom the action of the world has elevated and made keen do not live in isolation, but breathe a common air, and catch light and heat from each other's thoughts. There is a spirit of general elevation and enlightenment in which all alike communicate" (262–63).

Breathing a common air, catching light and heat from each other's thoughts, sharing a spirit of general elevation and enlightenment in which all alike communicate—this is the essence of the cult fiction experience.

THE FOUNDATIONS OF CULT FICTION

Cult fiction is a natural outgrowth of Romanticism, that revolutionary movement in art and thought that dethroned reason and objectivity in favor of emotion and intuition. Romanticism erupted first in Germany in the late eighteenth century, fueled by the philosophy of Emmanuel Kant, whose *Critique of Pure Reason* (1781) argued that the senses, not reason, were the conduit to the understanding of the essence of experience.

However, already in 1774, seven years before the publication of Kant's landmark treatise, young Johann Wolfgang von Goethe, the man who was to become the Shakespeare of Germany, had laid bare his heart in a highly emotional little book called *The Sorrows of Young Werther*. Never before in Western literature had a work of fiction inflamed an audience in quite the way this book did. Its effect on its readers was so extraordinary that the book defied categorization.

To describe *Werther* as a tale of unrequited love, overflowing with anguish and heartache and tragedy fails to distinguish it from countless similar books, none of which had the effect of visibly altering the behavior of their readers, of becoming the book by which their readers ordered their lives, of actually tempting their readers to commit suicide. An alarming number of *Werther* enthusiasts did just that. And not just in Germany, or even Europe. Indeed, the *Werther* cult spread all the way to China, where Werther dolls dressed in yellow coats and blue pants became a fad. Even Napoleon became a cult follower. It is said that he read the novel half a dozen times and even carried it into battle with him.

Cult fiction also owes a debt to the political revolutions that were taking place at the same time in France and the United States. These revolutions liberated the spirit as well as the body from bondage—whether real or imaginary—and ushered in an age of democratic idealism with all the promises and penalties that go with the dream of absolute freedom. The promises are of unlimited opportunities to pursue all possibilities, to try anything in the hope of reaching some ultimate joy or awareness. The penalties are the heartaches, the frustrations, the disappointments that are bound to accompany the relentless exploration of possibilities. What this means for cult fiction is that readers are eager for books that speak to their innermost concerns but worry that there is only so much time available to find the Right Book, especially when the next one just might be more "right" than the last one. Thus, avid cult readers tend to behave like gamblers who are sure their luck will change with the next deal.

Cult fiction was also influenced by a growing interest in the metaphysics of mythology. Instead of seeing myths as either religious fairy tales or charming little stories, Romantics were beginning to recognize the spiritual and psychological truths inherent in myths and myth-making. Research into folklore and fairy tales flourished throughout the nineteenth century, paving the way for more scholarly approaches to a subject once thought amusing but of little intellectual value.

Particularly noteworthy in the twentieth century have been the contributions made by such works as Carl Jung's *Psychology of the Unconscious*, Sir James Frazer's *The Golden Bough*, and Joseph Campbell's *Hero With a Thousand Faces* and *The Power of Myth*. The recognition of the psychological truth of myth and its influence on art and the subconscious raised the possibility of creating new myths for a new age, especially an age in which belief in absolute truths had given way to the more common assumption that everything is relative. It is not surprising, then, that in an age of what one commentator has called the "ephemeral verities," some cult books reinvent reality (i.e., reconstruct its features to conform to a preconceived idea) as a challenge to accepted patterns of thought and behavior.

Meanwhile, this Romantic energy has driven seekers every which way in their search for truth. Resistance to consensus has made their quests solitary and frequently frustrating. Asserting their individual claims has often trapped them in dizzying contradictions and costly ironies. They have been forced to share the beauty of the struggle with the bitterness of defeat. Insistence on the loneliness of the pursuit denies them the benefit of each other's experiences, not to mention each other's company, something they crave the more they deny it.

Cult books resolve this conflict between the solitary and the shared experience by speaking privately in a public voice, by creating the illusion of the fused experience, the illusion in which the reader forms a bond with a seemingly unique book because the book is as personal to the reader as a diary. The book's story becomes the reader's own private experience, even though scores of other readers are experiencing the same illusion. What you have is a number of people assenting individually to a book's "message" and then, when they discover that others feel the same, believing that it is purely a matter of coincidence. They are convinced that they have arrived at this feeling independently, and so their sharing is really a sort of "individual togetherness." If a number of readers just happen to arrive independently at a conclusion, their agreement is labeled coincidence, not conformity.

The truth, of course, is that not all cult followers experience such spontaneous—and simultaneous—initiation. Publicity of some sort or other usually creates a climate of curiosity and acceptance that can dispose readers favorably toward a cult book before they have actually read it. Even so, many will insist that they were skeptical, that no amount of proselytizing could convert them, that their acceptance of the book was strictly their own doing. Some degree of self-delusion accompanies all leaps of faith, and cult fiction would not be "cult" fiction if readers looked too carefully before they leaped.

This longing for the solitary conversion is another Romantic trait. Romantics crave loneliness, yet it is precisely the pressures of loneliness that drive them eventually to seek other minds of similar inclination. As long as the individuals remain convinced that their inclinations are their own, they will see no contradiction between private and collective assent. The fact that a contradiction does, nevertheless, exist but is stubbornly denied is what often gives literary cults their neurotic edge. Just as the hero of a cult book may see irony everywhere but in his own eye, so may gullible readers lack the sense of irony so necessary to see themselves clearly. They want things both ways and will convince themselves, at least for the time being, that they can have things both ways. Failure to have things both ways throws them into despair, and it is the luxury of this despair that is sometimes referred to as Romantic agony. This agony, pleasurable as it is in small doses, is eventually relieved by a process of emotional narcosis in which contradictions merge and opposites exchange meaning. For example, the hero who both loves and loathes himself soon relieves the tension by equating love with loathing. Thus, the pathway to love becomes hate, and salvation lies through destruction.

Democratic idealism is the fulcrum between Romanticism and myth, and as such it allows the cult follower to perform the delicate balancing act between illusion and reality. Life in a democracy is a gamble, and cult fiction flourishes when the risks are high. This explains why cult literature has long found particularly fertile soil in the United States, where it continues to excite what French historian Alexis de Tocqueville referred to a century and a half ago as the "restless spirit of Americans." In addition to the fact that cults arise where the equality of ideas is a political premise, they require even more the virtually unlimited opportunity that America has always been able to offer, especially in those halcyon years following World War II.

It is one thing to believe that all things are possible but quite another for any one person to be able to take advantage of all things. Americans, in their pursuit of happiness, have historically enjoyed the means of pursuing about as many avenues to happiness as they could squeeze into a lifetime. Socially, professionally, religiously, they have taken full advantage of their right to pursue their own destinies. Thus, they have changed jobs and neighborhoods, partners and faiths with astonishing frequency.

A Swedish observer once asked: "What is it that Americans will not try?" And Alexis de Tocqueville noted as far back as the 1840s that "the American has no time to tie himself to anything." Armed with affluence and turned loose in the supermarket of possibilities, Americans have become fickle consumers of the limitless brands of lifestyles available to them. It was inevitable that guidebooks to selectivity would arise and that they, like everything else, would come in a "wide variety of choices." These guidebooks, or cult books, offer a temporary means of coping with the conflict between the unlimited possibilities of the democratic feast and the limited energies of human beings.

People who are restless, ambitious, on the move do not want to be reconciled to some dreary concept of life as stable, as cyclical, as predetermined. When they respond to a cult book, it is because they find in it a scheme of things that breaks the mold, that offers them giddy new dimensions of belief and experience that transport them to realms remote from the tedium that they can now afford to escape. These books offer them either methods of overcoming traditional obstacles or excuses for making irregular detours. Either way they are moving, pursuing, exploring. There is always another avenue open somewhere, and half the fun is in finding it.

Finding "it" is what the American Dream is all about, and the postwar years promised to be the best time ever for finding "it." Jack Kerouac never gave up looking for it, but the question that began to haunt the pursuit and threatened to turn the dream into a nightmare was: What if "it" was not to be found? America had long since learned about the corruption of power, but it had never before encountered the corrupting power of freedom. It was to this new fear that cult fiction spoke, and it is probably because the postwar years were years of such affluent anxiety that cult literature had its golden age. Since that period is recent enough to remember yet distant enough to ensure historical perspective, a closer look at those times and the cult literature they inspired can contribute to a better appreciation of cult literature in general.

The history of America since World War II is the history of the alternate pursuit and abandonment of the American Dream. And that history is written within the pages of the cult books of the times. The banality of the years immediately following the war was oppressive to those too young to welcome the relief from a decade and a half of poverty and war. Instead of adventure and discovery, they were offered security and the suburbs. Rebellion smoldered. Those who dropped out of the system were called "delinquents" and treated as criminals. There was something wrong with the gingerbread world, but no one could quite put a finger on it. Then J. D. Salinger came along and did put a finger on it. Holden Caulfield, the adolescent protagonist of *The Catcher in the Rye,* called the life of the times and everybody who lived it "phony," but he offered no way out other than his own form of passive resistance: turn your back, bite your tongue, and bide your time.

In the fifties, Salinger's phony world gave way to William Golding's unregenerate one in *Lord of the Flies* and then to Jack Kerouac's existential one in *On the Road*. Then came the sixties and the moral ambiguity of Joseph Heller's *Catch–22*, the moral superiority of Hermann Hesse's *Demian* and *Steppenwolf*, the moral revolution of Robert Heinlein's *Stranger in a Strange Land*, and the moral indifference of Arthur Clarke's *2001: A Space Odyssey*. By the end of the sixties, Holden Caulfield's cry in the wilderness had become a howl in the firmament. Holden's dream of brotherhood and human fulfillment had been replaced by Bowman's fantasy of apotheosis and apocalypse.

Such is the gamut of myth that cult literature runs. Myths begin in rebellion and end in submission. Whether they end happily or unhappily, one is reconciled to the inevitable. The curious thing about cult literature is that while it draws so obviously upon myth for its theme and structure, it deliberately refuses to reconcile the reader to logical inevitability. While it may push relentlessly to an inescapable conclusion, it leaves the reader either belligerent or intoxicated. If the hero loses, the reader feels resentful and wants to risk the same loss as a gesture of defiance against injustice. If the hero wins, the reader rejoices in his arrogance and becomes supercilious.

Some cult myths are really anti-myths in that they often argue against acceptance of their own truths, leaving their readers dissatisfied with the way the universe is run. The "catch" of *Catch–22*, the "slaughter" of *Slaughterhouse-Five*, the phoniness of Salinger's New York, the seediness of Nathanael West's Hollywood, these are anti-myths that the authors invent in the hope of having them debunked. Other cult books (*Demian, Stranger in a Strange Land, 2001: A Space Odyssey*) imply that the laws of myth are not immutable and may be broken by those courageous enough to defy them and create their own myths. Either way, their message is denial and rebellion, and therefore, they gather together those who have privately dreamed of a different order in the universe.

Romanticism, democratic idealism, myth—dream, opportunity, truth—these, then, are the cultural components that interact to create the friction that generates cult literature. In addition, certain psychological components must be present, in full or in part, before a book can inspire a cult and qualify for the label of cult fiction. These psychological components include such things as idealization, alienation, ego-reinforcement, suffering, behavior modification, and vulnerability.

A figure must be present in the book with whom readers can identify strongly, a figure whose alienation from society matches the readers' real or imaginary isolation. This figure must be of the sort that permits readers to boost their own egos, to feel superior to those who do not know or care. So engaged must their egos become that they are willing to sacrifice something of themselves in an effort to become more like their ideal or to adopt the attitudes held by their ideal, willing ultimately to surrender to the cult that surrounds this figure. What they gain from this sacrifice is the collective power of the cult over the uninitiated, power which may range from indifference to them to open revolt against them.

Modification of their mental behavior is, of course, necessary if this power is to be wielded, but frequently there is an accompanying modification of physical behavior in terms of clothing, hair styles, and living arrangements. The magnetic core around which these components cluster is a mind-set that can best be described as vulnerable in the sense of being receptive to oversimplified solutions and susceptible to evasions of responsibility that pass for involvements.

THE COMPONENTS OF CULT LITERATURE

Idealization

Psychology defines idealization as overwhelming admiration for another person, admiration so intense that the idealizer wishes to become that other person. Such emulation frequently leads to imitation, the results of which are not necessarily bad. Idealization is not considered abnormal behavior. It can, in fact, be a quite wholesome mental attitude if the person being idealized sets a good example for the idealizer and if the idealization does not become obsessive. Imitation of a positive role model has sustained many people struggling to achieve a goal. Idealization of the heroes of cult literature, however, is usually neurotic, for two reasons: these heroes may behave in ways that are destructive to imitate, and their sexuality may be confused or perverted.

In cult books there seems to be a deliberate shying away from sexual matters, a deliberate preference either for sexlessness or for figures whose sexuality is ambiguous. The only cult figure who glorifies sexuality is Valentine Michael Smith (*Stranger in a Strange Land*), and his case is extraordinary. To begin with, he is a human who was born on Mars into a culture that knew nothing of sexual matters. When Smith is brought to Earth, he is sexually innocent. When at last he does learn about sex, he discovers in it the one thing that had been missing in an otherwise perfect Martian society. To him, sex is the ultimate expression of brotherhood. For people to become what he calls "water brothers," for them to "grok" (i.e., "harmonize perfectly with") one another, they must know each other sexually. The sex in *Stranger in a Strange Land* is heterosexual, but there are no limits to its variety, nor is deviant sexuality necessarily prohibited. The emphasis, however, is on sexuality itself, not the form it takes.

Even so, Smith remains a curiously asexual person himself. Perhaps it has something to do with his original innocence, which seems to cling to him even after he has discovered and exalted sexuality. His sexuality is unlike that of any other male character in the book, especially after he assumes leadership of a religious group and takes on more and more the appearance of a god. Smith is described in terms of androgynous beauty. He is slim and fair and smooth-skinned, well-built but not muscular, good-looking but not pretty. Both men and women find him attractive, and he gets along with both equally well.

Idealization is an even more potent ingredient in Hermann Hesse's *Demian,* the only book to enjoy two lives as a cult classic, first in Europe in the early twenties, then in America in the late sixties. The title character, Max Demian, is youthful beauty incarnate. The book's narrator, Emil Sinclair, admires Demian's face so much that he tries to paint it, even though he is not an artist. And in one scene he sees Demian barechested and is struck by Demian's fine build and smooth skin. Sinclair's idealization of Demian is never overtly sexual, although neither boy's sexual orientation is ever really clear. Rumors circulate about Demian's sexual conquests, but there is no evidence to support such rumors, and Sinclair's behavior, no matter how debauched, never violates his own ideal of celibacy. Hesse never really tells us anything directly about Demian's sexual life, but the implication is that there was none—that Demian was above all that. It is obvious from Sinclair's behavior that Sinclair does not think about Demian's sexuality and that his own is confined to the search for the ideal woman—a Beatrice on whom he wishes only to lavish spiritual adoration. Sinclair consigns sexual longing to the dark side of life and deplores the way in which his own body seems to work against his idealism.

Both Demian and Sinclair seem to find some sort of sublimation in Demian's mother, Eva. Rumors have even circulated about Demian and his mother, but since these rumors are presented as town gossip, they serve rather to expose the vulgar minds of the inferior mob who cannot possibly understand the paradox of passionate chastity. Still and all, Frau Eva does hold out the promise of sexual favors to those who are ultimately initiated into her select group. Although nothing happens between her and Sinclair in the story, the likelihood that something might happen is expressed in the parting kiss Demian bestows on Sinclair as a gift from his mother.

Cult followers of Demian seemed to find in him the expression of their own disdain for purely physical matters. These followers, often notoriously promiscuous themselves, seemed to share Sinclair's disgust with the purely physical. It was an appetite they would rather not know, but knowing it, they could not help surrendering to it. The more they detested the surrender, the more they idealized Demian. However, had Demian really been asexual, their response might have been less indulgent. As it was, they found something in the relationship between Demian and Sinclair. The two were not just mentor-disciple, they were blood brothers in that way Hesse had of intensifying the myth of male friendship.

Hesse exalts the mysteries of male friendship in many of his books but never in an overtly physical way. Although his male characters have physical appetites, they transcend them when they are together, and their interaction remains almost exclusively on a spiritual plane. One has only to think of Demian, the "high priest" of Abraxas, whose only physical contact with Emil Sinclair is the enigmatic kiss he places on Sinclair's lips in the field hospital at the end of the novel. Similarly high-minded relationships exist between male figures in *Narcissus and Goldmund, Peter Camenzind,* and even in *The Glass-Bead Game.*

The idealization of the androgynous represents a desire to return to a presexual, pure state of existence. In Greek mythology, the myth of the androgynous goes back at least as far as the legendary Tiresias, the blind prophet of Greek drama who lived for many years in the body of a woman. It has been suggested that the myth of the androgynous underlies the story of Adam and Eve. If Eve was made from Adam's rib, then Adam was once part female, and Eve, in being made from Adam, is partly male. Possibly as part of the punishment for disobedience, the original androgynous being then became two separate beings, one male and one female, with each retaining the memory of that perfect state and the wish, so the story goes, to return to it. Thus, it is postulated that the history of mankind has been the steady evolution of human beings toward that return, and continuing efforts to eliminate sexual stereotypes, to abolish sex discrimination, and to promote unisex fashions in clothing and hair could be seen as efforts to fulfill that prophecy.

Alienation

In most cult books one is likely to encounter at least one lonely figure living in self-imposed solitary confinement of either a psychological, emotional, spiritual, or intellectual sort—alone, aloof, apart; in a word, alienated. Of all the appeals of cult literature, alienation is the only one in which writer and reader truly meet, for there can be no misreading of the author's presentation of his main character. From Werther to Des Esseintes to Howard Roark, the hallmark of the cult hero has been his detachment from the world, his rejection of and by society, his self-consciousness, his alienation. Readers who succumb to the cult do so because they identify with this alienated hero.

There is a paradox inherent in the popular use of the word "alienated," especially in the way it used to be used to describe whole groups, as in the "alienated youth" of the sixties. When masses of people can be classified as alienated, the sense of aloneness usually associated with the word no longer seems to apply. Cult books help followers come to terms with this paradox by assuring them that they are essentially alone even though there are others who share their feelings. The fact that Holden Caulfield speaks for a lot of readers when he describes people as "phony" does not conflict with their conviction that he speaks for them individually. As long as cult followers feel they have arrived at a conclusion on their own, it does not matter to them how many others share that conclusion.

Cult books appeal to people who feel somehow cut off, socially disenfranchised, deprived of their rightful place in the community of man. Much as they may lament this condition publicly, many secretly prefer alienation, taking curious comfort in the knowledge that they are not alone in their loneliness. Cult fiction thrives on this paradox. The cult itself becomes the protective group to which individuals who feel alienated can belong, but since belonging does not necessarily mean interacting, they can have the best of both worlds.

It is not surprising that the first and probably most famous cult book of the postwar period was Salinger's *The Catcher in the Rye,* featuring one of modern literature's most alienated and most endearing antiheroes, Holden Caulfield. As a tall and gangly, worldly-wise sixteen-year-old with hair already turning gray, a sensitive loner at the mercy of a world full of phonies, Holden Caulfield stood for the forgotten generation that got sandwiched in between Glenn Miller and the Grateful Dead. While their older brothers came home from the war and took over, invading the universities and producing the "baby boomers" who would turn against them in twenty years, teenagers like Holden felt caught in the middle, trapped, voiceless.

The Catcher in the Rye appeared at about the time the word "teenager" was coming into common usage, and hangouts catering to teenagers were springing up across the street from high schools around the country. Holden, with his naive sophistication, appealed to the young who felt left out, ignored, invisible. Superficially cynical, yet deeply compassionate, Holden knows how tacky the world really is and how tragic that truth is. As he wanders around New York, just before Christmas, the city he inhabits reflects his somber mood, for it is not a marshmallow city of bustling shoppers and silver bells but a sinister presence that hovers, wintry and gray, a bleak backdrop to his desperate but defiant isolation.

The harrowing image in *Lord of the Flies* of Ralph, the last civilized human being, fleeing for his life before Jack and his warriors, running toward the beach as the island goes up in flames behind him, is perhaps cult literature's most graphic portrayal of man helpless in a depraved and absurd universe. The false rescue that follows, coupled with Ralph's sense of his own loss of innocence, only isolates him further. He knows something the boys do not yet know and the rescuers never will admit: Evil is not learned or acquired; it is innate and aggressive. While he realizes that he shares this evil side with all mankind, Ralph is nevertheless alienated from those who either deny it or let it blindly rule their lives. He can neither be the friend of ignorance nor the ally of destructive urges.

If most cult heroes affect a certain stature that enables their followers to look up to them, then Dean Moriarty of Kerouac's *On the Road* can only be called the exception that proves the rule. Although he is never cynical or bitter, he is totally insensitive to the feelings of those who admire him. In fact, his insensitivity seems to increase in direct proportion to their admiration. He challenges the rules of love, friendship, and sheer survival in a mood of happy, oblivious rebellion. The inner law that motivates him is never made clear, perhaps because Kerouac, through the adoring eyes of Sal Paradise, idolizes Dean too much to see his feet of clay. Dean's antics may seem irrational and pointless to most people, but to Sal—and by extension, to cult readers—they are divinely inspired.

In Hesse's *Demian*, Max Demian bears the mark of Cain, which for him distinguishes all who wear it from the masses who loathe and fear anyone who is different. This mark not only sets him apart but places him above all those who do not understand that society is sick and dying and ripe for destruction and rebirth. Emil Sinclair, like the cult reader, at first resists this inversion of the Cain myth but soon learns to accept it and rejoice in it. Later, others of the clan of Cain pass through the Demian household, but generally they remain aloof and go their separate ways. Emil and Demian see very little of each other, yet their spirits are so intertwined that Demian can sense when Sinclair needs him, and Sinclair can count on Demian to respond to a telepathic summons. This isolation of the spirit is the alienation of the monk who needs only to know that his soul is in communion with other souls. The bond that unites cult followers is not unlike a form of spiritual communion, since there are, after all, religious overtones in most cult novels.

In *Stranger in a Strange Land*, Valentine Michael Smith, as a Martian, is totally alienated from life on earth. Even when he learns the customs of the planet, he remains essentially alienated by virtue of his incredible mental powers. And when he becomes the leader of his own religious movement, he assumes the roles of teacher and prophet—and ultimately scapegoat. The possibility of the existence of someone so totally different, so wonderfully unique, encourages cult followers to see alienation as a sign of superiority and thus an attitude to be adopted.

2001: A Space Odyssey demonstrates the truth of the axiom "He travels furthest who travels alone." Frank Bowman, the solitary astronaut, sheds all human emotional encumbrances except curiosity as he journeys into space and time and the essence of being. And when he is privileged to see and know and understand all, he returns as a starchild, hovering alone within range of Earth, charged with the power to pull mankind up another rung on the ladder of intellectual ascendancy.

In *The Teachings of Don Juan,* Carlos Castaneda's drug-induced trips through the labyrinths of the mind are journeys as solitary and revealing as those of Frank Bowman. For Castaneda alienation becomes the only path to knowledge, for each man, he learns, must find his "spot," grapple with his "ally," and court his own "weed" on his way to the separate reality that can only be shared by means of special consensus. "Special consensus" is defined as the verification of nonordinary reality through shared perceptions of it. Special consensus might be a synonym for the communion of souls in which perception is shared by many but experienced alone.

Alienation has remained an important concept throughout the last half of the twentieth century partly because it has come to be used to describe the experience of whole groups of people who feel that their rights and their welfare have been either ignored or violated. During this time it has worn many faces: that of the defiant and the merely different, of the repressed and the rejected, of the lame and the lost; of free spirits, lost souls, proud rebels. Sometimes the cry seems shrill and the protest excessive, making one wonder how much of this appetite for alienation is not after all just another version of our eternal impishness, our resistance to conformity of any kind including the law, our wish to be anything but anonymous. To be alienated is to have an identity, to be noticed, to be someone and, in the case of cult literature, to be someone special.

Ego-reinforcement

Cult books stroke the egos of cult readers. This may, in fact, be the first law of cult fiction. A cult book must, above all, serve as the mirror in which the alienated see themselves reflected—and rejoice. To begin with, the reader who idealizes the book's hero will do so because of certain traits the two share (or the reader thinks they share) that enhance the reader's self-image. And if that hero is alienated from the world, rejected, ignored, a victim maybe of jealousy or fear, and has the look of the lost innocent, a reader who feels similarly estranged will step into the role and assume the mantle of the tortured outcast, condemned by virtue of his superiority.

Colin Wilson's *The Outsider* is a perfect example of this appeal to what one might call, accurately if unkindly, the snobbery of the self-appointed elitists of sensitivity. Other good examples would be Ayn Rand's *The Fountainhead* and Heinlein's *Stranger in a Strange Land*. Goethe's Werther, of course, initiated this competition over who is more sensitive or who suffers more acutely, but cult heroes of this century have been just as busy at the game of patting themselves on the back with one hand while beating their breasts with the other. Since they see being an outcast as proof that they are not part of the herd, rejection is ultimately as gratifying as flattery.

Ordinarily when an author's insights take on meaning for us and we think we see through others, we end up also seeing through ourselves, and this sobering discovery results in what might be termed "educated humility." We share the author's understanding of motives, and such understanding reminds us of our common humanity. When this happens, we realize that the reward for both author and reader is ultimately not pride but gratitude. Our self-image has been chastened through self-honesty. A cult book, however, shorts the circuit so that both pride and ego emerge unscathed, even bolstered. Readers who pride themselves on their intelligence easily identify with characters who take pride in theirs, and in this way one ego reinforces another.

Cult readers, for example, will argue that while Holden Caulfield is as phony as everybody else, at least he admits it. His argument is with those who will not own up to their own phoniness. Clearly he is callow and brash and somewhat supercilious, but these shortcomings—if indeed they *are* shortcomings—can be excused because Holden is ultimately accurate in his assessment of the phonies around him. Because they feel superior to the mob, many cult heroes are sorely lacking in civility, neglecting to let the rules of courtesy interfere with the frank expression of their opinions or the uninhibited exhibition of their moods.

Even Werther could be something of a bore with his tedious attention to the barometer of his innermost feelings. In more recent times one could point to Sylvia Plath's preoccupation with her own psychosis in *The Bell Jar*, to D. H. Lawrence's pedantic pornography in *Lady Chatterley's Lover*, to Jack Kerouac's self-centered rambling in *On the Road*, to Carlos Castaneda's multiple volumes recounting in excruciating detail his largely unsuccessful attempts to find that promised land called a separate reality. But tedium is a matter of taste, and cult readers are offended when their favorites are so labeled. Thus, those who are offended by Howard Roark's loftiness in *The Fountainhead* might have no problem at all with Meursault's callousness in *The Stranger*.

Golding's exposure of evil in *Lord of the Flies* came as a consolation to cult readers eager to take a dim view of human nature. Appalled by man's taste for violence, including his own, Golding located the cancer within man's own soul and declared the disease terminal. Cult followers wondered if awareness might not check the spread of the disease but doubted that most people were capable of such awareness. Thus, those who felt they were among the few people capable of appreciating Golding's grim message could look with contemptuous pity upon the unhappy fate of a world destined to destroy itself in spite of all its grand illusions about peace and brotherhood.

On the Road annoys many readers today because time has emphasized the selfishness of Dean Moriarty and his friends. Occasionally criminal, the characters in this book are always patronizing. They use people and places as if they were disposable rather than expendable. They lie and cheat and exploit with total disregard for any feelings but their own. Their incessant movement is the most graphically illustrated ego-trip in cult literature, and with Kerouac riding along as Sal Paradise, we have the most blatant example of an author's unashamed ego-reinforcement. In no other book is one so aware of how dependent self-gratification is on the emotional support of others.

Cult books also reinforce the ego at the expense of others. In them there are no moral absolutes. One is not simply good or wise or loyal; one is better or wiser or more loyal than someone who is bad, ignorant, or disloyal—or who is simply less good, less wise, and less loyal. Everything is relative. In an age of moral relativism, it is not surprising to find this assumption underlying these books. What is interesting is to see the way in which books that preach moral relativism can undermine their own philosophy or become self-fulfilling prophecies. It is when personal worth is based on a relative scale of values that the one-eyed man is crowned king. By the same token, if semi-blindness is the measure of the highest good, then it does not take much to make cult followers feel superior to the blindness all around them.

Thus, in *Stranger in a Strange Land* freedom begets anarchy and individualism degenerates into tyranny. In *Warlock*, bravery and arrogance combine to trigger vigilantism. Dixon in *Lucky Jim* slides from sensitivity into paranoia, and in *Fear and Loathing in Las Vegas*, what begins as eccentricity ends in an orgy of nastiness and mean-spiritedness. *The Fountainhead* makes no apologies for its assertion that self-interest is the first law of survival and of progress.

A cult book perpetuates the view that most people are blind, and it sets about demonstrating this by showing its heroes in conflict with hordes of philistines. However, since we live in an age that distrusts traditional heroes and prefers to debunk them, the heroes of cult literature often appear smug and superior rather than wise and valiant, for they cannot afford to have doubts. In an age of uncertainty, one's heroes must be absolutely sure of themselves. Instead, then, of educated humility, what their followers too often learn is smugness and vanity.

Suffering

Happiness is a fragile vessel easily shattered, but the cup of sorrow is bottomless, and many delight in drinking thereof. If the ordinary vicissitudes of life do not supply enough misery, masochists fill the gap with imaginary slights and veiled insults. Their cheeks are red with rebuke, and their hearts ache with unrequited love. If they fancy themselves as artists, they embrace the loneliness of the gifted and the burden of genius. And if they go unrecognized, then what greater pleasure than the sweet agony of failure itself? If one cannot be a success at anything else, the point is to be a success at suffering.

Ever since the dawn of Romanticism, suffering has been a sign of sensitivity, of deep feeling, of moral superiority. In fact, suffering could be said to be the very theme of many cults books, from *The Sorrows of Young Werther* to *The Catcher in the Rye*. Werther cannot wait to see Lotte married to someone else so that he can mourn his loss, and Holden Caulfield is never more delighted than when he is caught in the clutches of a "phony" or has just detected phoniness where one would least expect it. Holden finds it everywhere, of course, because he is always on the lookout for it and because he *wants* to see it. This is not to say that it is not there, just that his remote sensors are set to detect it where it might otherwise pass unnoticed.

While extreme mental suffering permeates Sylvia Plath's *The Bell Jar*, physical suffering dominates such works as George Orwell's *1984* and Anthony Burgess's *A Clockwork Orange*. The narrator of Carlos Castaneda's *The Teachings of Don Juan* submits to excessive physical discomfort in order to reach (with the help of peyote) a higher level of consciousness, while the teenagers in S. E. Hinton's *The Outsiders* involve themselves in gang wars (rumbles) in a ritual of macho sadomasochism that for them is one of the rites of passage. Hunter Thompson's crazy duo in *Fear and Loathing in Las Vegas* abuse substances, themselves, and their readers, while Jim Thompson, in *The Killer Inside Me*, terrorizes readers by making them psychological accomplices in unspeakable acts. In Robert Pirsig's *Zen and the Art of Motorcycle Maintenance*, the narrator picks at his psychosis like a sore, remembering its pain and enjoying the extreme anguish that always accompanies his excursions into the realms of metaphysical inquiry.

Suffering heroes would not be cult figures if they did not touch a responsive nerve in cult readers. The masochistic reader, of course, is not new to literature. Greek audiences might have preferred to hear about rather than witness violence, but Elizabethan audiences did not leave the theater satisfied until the stage was strewn with bodies. Since the advent of the Gothic horror story in the eighteenth century, fiction from Edgar Allan Poe to Stephen King has pandered to a taste for torture. Stephen King, in fact, said it all when he titled one of his most disquieting books *Misery*. What is different about cult fiction, however, is that the suffering in them is a result of mental and emotional anguish rather than external threats. Although horrible things happen, as in *Lord of the*

Flies or *A Clockwork Orange*, these works do not come under the heading of horror. Even Mary Shelley's *Frankenstein* contains much less actual horror than the movies would lead one to believe. The creature suffers what other cult heroes suffer: rejection, alienation, and loneliness.

Behavior Modification

One of the strong appeals of cult fiction is that it provides its readers with a program for altering the way they look and act. The Werther cult that spread throughout Europe and Asia following the publication of Goethe's *The Sorrows of Young Werther* is only the most notable example of this phenomenon. The calculated artificiality of Des Esseintes's suburban retreat in Joris-Karl Huysmans' infamous handbook of decadence, *Against Nature*, was emulated by Huysmans' contemporaries and has continued to influence bored sophisticates, jaded by excess and tired of the tyranny of the commonplace. During the heyday of decadence, affected young aesthetes agreed with Oscar Wilde, who said that it was the first duty in life to be as artificial as possible.

Except for those who patterned their behavior after the Beats of the late fifties, most cult readers of that decade exhibited little visible influence of the books they were turning into cult favorites. Books like *The Catcher in the Rye* and *Lord of the Flies* had little effect on overt behavior. The mood of rebellion that was to erupt later and make itself visible in dress and action was only smoldering at that time. These books inspired a lot of sneering and cynicism, and there were those who got drunk and angry, but such behavior was hardly distinguishable from routine youthful misbehavior. Holden's red hunting cap, which he wore backwards, never did catch on as a fad, but his desire to head for the woods and live out his days in a commune became the counterculture dream of the sixties. In *On the Road*, Jack Kerouac presented, for the first time, a pattern of behavior that was very much out of the ordinary in the late fifties. His thumb-tripping, pad-crashing, pot-smoking, boozing, mooching, frantically searching young men on the run reflected a lifestyle that continued to be imitated throughout the sixties and into the seventies until its influence became so commonplace as to become virtually invisible.

Valentine Michael Smith's "discovery" of sex as a means to the full realization of brotherhood and understanding is the most apparent contribution *Stranger in a Strange Land* made to behavior modification. Just as Hesse's *Demian* gave some enthusiastic readers permission to explore the darker sides of their nature, Heinlein's book did much to add momentum to the sexual revolution of its day. Heinlein's book condones all varieties of sexual experience as long as the participants are in complete harmony with themselves, each other, and the universe. Such harmony puts one beyond the restrictions imposed on ordinary mortals, and cult followers who believed this felt free to behave according to their own rules. It is easy to see how such thinking could lead to the sort of anarchy that rumbled through the sixties. Modification of behavior according to the lifestyle advocated in *Stranger in a Strange Land* found its most extreme expression in the Charles Manson cult, where sexual license was rampant, regard for law nonexistent, and murder not only condoned but exalted.

Vulnerability

In the cult fiction after World War II, there was a noticeable movement away from explicit social criticism toward criticism by implication. Those who once shook their fists at the world were replaced by those who simply turned their backs. It was the journey from Holden Caulfield's frustrated anger to Frank Bowman's stoic acceptance. In between, of course, there was a lot of sound and fury about social change, but the cult books of the sixties are curiously introverted. By the early seventies, cult followers who were once eager to change the system gave way to those who were content to dream rather than act.

This attitude of benign indifference, amounting almost to a paralysis of the will, ultimately renders a reader vulnerable to the doctrines and dogmas of the cult book in question. At one extreme, vulnerability becomes sheer gullibility, an eagerness to accept blindly and without question what the book is saying—or what the reader *thinks* the book is saying. "I read the book and it changed my life," is the sort of testament this response frequently elicits. A response like this is usually spontaneous and emotional, and all arguments against it only strengthen the believer's resolve. If, for example, a young man just discovering his darker impulses and feeling guilty about them should stumble across Hesse's *Demian*, he might find Max Demian's exaltation of this dark side a seductive way out of a moral dilemma.

At the other end of the spectrum, vulnerability resembles the faith of the converted, an acceptance of a doctrine based on emotion rather than reason. Students of Carl Jung, for example, might subscribe to the doctrine of *Demian* rationally because it illustrates Jungian theories of myths and archetypes. Cult readers, on the other hand, are more likely to succumb to the doctrine emotionally, seeing the myths and archetypes not as representations of ancient wisdom (Jung's "collective unconscious") but as new and exciting alternatives to oppressive Christianity. While authors of cult books cannot be held responsible for the reaction of their readers, some, like Hesse, cannot help betraying a burning desire to manipulate their readers. All writing is manipulation of one sort or another, but the difference between non-cult literature and cult literature is the difference between a fable and a tract.

It is here that author and reader meet in that mysterious alchemy that finally produces the phenomenon of cult fiction. The author supplies a central character who is close to what was once known as a *naïf*, someone a little too good for this world but whose charming innocence tempts us to follow in his path. There is something of the *naïf* in all great religious figures, and there is certainly a great deal of it in every cult hero from Werther and Eugene Gant to Holden Caulfield and Howard Roark, and even to a madman like Lou Ford in Jim Thompson's *The Killer Inside Me*, who becomes the victim of his own helplessness. When vulnerable reader meets vulnerable hero, their identities literally fuse, and a cult reader—and thus a cult book—is born.

Since cult books operate like temporary sedatives, those who search restlessly for the fulfillment that each new cult book promises resemble a machine that is constantly trying to find ways to shut itself off, as if one of its primary functions is to find excuses for not functioning. The mind of the cultist may not cease functioning exactly, but it shifts into neutral and idles. The motor runs, but the gears no longer mesh—until restlessness returns. In this respect, cult readers who move from book to book always hoping for "the answer" are reliving the Don Juan myth, searching fruitlessly for perfection and taking comfort in temporary gratification.

A weakness for causes and a willingness to ally oneself with them, often indiscriminately and irresponsibly, is one of the most puzzling traits cult readers possess. Even though such alignments are mostly cerebral, they do seem to contradict the cult reader's commitment to individuality. Here again, however, it is the paradox of "lonely togetherness" that conceals an innocent hypocrisy. Surrendering to a "higher principle" promises to enhance one's identity, not diminish it, for the immediate reward of surrender is power. There is power as well as safety in numbers, and the power that comes with surrender to a group is the power of sheer numbers. No longer alone, no longer in doubt about your identity, you can share the group's disdain for those who do not belong.

Cult books satisfy a desire for both surrender and power even if they seldom overtly preach it. Again, it is the perception of the reader rather than the intention of the author that determines the intensity of the desire. If a vulnerable reader is looking for an ideal to surrender to, that reader will find it regardless of whatever safeguards against surrender the author might have included in the book. By the same token, a blatant appeal to this desire is likely to have the opposite effect. Books that are too obvious, too shrill, too propagandistic are like those books that cater to depraved tastes and manage only to numb already jaded palates.

A cult book whets the appetite, but the degree of success of such appetite-whetting depends on the chemistry of all the elements of cult literature. The total appeal of cult literature, as we have seen, is cumulative. Thus, surrender and power depend on idealization (for something to surrender to and take power from), on alienation (for pressure to surrender and for the need for power), on ego-reinforcement (for incentive to surrender and for the desire for power), on suffering (for emotional involvement), on behavior modification (for a script by which to enact surrender and achieve power), and on vulnerability (for the psychological predisposition to surrender or to acquire power).

Within the components of cult literature vulnerability provides the emotional context for surrender and for the desire for power, but it also acts as the catalyst that precipitates the process whereby an ordinary book becomes a cult one. By isolating school children on a remote desert island and leaving them on their own, Golding, in *Lord of the Flies*, made vulnerability the means whereby the forces of darkness seized power. As the veneer of civilized behavior cracks, we watch in helpless horror as the children revert to savagery, torturing and killing with remorseless abandon. But this behavior is mere backdrop to the real horror it symbolizes as, one by one, all but three of the children surrender to the charismatic lure of the diabolical Jack.

The rescue by warships at the end of the novel is chillingly ironic because it signals only a hideous delay in the inevitable triumph of the dark forces over the light. Cult readers find the idea that man is basically evil appealing even if that is not exactly Golding's point. The idea that man fights so-called "just" wars with thinly disguised delight reinforces cult readers' skepticism about human nature. Thus, readers find a melancholy pleasure in contemplating a world bent on self-destruction, a world grown weary of its own sophistication and eager to set itself aflame.

Cult fiction is a barometer of our cultural history. By examining cult books and trying to figure out what makes their appeal so strong, we learn something important about the times in which a cult book first appears and about the frustrations and aspirations of the people who swear by it. It is gratifying to realize how many cult books have entered the mainstream of literature and continued to live beyond their times. By the same token, it is curious to note how many cult books, so ardently admired in their day, have become almost unreadable to later audiences. *The Sorrows of Young Werther*, the very first cult book of modern times, is readable today only to scholars of the Romantic movement who understand its excesses and appreciate its quaint charm. The same can be said of *René*, a novel so overwritten that it can only be read today with amusement. Books like *Axel* and *Against Nature* remain literary curiosities. And then there are those counterculture novels that are so much a part of the sixties that future generations are apt to find them totally mystifying: for example, a cryptic book like *Trout Fishing in America*, a dated book like *Been Down So Long It Looks Like Up to Me*, or an outrageous book like *Fear and Loathing in Las Vegas*.

The phenomenon of cult fiction in Western society might strike some as a symptom of cultural disintegration. As faith weakens and doubts increase, we grasp at straws but find nothing that lasts. On the other hand, the persistence of cult fiction could also be viewed as a sign of cultural health. As dogmatic systems of imposed belief and behavior give way to liberal philosophies based on questioning and individual responsibility, cult books are necessary waystations along the road to discovery and enlightenment. Their strength lies not so much in their answers but in the questions they raise or keep alive. And the fact that, in spite of their many differences, they have so much in common can be of immense comfort to those who fear that they send contradictory messages that cancel each other out.

On the contrary, taken as a whole, they tend to reinforce each other, especially in their reliance on myth, in their respect for leaders who are firm but fair, and in their underlying faith in one person's ability to make a difference. For ultimately, although these books are cult favorites, with all that implies, they are read in private, their messages are personal, and their ultimate appeal is to that stubborn individual inside all of us that will not be patronized—at least for long.

CULT CLASSICS

Against Nature (A rebours)

Joris-Karl Huysmans (1884)

Against Nature (also translated as *Against the Grain*) is the story of an effete character who turns to artificial pleasures as an escape from life's monotony. Des Esseintes, the hero, is fastidious, rich, disillusioned and lost in a world composed, "for the most part, of imbeciles and knaves." He feels a great scorn for humanity, and combines many features of Johann Wolfgang von Goethe's Werther (see *The Sorrows of Young Werther*) and François-René de Chateaubriand's René (see *René*). Women he finds boring, stupid, and vain, although he has seduced more than a few of them.

Enervated by a life of debauchery, Des Esseintes retreats to a remote place in the country and organizes his life "against the grain." He sleeps by day, lives by night. His living room is hung with dark draperies; his servants dress like medieval votaries; the paths of his gardens are powdered with coal; his plates are bordered with black; he drinks dark wines from dark cups; he grows monstrous artificial-looking flowers, reads decadent literature, and delights in abnormalities. This continues until his health fails and he has to resume ordinary living. *Against Nature*, a classic of late nineteenth-century "decadent" literature, became a cult favorite to those who found it a bracing antidote to Victorian hypocrisy and repression.

In Oscar Wilde's Faustian novel, *The Picture of Dorian Gray*, the diabolical Lord Henry sends young Dorian a "yellow book" (Wilde never mentions the title, but it is unmistakably *Against Nature*) that Dorian calls the strangest book he has ever read. Wilde describes its effect on Dorian thus: "It seemed to him that in exquisite raiment, and to the delicate sound of flutes, the sins of the world were passing in dumb show before him. Things that he had dimly dreamed of were suddenly made real to him. Things of which he had never dreamed were gradually revealed" (155).

Dorian sees this plotless novel with only one character as a psychological study of a wealthy and dissolute young Parisian nobleman who spends his life trying to escape his own dreadful times by trying to recreate the atmosphere and, thus, the passions of earlier times. He wants to sum up in himself, as he puts it, "the various moods through which the 'world spirit' had ever passed, loving for their mere artificiality those renunciations that men have unwisely called virtue, as much as those natural rebellions that wise men still call sin" (156).

Dorian Gray describes the style of the book as curiously jeweled after the fashion of the finest artists of the French school of *Symbolistes*, a style in which the metaphors are as "monstrous as orchids, and as subtle in color," a style in which mysticism is rendered sensually. "One hardly knew at times," he says, "whether one was reading the spiritual ecstasies of some medieval saint or the morbid confessions of a modern sinner." Ultimately, overcome with fascinated loathing, he calls it a "poisonous book," adding that "the heavy odor of incense seemed to cling about its pages and to trouble the brain." As he reads on, unable to put the book down, "the mere cadence of the sentences, the subtle monotony of their music" induces in his mind "a form of reverie, a malady of dreaming, that [makes] him unconscious of the falling day and creeping shadows" (156).

" 'I thought you would like it,' says Lord Henry.

" 'I didn't say I liked it, Harry. I said it fascinated me. There is a great difference' " (157). It is not uncommon for cult readers to be fascinated by books they really do not like, to resist even as they know they are being drawn in. If any book has the power to offend and seduce simultaneously, it is this one; and it continues to exert this attraction today.

Wilde explains that for years Dorian "could not free himself from the influence of this book. Or perhaps it would be more accurate to say that he never sought to free himself from it." So powerful is its hold over him that he sends to Paris for nine copies of the first edition and has them bound in different colors "so that they might suit his various moods and the changing fancies of a nature over which he seemed, at times, to have almost entirely lost control." Des Esseintes, the effete young man in whose temperament the romantic and scientific are so curiously blended, becomes the person Dorian sees himself becoming. "Indeed, the whole book seemed to him to contain the story of his own life, written before he had lived it" (158).

The effect *Against Nature* has on Dorian Gray is indicative of the powerful hold this novel had on young men throughout Europe from the moment it appeared in France in 1884. Just as *The Sorrows of Young Werther* a century earlier had spoken to the unbridled romanticism of youth straining against the strictures of neoclassicism, *Against Nature* spoke to the jaded romanticism of youth straining against the strictures of oppressive middle-class morality. In fact, Des Esseintes, the enervated hero of *Against Nature,* rebels against romanticism itself, announcing that "nature has had its day" and retreating into a world of almost total artifice.

If Werther is the naive young man, pure of heart and noble of spirit, who dies by his own hand for loss of the unattainable, Des Esseintes is the man of the world, impure of heart and ignoble of spirit, who hangs onto life by a thread after having attained everything he thought he wanted and more. Such supreme disillusionment had a fatal attraction for readers eager to turn their backs on a world as ugly and boring as the syndicated sins it purveyed.

In fact, the overall appeal of *Against Nature,* at least to those who took is as seriously as Dorian Gray did, was its total rejection of anything remotely resembling the normal, the wholesome, the moderate. Its message was to those who were tired of Victorian platitudes about duty and piety and respectability. The call of duty, like the call of nature, was anathema to them. (Des Esseintes is never happier than when his body's digestive system is given over to an artificial system of tubes and pumps.) And whatever value "the importance of being earnest" might once have had was seriously undermined by Oscar Wilde's wickedly funny satire. More so than in any other cult book, *Against Nature* repudiates all accepted norms and commonly held values. But it does so not in the spirit of criminal rejection but in the spirit of intellectual superiority, of monumental disdain for the world's banality expressed in an attitude of sardonic aloofness.

There is never a flicker of doubt in Des Esseintes's mind that he is above the herd. Much of the charm of the book for the ordinary reader is in listening to Des Esseintes speak his opinionated mind about the cultural and social issues of the day and, for that matter, about the intellectual history of the Western world. To the cult reader, these opinions take on the power of truth. When Des Esseintes finds luminaries like Voltaire, Rousseau, and Diderot "remarkable for the number of moralizing inanities and stupid aspirations they contain" (148), the common reader is shocked while the cult reader is thrilled. How liberating it is to a believer to read that Des Esseintes finds Honoré de Balzac too bourgeois or Charles Dickens nerve-wracking; that, instead, he prefers the neurotic nightmares of Edgar Allan Poe or the fevered fantasies of Charles Baudelaire, "sickly books, undermined and inflamed by fever."

Des Esseintes is so much the consummate snob in matters of taste that it is easy to see why he can inspire only extreme loathing or extreme admiration in the book's readers. Diamonds are dismissed as commonplace gems fit only for the fat fingers of butchers' wives, and although he dislikes artificial flowers that "look real," he prefers real flowers that look artificial. And whereas those who spend a lot of money on interior decoration usually want to show off their investment, Des Esseintes goes to great expense to make his bedroom resemble a monk's cell, including using hand-loomed fabrics on the wall that simulate the texture and color of plaster and having expensive carpet worn down to make it look as if a monk had spent a lifetime pacing the floor in solitary prayer and meditation.

Des Esseintes's fondness for using church furniture in secular situations contributed to the vogue for using pews as benches in town house foyers and prieu-dieux as desks in town house nurseries (but not for concealing chamber pots, as Des Esseintes did). Likewise, his preference for solitude encouraged cult readers to adopt an attitude of patronizing aloofness, an attitude reflected not only in Lord Henry Wotton but also in such contemporary fictional personalities as Phileas Fogg in Jules Verne's *Around the World in Eighty Days* and Henry Higgins in George Bernard Shaw's *Pygmalion*, gentlemen who prefer the pleasure of their own company.

Des Esseintes also foreshadows the antiheroes so popular in the twentieth century, particularly the ones who turn their backs on society and go their own way. Des Esseintes, in fact, is a reverse image of the monomythical hero who goes out into the world, fights the dragons, and brings back the message of hope to the masses. When we are first introduced to Des Esseintes, he is just returning from his sojourn into the world, but his encounters have been surrenders to, not victories over, the hedonistic pleasures that some call vice. His retreat into the suburbs is more to repair his body than to regenerate his soul. It is physical exhaustion, not moral disillusionment, that forces Des Esseintes to retire. He hopes that his impotence is temporary, as had previously been the case when he gave what he called a *dîner noir* (black dinner-party) in memory of his lost virility.

The myth that underlies this provocative work is a parody of the quest myth in which the hero searches for everything from a lost father (Telemachus in search of Ulysses) to the Holy Grail (Parsifal). It is a parody because Des Esseintes goes on this quest while never setting foot outside his suburban house, except for one attempt to travel to England, an exception in the story that truly proves the rule. (The atmosphere in the waiting room of the train station is so "English" that he knows the real thing would only be a disappointment, and so he returns home.) In his self-imposed solitary confinement, Des Esseintes searches through art and literature, philosophy and religion, even music for some truth that will make life, if not meaningful, at least bearable. That the end of all this searching is something of a disappointment never bothers cult readers who then move on to the next possible answer. In fact, it is disappointing only if you naively expect a book to *have* the answers.

When Barbey d'Aurevilly, a contemporary of Huysmans, finished reading *Against Nature*, he declared that its author would now have to choose between "the muzzle of a pistol and the foot of the Cross." It is not known what ultimate effect *Against Nature* had on its readers, but while we may speculate on the number who might have reacted as Dorian Gray did in ending his own horrible life, we do know that Oscar Wilde converted to Catholicism shortly before he died and that Huysmans himself became devoutly religious and even, so the story goes, had his eyelids sewn shut near the end of his life to spare him the agony of looking upon the evils of the world.

Cult readers are attracted to carefully detailed worlds that are radically different from the world they inhabit. Huysmans provides such a world in the fastidiously appointed house to which Des Esseintes retreats in a suburb of Paris. Everything from the church stalls where bill collectors are kept waiting, to the organ that dispenses liqueurs, to the jewel-encrusted tortoise that dies of the weight of its costly adornment, is presented with striking verisimilitude. Ultimately, it becomes the fully realized dreamworld of the sensitive soul that pines for solitude and a life of quiet meditation, "far from the madding crowd." That this dream can become a nightmare—as, indeed, it does for Des Esseintes—is conveniently overlooked by cult readers convinced that they can avoid their hero's "mistakes."

Considering the shock value *Against Nature* still has today, it is almost impossible to imagine the impact it had on readers when it appeared at the height of Victorianism. Although the French were much less inhibited than the English, French artists still chafed under the leadership of a bourgeois monarch surrounded by boorish social climbers from the rapidly growing ranks of the middle class. "Citizen-King" Louis-Philippe had nothing of the stamp of royalty about him, and France's repeated attempts to install republicanism only produced equally colorless and narrow-minded leaders. All over Europe mediocrity and hypocrisy were stifling artists and thinkers, anyone with a creative mind and refined sensibilities. Against this tide of mediocrity and hypocrisy Huysmans' voice was a clarion call, for he had the audacity to denounce bad art and bad taste where he saw it and at the same time exalt the senses with perversions that were themselves only parodies of the mockery that middle-class hypocrisy had made of healthy appetites. The combination was irresistible to those who were suffocating in the fetid air of an age that seemed to be stretching into one long endless Victorian Sunday.

Against Nature also revived the flagging importance of the ego. The

Romantics had proclaimed themselves as "unacknowledged legislators of the universe" and been proud to hail the individual spirit as the protector of liberty and equality and all that was good and true and beautiful in the world. But the Victorians had preferred committees to personalities, and by the 1880s had pretty much relegated the individual to the status of eccentric—tolerated but not encouraged. Huysmans did not single-handedly change all that, but he contributed to the temper of the times by exalting the virtue of individual taste versus mass tastelessness and thereby helped to stimulate a renewed respect for aesthetics. That Oscar Wilde could campaign successfully for restraint and purity in art in opposition to the excesses of Victorian gingerbread and clutter can be attributed as much to the influence of Walter Pater as to the iconoclasm of Huysmans, whose books, at least for a significant number of devoted readers, helped topple the purveyors of bad taste.

Henry James called *Against Nature* monstrous and mocked it in "The Author of Beltraffio," while his friend Paul Bourget, a French pioneer of the psychological novel, thought it wonderful. The book quickly became the favorite of the expatriate American artist James McNeill Whistler, who congratulated the author the day after the book came out. Oscar Wilde thought it was the best thing he had seen in years, and such prominent literary figures as George Moore and Arthur Symons joined French poet Paul Valéry in making it their "Bible and bedside book." Symons, in fact, called *Against Nature* "the breviary of the Decadence," and when he later renounced decadence as a "strange and beautiful disease," he also renounced Huysmans. It is an attitude not uncommon among cult readers who, failing to find the answers they want in one cult book, turn on it in anticipation of the next.

Against Nature is still in print and never fails to make a profound impression on all who read it, especially those who are amazed to find a century-old book brimming with the sort of irreverent style moderns always think is exclusively theirs. However, its sheer erudition tends to set it apart from the sort of book that cult readers usually prefer. Ultimately its appeal is to the dandy, not the Bohemian, and cult readers, at least in the last half of this century, tend to fall almost exclusively into the Bohemian camp.

FOR FURTHER READING

Ellmann, Richard, *The Uses of Decadence: Wilde, Yeats, Joyce*. London: Macmillan, 1988.

Lloyd, Christopher. "French Naturalism and the Monstrous: J.-K. Huysmans and *A rebours*." *Durham University Journal*, Durham, England (1988): 111–121.

Whissen, Thomas. *The Devil's Advocates: Decadence in Modern Literature*. Westport, Conn.: Greenwood, 1989.

Ziegler, Robert. "From Body Magic to 'Divine Alchemy': Anality and Sublimation in J.-K. Huysmans." *Orbis Litterarum: International Review of Literary Studies* 44. 4 (1989): 312–326.

Animal Farm

George Orwell
(1945)

Animal Farm is a fable that satirizes the failure of communism, a prophetic book that it took history forty-four years to prove right. Looked at half a century later, the book's attack on the Soviet Union seems clear. At the time, however, and for many years thereafter, the book was read by many as a criticism, not so much of events behind the iron curtain, but of tendencies in Western society to drift toward totalitarianism of any sort. In the backlash against America following World War II, there was a feeling that those who had won the war were beginning to resemble those who had lost, particularly given the repressive atmosphere during the McCarthy era in the early fifties. The premise of the book, that revolutionaries become carbon copies of the rulers they overthrow, was used as a stick to beat ourselves with. Together with *1984*, Orwell had aimed a double-barreled shotgun at "Western imperialism."

Some of this confusion arose because Orwell had a reputation as a liberal socialist. His encounter with the unpleasant side of imperialism as a member of the Indian Imperial Police in Burma and his experiences living among working-class people in Paris turned him toward socialism. His sympathies were deepened by a prolonged visit to a depressed industrial area in England (recorded in *The Road to Wigan Pier*) and by his experiences in Spain during the revolution, where he went as a journalist and ended up joining the International Brigade (recorded in *Homage to Catalonia*). His disenchantment with Soviet communism and with Stalin had already begun in the thirties and was only aggravated by the Soviet Union's duplicity during the early days of World War II. Possibly because he maintained a distinction between Stalinism and Marxism, his readers were not prepared to see *Animal Farm* as a total defection to the capitalist camp. Rather, they saw it as a warning to any socioeconomic system corrupted by power.

Animal Farm is such a classic of its genre that its story tends to get in the way of its message. Under the repressive regime of Farmer Jones, the animals are driven to overthrow him and try to run things themselves. Soon, however, a new hierarchy takes charge, with the cunning, selfish pigs lording it over the more docile and less assertive animals. The high ideals of animal equality and sovereignty proclaimed at the beginning of the revolution are quietly ignored, and the lot of the other animals under the oppressive hoof of the power-hungry pig Napoleon becomes as wretched as it had been under Farmer Jones. The most memorable line from the story is also the book's most bitterly ironic one. When the oppressed remind their new rulers of the promise of equality, they are told that while all are equal, "some are more equal than others."

There is an irony surrounding the reception of *Animal Farm* that would be tragic were it not so predictable. Like Jonathan Swift's *Gulliver's Travels*, it has suffered the fate of the political fable that time has turned into a child's fairy tale. Orwell has often been compared to Swift, and rightly so, but not for the reasons usually attributed. The similarity is less in what the scholars see as two writers of brilliant, incisive, witty, political satire than in the fact that they are both cynics whose works have been frequently misinterpreted and usually read for the "wrong" reasons. Swift's notorious essay "A Modest Proposal" is promoted as a heartfelt plea for aid to the starving when, in reality, it is a wicked exercise in merciless black humor, made all the more delectable by its poker-faced style and by Swift's obvious delight to be living in an age so rich in material for satire. Like contemporary satirists from Mark Russell to Tom Wolfe, he was never happier than when he had something—or preferably somebody—to poke fun at.

In Orwell's case, although most scholars maintain that his target in both *1984* and *Animal Farm* is the excesses of the political left, most "Orwellians" view both novels as attacks on the political right. At least they did when the two books first appeared, for in spite of the Berlin Blockade, the rise of the Eastern bloc, and the cold war, they feared the specter of Senator Joseph McCarthy and saw him as the embodiment of Big Brother. While it was hard not to see that *Animal Farm* was, at least on the surface, a mockery of left-wing socialism, to cult readers the enemy was still right-wing conservatism. To their way of thinking, conservatism stood for elitism and privilege, and these were precisely the evils that Orwell seemed to blame for the reappearance of inequality among the animals once they had taken the farm from its capitalistic owners. The animals would have to be reeducated in order for them all to learn how to cooperate in harmony and equality. In the meantime, as far as avid Orwellians are concerned, there could be no better slogan of fat Western capitalist imperialist pigs than "some are more equal than others."

Orwell was impressed with Charles Dickens and the way Dickens could recreate a child's view of reality. This is exactly the sort of reality Orwell recreates in *Animal Farm,* and its appeal to cult readers is the same as the appeal of *Lord of the Rings, Jonathan Livingston Seagull,* and *Watership Down,* as well as the darker fantasy worlds realized in works such as *The Catcher in the Rye* and *Lord of the Flies,* images of a world where complexities have been simplified. When, for example, in *A Canticle for Leibowitz,* the post-nuclear survivors refer to the nuclear holocaust as "The Simplification," Walter M. Miller, Jr. is doing in jest what these other authors have done in earnest: reducing the world to a place controlled by any one of a number of cynical abstractions (i.e., power, greed, aggressiveness,deceit, ambition) depending on which book you consult.

This is not to say that the authors necessarily intended to be read this way. But what they intended is not always easy to figure out even when you have the author's own word for it. The truth is that the mystery of intentions requires that we not take much stock in guesses about what motivates an artist, when artists themselves, if they are honest, are pretty much in the dark about it. And when their books become cult favorites, it matters still less what the authors might have been up to, even when we can make educated guesses.

In Orwell's case, it is reasonable to assume that *Animal Farm* really is a satire on the history of communism in the Soviet Union since the 1917 revolution. The animals match real-life characters in modern Russian history, and the circumstances are historically accurate. Nevertheless, readers are perverse, none more so than cult readers, and cult readers chose to see the fable as relevant to fascist demagoguery rather than communist misrule. In fairness to all readings, it must be said that if the novel is to survive its life as a political tract and merge with the mainstream of significant literature, it must be able to accommodate disparate but defensible interpretations. Within the larger and quite obvious themes of treachery, greed, and demagoguery, the narrowness of a particular response simply testifies to the novel's ability to have an effect on many different audiences, thus broadening its ultimate impact.

One reason that cult readers preferred to read Orwell as an enemy of the political right is that they were loath to abandon the idea of utopia. *Animal Farm,* like *Brave New World* and *1984,* is also a utopian—or dystopian—novel since it takes as its premise the hypothesis that an overthrow of a bad government will result in the establishment of a good one. Given Orwell's earlier political leaning, cult readers had difficulty imagining that he could abandon them or, worse yet, convert to the enemy camp. Orwell did *not* convert, however (an assumption that conservative readers often mistakenly make). Rather, he did what neither side appreciated: He declared a pox on both houses and denounced extremes on either side. What is more, he managed to go beyond politics to explore the darkness of the human heart, and it was in such apparent cynicism that cult readers could not—and still cannot—join him.

It cannot go unmentioned that there is something irresistible to many readers, not just cult readers, about animals that behave like humans. Probably for the average reader, the attraction is much like that of a cartoon: a chance to laugh at human foibles without directly laughing at human beings. Most animals inspire some sort of sympathy in people that makes their human traits less disagreeable while still being fairly representative. But cult readers go a step farther by not really identifying with any of the animals in *Animal Farm*. They see others represented in the behavior of the animals, while they see themselves as safely outside the farmyard orbit and thus, like the author, capable of appreciating the joke from a comfortable distance. They look upon it all, of course, with an air of sad superiority, wishing it were otherwise but secretly doubting that it will ever change. This, in fact, is the cultists' dilemma: feeling they have the answer to what is wrong with the world while at the same time wondering if anyone will listen. They tend to see themselves as prophets without honor in their own—or any—land.

Animal Farm has survived its popularity as a cult book and even as a children's book to be a reminder as the century ends of an illusion that darkened so much of the century's history.

FOR FURTHER READING

Paden, Frances Freeman. "Narrative Dynamics in *Animal Farm*." *Literature in Performance: A Journal of Literary and Performing Art* (April 1985): 49–55.

Smyer, Richard I. *Animal Farm: Pastoralism and Politics*. Boston: Twayne, 1988.

Solomon, Robert, and Robert Mulvihill, eds. *Ant Farm: An Orwellian Allegory*. In *Reflections on America*, 1984: An Orwell Symposium. Athens, GA: University of Georgia Press, 1986.

Another Roadside Attraction

Tom Robbins
(1971)

No book expresses the post-sixties sensibility better than Tom Robbins's *Another Roadside Attraction*. In the aftermath of the trial of the Chicago Seven, the invasion of Cambodia, and the shootings at Kent State University, the mood of the counterculturists had changed dramatically. Whereas moral indignation had previously inspired bitter satire, a feeling of utter frustration now resulted in absurdism. Lampooning laced with gallows humor became the tone of protest, and Robbins appeared fortuitously to become its leading voice.

To understand Robbins's appeal, one must first understand the shift in the nature of protest itself that took place in the early seventies. While there was still a great deal of bitterness about the war in Vietnam and much dissatisfaction with social and political conditions in the United States, the momentum of dissent slowed considerably after the incident at Kent State. It was almost as if the gunfire in Dallas in 1963 and the gunfire at Kent State in 1970 were parentheses between which the sixties as we remember them occurred. After 1970 the situation looked so utterly hopeless that protesters simply threw up their hands and adopted an attitude of pessimistic contempt leavened with the laughter of despair.

Such a souring of attitude was predictable given the self-centeredness and sense of alienation common to the young at the time. Add to this the natural restlessness of youth and the tendency to oversimplify, and it is easy to understand how quickly young dissidents could lose patience with a system that would not gratify their wishes upon demand. In anger and frustration, the disenchanted turned their backs on the system and retreated into their own world to sulk and sneer. And one good way to sneer was to read Tom Robbins, for Robbins, with deliberate ingenuousness, quite offhandedly said all those things calculated to infuriate parents and thus endear him to their rebellious children.

Another Roadside Attraction is about a band of eccentrics who operate a roadside attraction on Puget Sound, Washington, known as Captain Kendrick's Memorial Hot Dog Wildlife Preserve. The attraction is the brainchild of John Paul Ziller, a man of many curious talents who goes around in feathers and hides in the company of a baboon named Mon Cul. Among other things, Ziller is an artist whose enormous painting of a hot dog graces the roof of the memorial. Others in his company include Amanda, an earth goddess devoted to butterflies, magic, mushrooms, and motorcycles; Plucky Purcell, holy man, crazy man, well versed in both the esoteric and the erotic; and Marx Marvelous, either a mystical skeptic or a skeptical mystic.

The book is a fairly formless series of improbable events richly embroidered with imaginative commentary in Robbins's inimitable voice. The style is highly anecdotal, meaning that the book can be picked up at almost any point and enjoyed—even made sense of—although "making sense of" is not quite Robbins's point. In a pointless world, sense itself no longer makes sense. The only defense against the dread of modern life is to adopt a party mood, thumb your nose at the world, and have fun. The mood in Robbins is similar to the mood in the old Beatles films, a feeling of happy irresponsibility, an embodiment of the sixties injunction to "do your own thing as long as you don't hurt anyone else." It is an attitude that dissipated quickly during the seventies into a menacing "me-first" posture that said the world must not only tolerate but subsidize my pleasures, no matter how destructive to me or to society.

This is what makes Robbins's book seem a little ridiculous today. When Amanda says, "I believe in birth, copulation and death. . . . Today I think I'll copulate" (10), the threat of AIDS did not exist. Back then her remark was daring; today it is merely stupid. As is this one, also from Amanda: "There is no such thing as a weird human being. It's just that some people require more understanding than others" (10). At one point Amanda's father, dismayed by her marijuana breads and her reputation as the Betty Crocker of the underground, asks her what he is to tell their relatives and friends. Amanda replies, "Let them eat cake" (11).

Although he is something of a parody of the monomythical hero, John Paul Ziller does, nevertheless, retain some of the qualities of that sort of figure, and it is this fact that helps account for the appeal of *Another Roadside Attraction* as a cult book. He is described as "a dreamer who entertained exotic visions of himself" in which he saw himself as someone from not only another zone but perhaps even another time. He keeps a sort of psychedelic journal containing entries that would have had strong appeal to the late-blooming flower children of the early seventies. For example: "We breakfast at the All-Night Sanskrit Clinic and Sunshine Post. Phosphorescent toadstools illuminate the musicians. Ghost cookies sparkle with opium. We learn the language of the Dream Wheel" (27).

The antiestablishment paranoia prevalent at the time is clearly part of the reinvented reality of the book and might even be said to underscore its basic myth of the outcast at odds with society. One scene in the book takes place at the Pelican, a gin mill in a small California town that attracts redneck bigots with names like Bubba. Their remedy for the scourge brought on by weirdos full of LSD invading their community is to "get us some ax handles and ball bats and . . . clean house. Put the fear of God in 'em. They're just germs, you know, no more than germs or flies or rats. People that sink to that level ain't fit to live in a country like this. Let's do Uncle Sam a favor and clean out that rat nest" (33).

Enter Plucky Purcell, who proceeds to mouth the received wisdom of the day that the United States is no more a democracy than the Soviet Union is a communist state. He argues that the only difference between the two governments is in the degree of economic totalitarianism each demonstrates. "Economy *über alles,*" ("Economy above all") says Plucky with all the negative meanings that phrase connotes.

This book's central conceit is the outrageously irreverent account of Jesus' second coming, an event that occurs in the last section of the book but which is foreshadowed earlier by occasional allusions to "the Corpse." The episode is in decidedly bad taste, but even its tastelessness is dissipated by its sheer foolishness. Having Moses drop a tablet containing five additional commandments, as happened in *Monte Python's The Meaning of Life,* has a roguish charm to it, and certainly religion can take (and often deserves) some good-natured ribbing, but to bring Christ back as a mummified corpse discovered in the catacombs of the Vatican after an earthquake looks suspiciously like a desperate attempt to outrage, a gimmick calculated more to offend than to amuse.

Plucky Purcell is the character who happens to stumble onto the corpse, which is described as short, with the swarthy complexion of a Greek olive and a nose the size and shape of a buzzard's. Plucky manages to spirit the corpse out of the Vatican and to the studio of a friend of his who specializes in plaster-of-paris pop art sculpture. The friend agrees to disguise the corpse, and the next day it crosses the ocean in the hold of a plane bound for Puget Sound, where it ends up at Captain Kendrick's Memorial Hot Dog Wildlife Preserve.

These heretical hijinks soon turn into metaphysical high comedy as John Paul Ziller, Plucky Purcell, Amanda, and Marx Marvelous debate various ways of dealing with their earthshaking discovery. Plucky is all for displaying the corpse and exposing Catholicism (and thus all of Christianity) as a hoax, while Marx proposes a system of selective blackmail whereby the Pope and certain celebrated world leaders would be pressured into introducing extensive liberal reforms affecting human rights, the environment, peace, and love. Amanda, with her curious mixture of poetry and practicality, suggests a simple, secret burial on a secluded mountainside, arguing that neither exposure nor blackmail would work since most people would probably refuse to accept the death of Christ, and the Church would probably refuse to admit the presence of His corpse.

In the meantime, the FBI is hot on the trail of the corpse, and the agent who comes to spy on the merry pranksters at Ziller's zoo speaks in the voice of the hated establishment: "I can't understand you young people. I mean I just can't understand you. I guess you've just had it too easy, we've spoiled you 'til you're soft and rotten. . . . You never learned to respect authority" (250–51). Amanda holds her own against him, though, speaking with the true voice of a flower child: "In order to be respected, authority has got to be respectable," she says. "The only authority I respect is that one that causes butterflies to fly south in fall and north in springtime" (251).

The idea of rescuing the true meaning of Christ from the corruption of the Church is one of the strongest appeals of this book. It was a common complaint of the time that the Church had lost touch with its roots. Popular musicals of the day like *Jesus Christ Superstar* and *Godspell* were attempts to rediscover the church's original vitality. The true Christ, it was argued, behaved (and looked) a lot like a hippie. The last thing he wanted was to establish a religion, to be responsible for an institution, to be a dreaded authority figure. Plucky insists that he has nothing against Jesus and that he does not think Jesus should be blamed for all the crimes that have been committed in his name. He thinks of him, in fact, as one of the greatest dudes of all time, living what he preached, teaching by example, going all the way without compromise and without hypocrisy. He admires the fact that Jesus was against both authority and private property. "Anybody who opposes authority and property is sweet in my heart. Jesus? Hell, I *love* the cat" (290).

It is the Catholic Church that has perverted Christianity, argues Plucky, but now he sees the Church in a state of crisis, isolated, defenseless, powerless, out of date. Revolt is rampant, he says, on a hundred different fronts from civil rights, war, celibacy, and poverty to repressive dogma, superstitious doctrines, and fascist politics—in short, the whole familiar shopping list of counterculture concerns. He denounces Church and State as twin authorities that have been on a two-thousand-year power trip, calling them "control freaks, reward-and-punishment perverts and power mongers" whose authority would crumble if the hoax of Christianity were exposed. When Marx worries that it would "freak out some people," Plucky says, "The young would go for it. They'd eat it up" (289). And the young, as Marx notes a little later on, "were increasing in number and influence" (308).

In the modern metaphysical supermarket, where each aisle offers a new and more exciting ideology, Robbins's anti-authority, pro-pagan philosophy is a highly attractive commodity. Plucky's arguments against the Church become particularly persuasive when he pits the Church's history of sexual (and thus, most physical and emotional) repression against the image of the Greek god Pan who symbolizes a healthy balance between body and soul.

In a highly imaginative encounter in the desert between an itinerant Tarzan and a fasting Jesus, Jesus comes across as dogmatically uncertain and thus unsympathetic. Tarzan, on the other hand, who sings the praises of Pan as the god who represents the union between nature and culture, between flesh and spirit, says what the young want to hear. In the beginning was not the word but the orgasm, he explains, and there was a balance between the phallus and the womb. Coming in the wake of the sexual revolution of the sixties and well before the plague-stricken eighties, such a pronouncement amounted to a manifesto. Christ warns Tarzan that if you think carnally, then you are carnal, but if you think spiritually, then you are spirit. Tarzan's retort is simple and compelling: "Any law against thinking both ways?" (306).

The dilemma of what to do with the corpse of Christ is resolved when Ziller and Plucky, in the company of the baboon, Mon Cul, spirit the corpse away to Florida and sneak it aboard a helium weather balloon whose mission is to test the effects of solar radiation on living tissue. As the balloon ascends, any creature within it will eventually disappear literally into thin air. This is presumably what happens to John Paul Ziller, to Plucky Purcell, to Mon Cul, and to the corpse of Jesus Christ. With all hope of salvation for mankind gone, the world is thus doomed to the misery of its economically-motivated perversion of life—except, of course, for cult readers, for they are now in possession of a truth by which they can at least save their own lives. Such melancholy awareness of one's own impotent omniscience is but one of the pleasures a cult reader receives from a book like this. "The best lack all conviction," says William Butler Yeats in "The Second Coming," and cult readers enjoy the sense of being privy to secrets that permit them to feel simultaneously superior and powerless.

Amanda has the last word, and what she says hits that precise tone of arrogant humility and unclear simplicity characteristic of all dogmas that are ultimately merely rationalizations for continued self-indulgence. To say that life has no meaning is not to say that it has no value, she says, but to her way of thinking, the ultimate "cop-out" is to say that the universe has meaning but that mere mortals are incapable of understanding it. "Mystery is part of nature's style, that's all," she says.

"It's the infinite Goof. It's meaning that is of no meaning. That paradox is the key to the meaning of meaning. To look for meaning—or the lack of it—in things is a game played by beings of limited consciousness. Behind everything in life is a process that is *beyond* meaning. Not beyond understanding, mind you, but beyond meaning" (335).

Tom Robbins is a dazzling stylist with a message that would have been labeled, at the time this book came out, "mind blowing." For this reason alone, *Another Roadside Attraction* cannot be as easily dismissed as some cult books. By the same token, because it is so much a product of its times, and thus curiously dated, it now seems destined to take its place alongside other cult books of the period as merely "another roadside attraction."

FOR FURTHER READING

Siegel, Mark. "The Meaning of Meaning in the Novels of Tom Robbins." *Mosaic: A Journal for the Interdisciplinary Study of Literature* (Summer 1981): 119–31.

Wheeler, Elizabeth Patricia. "The Frontier Sensibility in Novels of Jack Kerouac, Richard Brautigan and Tom Robbins." *DAI* (October 1985): 985A.

Axel

Philippe Auguste Villiers de l'Isle-Adam
(1890)

What Joris-Karl Huysmans' *Against Nature* was to the decadents of the late nineteenth century, *Axel* was to the symbolists of the same period. And just as Johann Wolfgang von Goethe's *The Sorrows of Young Werther* had expressed the yearnings and frustrations of the Romantics a century earlier, *Axel* inspired a wildly enthusiastic cult of youthful followers who found in it a welcome antidote to the dreariness of Naturalism, a cynical new movement that saw man as a helpless pawn of nature, chance, and an indifferent God.

Several things conspired to turn *Axel* into a cult classic. A year or two before its publication, Villiers de l'Isle-Adam's name had appeared in *Against Nature* as one of Des Esseintes' favorite decadent writers. The specific book mentioned was *Les Contes cruels*, a book that had appeared just a year before *Against Nature* itself and about which Huysmans said that its "poignant irony enraptured Des Esseintes." Villiers de l'Isle-Adam's popularity with the young increased as more of his works appeared in rapid succession, including *Nouveaux Contes cruels* in 1889. In the meantime, *Axel* was being published in five parts in the review *Jeune France* (1885–86). At the time of his death in 1889, Villiers de l'Isle-Adam was in the process of correcting the proofs of *Axel*, which he had restructured into four parts and which was published in a single volume in 1890. Villiers de l'Isle-Adam was fifty-one when he died, and although that was not exactly young in romantic or decadent terms, his death occurred at a critical point in his life when it seemed as if he had been snatched away at the very pinnacle of success and thus died prematurely. Today wags would say, as they did about the untimely death of Elvis Presley, "Great career move."

Villiers de l'Isle-Adam's philosophical attitude was also in tune with the times. The French called *Axel* a bible of symbolism and a "true summa of mystical idealism," while the Germans gave it their inimitable stamp of approval by calling it the only true example of a French *Weltanschauungstragödie* (ideological tragedy) in the nineteenth century. Jacques Guicharnaud, in the afterword to his 1970 translation, calls it "a summa not only of the trends of thinking of an entire period but of a series of personal inner experiences. For towering over this proud and lofty work, marked by renunciation and the blackest of pessimisms, is the profile of its aristocratic author, desperately in search of the absolute" (192). What appealed to cult readers above all else was Villiers de l'Isle-Adam's disgust with the degradation of man in modern society. The attitude sounds commonplace today, but in the early days of the "age of progress," attitudes that questioned the virtues of mechanization, utilitarianism, industrialization, or any other contribution to the "greatest good for the greatest number" were met with profound disapproval from the firmly entrenched middle-class. Artists, however, felt that their sensibilities had been bludgeoned by the legacy of the factory and the smokestack and that matters of taste, beauty, and culture were being progressively devalued. Worst of all, there was no place for them in this world. They felt left out.

The best way for modern audiences to understand the appeal of *Axel* is to take a close look at what actually goes on in the story. Absurd as much of it now seems, it is still possible here, as with *Werther*, to get a feeling for what it was that captured the imagination of a bygone age.

Count Axel of Auersburg is a young man of astonishing beauty with a pale, translucent complexion and a pensive, somewhat mysterious demeanor. He inhabits an ancient, isolated old castle deep in the Black Forest where, in a setting half-Gothic, half-Wagnerian, he is devoting himself to the study of the hermetic philosophy of the alchemists and is being tutored by a Rosicrucian to receive the sacred solution to the ultimate mysteries of existence. But the castle has secrets of its own. At the time when Napoleon's armies were laying siege to Frankfurt, the people from the surrounding area brought in gold, jewels, and other valuables to be deposited in the Frankfurt National Bank. For safer keeping, it was decided to send the entire treasure, under an escort headed by Axel's father, to a secret place, but certain corrupt government officials had plotted to murder the Count, steal the treasure, and blame the whole thing on the French. Before succumbing to this treachery, however, the Count had an opportunity to bury the treasure deep in the underground recesses of his vast estate. Only his wife knew where the treasure was hidden, but she died before she had a chance to divulge the secret.

During the winter when the drama opens, Axel's cousin, Commander

Kaspar, has come to the castle and got wind of the treasure. The Commander is an insufferable vulgarian who is given to exclaiming, "I am *real life*!" Axel's life of pure reflection and imagination seems morbid and pointless to him, and so he tries to tempt his cousin away by telling him of the glories of the court and the pleasures of amorous conquest. But the stalwart young Count brushes these suggestions politely aside. When, however, the Commander happens to mention the treasure and urges Axel to try to recover it, Axel calls for swords to be brought and challenges the Commander to a duel. Before running his cousin through, however, Axel takes time out to express his contempt for the Commander's mockery of the concepts of honor and pleasure, and boasts of the loyal forces he can call to his defense and of the impregnable defenses that surround his castle.

In the meantime, Sara, a young French noblewoman who has been put in the convent, discovers the secret of the whereabouts of the treasure in a Book of Hours that had been bequeathed to the convent by Axel's mother. Just as she is about to be forced to take the veil, Sara escapes from the convent and makes her way to Axel's castle, where Axel offers her lodging for the night. During the night, when she thinks everybody is asleep, Sara steals down to the family tombs in the crypt below the castle. Following the instructions in the Book of Hours, she locates a certain heraldic death's-head and, with the point of a dagger, presses a button between its eyes. Instantly, a panel slides away and the treasure comes cascading forth in a mountain of gold, pearls, and diamonds. Suddenly she is aware that Axel is watching her, and before he knows what is happening, she draws two pistols of steel from the folds of her cloak and fires them at him one after the other. Fortunately for him, the wounds are slight, and he is able to seize her wrists and pry loose the dagger before she can use it against him. In the midst of the struggle, Axel suddenly realizes how beautiful she is, and Sara realizes how handsome he is, and in a moment they have fallen in love.

Sara turns out to be a Rosicrucian, too. In fact, her escape from the convent has been heralded by the blooming of the mystic rose. She and Axel embrace passionately, rejoicing in the unexpected bliss of having found, at last, objects worthy of their passion. Sara asks Axel dreamily if he would travel with her to distant lands where caravans "pass in the shade of the palm trees of Cashmir or Mysore" or to Bengal "to choose in the bazaars roses, stuffs, and Armenian maidens as white as the ermine's skin." She rhapsodizes about sailing to Ceylon "with its white elephants carrying vermilion towers, with its fiery macaws in the trees and with its dwellings all drenched in sun, where the rain of the fountains falls in the marble courts" (176). In a speech that goes on for pages, Sara and Axel fantasize about the possibility of realizing all their dreams now that they have miraculously found each other.

But here Axel strikes an unexpected note. "Why realize them?" he asks. "They are so beautiful!" And to her plea of "come and live!" he replies: "Live? No. Our existence is full—and its cup is running over! The future? . . . Sara, believe me when I say it: we have just exhausted the future. All the realities, what will they be to-morrow in comparison with the mirages we have just lived?" (182). He tells her that the quality of their hope is greater than anything Earth can sustain. To remain on Earth, he says, would afford them nothing more than a pale reflection of moments now lost to memory and melancholy. "What has the Earth ever realized, that drop of frozen mud, whose Time is only a lie in the heavens?" he asks. "It is the Earth . . . which has now become the illusion!" (182–83). He admonishes Sara to admit that the two of them have destroyed, in what he calls their "strange hearts," the love of life. To live after this, he argues, would be sacrilege against themselves.

Axel implores her not to be duped by the false allures of the external world, a world that promises "the keys to a palace of enchantments when in its clenched black fist it hides only a handful of ashes" (184). The cities of her dreams—Baghdad, Palmyra, Jerusalem—are, in reality, nothing but piles of uninhabitable stones, sterile deserts, wretched places that seem glamorous only from a distance because they are shrouded in the mists of her imagination. These "paltry villages" exist only in an Orient "which you carry within yourself," he tells her. "And what tiresome sadness the mere sight of them would cause you!" (184)

He proposes that they kill themselves at once, but Sara demurs, suggesting one more night of love. Axel begs her not to be frivolous and argues that their love could never endure, that it would eventually burn itself out. She pleads with him to reconsider, but he remains adamant. She is obviously reluctant to die, but her pleas are powerless against his nobler logic. When she argues that "to kill oneself is to desert," he calls this the "verdict of beggars for whom God is but a means to earn their bread" (186). "Perhaps it would be nobler to think of the common good—the good of all," she pleads, but he dismisses this, saying, "The universe devours itself; that is the price paid for the good of . . . all" (186). Still she persists. What about the treasures they will be leaving behind? she asks, but he calls them empty husks. The true treasures, he says, are within oneself. "We know what we are leaving: not *that* which we shall find!" she cries, but he counters with the argument that facing death is a returning to "*that* which inspires us with the dizzying heroism of confronting it" (186). Her resistance overcome, Sara agrees to share a goblet of poison with Axel, and the two lovers perish in a rapture.

The spirit of the play and Axel's quest for the Infinite, quite as much as the symbols, left their mark on a whole generation. Remy de Gourmont said that *Axel* "reopened the closed doors of the beyond, with what a crash, and through those doors a whole generation rushed toward the infinite. . . . He was the doorman of the ideal" (*Axel* 198–99). And, indeed, Axel—with his aristocratic haughtiness, his rejection of an earth that had become illusion, and his metaphysical narcissism, which leads him to conclude that the only reality is the soul—sets the standard for the alienated who, as Edmund Wilson put it in *Axel's Castle*, "drop out of the common life" and choose the often tragic way of realizing the spirit within themselves (266).

The dangers that Wilson saw as the consequence of taking *Axel* too seriously are dangers that all readers face when they fall under the spell of a cult book. "If one chooses . . . the way of Axel," he says, "one shuts oneself up in one's own private world, cultivating one's private fantasies, encouraging one's private manias, ultimately preferring one's absurdest chimeras to the most astonishing contemporary realities, ultimately mistaking one's chimeras for realities" (287). Readers today who laugh at Axel and find his fancies too absurd to mistake for realities need only remember that each age prefers its own chimeras, no matter how absurd, and can just as easily mistake them for contemporary realities, no matter how astonishing.

FOR FURTHER READING

Anzalone, John. "Timeless Tomes: Occult Libraries in Villiers' *Isis* and *Axel*." *L'Esprit Createur* (Spring 1988): 87–94.

Wilson, Edmund. *Axel's Castle*. New York: Scribner's, 1931.

Been Down So Long It Looks Like Up to Me

Richard Fariña
(1966)

Like other cult books of its time, *Been Down So Long It Looks Like Up to Me* is part diary, part fantasy, part parody. Like Jack Kerouac before him and Hunter S. Thompson after him, Richard Fariña recreates a series of personal experiences with vivid immediacy, yet the reality he perceives so graphically is filtered through a lush narrative style and an unfettered imagination that heighten his perceptions to an almost surrealistic plane. At the same time, the events he recounts are in essence so banal that the effect is a novel that reads at one moment like an absurdist takeoff on the "varsity drag" college frolic genre and the next like a satire on post-pubescent angst. The cute coeds are there, but this time around Miss Kneesox carries condoms in her rucksack, and her resistance is overcome not by a pledge of matrimony but a pinch of "snow."

Although Fariña is better than most at writing about the college scene, one gets the feeling in many passages that behind them lurks the specter of the maudlin inanities of the campus literary magazine with all its pretense and precociousness. Certainly there is a sense of parody in the passage in which Kristin is puffing "with languid abandon on an after-dinner cigarette" while Gnossos, stretched out beside her, his boy scout shirt open at the throat, watches shadows flickering on the ceiling that resemble "hybrid animals leaping among the shadow and flame." Then, as he feels Kristin's hand in his, he thinks "*How can those terrified vague fingers?*" And as their passion intensifies, Fariña tells us that Gnossos "measured her body with the fleshy caliphers of his mind's vicarious eye, matched it against the feral silhouettes of his Radcliffe muse" (186–87). What follows is a scene of comic seduction during which Gnossos, the celebrated make-out artist, claims he is a virgin because he has never truly surrendered himself.

It is clearly 1958, even if there are drugs around and the atmosphere seems anachronistically permissive. Fariña describes a typical college party of the day, a party that takes place in a tidy loft at the top of well-scrubbed stairs. Through the heavy oak door that leads to the loft, approaching guests hear only murmuring and quiet laughter and the muted tinkling of glass rather than the coarse voices and loud music of a decade later. Although there is an "increasingly stronger scent of smoldering pot," the zombies Fariña describes could just as easily be "smashed" on booze as "stoned" on grass (128). One of them is a "hairy little man" who is squatting "on a silk pillow in the middle of the floor, wearing a V-necked teeshirt, holding a guitar limply in his hands." A "bubbling narghile . . . on a brass platform" is at his side, "one of its many mouthpieces pursed in the man's lips." Other zombies recline on pallets "covered with Indian prints and burnt-sienna burlap" or on Japanese bamboo mats. Scattered here and there are foam rubber cushions "stained with spilled liquids, crushed fruit, spent love" (129).

The music coming out of the stereo is apparently something exotic, something Oriental or possibly Indian, for two girls described as "twin vampires with Egyptian eye makeup" are kneeling before the speaker, "digging sounds too muted to distinguish." Even the dancing is not the frenzied disco style of later years. Instead, as couples dance on the bare floor, Fariña says it is "not exactly dancing, more like shifting their weight around the common focus of their welded navels, rubbing" (129). There is also a spider monkey present named Proust who gets turned on "only by stages" by LSD (130–31).

In his introduction to this book, Thomas Pynchon, friend and classmate of Fariña's, describes the undergraduate consciousness as resting in part on a frivolous misunderstanding of the meaning of mortality and blames the elitism and cruelty so characteristic of college humor on a belief in, to use Gnossos's term, one's own Exemption. This faith in one's Exemption included, he says, not only exemption from mortality but also exemption from the ordinary demands of life. It is this illusion of Exemption, he says, that both bothers and bewitches Gnossos Pappadopoulis. As he tries all the hip trips of the late fifties and early sixties—Eastern religion, road epiphanies, mescaline, love—Gnossos thinks, "I am invisible . . . and Exempt. Immunity has been granted to me for I do not lose my cool" (4).

The shadow of Jack Kerouac's *On the Road* falls across the very first page of *Been Down So Long It Looks Like Up to Me*. Here is Gnossos, "furry Pooh Bear" and the "keeper of the flame," voyaging back "from the asphalt seas of the great wasted land." On those main arteries of pre-interstate America "highways like US 40 and legendary route 66 [get your kicks!]", Gnossos associates himself with the vastness of the United States as he thinks to himself, "I am home to the glacier-gnawed gorges, the fingers of lakes, the golden girls of Westchester and Shaker Heights. See me loud with lies, big boots stomping, mind awash with schemes" (3).

He equates his return to his college campus, Athené, with Ulysses' return home to Penelope lying in an "exalted ecstasy of infidelity," to Telemachus, the son who hates him and who "aims a kick at his groin," and to his faithful old dog, Argus, who "trots out to greet his weary returning master and drives fangs into a cramped leg, infecting him with the frost of some feral, hydrophobic horror" (3). The sardonic tone is pure Fariña and pure fifties half-hearted cynicism, reminiscent of J. D. Salinger's tone established early and maintained throughout *The Catcher in the Rye*—a certain irreverence, a certain brassiness, a certain disappointment that people don't play their parts better or that the script of life is not better written.

But the book also shares a similarity with *On the Road* in its implicit insistence on the presence of some kind of corny silver lining, a pervasive optimism that shines through all the frenzy and frustration of aborted journeys and failed quests. What a far cry it is from *Less than Zero*, Brett Easton Ellis's dreary dirge for the pampered overindulgers of the eighties. Today the book seems deceptively more innocent than it is precisely because of books like *Less than Zero* and other so-called hip urban novels of young-white-male, middle-class angst. There is, in *Been Down So Long*, an ingenuous honesty, even a wholesomeness, to the goings-on in spite of the amplified dope/sex/rock 'n' roll motif. Even the mock communion the students celebrate using Red Cap Ale and goat cheese is more Greek blast than gross blasphemy.

In *Been Down So Long*, as in many cult books, women are sacrificed to the masculine ego. Although they are not humiliated the way they are in, say, Hunter Thompson's *Fear and Loathing in Las Vegas*, they are often manipulated or treated as if they are a little slow to catch on, like bumptious little Betty Coeds, forever the bubble-headed butt of coarse, stale jokes. For example, they ask guileless questions (Will this drug make me do anything I don't want to do?) as if they honestly expect to get any kind of warning from some horny Harry. They fall for obvious seduction techniques, they're easily fooled, yet they can (and do) break hearts.

Fariña's coeds are not unlike the women in other cult books who exist on the fringe, not necessarily abused or mistreated in a physical way, but simply ignored or forgotten. Or if their presence is noted, these women are usually transient, passive, incidental. Even the strong-willed

Dominique Francon in Ayn Rand's *The Fountainhead* suffers an obvious lack of fulfillment until she can surrender to the overwhelming masculine presence of Howard Roark.

There are, of course, exceptions. Phoebe is Holden's salvation, Lotte is Werther's exalted love, Daisy is Gatsby's idealized love, Frau Eva is Demian's mother love. However, in novels like *Against Nature, A Clockwork Orange, Fear and Loathing, The Killer Inside Me, On the Road* and *Lolita,* women are used, abused, conned, and even killed. Elsewhere, with few exceptions, women have little or no place in the story. In most science fiction they are at best stock characters, and in novels like *On the Road, Catch–22, The Outsiders, The Teachings of Don Juan, A Separate Peace, 2001: A Space Odyssey,* and *Zen and the Art of Motorcycle Maintenance* they hardly figure at all.

Exemption and cool are two naive pretensions that Gnossos loses in a hurry in the novel's climax in war-torn Cuba. There, he finds, no one is exempt from the revolution that is replacing an autocratic dictator with what will turn out to be a Soviet puppet. Fariña uses different names for the two leaders, but this is clearly the Cuba of the 1950s where Fidel Castro is locked in combat with Batista, a conflict that caught the imagination of American youth with a curious passion. Even though they saw Castro as a comic figure in battle fatigues and bandolier, a heartily insincere smile breaking through the unruly beard, itself a symbol of resistance, young Americans still admired his style and that of his sidekick, Che Guevara. Something in their irrepressible spirit, in the comic-book way they conducted their war, and in the offhand style of these two scruffy "banditos" overturning a corrupt tyrant appealed to the adolescent prankishness of young Americans. That the reality was something quite different hardly mattered to these admirers—the same admirers, incidentally, who had laughed when a gang of Cuban dissidents had terrorized the House of Representatives ten years earlier.

"Lost my old Exemption button," Gnossos says just minutes before a stray bullet from a passing army vehicle results in the death of his buddy Heffalump (299). Suddenly the party's over, and Gnossos and his friends find themselves in the midst of terrifying reality that makes the campus riots that follow a few pages later seem like child's play. Thomas Pynchon maintains that the true climax of the book takes place in Cuba. Fariña had gone through a Hemingway phase a few years earlier, a not uncommon experience among aspiring writers in the fifties, and it was a Hemingway axiom that every true story must end in death. "Death, no idle prankster, is always, in this book," says Pynchon, "just outside the window." He finds cosmic humor in Gnossos's futile attempts to thwart the inevitability of death, to come to terms with Thanatos, as it were, "to find some kind of hustle that will get him out of the mortal contract we're all stuck with." The cosmic humor is really the result of a cosmic paradox: Gnossos is so much in love with life and wants so much to experience it firsthand that he is driven to take chances, to tempt death, not entirely aware of the fact that, as Pynchon puts it, "the more intensely he lives, the better the odds of his number finally coming up" (xiii).

Fariña's number actually did come up just two days after publication of *Been Down So Long,* when he was thrown from a motorcycle and killed. His death inevitably added to the book's mystique, almost as if he had died as a martyr to the cause. Certainly, the book stands on its own as one of the best expressions of the counterculture mentality, but Fariña's early death has given this, his only novel, a kind of untouchable status, rather like *A Confederacy of Dunces* or *The Bell Jar,* as if writing this book, making permanent this incomparable moment in time, was the only thing Richard Fariña was meant to do. It resides in what he calls in the book, "the lymphatic grottos of limbo," a phrase more to the taste of the stoned than the sober—and typical of Fariña's style.

Been Down So Long is gratifyingly unstuffy. Underneath there's a persistent sense of fun even in the darkest moments. In this respect, the book represents that side of the counterculture exemplified by the Beatles, four happy-go-lucky lads bopping around, having a good time, taking their music and their performances seriously but not (as yet) themselves. Though detractors might see signs of incipient destructiveness, cult followers quite innocently saw the lifestyle depicted in this book as the least harmful and offensive way of dealing with a world troubled by an unjust war abroad and civil unrest at home. Here was the cool way to cope, and Exemption, the illusion of immunity, was the closest one could come to some sort of idealized Oriental detachment.

FOR FURTHER READING

Fariña, Richard. "Baez and Dylan: A Generation Singing Out." In *The Age of Rock: Sounds of the American Cultural Revolution: A Reader*. New York: Random House, 1969: 200–7.

Stephenson, Gregory. "Toward Organized Innocence: Richard Fariña's *Been Down So Long It Looks Like Up to Me*." In *The Daybreak Bug: Essays on the Literature of the Beat Generation*. Carbondale: Southern Illinois University Press, 1990: 131–38.

The Bell Jar

Sylvia Plath
(1963)

The Bell Jar was first published in England in 1963 under the pseudonym of Victoria Lucas. Sylvia Plath was living in England at the time, and less than a month after the book appeared, she took her own life. The novel was then published in the United States eight years later, in 1971, under Plath's own name, and has known popular and critical acclaim ever since that second publication.

The Bell Jar filled a vacuum in American literature, for until its appearance in 1963, American literature had produced very few heroines who could be said to be extensions of their authors, in the way Elizabeth Bennett speaks for Jane Austen in *Pride and Prejudice* or Jane Eyre for Charlotte Brontë. But Esther Greenwood, the heroine of *The Bell Jar*, is more than just an extension of Sylvia Plath; she is as much a product of her times as Holden Caulfield is of his, and thus *The Bell Jar* became, for many women, their version of *The Catcher in the Rye*. Although Esther's mental problems become more severe than his, it must be remembered that Holden is telling his story from inside a mental institution.

In terms of its cult appeal *The Bell Jar* is also very close in spirit to a number of other novels to come out of the changing sociopolitical energy of the 1960s, such as Ken Kesey's *One Flew over the Cuckoo's Nest*, Joseph Heller's *Catch–22*, and Kurt Vonnegut's *Slaughterhouse-Five*, all of which achieved immediate cult status. In these and other essentially 1960s works, the focus is on the relationship between the individual and society, and war and madness become metaphors for the human condition as hospitals (or the army) become both microcosms of and escapes from the insanity of society. Like a number of novels that followed it, *The Bell*

Jar focuses on the individual lost in a society that can no longer respond to individual needs and whose institutions no longer seem to work.

The Bell Jar describes Esther Greenwood's descent into a private, schizophrenic hell and details the first steps of her recovery. The novel is divided into two uneven parts, as if its very structure were a reflection of Esther's divided mind. in the first section, Esther describes her frantic month in New York City as one of twelve student editors for a special college issue of *Ladies' Day*, a leading women's magazine. Like *The Catcher in the Rye*, this section has an atmosphere about it that is peculiar to the place and the times. For *Catcher*, it is the New York of the late forties; for *The Bell Jar*, it is the same city in the fifties. While there are significant differences between these periods, Holden and Esther are similar in their naivete, both of them telling their stories with a mixture of wry humor, embarrassed pathos, and painfully transparent bravado. Like Holden, Esther is slowly coming apart in the city, but whereas Holden orchestrates his own misadventures, Esther seems swept along by forces beyond her control as she rushes through the frenetic life of a junior staff member on a leading women's magazine. As this first section ends, it is Esther's last night in Manhattan, and in a solitary gesture of hysteria and revolt, she stands on the roof of the Amazon hotel, deliberately tossing her new wardrobe piece by piece over the edge.

At this point Esther begins her frightening descent into the nightmare world of schizophrenia, and the second section of *The Bell Jar* is more like a separate, almost unrelated novel, as if the reader had abandoned the sardonic world of Holden Caulfield for the neurotic world of Franz Kafka. Esther returns to Boston, jobless and friendless, and there, during the summer before her senior year in college, she wanders the city searching for her identity and contemplating suicide. After swallowing a bottle of pills, she is hospitalized, and as she begins the slow, painful process of recovery, including shock therapy, she feels at first that she has merely traded one agony for another. However, once she comes under the care of Dr. Nolan, a physician of great sensitivity and understanding, Esther begins to discover her own identity, and it is at this point that the "bell jar" that has enclosed her and threatened to smother her begins to lift.

Part of Esther's problem is simply that of growing up in the conservative fifties and yearning to break free. But at a deeper level, the problem is Esther's sexual identity, or lack of it. As Esther says, "pureness" was a big issue in the 1950s, and it was an even bigger issue for a sheltered young woman whose father had died when she was a child and whose mother had to work merely to survive. Esther has never been able to come to terms with her own sexual identity; she associates sex with babies and cannot shake the image of the fetuses in bottles that she had once seen on a visit to a friend who was a medical student. In a way, the fetus in the bottle is a metaphor for Esther in the bell jar, her psychosexual development stunted, her whole emotional self frozen in time.

Her recovery is marked by two significant events. First, she initiates herself into sexuality by seducing a young Boston math professor, but as luck would have it, she hemorrhages badly and is rushed to the hospital, where the doctor tells her that her case is "one in a million." Second, when her closest friend, Joan, commits suicide, she learns not to blame herself. We know at this point that she will convince the hospital board to release her and that she will recover. Actually, from the clues dropped at the beginning of the novel, we know that she has married and had a baby by the time she sits down to write her story.

Esther Greenwood is possibly the only *heroine* in cult literature, and as such she presents a unique case that raises special questions. For one thing, there is the contradiction between the upbeat ending of the novel and the suicide of its author a month after the novel's publication. For another, there is the nature of Esther's "sickness," which seems to be, among other things, an inability to make choices. A final question has to do with her unique status as a cult heroine. How much weight must be given to Esther/Sylvia as a voice for women? Ordinary readers tend to believe that Sylvia Plath's suicide undermines the point of *The Bell Jar*, while cult readers feel just the opposite. They think that by committing suicide, Plath not only pokes bitter fun at the myth of the happy ending but reinforces the hopelessness and frustration of the reality of trying to grow up in the bell jar of the fifties or, by extension, in any period when women feel repressed.

Thus, this book owes something of its cult status to the growth of the women's movement in the United States. In *The Bell Jar*, Sylvia Plath wrote an initiation novel that coincided with the emergence of feminist literary consciousness in the United States, and since its publication the novel has stood at the top of a long and growing list of works by women writing about themselves in that society. Whenever the feminist initiation novel is discussed, *The Bell Jar* is cited as a beginning. In a number of ways, the novel captures the experience of growing up female in America. To feminists, the tragic story of Esther/Sylvia says something about the difficulties of the literary life for women in America. However, if feminism were really to account for the cult status of *The Bell Jar*, then the question arises about the status of other titles on the feminist list, not one of which has become a genuine cult classic. What is closer to the truth is that *The Bell Jar*, while it may speak to feminists, speaks to a lot of other people as well—even speaks *for* them, in fact, in a way few books do.

As a rule, cult books are not limited to audiences of a particular sex or race. The limitations imposed on the full appreciation of a particular work by restricting its interpretation to any special interest group can be seen in the critical reception of *The Bell Jar* both by feminists and by female critics. Feminists see Esther as a victim, a sensitive woman/artist denied expression, repressed, driven to despair by an unfeeling society bent on turning her into a Stepford wife and mother. Female critics, on the other hand, finally get annoyed with her because they cannot find a solid core, only a neurotic surface. She exasperates them because she is so self-centered and so self-destructive. She finally "acts like a woman"—emotional, neurotic, spoiled—and even if she is deviant, she cannot come to terms with it as they think a modern woman should. Her way out is the way out of Anna Karenina, Emma Bovary, and Hedda Gabler—playing a man's version of a woman right up to the end.

But Esther Greenwood is a tormented soul to whom any sensitive reader can relate. Early in the novel, Esther describes her life as a fig tree in a story that she had once read, saying that from "every branch, like fat purple figs, a wonderful future beckoned and winked" (84). Yet Esther feels powerless to pick from this tree and is able only to imagine herself sitting "in the crotch of this fig tree, starving to death, just because I couldn't make up my mind which of the figs I would choose" (85). In this respect, Esther is like a cult follower herself, but instead of being one who skips from book to book in search of the ultimate answer, she can only sit paralyzed before possibilities too plentiful to choose among.

It is possible, of course, that the symbolism of the fat purple figs is sexual, although it can also quite reasonably be extended to such things as career choices and matters of belief. The irony in Esther's case is that although it is tempting to see her as repressed by the "Eisenhower society" she inhabits, it is something else entirely that inhibits her, and she knows it. After all, a person cannot look at a fig tree laden with temptations and call that tree repressive. It is not logical that the very tree that is offering her its wonders is also telling her to refuse what it offers. That she finds choices intimidating is entirely a personal problem, and obviously a psychological (not to mention universal) one.

Like Kafka, Lawrence, Virginia Woolf, and other artists afflicted with ailments that had nothing to do with the times in which they lived, Sylvia Plath was similarly afflicted, in her case with what medically trained readers think was probably endogenous depression, a congenital condition that would have driven her over the edge in any age. However, because Plath's life intersected with the emergence of the feminist consciousness, it has been appropriated as a metaphor for sensitive women artists frustrated by a world that they find cruel, demanding, seductive, and bewildering. Cult readers, generally unaware of the physiological problems that might lie beneath Esther's (Sylvia's) emotional problems, see only a tortured woman who represents what they think they are or might become.

Even though responsibility for her unhappy fate seems to rest ultimately with Sylvia Plath herself, there are many who insist on finding someone guilty of her suffering as well as her death, someone to blame and to punish. Society is the most convenient target, that faceless crowd that never seems to include the accusers and that is somehow forever in conspiracy against sensitive artists and thus responsible for their misery.

However, in all fairness to those readers who want to see society take its fair share of the blame for the suffering of a cult figure, it must be admitted that the fifties sent contradictory signals that were particularly painful to the soul of any artist—but particularly a woman—who wanted to be taken seriously. This was the age of the "sex symbols" (Monroe, Mansfield, Bardot, and others), the notorious teases who made it their business to remain both alluring and aloof, delectable but untouchable, seductive but never seduced. In a way, Marilyn Monroe and Sylvia Plath were alter egos. Whereas Monroe maintained that her image as a sex symbol blinded people to her intellectual side, Plath is obviously bothered by the fact that her image as an intellectual blinds people to her sensual side. The world was not yet ready to accept both sides in one woman. Thus both Marilyn Monroe and Sylvia Plath suffered from stereotypes that suffocated them the harder they fought to escape, and both ended up taking their lives in an act of frantic desperation.

The Bell Jar has multiple layers of meaning, and its mythical allusions are many, from the myths of initiation and quest found in so many cult books, to the modern psychosocial myths of repression and sublimation and projection. As a novel of initiation, it is a book about growing up female (but not exclusively) in America, with all the role restrictions and psychological hurdles that a woman (again, not exclusively) may face. At its psychological level, *The Bell Jar* describes the world of the schizophrenic from the inside, and the power of Sylvia Plath's poetic language brings this nightmarish world to vivid and astonishing light and turns it into a powerful symbol of the hidden hopes, the latent talents, all the quivering frustrations of the buried life struggling to be reborn.

Images of babies in bottles, fetuses and figs, bell jars, and scenes of electroshock and drowning all convey that heightened sense of reality that is also common to cult books. The image of Esther curled up inside a plastic bag, stuffed under the breezeway of her mother's house, is one that cult readers find central to their identification with the novel, for it symbolizes not only their feeling of entrapment but also their own scarcely admitted but nevertheless undeniable death wish. This is certainly not the first novel to rationalize the taking of one's own life, but it is the first to justify it as a viable option.

Ultimately, this extraordinary "confessional" speaks to cult readers at the point where Esther's psychosexual history intersects with the spirit of the fifties, again in much the same way that Holden Caulfield's lonely figure finds its spiritually accurate backdrop in the world of the late forties. Both seem caught in the flypaper of social conformity and hypocrisy, and although most cult books do end up suggesting a similar conflict between protagonist and society, their authors invariably manage to breathe new life into what could easily become banal and repetitious. But the secret to *The Bell Jar*'s cult status lies finally in the intensity of Esther's experiences, an intensity made so personal and so powerful by virtue of Plath's rich prose style that readers—men as well as women—read this story as if it were their very own.

This kind of neurosis that afflicts especially the young is viewed by some authors as immaturity, something that can be cured merely by growing up. Others see it as a budding rebellion against an unjust society, while still others see it as "the sickness of youth" with the outcome primarily a matter of character. In *The Bell Jar* we never see Esther getting beyond this intense preoccupation. She does not grow up, she never stops rebelling, and her character seems somehow flawed, stuck, preoccupied with itself.

One explanation for this narcissism could be that Plath's neurosis was simply the style then, a style that we also see in *The Catcher in the Rye*. The inability to make choices or to take responsibility along with the tendency to fragment one's emotions were not uncommon responses to the relatively rigid and conservative fifties. It is entirely possible that Esther surrenders to mental illness partly because it is available to her and trendy, only to get caught in her own game and become suicidal because she cannot find her way back. Her narcissism has trapped her. She has pursued success and happiness to a dead end. In losing touch with the past, which she can no longer see objectively, she is incapable of envisioning the future, for it has become totally beyond her imagining. She is lost, adrift, and anything the future might hold for her seems to be either distasteful or impossible to achieve. In that state of mind, expectations have not only diminished but disappeared. Death, then, seems the only solution, suicide the only means.

Exaltation or damnation ("the foot of the Cross or the muzzle of a gun"): these are the alternatives cult books offer; and although most readers prefer the former, *The Bell Jar* is one of a handful of cult books that cater to the dark side of the cult mentality where narcissism and masochism merge into madness and self-destruction.

FOR FURTHER READING

Deer, Irving. "Sylvia Plath's *The Bell Jar*: Searching for Openness." In *Youth Suicide Prevention: Lessons from Literature*. New York: Plenum, 1989.

Tanner, Tony. *City of Words: American Fiction, 1950–1970*. New York: Harper & Row, 1971.

"Victoria Lucas and Elly Higginbottom." In *Ariel Ascending: Writings About Sylvia Plath*, ed. by Vance Bourjaily and Paul Alexander. New York: Harper, 1985.

Wagner, Linda W. "Plath's *The Bell Jar* as Female Bildungsroman." *Women's Studies: An Interdisciplinary Journal* 12.1 (1986): 55–68.

Brave New World

Aldous Huxley (1932)

"O brave new world, / That has such people in't" exclaims Miranda on the enchanted island that is the world of Shakespeare's *The Tempest.* In *Brave New World,* Aldous Huxley's cult classic in which utopia is portrayed as totalitarian nightmare, Miranda's happy cry becomes an Edvard Munch cry of anguish over a world in which human values have been irredeemably perverted.

Unlike Orwell's *1984,* which postulates a world order based on terror and fear, Huxley's "new world," while anything but brave, is based on comfort. Unable to confront the realities of pain and dying, its citizens are permanently tranquilized by a drug called "soma" and are thus protected against anything unpleasant. Living to them means feeling good, and this to cult readers is the same as feeling nothing. In fact, one thing cult readers like about this book is its anti-utopian point of view. They believe, along with Huxley, that living is feeling and that much (maybe most) of feeling is pain. Thus, a utopian dream is a false dream because a painless life would be a life not worth living.

In the tradition of the utopian novel, *Brave New World* projects into the future the tendencies of the present. The things that most disturbed Huxley—and that attracted cult readers to this book—were mindless technology, promiscuity, the loss of the values of valor and honor ("civilization has absolutely no need of nobility or heroism"), and an overall paralysis of any aesthetic sense. In Huxley's "brave new world," everything is machine-made, mass-produced, and sterile, and as a consequence civilization has lost touch with the qualities that once gave life zest, qualities of passion and vitality, of irrationality and excess that were both its peril and its promise.

In this new world, test-tube babies are genetically engineered to perform specific functions, and children are conditioned to satisfy the demands of the marketplace. Such "standardization of the human product," as Huxley puts it, is a horror perceived even by Bernard Marx, one of the ruling elite. Indeed, the objection to utopia is no longer that it is an unrealistic dream but, on the contrary, that it is coming true and turning out to be a nightmare.

The utopian myth is an enduring and familiar one, from the Garden of Eden to Homer's Land of the Lotus-Eaters, from Sidney's Arcadia to More's Utopia. Its most famous realization in recent times is James Hilton's Shangri-La, that lost land of harmony and peace hidden deep in the Himalayas that so fascinated readers in *Lost Horizon,* a book that, as it happens, appeared the same year as *Brave New World.* In common usage the word "utopia" (meaning "nowhere") connotes a never-never land of eternal bliss that can take the form of anything from a tropical paradise of pure sensual pleasure to a scholarly retreat where the mind is free to meditate uninterrupted.

The inversion of this myth is a modern invention that had its start with Samuel Butler's *Erewhon* in 1872, and it has flourished in the twentieth century probably as a result of the proliferation of totalitarian regimes that have perpetrated unprecedented horrors in the name of social progress. Only in this century, then, has the cost of such progress in terms of human dignity, moral independence, intellectual freedom, and emotional liberty been assessed and found exorbitant.

What appeals to cult readers about such dystopias is that they bring out in bas-relief the evils of contemporary life and make them shockingly clear. *Brave New World* follows in the tradition of H. G. Wells's classic *Things to Come* as one of the earliest science-fiction utopias to project a future that readers see as practically here. Ever since its publication, the fears that the book aroused have been steadily reinforced: fears of being victimized by such things as genetic engineering, massive sedation, controlled insemination and sterilization, programmed pregnancies, in vitro fertilization, brainwashing—the list goes on as each scientific "breakthrough" adds to the growing list of possible horrors.

In fact, some cult readers today claim they are not reading prophecy but history. In Huxley's utopia, just as in modern society, they say, happiness is equated with sensual pleasure, and every desire must be gratified at the moment of its inception. Likewise, they see in the attempts to condition children against the fear of death by having them frolic among the terminally ill a symptom of the modern desire to desensitize human beings not only to painful emotional realities like loss of loved ones but also to unpleasant physical realities such as pregnancy or disease. Soma, the tranquilizer that makes anything bearable in Huxley's new world, is reflected in the modern tendency to rely heavily on prescription drugs or alcohol as well as on the illegal use of so-called "controlled substances."

Thus, there is more than a superficial resemblance between today's world and Huxley's newer one in which people find themselves hedonistically searching for one superficial pleasure after another, from wallowing in sensual movies called "feelies" to ingesting large doses of soma. The shift in emphasis, as the Controller puts it, has been "from truth and beauty to comfort and happiness."

Cult readers may not find the traditional monomythical hero in *Brave New World*, but they tend to respond even more enthusiastically to any remnant of Rousseau's "noble savage," and John Savage, the halfbreed rebel from New Mexico, is their man. When Bernard Marx first takes John back to London, John becomes a great social success. All the jaded sophisticates of London want to meet him and are even willing to put up with Bernard, whom they always found somewhat of a bore (too shy and misanthropic), in order to do so. Lenina, Bernard's sometime girlfriend, also finds herself greatly attracted to this natural young man and does her best to seduce him. But although he lusts after her, John sternly rejects her because she is representative of the loose morality of civilization.

Huxley's Savage differs from those other exotic intruders into "civilization" in that he can make a choice: he can accept God, poetry, real danger, freedom, goodness, and sin—in short, "the right to be unhappy," as Mustapha Mond remarks—or he can relieve all anxieties by approving the new world. If the former, he would then have the "right to grow old and ugly and impotent; the right to have syphilis and cancer; the right to have too little to eat; the right to be lousy; the right to live in constant apprehension of what may happen tomorrow; the right to catch typhoid; the right to be tortured by unspeakable pains of every kind." After a pause, Savage answers, " 'I claim them all,' " and by choosing life, he ironically selects the path to self-destruction (163).

Nevertheless, choosing life does mean surrender to its cheap temptations. John is appalled by the hedonism of so-called civilized society and longs to return to the stricter morality of the primitive life. At the hospital where his mother is dying of cancer—and the children are running around being desensitized—John goes berserk and tries to destroy the soma rations that are being doled out to the hospital workers. He argues with the angry Deltas, trying to get them to see how reliance on soma is making them less than human. They mob him and nearly kill him before the police arrive and quell the riot with water pistols that shoot tranquilizers.

John is arrested, but instead of sending him into exile or imprisoning him, Mustapha Mond, the urbane World Controller, engages in long philosophical arguments with him. He explains to John that the Brave

New World has no room for art, science, or religion because these are disruptive forces that require social instability and occasional misery in order to thrive. In a world dedicated to feeling good, there is no room for visionaries, cranks, and egoists who were the great culture heroes of the past. Eloquent as Mond is, however, Savage remains unconvinced. He still feels that Shakespeare, suffering, motherhood, and God are important values, and he decides to become a hermit in a lighthouse on the coast of Surrey. There he goes, determined to be self-sufficient and independent of the gadgets and creature comforts for which everyone else exists.

Soon, however, word of John's eccentric behavior gets around, and curiosity seekers descend on him in helicopters. John tries to kick them out, but eventually they become too much for him. They have heard that he whips himself when he feels lust for Lenina, and they would like to make a public display of this spectacle. In his rage, John turns on Lenina and whips her to death. When his pursuers learn of this and come after him, they find that he has hanged himself in the lighthouse, unable to bear the burden of living in the Brave New World.

John's fate is the sort of grand gesture, the supreme and noble martyrdom that has an irresistible appeal to the cult reader who has long since taken John's side against so-called civilization and its schemes to reduce man to a grinning robot. John's savageness is his naturalness, what would *seem* savage to the pseudo-civilized. The life he is asked to accept is a prison in which the flesh can exist only at the expense of the spirit. His bloody self-flagellation is his way of trying to redeem the spirit, to take onto himself the sins of a world that no longer seems brave or godly or beauteous. His sensual feelings for Lenina—which he believes to be unpure—have to be overcome, and this he does by beatings and hard work. He is, in essence, the kind of Blakean hero Huxley has presented elsewhere, a figure who disdains the mechanistic and consciously determined world in favor of a natural existence based on ideals of purity and integrity and a deep respect for life.

At the center of this book's appeal to cult readers is Huxley's concept of the nonattached man. This man, as Huxley describes him elsewhere, would be uncommitted to fame, love, position, power, even to art and intelligence. The nonattached man puts an end to pain not only in himself but also to such pain as he might inflict on others. He becomes the happy as well as the good man. This man, obviously, must be educated in a free society that is cognizant of individual needs as opposed to a totalitarian society that educates the masses to obey. This is about as close as Huxley gets to the monomythical hero, in this case a hero who exists within, a concept increasingly appealing to modern readers as external solutions seem doomed to failure. Especially in the thirties, when the world's problems seemed unsolvable, the retreat inward grew more attractive, and Huxley offered a hope not unlike the Christian hope of individual redemption as the first step toward universal salvation.

That this retreat inward can easily degenerate into self-centeredness is not a transformation cult readers are likely to detect, since by the time they have reached the narcissistic core of the belief in the self, they are quite beyond subtleties. Thus, another aspect of the appeal of *Brave New World* is the self-congratulatory possibilities of looking around at the world, much as Holden Caulfield does, and finding it worthy of scorn. The world that Bernard Marx and John Savage inhabit is one that cult readers think describes their own, a world full of desensitized, programmed, subservient people willing to sacrifice their integrity for instant gratification. In Huxley's brave new world of the future, cult readers see a mirror image of their own, only heightened and intensified.

Huxley revised his thinking somewhat in *Brave New World Revisited* (1958) to amplify his understated concerns about overpopulation and overconsumption. Basically, however, his fears remained unallayed. However, in *Island* (1962), he displayed a mellowing of his outlook, a cautious optimism made up of generous portions of drugs, mysticism, and wishful thinking. In the meantime, his experiments with mind-altering drugs and oriental mysticism had turned him into something of a cult figure, with a devoted following among the disaffected youth that gained strength following his death on November 22, 1963, the day John F. Kennedy was assassinated.

FOR FURTHER READING

Aldridge, Alexandria. "*Brave New World* and the Mechanist/Vitalist Controversy." *Comparative Literature Studies* 17 (1980): 116–32.

Meckier, Jerome. "Our Ford, Our Freud and the Behaviorist Conspiracy in Huxley's *Brave New World*." *Thalia: Studies in Literary Humor* 1.1 (1979): 35–39.

Sexton, James. "*Brave New World* and the Rationalization of Industry." *English Studies in Canada* (December 1986): 424–39.

Thiel, Berthold. *Aldous Huxley's* Brave New World. Amsterdam: Gruner, 1980.

Watt, Donald. "The Manuscript Revisions of *Brave New World*." *Journal of English and Germanic Philology* 77 (1978): 367–82.

Wheeler, Wayne Bruce. "The Horror of Science in Politics: Prophecy and the Crisis of Human Values in Mary Shelley's *Frankenstein* and Aldous Huxley's *Brave New World*." *DAI* 40 (1979): 2246A.

A Canticle for Leibowitz

Walter M. Miller, Jr.
(1959)

When *A Canticle for Leibowitz* first appeared in novel form, it did not carry the science-fiction label even though its three parts had originally appeared (in a somewhat different form) as stories in the *Magazine of Fantasy and Science Fiction*. Today it is considered one of the very best science-fiction novels ever written, although it is quite possible to read it as an allegory of the history of Western civilization because it merely repeats in the future the events of the past. Its three parts, set at six-hundred-year intervals, parallel the actual historical periods we designate as the Middle Ages, the Renaissance, and Modern Times.

With the Catholic Church at the center of the narrative, the parallels with the past are inescapable. In part one, "Fiat Homo," the Church is desperately clinging to whatever is left of previous civilization by assigning monks to copy at great labor all existing fragments of texts or drawings even though the Church has no idea what these fragments mean. Except for the references to radiation and fallout, one could easily be within the walls of a medieval monastery where monks ruined their eyesight copying what remained of Greek and Roman literature.

In part two, "Fiat Lux," learning has advanced to the place where scholars are emerging who can translate the cryptic fragments of old texts into scientific meaning. Although a tug-of-war exists between science and religion, throughout this section there is a balance between the two that makes for the sort of social stability characteristic of the Renaissance.

In the last section, "Fiat Voluntas Tua," science has gained supremacy, the Church, by preserving knowledge, has unwittingly contributed to dangerous advances in technology, and the world is once again devastated by nuclear war. Although in reality such nuclear devastation has not yet occurred, the book is clearly a warning that it might occur, and even something of a prophecy that it will.

When it first appeared, *A Canticle for Leibowitz* addressed the fears of a nation locked in a cold war with an implacable enemy and surrounded by a growing number of nations with growing nuclear capabilities. When, soon after the book's appearance, the Cuban missile crisis panicked the nation, the book's projections seemed as probable as they were possible. With schools practicing evacuation drills and fallout shelters being sold at shopping malls, a book like *A Canticle for Leibowitz* took on chillingly realistic overtones. The very fact that its science-fiction elements could be ignored gave the book the power that outer-space adventures lacked.

The story opens in the former United States of America, six centuries after a devastating nuclear war. The first third of the novel concerns an exciting discovery made by Brother Francis Gerard, a novice monk. Scrabbling in some ancient ruins, he finds a fallout survival shelter that contains a few relics of the blessed I. E. Leibowitz, legendary founder of his Order. The most valuable item is the blueprint of a circuit design, although the relics also include a grocery list and racing forms. Almost all books and documents had been destroyed during the Age of Simplification that followed the nuclear war.

Brother Francis's findings, fragmentary as they are, represent a treasure trove to the monks, who are slowly, painfully, almost blindly, trying to accumulate and preserve the scattered knowledge of the past. Francis spends fifteen years copying the precious blueprint and illuminating his copy with gold leaf, even though he is utterly ignorant of the document's meaning. He then departs on a pilgrimage to New Rome and is robbed of his life's work along the way. But Leibowitz—one-time weapons scientist turned "booklegger"—is canonized. Francis's discoveries have not been in vain.

There is a strong appeal in this first section to the mythical need for a hero in an age that has devalued the meaning of the word. Cult readers find in Leibowitz a man they can respect, for he obviously went from being an unthinking participant in the world's destruction to becoming a martyr in the cause of human dignity and the sanctity of the soul. We learn that he has suffered for his beliefs, that he has inspired others to endure, and that he has even performed miracles. While much of this is obviously apocryphal, the Church is tough enough in its use of the devil's advocate to ensure that the man who is eventually canonized is someone of proven strength and faith. While Leibowitz may not qualify as a monomythical hero, the spirit of a man who turns his back on the amorality of science and becomes a humble servant of God pervades the novel and speaks powerfully to those who wish more scientists would make the discovery before it is too late.

In the middle section of the book another six hundred years have passed, and Church and State are in equilibrium. The leading natural scientist of the day, a scholar-aristocrat called Thon Taddeo, visits the monastery of St. Leibowitz and is astonished to find that the monks have built a workable electric arc light, powered by the muscles of novices. He is even more astonished when he examines the Leibowitz Memorabilia: ancient texts and blueprints, scraps of scientific papers, mathematical equations–all dating from the mid-twentieth century. The artificial illumination enables the scholar to read—and misread—the memorabilia. Following this, a number of cross-dialogues occur involving the Abbot and the Scholar along with a parasitic one-eyed Poet and the Wandering Jew. These dialogues reveal the misunderstandings that result from differing premises,but they also reveal the stability that results when powers are evenly matched.

The third section, which is an allegory of contemporary history, has had the greatest impact on cult readers. Therefore, it is to this section that one must turn to find the essential ingredients that make *A Canticle for Leibowitz* a cult book. As nuclear war erupts again ("Lucifer is fallen"), the Abbot resists euthanasia clinics, while Brother Joshua prepares to lead a remnant of clergy and children to Alpha Centauri, where another attempt will be made to temper technology with wisdom. In addition to allusions to the Greek myths having to do with cursed houses and proud kings, of vengeful gods and disobedient men, *A Canticle for Leibowitz* is grounded more obviously in Christian myth, particularly as it manifests itself in the tenets of the Roman Catholic Church. Although these tenets are sometimes held up to severe scrutiny, even mockery, they are essentially intact throughout the book and are given new luster in section three. Here the essential question is raised about the relationship of convenience to salvation—or how much of the soul we are willing to sacrifice for the comfort of the body.

Dr. Cors, the physician who favors euthanasia for hopeless victims of radiation, sees suffering as the root of evil, but the Abbot argues that it is not suffering but the unreasoning fear of suffering, together with the craving for worldly security, that is the root of evil. He staunchly maintains that "Nature imposes nothing that Nature hasn't prepared you to bear." No worldly evil exists, he maintains, except that which has been introduced into the world by man—"with a little help from the father of lies." But what cult readers find particularly challenging is the Abbot's summation of what is essentially wrong with the world. "To minimize suffering and to maximize security were natural and proper ends of society and Caesar," he says, "but then they became the only ends, somehow, and the only basis of law—a perversion. Inevitably, then, in seeking only them, we found only their opposites: maximum suffering and minimum security" (312). He sees euthanasia as merely a convenient way for modern society to get rid of superfluous people.

This book is unflinching in its moral perspective, and for this reason it appeals to cult readers who are likely to favor a conservative religious point of view. However, it also attracts those who find that its despair over the perpetuation of human folly matches their own. These are the people who, no matter what their religious beliefs, hold out little or no hope for the earthly salvation of mankind. They disagree with Santayana about the study of history as a way to avoid making the same mistakes. They believe that man is condemned to repeat his mistakes regardless of what he knows of the past—in fact, maybe precisely because he *does* know the past and either wants to try it for himself or fools himself into thinking that times have changed and things are different. A book like *A Canticle for Leibowitz,* then, also appeals to those who would like to see the world punished.

Some argue that the religious element of the book is ambiguous and that its message, if there is any, is tempered by a generous amount of humor. The humor ranges from puns to slapstick comedy to central symbols of misunderstanding. Elaborate jokes escape the confines of one book to echo in another (the blueprint of section one, the dynamo and a fragment of *R.U.R.* in section two, the Poet's satiric verse in section three). Cult readers, however, see the comedy merely as comic relief in an attempt to soften the intensity of a clear moral mandate. Miller's careful attention to the fine points of church doctrine and his fidelity to the particulars of the Judeo-Christian tradition do seem to override any dismissing of his generous use of Hebrew and Latin as mere window dressing. Miller is a Catholic convert, and his teasing of the tenets of Catholicism is done in the spirit of Graham Greene, who puts his faith to the test in the blessed assurance that his faith will triumph. The fact that the novel is organized to resemble a religious triptych seems to be much more than accidental.

Most readers get so involved in the story that they neglect to look at things it conveniently leaves out. So absorbed do they become in Miller's absolutely convincing representation of the post-nuclear world that they easily ignore the fact that it seems to be only the Catholic Church that has survived, and survived in style. There is no mention whatsoever of the other religions of the world, but the Catholic Church not only remains but flourishes, complete with a Pontiff who resides in a place called New Rome and a thriving network of abbeys and monasteries (although no mention is ever made of convents, curiously enough). Cult readers are quite willing to overlook any incongruities in a myth and accept it uncritically if its appeal is powerful enough. In this sense, *A*

Canticle for Leibowitz assumes the status of an object of faith, like a book of the Bible whose message far outweighs any inconsistencies it may contain. Cultists even argue that it is precisely these inconsistencies that give the myth its honesty and thus its validity.

Ultimately, the appeal of a book with a religious point of view is not difficult to understand when one thinks of such classic "cult" books as the Book of Morman as well as the writings of Mary Baker Eddy and Emmanuel Swedenborg, not to mention the dozens of lesser books by divines of all persuasions that have spoken not only *to* but *for* the devout. After all, the Holy Bible itself was a cult book long before it achieved the respectability of holy writ, and the early Christians who were martyred in its name were dismissed as nothing more than members of an Oriental cult.

A Canticle for Leibowitz, however, is similar only in its religious sensibility. Other than that, it bears no resemblance to the books that proselytize or urge others to. In short, it is not a religious book but a book with a religious edge. But because of the honesty of its convictions and the breadth of its learning, it does not offer the easy answers that so many cult books do.

The book ends on a haunting note. The grotesque, two-headed Mrs. Grales reappears and unsettles everyone with her "quest" to have her second head blessed by the Abbot. Until near the end of the story, this second head, to whom she has given the name Rachel, seemed to have no life in it—except for an occasional fleeting smile that onlookers suspected was their own inflamed imagination. Then the bombs begin to fall again, and the Abbot is pinned beneath the rubble. At that point Rachel awakes and blesses the Abbot because she alone is untainted by original sin. It is with that disturbing image (and the rockets taking off for Alpha Centauri) that the book ends. Miller has written nothing since.

FOR FURTHER READING

Dunn, Thomas. "The Deep Caves of Thought: Plato, Heinlein, and Le Guin." In *Spectrum of the Fantastic*. Westport, Conn.: Greenwood, 1988.

Kievitt, Frank David. "Walter M. Miller's *A Canticle for Leibowitz* as a Third Testament." In *The Transcendent Adventure: Studies of Religion in Science Fiction/Fantasy*. Westport, Conn.: Greenwood, 1985.

Manganiello, Dominic. "History as Judgment and Promise in *A Canticle for Leibowitz.*" *Science-Fiction Studies* (July 1986): 159–69.

Tavormina, M. Teresa. "Order, Liturgy, and Laughter in *A Canticle for Leibowitz.*" In *Medievalism in American Culture: Special Studies*. Binghamton, N.Y.: Center for Medieval & Early Renaissance Studies, 1987.

Young, R. V. "Catholic Science Fiction and the Comic Apocalypse: Walker Percy and Walter Miller." *Renascence: Essays on Value in Literature* (Winter 1988): 95–100.

The Catcher in the Rye

J. D. *Salinger*
(1951)

Ask anyone to name a cult novel and the answer you are most likely to get is *The Catcher in the Rye*. Just as Johann Wolfgang von Goethe's *The Sorrows of Young Werther* is the prototypical cult novel of all time, J. D. Salinger's book is the prototypical cult novel of modern times. The book continues to cast a spell over young readers, and its popularity shows no signs of waning. It has long been required reading in many high school and college English classes, but it has somehow managed to avoid the fate of other books that have been caught in what has been called "the deadly embrace of the academy."

Ian Hamilton, in his unofficial biography of Salinger, says that when he first read *Catcher*, he felt as if he had stumbled upon a book that spoke not just *to* him but *for* him. No one has described the appeal of cult fiction better than this, for a true cult book is one that seems to address the reader directly and to say things in a way the reader would wish to say them. Not all readers, regardless of their enthusiasm, respond to this unique book in the same way. While some find Holden Caulfield a lonely misfit worthy of extreme sympathy, others admire his sardonic wit in the face of insurmountable odds. Still others admire his stoicism, for although he has much to resent about the world he inhabits, he accepts its irritations with grace and humor.

One of the most immediate appeals of the book is Holden's way of classifying people as phonies. Few in the novel escape the label, although Holden does seem to allow for degrees of phoniness. The nuns he meets are perhaps the least phony (except for his dead brother, Allie, and his kid sister, Phoebe), whereas cute little Sally Hayes is described as the "queen of the phonies."

A phony, apparently, is someone who is only out to impress others, someone whose opinions are secondhand, someone who is unable to just "be himself." Just about everyone Holden has any contact with during this three-day sojourn between leaving prep school and arriving home fits into this category. To him, the most pathetic thing about it is that the phonies do not know they are phonies. Holden's own phoniness—his red hunting cap, his lies, his gut-clutching routine—is at least deliberate. His excuse, of course, is that the *real* phonies leave him no choice. Here, however, even he is self-deceived, and it is this gap between self-deception and self-awareness that accounts for the tone of melancholy smugness in the book, arising from what cult readers see as a sad but honest view of the world.

The only people Holden knows, then, who are not self-deceived phonies are Allie and Phoebe. In Holden's world, the good die young, and Allie's premature death has removed any hint of phoniness from his character and made him something of a saint in Holden's memory. Phoebe plays childish games with her name,but childishness itself excuses phoniness, and Holden holds out great hope for her, provided she is not corrupted by the phoniness that waits ready to seduce us all. Phoebe's innocence is the goal of Holden's quest. His journey through the world of phonies leads him to her as his last hope. It is, of course, to her that he has wanted to return ever since he ran away from Pencey, but when he finally does get to see her, it is clear that for him there is no one left he can turn to. Her innocence can redeem him, for he considers himself lost. His wish to catch others from falling over the edge is the wish of the reformed sinner, not the blessed innocent. Holden might be able to break their fall, but only a Phoebe can lead them back into the light. His older brother, D. B., is a lost cause. He has grown up and sold out to Hollywood, and at the end of the book we see him squiring around a phony English actress and offering platitudes to Holden.

The basic myth behind this story is clearly the myth of initiation. Holden takes what Pencey has led him to suspect and applies it to life only to have it reaffirmed that life is a disappointment. This disappointment, however, leads to a deeper mythical level in which the hero attempts and at times even seems to effect a return to innocence—in Holden's case in his return to Phoebe and his reinforced appreciation for her genuineness. *The Catcher in the Rye* also has strong elements of the odyssey in which the hero travels geographically and spiritually through a world of temptation and deception on his way "home." It also suggests the horrors of the vacuum between death and resurrection when death seems so terribly final and resurrection so frighteningly uncertain. In this respect it becomes something of a "dark night of the soul," certainly no less painful—and perhaps a great deal more—by being an adolescent one.

The Catcher in the Rye thrust its rebellious way into a postwar society that was torn between those who were tired of chaos and longed for tranquility and those who felt that for them life was just beginning. On one side were the older people, the ones who had just endured nearly twenty years of depression, war, and uncertainty, and who were emotionally drained. On the other side were the younger people, aware of the past but too young to be intimidated by it, and they were in no mood to settle down. Although they talked a lot about security, they also sensed a beast within themselves restless to be freed.

Rebellion, however, seemed wrong somehow. These young people respected their parents' desire for stability, and so they tried to find excitement in the postwar booms in construction, education, and recreational activities. Meanwhile, it seemed to them that everything was settling into a rut. They had been raised on dreams of a better world, but the better world was taking on the shape of dreary, look-alike subdivisions and shopping centers. There was plenty of comfort and convenience and very little "life." As rebellion smoldered inside them, society around them became increasingly dull. They began to feel smothered, yet they did not quite know what to do. Something was wrong, but they did not know exactly what. Often they wondered if something was wrong with *them*, and they felt guilty about feeling so discontented in the midst of growing affluence and opportunity.

It was in the hearts of these young people that *The Catcher in the Rye* struck a responsive chord. It put into salty, daring language all their pent-up hostility and frustration and gave them the label they had been looking for to describe the society that threatened to stifle them: phony. No society, no matter how rich, how comfortable, how secure, could have much meaning or substance to it if it was "phony." The book's uninhibited language was its most immediate appeal. Every "goddam" or "Chrissake" was a slap in society's sanctimonious face. The fact that the book was censured and even banned only added fuel to the fire. Such actions proved Holden—and all his admirers—right. It's just what some "goddam phony" *would* do, "for Chrissake!"

Although *The Catcher in the Rye* seems to take place in an easily recognizable world, Salinger is selective in his details in a way that creates a tension between the sharply etched close-up and the vague, impressionistic long-shot. Things like Ackley's pimples, Stradlater's dirty razor, Mr. Spencer's white chest hairs, and the hats the girls from Seattle wear are well-focused and enlarged. Pencey, though, seems to be seen from the hill from which Holden watches the football game. And New York City is not a bustling metropolis full of cars and people but a wintry, desolate place, a murky backdrop against which Holden is dwarfed and isolated. It is eerily quiet and deserted, as if Holden's cab is the only vehicle on the streets and the few people he encounters are the only people in the city.

Even within the vagueness, however, there is precision. Holden's cab may be the only car on the street, but it has a vomity smell to it. An empty hotel lobby smells of 5,000 dead cigars. And when the snow falls, it is like real snow dropped onto a stage setting. Sometimes Salinger creates the opposite effect. When his mother enters D.B.'s room, where Phoebe is sleeping, her presence in this precisely described room is as evanescent as the smoke from the cigarette that Holden has just hastily put out.

When we put these impressions together, we realize that Salinger has created a world of blurred edges and detailed interiors that conveys the illusion of reality but that is actually a very clever distortion of it. Central Park, for example, is not the park of muggers and bums and assorted vagrants (as it was even then), but rather an empty stage on which Salinger places ducks or children at play or a lonely Holden Caulfield forlornly watching the children and worrying about the ducks. The scene is described with such precision, however, that we accept it without question. It is the reality of perpetual twilight where untroubled children laugh and skate as the sky grows darker and where grim forces that lurk in the shadows prepare to pounce.

Early in the book we see Holden on a hilltop, looking down at a football game in which he has no real interest, either as player or fan. This scene establishes both the fact of his alienation from others and the reason for it. He alienates himself by choice, sometimes because he cannot stand the company of others, sometimes because he becomes disappointed with their company, and sometimes because his actions seem calculated to drive others away.

In all these situations, however, he is ambivalent. He dislikes Ackley and Stradlater, yet seeks them out, only to find further reason for dislike. He visits Mr. Spencer and Mr. Antolini, only to find their company disagreeable. And after forcing himself on Sally Hayes or Carl Luce, he is at pains to be his most obnoxious. His wanting people close to him yet keeping them at a distance is one of the attractions the book continues to have for readers who share his need for people and, at the same time, his distrust of them.

Holden's alienation, however, goes deeper than his ambiguous relationships with people. His family, for one thing, has come apart at the seams. There is no longer a unit he can rejoin. The various educational institutions he has attended promise one thing and do another. Thus, they become things from which he must disengage himself. He cannot tolerate cheap entertainment, yet that which is not cheap is cheapened by those who praise it without understanding it. And even those who do not need to pander to an audience—people like the Lunts and even the Greenwich Village piano player—show off shamelessly. Holden is heading down a road that has only ruts. Twenty years later, in the late sixties or seventies, Holden might have carved his own rut, followed his dream of dropping out and drifting, and nobody would have stopped him or, for that matter, cared. But in his day such a departure was tantamount to social suicide.

Holden is a fledgling existentialist, learning where he is going by going there. He sees that it is up to him to create values in a world that seems to have lost or abandoned its. This is why his frustrated "escape" spoke to those at the time the book appeared who longed for a new direction but simply did not know which way to turn. All they could do was to follow his example and turn inward and risk being called neurotic—or worse.

Holden Caulfield is too troubled a young man to honestly enjoy feeling superior to others, but many readers see only the brashness and none of the humility. Granted, he is adolescent enough to patronize others at times, but he is also mature enough to know that he, too, is vulnerable. Cult readers, however, identify with the adolescent side of Holden's character without seeing the mature side in true perspective. This reaction is as much Salinger's fault as it is the reader's, for Salinger succeeds almost too well in supplying us with an irresistible way of observing—and abusing—all those phonies who seem all of a sudden to be coming out of the woodwork. Holden's insight seems uncanny for his age, and perhaps the first thing that intrigues us is his precociousness. It makes us wonder why we never saw things so clearly or expressed things so well.

It is easy to see why a cult reader would be overwhelmed by the accuracy of Holden's cold, appraising eye. Even those readers who are not cult followers find that the book seduces them into seeing people through Holden's eyes and analyzing them as he might. The uncritical reader, however, has no problem seeing Holden's fits of depression, even his ultimate institutionalization, as the result of social injustice rather than personal psychosis. And if that same reader sees beyond the black humor to the black despair beneath, then it is easy to see how that reader can feel smugly sympathetic, nodding in silent commiseration with a fellow victim of life's callous ironies.

All cult books reinforce the egos of their readers, otherwise there would be no cult. Cult books are mirrors in which committed readers see themselves reflected in only the most flattering sense, in the way Narcissus felt when he spied his own image in a pool of water, and it was love at first sight. Cult followers must feel superior to others, and one of the best ways to feel superior is to be in possession of knowledge others are too ignorant or too stupid to share. To be able to convince Mrs. Morrow that her son is an angel when he knows him to be an obnoxious little nerd is a pleasurable intellectual game for Holden. It is a game his admirers also enjoy, for they become fascinated with the power to manipulate someone for whom they have no regard. *The Catcher in the Rye* has encouraged many to enjoy such power by indulging in similar manipulation. What greater self-satisfaction than to feel oneself a genuine among the phonies—or better yet, a "real" phony among all the second–rate fakes?

Although Holden suffers intense loneliness and alienation, and seems to enjoy every painful pang, he also knows how to make others squirm. His insults range from the subtle and calculated way in which he annoys Carl Luce during their conversation at the hotel bar to the direct and deliberate way he concludes the afternoon with Sally Hayes by telling her that she is a "pain in the ass."

The scene between Holden and Ernest Morrow's mother on the train to New York is an example of manipulation that is cruelly dishonest. By building up her son in her eyes, Holden's lies can only result in worse disillusion for the mother. His premise is that a mother's blindness is phony and, therefore, worth exploiting.

Although Holden does not seem to think that the sort of lie he tells is destructive, he is quick to pounce on institutional lies ("This school builds character," "You've got to play the game") as slogans that deceive and thus do harm. Such high-handed double-think give cult readers carte blanche to lie and insult whenever they feel they are in the presence of a phony. In fact, cult readers in the fifties got a kick out of "turning somebody on," a phrase that back then meant to put someone on the defensive.

Holden's masochism is more obvious. When he is not courting abuse from others, he is punishing himself with exhaustion and too much smoking. He enjoys suffering because it helps him feel sorry for himself. Sometimes he even fantasizes that he has been shot in the stomach and is dying. But it is during his serious fits of depression that we see him most painfully critical of himself. He lies about himself, saying that he is "very sexy," and then confesses that he is a virgin. He struts and brags and then collapses under the weight of his own self-deception. It is this arrogant self-doubt, of course, that has continued to endear him to his many admirers over the years. They share his disdain for a phony world, but they also suffer moments of severe doubt about their supercilious attitudes and wonder sometimes if they are as genuine as they would like to pretend. Many of them ultimately identify with Holden's neurosis, convinced that it is they who are sick and out-of-step, and that there is no place for them in this world. In the sixties and seventies, they showed contempt for society by mocking it and contempt for themselves by surrendering to the facelessness of mass protest and communal living.

Salinger's description of reality led many readers to adjust their behavior in accordance with that description. Following Holden's example, many young people of his generation became psychological dropouts. They did not throw rocks at schools or try to close them down. Instead, as good disciples of Thoreau, they offered what they liked to refer to as "passive resistance." They simply ceased to believe in the ideals given them and expressed their rejection by refusing to cooperate. If they stayed in school, their grades dropped as their cynicism increased. If they left school, it was to try to "make it on their own." Few succeeded. Their forces were too scattered, and society was not yet ready either to accept or to ignore them.

Salinger set out to do one thing, his readers another. What Salinger did was to give us an accurate picture of a young man submerged in a society that threatened to crush rather than release his potential. Holden is being flattened out, steamrolled, and his energies are directed toward mere survival. He is suffocating and clawing for air. He is at the bottom of an abandoned well with no idea of how to get out.

Salinger's early readers, however, saw a way out. By misreading Holden's persistent abuse of the world, they could adopt an attitude of convenient smugness and thus dismiss rather than rearrange the world. They could at the same time become sentimental. Salinger sentimentalizes Holden's family, or at least his brothers and sisters. Holden's grief over Allie's death and his concern for Phoebe's future offered a way for self-pity to be excused as brotherly love. From here it is but a short step to the luxury of *Weltschmerz,* that feeling of melancholy compassion for the whole wide suffering world. At one point Holden confesses that he misses the very people he loathes. How easy, then, if you feel that way, to go around carrying the burden of world sorrow on your shoulders and at the same time to feel that there is nothing you can do about it.

Of course, such an evasion is simply another part of the inward retreat. From the privacy of one's own clenched self it is easy to look out upon a lost world and feel helpless. This is probably the way a humanitarian felt in the days when the masses were so hopelessly destitute that their salvation was an equally hopeless dream. A feeling of futility is excusable when social forces seem marshaled against you, but in times of relative affluence, futility is as phony as the tears of the woman Holden observes weeping buckets over a tearjerker at Radio City Music Hall while her child begs to be taken to the bathroom. It is, however, not unusual for cult followers to fancy themselves as romantic victims at the mercy of oppressive forces eager to crush their spirit.

Ultimately, the attraction of such an indulgent attitude lay in the very ideal cult followers so vocally disavowed: the desire for security. To act is to risk. Thoughts can be altered, denied, revoked; deeds are visible and irrevocable, and they can also be embarrassing. In a world so recently restless, the odds against overt rebellion were simply too great.

With rebellion ruled out, Holden is left with three options, none of them very realistic. He can try to recapture the past, he can hope to remain stuck in the present, or he can run away and face some unknown future. His dream of recapturing the past is summed up in the phonograph record he buys for Phoebe. A phonograph record preserves music "under glass." The moment is caught, but of course, times change, so the music is never really the same. When the record gets broken, it is the dissolution of a dream. The song can only be remembered, as Allie is remembered, even though time, meanwhile, is working its effect on memory.

The dream of the present is revealed in Holden's concern about where the ducks in Central Park go in the winter. They must be somewhere, and he wants to know where, because if they are away somewhere free, then it is possible to escape the chill of the present. But what if they have been taken inside somewhere? That would be imprisonment. Holden never learns the answer, and it is highly probable that he does not want to. Imprisonment he knows; escape he is incapable of.

He makes his dream of the future—to run away to New England and live off the land—depend upon Sally Hayes's cooperation. He lacks the courage to pursue this dream (a dream that a later generation would pursue) but he can blame Sally for the loss of this dream.

Thus, both reform and escape are impossible dreams, and Holden, trapped in utter frustration, forfeits his sanity because he cannot face that demoralizing truth. Meanwhile, his admirers, unwilling to follow him all the way, shrugged their shoulders, hocked their dreams, and trudged to the suburbs. A generation later, their children came about as close as a body can to turning those "impossible" dreams into reality.

FOR FURTHER READING

Bloom, Harold, ed. *Holden Caulfield*. New York: Chelsea House, 1990.

Daughtry, Vivian F. "A Novel Worth Teaching: Salinger's *The Catcher in the Rye*." *The Virginia English Bulletin* (Winter 1986): 88–94.

Nadel, Alan. "Rhetoric, Sanity, and the Cold War: The Significance of Holden Caulfield's Testimony." *The Centennial Review* (Fall 1988): 351–71.

Steinle, Pamela Louise Hunt. "If a Body Catch a Body: J. D. Salinger's *The Catcher in the Rye* and Post-World War II American Culture." *DAI* 49 (1988): 107A.

Catch–22

Joseph Heller
(1961)

Catch–22 is a Kafkaesque satire on the bureaucratic madness of the military and on the logical inanity of the military mind. In a curious twist of fate, this peculiar antiwar novel managed to attract two otherwise incompatible audiences. To veterans of World War II, it was a hilarious reminder of the chaos and disorder that seemed always to hover just beneath the structured surface of military life. For them it was the way things were, and if it poked fun at the military, it was simply stating the obvious, not grinding an ax.

To others, however, especially as the decade of the sixties progressed and the war in Vietnam escalated, it was the ultimate pacifist tract, the best reason yet presented for turning one's back on war of any kind and lighting out for neutral ground. The very catch in military logic that it ridiculed—the infamous "Catch–22"—was also their way out. "Be crazy, it's all crazy anyway." As disenchantment with American foreign policy abroad and domestic "oppression" at home mounted, "Catch–22" became the rationale for opposition, desertion, draft-dodging, dropping out, whatever it took to lodge a passive protest against what many considered an unjust war.

Catch–22 is set on the imaginary island of Pianosa during World War II and focuses on Captain Yossarian and his attempts to survive the fanatical lunacy of his bomber squadron's commanders long enough to get home. As the death toll rises, the quota of bombing missions required for home-leave is repeatedly increased. By pleading insanity, Yossarian hopes to find a way out until the doctor quotes the infamous Catch–22, which goes something like this: Flying missions is crazy. To get out of flying them, you must plead insanity. However, since wanting to get out of flying them is proof of sanity, the minute you say you don't want to fly, you have to.

Although Yossarian does not want to fight, he is not a coward, and this was an important part of his appeal to cult readers. He is often called an antihero because he was on the wrong side in a popular war, but in reality he has all the attributes that make up the idealized monomythical hero. He loves life, culture, travel, and adventure, and he is cursed (blessed?) with such a sensitivity to injustice, irrationality, and inhumanity that he ultimately finds himself in opposition to all the powers that be. He is slow to realize the full implications of his predicament, but when he does, he has the courage to take the only definitive action still open to him.

Yossarian has been called one of the great "drop-outs" in American literature, and those who responded to Timothy Leary's exhortation to "tune in, turn on, and drop out" were drawn to him. In his opposition to forces he distrusted, he comes up against the two chief enemies of the counterculture: the Establishment and the System. Yossarian, like his admirers, finds it impossible to live within the Establishment, even to reform it, because he feels, as his admirers did, that it tends to treat human beings as mechanisms, to value conformity above creativity, to regard people's files as more important than the people themselves, and to indulge in official lying as a matter of policy.

The way he sees it (and his admirers shared his vision), the System tends to use war not so much to fight a national enemy as to regulate its own people. It fosters power struggles that victimize the fighting man in wartime and the creative person in peacetime. On every level, the System needs scapegoats and always finds them. The Establishment formulates humanitarian policies not for its own practice but for use in measuring the enemy, for propaganda purposes. Corruption runs rampant in all professions and institutions because private greed is sanctified.

Yossarian's principles accurately reflect the principles of the counterculture. To begin with, Yossarian values individuality and freedom more than status or official recognition. And he thinks of money and machinery as means, not ends. He is also more interested in humanity than in organizations, and when The Organization turns against human values, Yossarian has the courage to remember that there is a higher law than the state and that there are times in history when the state is the villain, when what is needed is a new kind of hero.

Yossarian is this new kind of hero, and the notorious Catch–22 is his dragon. In every written law it is the unwritten loophole that empowers the authorities to revoke one's rights whenever it suits their cruel whims. Because of Catch–22, justice is mocked, the innocent are victimized, and

Yossarian's squadron is forced to fly more than double the number of missions prescribed by air force code.

Cult readers had no trouble finding parallels to Catch 22 in civilian life. A policeman might make an illegal arrest in order to break up a demonstration, but the demonstrators must submit to arrest or else they would be guilty of disobeying the police. By the time the courts assert the law and free the demonstrators, the police have accomplished their purpose.

Orr, the combat pilot and Yossarian's tent-mate and alter-ego, is also the "alter-hero" of the book. In Orr there is something of the real "prophet," for it is he who prepares the way for Yossarian. From the beginning, he has been Yossarian's double, acting in many ways like the ego to Yossarian's id. Orr operates objectively and rationally to their common predicament while Yossarian behaves subjectively, whining and protesting and acting moody. Orr is resourceful and cunning, having lived among his enemies in the guise of a shallow-minded joker while plotting his revenge, while Yossarian has trouble getting beyond his own moods and emotions.

Of course, hovering always in the background and overriding all other symbols is the haunting, mysterious, anonymous Soldier in White, bandaged from head to foot and kept alive by an endless rotation of body fluids. What begins as a grotesque joke—what is excreted at one end is what is injected at the other—becomes a grim symbol of the mechanical regulation of human life: facelessness, self-containment, the withdrawal and isolation of the patient who is thoroughly dehumanized yet kept alive because it has become possible to do so. With the Soldier in White there is even doubt about whether someone actually exists beneath those bandages. And if he does exist, does he hear what is going on around him? Does he think? Can he feel? These are horrible questions that carry the madness of war beyond the battlefield.

Thus the appeal of *Catch–22* as merely another antiwar novel would not account for its cult status. It needed this extra dimension to attract readers to its premise that military methods make a mockery of political goals. Because of the very nature of war, even a "good war" will become an evil, extremist enterprise. It seems safe to conclude that for Heller and his hero, World War II began as an idealistic war, with justifiable, humanitarian aims, and degenerated into just another self-negating, militaristic crusade. No matter how noble the ends, the means become identical with the enemy's. This was the message the counterculturists wanted to hear and the argument still used to oppose any military action, no matter how seemingly justifiable.

This tragic but inevitable corruption of purpose is demonstrated in the scene in which Dobbs proposes to Yossarian that they assassinate

Cathcart because of his illegal treatment of his men. Dobbs is carried away by the idea and soon envisions a blood-bath. Although his desire to punish a guilty commander is understandable, it is clear that Dobbs would soon out-Cathcart Cathcart in his thirst for revenge.

Dobbs's misguided fanaticism is symptomatic of the larger fanaticism that informs the entire narrative of *Catch–22*. A democracy has declared war on the fascist powers because they are aggressively antidemocratic, inhumane, and uncivilized. But the U.S. military establishment is repeatedly revealed as being antidemocratic and quasi-fascist. Clevinger, for example, believes that Scheisskopf is sincere in asking for suggestions, and he responds accordingly with several sensible proposals. As a result, he is punished for his presumption, even framed and humiliated in a travesty of justice worthy of the most heinous of Nazi court trials. Cathcart's contempt for enlisted men, Dreedle's flaunting of his privileges, the way Korn insists that disagreement with him is tantamount to disloyalty to the flag, and the sadistic Star Chamber tactics of the men from the C.I.D. all demonstrate that the military is not defending democracy but undermining it.

Added to this are other crimes dear to the hearts of counterculturists eager to tarnish the image of America. How can the army Yossarian is serving be called antifascist when Captain Black considers a certain corporal to be un-American because he disapproves of Hitler? Furthermore, the Texan and Cathcart both feel free to express racist attitudes, while the tribal history of the native-American White Halfoat makes it clear that the American people are themselves guilty of genocide.

If these examples of latent American fascism are reminiscent of the attitudes expressed in Kurt Vonnegut's cult classic *Slaughterhouse-Five*, the suggestion that perhaps there is a dark side in all of us that war releases is reminiscent of the premise of William Golding's cult classic *Lord of the Flies*. Scene after scene in *Catch–22* postulates the likelihood that war so brings out the worst in men that it can turn humanitarians into butchers. War triggers the release of the sadistic impulses of men like Havermeyer, Aardvark, and Black and creates a climate favorable only to cynical people like Korn and Peckem, exploitative people like Minderbinder, and manipulative people like Wintergreen. War allows military policemen to commit arbitrary, illegal acts simply because there is no way to stop them. In the name of efficiency, armies convert people into mechanisms, as typified by the activities of Scheisskopf and the fate of the Soldier in White. The ultimate antihumanitarian aspect of even a "good war" is shown in the decision to bomb an unwarned civilian population in an undefended village purely for military purposes. An act of this sort makes it impossible for the uncorrupted to see any difference between the enemy and themselves.

An especially curious thing—among a multitude of curious things—

about *Catch–22* is that as the action unfolds, we see or hear almost nothing about an actual enemy. Peckem's "enemy" is Dreedle, the military court's enemy is Clevinger, the C.I.D.'s is the Chaplain, Minderbinder's is his own squadron. One effect of *Catch–22* not lost upon the cult reader is the suspicion that governments on either side use war less as a defense against an enemy than as a means of controlling the lives of their own people.

Although a synopsis of *Catch–22* makes it sound like a routine World War II novel, it is really much more. This is why veterans of that war could appreciate it so much. They understood its target to be the military mind regardless of nation or cause. For them, World War II was a necessary evil, but they did not kid themselves when it came to assessing the virtues of armies on either side. Thus, the wisest of them found much to admire in a desert fox like Rommel and much to deplore in the petty malice of some of their compatriots. They knew evil to be the most egalitarian propensity.

However, younger readers who took it to heart as an antiwar novel saw the scale of evil tilted toward their fathers who, they felt, had whitewashed their wartime misdeeds in the blood of Auschwitz, pretending to have waged a holy war when in reality they found out about the holocaust only after they got back home. Heller wrote the novel during the Korean War, but it appeared at the dawn of the Vietnam War and found its greatest popularity during the time that that war was heating up. The time was right, then, for an assault against the rationalization of what Dwight Eisenhower had called the "Crusade in Europe" and for a blanket denunciation of war for any reason and against any enemy. In this respect, it became the definitive statement of the modern antiwar position, much as Erich Maria Remarque's *All Quiet on the Western Front* (1929) had expressed the pacifism of the post–WWI generation.

Nevertheless, cult readers are sophisticated enough to demand more than the elements of a tract in the literature they take to heart, and in this respect *Catch–22* contains its share of the conventional components of cult fiction. Throughout this book there are numerous references to mythological and literary parallels. Yossarian is Everyman, Aeneas, Christ, Ulysses embarked on an odyssey, a quest, a descent into hell in order to bring back a message, a plan for our salvation. He is the antihero who becomes the hero of this reinvented myth that offers a blueprint for resistance and survival and sanity in a world that insists on repeating its mistakes. Yossarian is a modest man with a wholesome attitude toward life, but because he is sensitive to injustice, irrationality, and inhumanity, he finds himself in opposition to the established authority.

Yossarian describes himself variously as Tarzan, Mandrake, Flash Gordon, Shakespeare, Cain, Ulysses, the Flying Dutchman, Lot in Sodom,

Deirdre of the Sorrows, Sweeney among the Nightingales, and *Supra*-man. Except for the last, these are all heroes who are also outsiders. By calling himself *Supra*-man, Yossarian is saying that he hopes to *surpass* man. In this respect he resembles Frank Bowman of *2001: A Space Odyssey*, Valentine Michael Smith of *Stranger in a Strange Land*, the title character in *Demian*, Howard Roark in *The Fountainhead*, and even Jay Gatsby in *The Great Gatsby*.

All of these are characters who are (or seem to be) larger than life. Yossarian possesses many of the traits that set these people apart and above, one of them being his ability to question clichés and shibboleths, to think for himself, to know what and what not to value from the past. Like his counterparts in other cult novels, Yossarian prides himself on his individuality and is jealous of his freedom, which he values more than mere status or official recognition. He would agree with the famous abolitionist who argued that that which is not just is not legal.

"I'm not running *away* from my responsibilities," says Yossarian as he takes off for Sweden at the end of the novel, an ending that upset some critics. "I'm running *to* them." To war protestors, of course, Yossarian's decision pointed the way for their own escape from an immoral obligation. Running away they found to be much braver than going off to fight a war they did not believe in. As far as they were concerned, personal refusal was the only heroism left, and Yossarian was the hero who would lead them to "a new morality."

While it is true, as some insist, that Yossarian resembles Dr. Strangelove more than King Arthur, it is equally true that simply recycling the same old antiwar message would have failed as surely as those messages themselves had so obviously failed. What good has *The Good Soldier Schweik* or *All Quiet on the Western Front* done? What readers needed to encounter was a Colonel Cathcart, that model of robot-like conformity, a person who measures his happiness according to the "quotation of the day," always trying to adjust to the dictates of the bureaucracy and to avoid confrontations with officialdom. What readers also needed was to encounter a Soldier in White, possibly Heller's most inspired creation, for in this anonymous victim we have the perfect symbol of the rational absurdity of war.

Although the term "Catch–22" has become a permanent part of the language, and the novel continues to attract new readers, by and large its day has passed and its message has no more impact than that of the antiwar novels it tried to surpass. Perhaps the ultimate "Catch–22" is to be found in the fact that war's very absurdity is at bottom its most irresistible attraction and that antiwar novels, like all warning labels, only whet an appetite for the thing they warn against.

FOR FURTHER READING

Merrill, Robert. *Joseph Heller*. Boston: Twayne, 1987.

Potts, Stephen W. *From Here to Absurdity: The Moral Battlefields of Joseph Heller*. New York: Borgo Press, 1982.

Seed, David. *The Fiction of Joseph Heller: Against the Grain*. New York: St. Martin's, 1989.

Tanner, Tony. *City of Words: American Fiction, 1950–1970*. New York: Harper & Row, 1971.

A Clockwork Orange

Anthony Burgess
(1962)

On the surface *A Clockwork Orange* is a novel about juvenile delinquents in a near-future Britain, but on a deeper level it is a novel about conditioning and free will. The "clockwork orange" is a metaphor for that fantasy of modern science, the perfectly programmed man. Stanley Kubrick, who had already made Arthur Clarke's *2001: A Space Odyssey* a cult film classic in 1968, did much the same thing for *A Clockwork Orange* when he adapted it into a highly successful film in 1971. Dispute continues over whether this is a cult film or a cult book, but the question is really moot. What matters is that Anthony Burgess's basic concept, by either means, became a definite cult favorite.

What partially accounts for the popularity of *A Clockwork Orange* as cult fiction is its highly imaginative representation of the generation gap, an expression that had been given new meaning by the seemingly unbreachable rift that had divided parents and children into hostile camps by the early seventies. On the one side stood parents, all of whom had experienced in varying degrees of severity the deprivations of the Great Depression and the horrors of World War II. They looked upon themselves as proud survivors and were wont to parade the virtues of asceticism before their spoiled and ungrateful children. On the other side were the children who felt bullied by all the stories of suffering and sacrifice, who felt they were being told that they could never measure up, that no experience of theirs could ever compare with the Depression and the war, that anything that happened to them would pale by comparison. When at last they had heard enough about "making do" and "doing without," about "pitching in" and "muddling through," when they thought they would scream if they heard one more Glenn Miller record or one more comment about how "they don't make 'em like that anymore," they rebelled.

Sick of the Depression, sick of the war, sick of big bands and crew cuts and Peter Pan collars, they turned their backs on the past, despised on principle anything that happened before Elvis, and set about systematically driving their parents crazy. It was easy. All they had to do was follow one simple principle: If it bugs 'em, do it. Thus, when parents tried to reason with their children, they continued to miss the point. They never saw that their children took the opposite point of view only because it *was* opposite, that they would never give in simply because they were determined not to, regardless of what they might think privately.

When parents pointed to Nazi Germany as an evil enemy, their children spelled America "Amerika" and pointed to the way the United States was treating minorities and third-world nations. When parents boasted of winning a war, their children made it a matter of honor to lose one. When parents derided their former enemies, Germany and Japan, their children turned the Volkswagen "beetle" into the "love bug" and could not buy Japanese gadgets fast enough. When their parents made fun of the British, calling them "Limeys" and other derogatory names, their children welcomed the Beatles and the Rolling Stones with nose-thumbing enthusiasm and made "swinging" London the hip fashion capital of the world with Carnaby Street at the epicenter. In other words, the children of the World War II generation set about systematically dismantling the value structure in which their parents had—innocently, proudly, but relentlessly—imprisoned them.

The story of *A Clockwork Orange* takes place sometime—in the near future when teenage rebelliousness has provoked police-state response. The teenagers speak a street slang laced with graphic neologisms and bastardized Russian called "Nadsat." Street gangs mug and rape at will, and kids drink narcotic-laced milk. The story is narrated by fifteen-year-old Alex, who, along with his three mates, is given to mugging lonely pedestrians, robbing tobacconists' shops, and the like. Alex explains how his buddies ("droogs") got him arrested for beating up ("tolchocking") an old woman ("starry ptitsa") whose death gets him imprisoned. To get out, he volunteers for the "Lodovico treatment," which conditions him to avoid his three main joys: sex, classical music, and "ultra-violent" behavior. The treatment consists of watching the most appalling torture films while under the influence of an emetic drug. One film, a documentary about Nazi atrocities, is accompanied by the music of Beethoven, whose Ninth Symphony is Alex's favorite.

This aversion therapy cures Alex of his violent impulses—and of his love for great music. On his release from prison he becomes the pawn of a protest movement dedicated to the abolition of forcible conditioning for violent criminals. Some readers find the Burgess dilemma too equivocal: Which is worse, the disease or the cure? Burgess blames society for both, and cult followers tend to prefer to draw this conclusion, insisting that society creates the conditions in which criminal behavior flourishes and then, in an attempt to cure the problem, devises methods of conditioning that dehumanize those whose behavior is labeled criminal.

There is a pertinent parallel to this idea in Walker Percy's 1987 novel, *The Thanatos Syndrome*. In this provocative work, Percy presents the reader with a 1990s society that has cured its social problems simply by increasing the sodium content of its drinking water. Almost overnight teenage pregnancies cease, violent crime becomes nonexistent, and AIDS disappears, pornography ceases to sell, and drug dealers go bankrupt. Moreover, worker productivity increases, athletes break previous records, teams experience winning streaks, and people take pride in keeping busy and tidying things up. The only disadvantages to the treatment are the occasional eruptions of "rogue" behavior (unmotivated acts of violence), diminished powers of communication, and the widespread use of infanticide and euthanasia to get rid of the unwanted. It is a "brave new world" that is extremely attractive to the fearful citizens of the nineties for whom the daily news is nothing but a repetition of random acts of violence, serial killings, abortion, and drug-related crime.

In a curious way, Percy's "conservative" novel takes an even more liberal attitude than Burgess's "liberal" novel. In *The Thanatos Syndrome*, Percy strongly opposes conditioning of any sort, regardless of how attractive the results might be. Even in an age of rising crime and irresponsibility, he prefers human nature in the raw to human nature made unnatural through chemical alterations or any other sort of "human engineering." Burgess, on the other hand, has it both ways. While he deplores brainwashing and blames society for Alex's problems, he is reluctant to endorse human nature in the raw. It is a position that many cult readers find attractive, a "pox on both houses," a curiously passive attitude that makes them feel morally superior at no spiritual expense.

Burgess blames the excesses of human nature on a repressive society that corrupts its citizens—and primarily its youth—by restricting their liberty and force-feeding them outmoded values. Thus, their natural rebellion gets out of hand and only leads to more repression. It is a vicious cycle, and at the end of *A Clockwork Orange*, Burgess seems to wash his hands of the whole thing. In fact, he later labeled the book "too didactic, too linguistically exhibitionistic," thus justifying the complaint of some critics that he both raised and rendered moot the question of good and evil. What he is doing is nothing more than following in the footsteps of cult authors like Goethe and Walter Pater, and even

J. D. Salinger, who, after publishing works that inspired cult followings, later had second thoughts about what they had done.

The fact that both the film and the book shocked older readers was all it took to make *A Clockwork Orange* attractive to young people. What they saw that their elders tended to miss was the spirit of black comedy that informs the work. Alex and his "droogs" are a parody of street gangs, and the crimes they commit, whether they are exaggerated or accidental, are stylized in a way that is more theatrical than threatening. Indeed, many of the scenes have a choreographed look, like an intergalactic road-show version of *West Side Story*.

Cult readers (and viewers) also enjoyed the mockery of classical music. Having been brainwashed to believe that all great music is uplifting, they delight in watching Alex do unspeakable things while under the influence of Beethoven's Ninth, with its hymn to joy vibrating through the Dolby speakers as Alex mugs and maims. Later, when the same music is used to accompany films of Nazi atrocities, and to condition Alex to vomit at the sound, cult enthusiasts were delighted to see classical music thus desanctified.

Thus, cult followers in general ignored both Kubrick and Burgess in turning this work into a cult favorite. They were too busy enjoying the rebellion to worry about its cause or to want to change things. They were enjoying a liberation that their sheer numbers and an affluent society were making possible to a degree never before imagined. They were having too much fun fighting their own little fantasy war against the hopelessly square refugees from the swing era. Alex reminded them of Mick Jagger, one of the heroes of this war, a war that counted among its casualties such idols as Jim Morrison, Jimi Hendrix, and Janis Joplin.

It is interesting to note that the movie version of *A Clockwork Orange* had to be edited down to an R-rating after receiving an X-rating that excluded the only audience young enough to be interested in it. There is classic irony operating here, because both the book and the movie are serious, adult fare; yet the audience for both was the same audience that would later turn *The Rocky Horror Picture Show* into the top cult movie classic of all time. This serves as a reminder that cult books (and films) are defined by their readers and audiences, not their authors and producers.

Burgess's work has been dismissed as a minor dystopia, an allegation more in keeping with the spirit of cult followers than that of the general reader who might fear the consequences of a permissive society that has gotten completely out of hand. Rather than blaming Burgess's grim forecast on a society that is too repressive, the general reader is more likely to believe that society has not been repressive enough. Cult followers of the early seventies, however, had little interest in concepts like utopia or dystopia, for they had no historical perspective with which to judge such things. They would have agreed with Henry Ford when he said, "History is bunk." As far as they were concerned, the past was ancient history—and bad example. Depressions? Wars? Why couldn't older people get their act together?

What cult followers saw in *A Clockwork Orange* was an electronically charged age in which teenagers ruled the roost and quadraphonic sound systems could reach hitherto unheard of decibel levels. Of course they also saw the inevitable assault of the storm troopers in the form of parents and other leaders of society who swoop down on fun-loving teens and drag them off to concentration camps that hide under such euphemisms as rehabilitation centers, detox clinics, correctional facilities, and intervention programs.

Alex thus took on the status of a heavy metal hero, psychologically lobotomized by an insensitive society. If his appearance and behavior flirt with fascism, it is something cultists are not likely to admit, even though this is not the first cult book to suggest such a leaning. Cultists are extremists, and extreme political positions are often indistinguishable. The fact that Burgess puts his "fascist" thugs in a "communist" setting and attracts a cult illustrates this point.

One popular myth that helps explain the appeal of *A Clockwork Orange* is the myth of the gangster as hero. The criminal as outcast was one of Fyodor Dostoevsky's favorite motifs, and ever since Romanticism glamorized the misfit, outlaws have seized the imagination. It is not the lawlessness of the gang that matters as much as the gang as outcast, as an outnumbered few pitted against the tyranny of the majority.

The classic western (book and movie) thrived on this myth, and its presence could be felt in the age of the gangster film. And, of course, it was glorified for all time in *West Side Story*. In more recent times, it has found its way into such youthful favorites as *The Outsiders* and *Colors*, not to mention dozens of forgettable sci-fi stories in which teams of vigilantes confront lawless hordes.

In *A Clockwork Orange* there is the presence of yet another myth, one that can be found only between the lines. This is the myth of the Pied Piper. Burgess was in his mid-forties when he wrote this book. Whatever his avowed purpose, he succeeded in becoming a modern-day Pied Piper who led great numbers of children down a very strange path. But he must share the dubious honor of leading the willing young down the primrose path of protest with that sly old trickster Kurt Vonnegut, Jr.

Orwell's *1984* still chills the blood of readers young and old, and Huxley's *Brave New World* leaves most readers feeling decidedly uncomfortable, but the reaction then, and to some extent now, to *A Clockwork Orange* can be summed up in the comment made by one young man, a college freshman who had read the book and just seen the movie: "Groovy!" Nobody has ever said that about the Orwell or Huxley books.

FOR FURTHER READING

Coleman, Julian. "Burgess' *A Clockwork Orange.*" *Explicator* (Fall 1983): 62–63.

Gorra, Michael. "The World of *A Clockwork Orange.*" *The Gettysburg Review* (Autumn 1990): 630–34.

Ingersoll, Earl. "Burgess' *A Clockwork Orange.*" *Explicator* (Fall 1986): 60–62.

The Day of the Locust

Nathanael West
(1939)

The Day of the Locust falls into a special category reserved for those books that have achieved cult status even though they lack some of the components seemingly indispensable to cult literature. The novels of William Burroughs fall into this category, as do those of Hunter S. Thompson and Kurt Vonnegut, all cult favorites. The works of these writers have extraordinary main characters, for example, but they are characters who lack the charm or charisma we usually associate with a traditional hero—or even antihero. In the works of these authors, the leading characters are more likely to be simply points of view or convenient centers around which the action takes place.

Tod Hackett, the set designer and central character in Nathanael West's *The Day of the Locust,* is little more than a useful fixture in the novel, a typical Hollywood flunky who hangs around in the novel but gets no more involved than anybody else, who is, in fact, less interesting than characters like Faye Greener or Homer Simpson or the dwarf, Abe Kusich.

The appeal of a novel like this is a lot like the appeal of absurdist theater. It is easier in the theater to bypass the necessity for a point of view and transfer the angle of vision directly to the audience. In other words, instead of inventing a Nick Carraway (*The Great Gatsby*), through whose eyes the reader judges Gatsby and his friends, a playwright can simply present Gatsby and his friends and let the audience watch them the way Nick might. The movies do this, too, making the camera the point of view. In fact, since the camera is a more persuasive instrument of control, it can take the place of the narrator with extraordinary effectiveness.

The Day of the Locust is a literary version of that classic thirties movie genre, the screwball comedy. Ordinary readers, accustomed to more authorial intrusion and expecting to read about the Hollywood of the glossy movie magazines, were put off by the novel's eccentric and irreverent tone and treatment. Cult readers, however, relished the chance to witness the inanities of tinseltown from the catbird seat, as it were, feeling that West had painted a picture as wickedly accurate as any Hieronymus Bosch nightmare, one in which they fortunately had no part. This marks an important departure from the usual relationship between cult books and their readers. Ordinarily, where cult books are concerned, readers are anything but detached observers. They usually relate closely to the main character or to the events depicted, and experience intense involvement in the mood and action of the book. In novels like *The Day of the Locust*, the reader is never a part of the action but merely an onlooker, peering as if through the thick glass window of a recording studio.

The perception of reality in *The Day of the Locust* is presented in a way that is also different from the heightened reality of most cult books. In the West novel, the reality is again closer to the reality of a movie set: a reality that looks even more real than life itself but that is constructed of artifice and practiced deception, a matter of painted canvas, false fronts, and clever lighting. The characters that crowd this novel seem to come straight out of old Marx Brothers or Three Stooges comedies or out of that old Olson and Johnson exercise in celluloid frenzy, *Hellzapoppin*.' Words like "zany" and "screwball" and "madcap," all part of the Hollywood slang of the thirties, describe perfectly the bizarre antics of the oddballs who inhabit the cardboard world of the movies that West recreates as if on the back lot of a back lot.

For cult readers, it is the very phoniness of the "real" Hollywood that symbolizes the phoniness of all society. To them, West's Hollywood is a microcosm of what they see (or think they see) around them. The book has always had an avid following, but it was not until it was reissued in 1957 that it really caught on as a cult book. What readers saw then was the tawdry truth behind the crumbling facade of decaying American cities and the despair beneath the vain ambitions of people chasing neon rainbows. Finding fault with America was just beginning to become a popular pastime with the restless young, a pastime that started in beatnik rebellion only to erupt a decade later in hippie revolution. *The Day of the Locust* provided the incentive for welcoming, even encouraging, violent change.

The vision in *The Day of the Locust* is, after all, apocalyptic. The actual "day of the locust" itself is the day God's wrath descends on the wicked city and its depraved inhabitants and wreaks havoc. And the invasion of the locusts is only one of many plagues God sends to punish transgressors who choose to ignore his warnings and violate his commandments. In the years since the publication of *The Day of the Locust,* there has been a steady stream of science-fiction movies, from the mutant fly and monster tarantula movies of the fifties to the more sophisticated space adventures of the seventies and eighties. Today if a movie were to be made titled *The Day of the Locust,* audiences would expect a movie about some sort of invasion, either of killer locusts that attack people or of mutant locusts that emerge full grown from giant pods. There is an irony here that West would have appreciated, maybe even anticipated. For just as he gave *Miss Lonelyhearts* a title right out of the syndicated advice columns of the daily tabloids, he could not have chosen a better title for a novel about Hollywood than *The Day of the Locust* with its suggestion of a trashy movie about an invasion of hordes of predatory bugs.

The Day of the Locust also appeals to a taste for black comedy that is shared by cult readers who favor this sort of book. The humorous aspect of cult literature is a curious one because sometimes the humor is entirely in the eye of the beholder, as with those who laugh at *Lord of the Flies;* sometimes it is to be found mostly between the lines, as in *A Canticle for Leibowitz;* or it may be an integral part of the narrative, as in *Catch–22.* Seldom is it as blatant as it is in Hunter S. Thompson's *Fear and Loathing in Las Vegas.*

Nevertheless, Robert Stone calls this book "one of the funniest of great American novels"(5). He is probably right, but it must be admitted that the antics of the characters West lets loose in *Locust* are funny only to those with a taste for mordant wit. To others the humor might seem tasteless or merely blatant. Just as some people cannot laugh at Charlie Chaplin, and others find Bette Midler merely gross, there are still others who find these comedians genuinely hilarious. Those who have a taste for cynical wit are usually those who consider themselves to be far above the idiocy of those they are laughing at, and their scorn is mixed with a sort of patronizing pity. Part of them envies the uninhibited lifestyle of the Hollywood hustlers, regardless of risks to sanity and soul, and wonders if it is not after all better to be a drunk on the make in the land of broken dreams than to be a shifty stockbroker or crooked politician. Readers who discovered West in the fifties were fond of "bourgeois bashing," and they tended to favor any way of living that shocked middle-class mores. *The Day of the Locust* offered them a cast of characters who might have set out from Dubuque but who would never have been allowed back in.

Today, after so many Hollywood biographies, so many books about stars and studios, about directors and designers, about every facet of life in the movie capital of the world, *The Day of the Locust* has lost much of its sting, certainly much of its power to shock. By now everyone has seen the Moorish palaces, the pink stucco and fake palms, the frenzied galas and tawdry publicity stunts. We have even lived to see it immortalized, not just in Hollywood–where it is possible to take a "Grave Line" tour of the sites of celebrity suicides and murders—but also in Orlando, Florida, where the Disney corporation has transplanted a Hollywood studio with all its attendant tastelessness and gimcrackery intact. What was once a sign of the decay of Western civilization is now a theme park with the squeaky clean stamp of approval of the Disney imprimatur to give it style—and yes, even a certain class. Cashing in on a growing penchant for self-parody, the Disney studios at Orlando might decide to film *The Day of the Locust*. It could be a delightful comedy, richly layered to satisfy various levels of the viewing public. It might even become a cult classic.

But in spite of the overexposure Hollywood has received, in a town that thrives on excess, overexposure is ultimately impossible. In an introduction to a 1989 edition of *The Day of the Locust*, director Robert Stone writes: "No one with unambiguous feelings about 'the Coast' could have written a work so lyrical with fascinated loathing, and no one but West could be so lyrical and so wry at once"(6). To read the novel today is to be taken by surprise at its freshness, the way one sometimes is at a videotape of an old favorite that has not, as one feared, faded and gone fuzzy but remained amazingly crisp and clear to the point that one can almost forget that all the characters in it are now dead.

Budd Schulberg reread this novel in order to write an introduction to the 1965 Time-Life edition of it, and this was his reaction: "From the opening pages I was drawn back into this bleak fantasy of life in the lower depths of the Hollywood inferno. There was the Westian boardinghouse, 'the color of diluted mustard,' with its 'pink Moorish columns which supported turnip-shaped lintels.' There was the outrageous, arrogant dwarf, Abe Kusich, the local bookie. And Faye Greener, who is all the teenage voluptuaries who ever flaunt themselves at the studio gates; how deftly West rolled them all into one delicious, malicious bundle. And her father, the ex-vaudevillian to end them all, reduced to selling silver polish door to door, for whom every strange hallway is a stage as he hams his way into the grave. His death scene, with his daughter indulging in narcissistic primping with her back to him, is only one of a hilarious collection of mad vignettes" (Skillion 191).

Finally, something needs to be said about the appeal to cultists of writers whose untimely deaths leave readers with two cherished things: (1) a curiosity about what the author might have gone on to write; and (2) the convenient reality of a limited output. This was unfortunately not true in the case of Thomas Wolfe, who left trunks of unpublished manuscripts behind, far too much for any but the most ardent fan to wade through. Had what he published before he died at thirty-eight been all there was, or had there been a few modest scraps left around, chances are fans would have been secretly relieved and thus more enthusiastic. As it was, Wolfe's editors carved three fat tomes out of what they found, and no one hoped to find any more. In the case of F. Scott Fitzgerald, the output was just about right, with the unfinished *The Last Tycoon* just titillating enough to leave the question of what he might have gone on to write, had he lived, hanging fire. West had completed even less by the time he died in an auto accident at the age of thirty-six: four relatively short novels (*The Dream Life of Balso Snell, Miss Lonelyhearts, A Cool Million,* and *The Day of the Locust.*) So the guesswork about his future remains an idle, academic exercise.

Thus, like James Agee, Nathanael West is praised as much for what he accomplished as he is for what it is thought he might have accomplished had he lived. "It is my hunch," says Budd Schulberg, "that a more fulfilled better adjusted Pep [his nickname] West would have gone on to ever greater works, just as I thought Fitzgerald's most mature work might have been ahead of him, if only he could have hung on. But Scott was at the far edge of his physical resources. Pep was in his prime. One eye was focused on the tragedy of cornered modern man, the other on the comedy, with the double image blended in a rare, apocalyptic vision. What a shelf of books he might have given us in his next thirty-six years!" (Skillion 193).

One wonders. Our culture has long had a passion for idealizing artists who die young. Early death gives these figures a romantic dimension that makes them larger than life. It also means that they are safely out of harm's way, safely beyond embarrassment, and we are free to speculate on what might have been and can even give them credit for the promise. Chances are Nathanael West would have gone the way of J. D. Salinger or Walter M. Miller, two cult figures whose following has grown exponentially since they stopped writing. For whatever reason, it seems, an aborted career adds to the mystique of a cult author. In Nathanael West's case, the status of *The Day of the Locust* as a cult book would stand regardless of what he wrote later, much as Hermann Hesse's earlier works, written more than thirty years before his death, are the ones that continue to attract cult followers while his later books are largely neglected.

FOR FURTHER READING

Allmendinger, Blake. "The Death of a Mute Mythology: From Silent Movies to the Talkies in *Day of the Locust.*" *Literature/Film Quarterly* 16.2 (1988) 107–11.

Fine, David. "Nathanael West, Raymond Chandler, and the Los Angeles Novel." *California History* (Winter 1989–1990): 196–201.

Petite, Joseph. "Demonic Imagery in *The Day of the Locust.*" *Journal of Evolutionary Psychology* (March 1986): 137–41.

Scherr, Barry J. "Phallic Inadequacy, the Death of Eros and the 'End of the World': A Lawrentian Interpretation of *The Day of the Locust.*" *Recovering Literature: A Journal of Contextualist Criticism* (Summer 1986): 19–49.

Weltzien, O. Alan. "Constructing the Presence of Irony in *The Day of the Locust.*" *West Virginia University Philological Papers* 33 (1987): 58–67.

Demian

Hermann Hesse
(1919)

Demian has had two lives as a cult favorite. When it first appeared in Germany at the end of World War I, it struck a responsive chord in the hearts of young people disillusioned by war and disheartened by the specious promises of a system that seemed based on false principles. In his introduction to the first English translation of the novel, Thomas Mann speaks of the "electrifying" impact *Demian* had on the post–WWI generation in Europe. The youth of this generation, he says, responded to the "uncanny accuracy" of the work and felt that at last someone had emerged who could interpret the longings and misgivings of their innermost being. They thought this spokesman was someone from among themselves, whereas in reality Hesse was already forty-two years old when this book took Europe by storm.

In the early sixties, when it surfaced in America as a cult favorite of the rising tide of disenchanted youth, it offered them a way of looking at a world hopelessly divided, its alternatives equally unsatisfactory. Disillusionment was rampant, revolution was in the air, and there was widespread contempt for an industrial civilization that was drowning mankind in its own prosperity. The Cuban missile crisis, the assassination of John F. Kennedy, the shaky détentes and shifting alliances of the cold war, the chronic unrest in the Middle East and the escalating unrest in Southeast Asia, the indifference of Americans to civil rights, ecology, values—indifference to anything, it seemed, but their own self-aggrandizement—were concerns that troubled the young of the early sixties and made them restive.

If any one event threw things into sharp focus—and, paradoxically, into dire confusion—it was the erection of the Berlin wall. The wall was the physical representation of the symbolic iron curtain, for it made real and visible and inescapable the fact that the major powers of the world were divided into enemy camps. It forced one to take sides, but to many young people it was a Hobson's choice. It not only pitted former allies against each other, it made bedfellows of former enemies. To the young, there was something morally suspect about such cavalier alliances. To them, such fickleness bespoke the manipulation of the masses by those in power whose weapons were fear and false hope rather than freedom and love.

Hesse's description in *Demian* of a society mired in hypocrisy and deceit seemed directly applicable to the America of the sixties. Although he was describing Europe on the eve of World War I, the young readers of the counterculture saw history repeating itself with a vengeance. Like Hesse, they lamented the triumph of the herd instinct, the disappearance of freedom and love and, above all, the false communion that struck him as the inevitable consequence of a community "born of fear and dread, out of embarrassment, but inwardly rotten, outworn, close to collapsing" (115).

Technology was the ogre threatening to regiment men's lives and turn them into button-pushing robots. Universities were only processing plants where talents and dreams were butchered and cooked and packaged for a researched and engineered market. Hesse offered not so much a program for revolution as a climate for it. And the disillusioned of the sixties found this climate most compatible with the desolate wasteland to which they felt they had been exiled.

The fear of nuclear warfare and the embarrassment of affluence, the scandal of pollution and the injustice of discrimination, outworn value systems and archaic social structures—all pointed to imminent collapse. Demian applauds genuine communion as a beautiful thing, but he sees nothing like it flourishing anywhere. He argues that the true spirit will spring "from the knowledge that separate individuals have of one another" and that this special communion will eventually "transform the world." This is the sort of message that cult readers respond to, for it speaks to the alienated and promises them a spiritual bond with others equally alienated and just as eager to change the world. It also includes the irresistible paradox of surrendering to attain power. Demian says that he can "feel the approaching conflict," that it is coming soon, that it is going to expose the "bankruptcy of present-day ideals," and that it will result in the "sweeping away of Stone Age gods" for, he says, the contemporary world, the world as we know it, "wants to die, wants to perish—and it will" (115–16).

A few pages later he adds an element of danger to his prophecies that makes them all the more exciting. He says he smells death in the air but that "nothing can be born without first dying." He also predicts that the coming upheaval will be "far more terrible than I had thought" (131). The smell of death was in the air of the sixties, from the gunshots in Dallas in 1963 to the gunshots at Kent State in 1970, with assassination, murder, and warfare rampant. Add to the bloodshed at home the unimaginable carnage in Vietnam, and the history of the sixties was, indeed, far more terrible than anyone would have thought.

Because *Demian* purports to describe pre–WW I Europe, yet seems to describe America in the sixties, it becomes clear that the reality it describes is, in fact, a condition in which more than accuracy of observation is at work. One can observe rottenness and bankruptcy and false communion, but one can only "feel the approaching conflict" and surmise a death wish. It is an interesting stylistic jump from what is seen ("bankruptcy") to what is sensed ("smell of death in the air") to what is assumed ("nothing can be born without first dying") to what is guessed at ("far more terrible than I had thought"). The rapid succession and ultimate fusion of these four vastly different methods of description are what make the accuracy "uncanny," to use Thomas Mann's apt modifier. In varying degrees, it is this sort of highly impressionistic description within a cult book that seduces readers into unquestioning acceptance.

Few books speak to the alienated the way *Demian* does. Pistorius, Sinclair's organist friend and mentor, tells Sinclair that although people like them are quite lonely, they still have each other as well as the satisfaction of knowing that they are different, that they are rebels who crave the unusual. Such people, he says, may strike others as sinister, but they are the courageous ones, the only ones of true character.

As Demian tells it, those who wear the sign of Cain might well be considered odd by the rest of the world, maybe even crazy or dangerous, but they are constantly moving toward a more complete state of awareness while others strive to restrict their thinking to conform to the opinions of the herd. In *Demian* those who bear the mark of Cain are aloof, different, superior—in a word, alienated. It requires no effort at all for a willing reader to reverse the definition and feel that those who are alienated must then bear the mark of Cain. Alienation now becomes justified, coveted, desirable, for it is a mark of distinction, not of weakness. Here, as elsewhere, we see the familiar Emersonian inversion at work: If to be great is to be misunderstood, then it stands to reason that to be misunderstood is to be great.

People who bear the mark can never be part of the crowd because they could never share its shallowness and self-deception. The only reality is the one contained within you, Pistorius tells Sinclair, and that explains why so many people live unreal lives. They are what the world tells them they are, not what they really are inside. For those who acknowledge the only reality to be the one within themselves, there can be no communion with those who never allow the world within to assert itself. You can be happy in such ignorance as long as you know nothing else, says Pistorius, but once you look inside, you no longer have the choice of following the crowd. It is easy to take the path of the majority, he tells Sinclair, but difficult to travel alone, firm as one's resolve may be.

Since traveling alone is infinitely preferable to the company of philistines, cult readers take comfort in uncovering evidence of the boorishness of the herd. Like Holden Caulfield, finding a phony makes their day. When he is at school in Heidelberg, Sinclair obviously enjoys his heightened awareness of the emptiness of student life. At one point he stands on a street corner listening to the "methodically rehearsed gaiety" coming from some nearby hangouts. He brands it "false communion" and thinks of it as "shedding the responsibility of fate" and taking "flight to the herd." One wonders just how it is possible to escape fate that, by definition, is inevitable. However, sandwiched in between "false communion" and "flight to the herd," that sort of enigmatic phrase slips between the cracks and into the mind almost subliminally. Apparently, those not of the herd may somehow choose to accept the responsibility of fate, which sounds oddly like choosing to accept the law of gravity. (For some startling observations on this subject, see Robert Pirsig's *Zen and the Art of Motorcycle Maintenance*.)

There is a psychotic element in such thinking that has been known to lead to delusions of grandeur. In cult followers, it usually results only in a severe case of enlarged ego. Those most susceptible to the attractions of a cult book feel not only alienated but inferior, and seek some means whereby they may invert the low image they have of themselves and feel above rather than beneath others. Emil Sinclair recounts the effect of Beatrice in terms analogous to the effect of a cult book on such a reader. Claiming that the "cult of Beatrice" has completely changed his life, he says that in the space of a day he has changed from "precocious cynic" to "acolyte whose aim was to become a saint." The path to sainthood is the same as the path to selfhood. This is a path that Sinclair takes eagerly because its difficulty allows him to yield to his own vanity and because his idol Demian is there to lead him. Demian convinces Sinclair that there are some—those with the mark of Cain—who are not only superior to other people but above the law.

Once Sinclair has been indoctrinated, has passed from hedonism to mysticism, and has been accepted into Frau Eva's select company, he makes his own declaration of independence from the herd. He now dedicates himself to representing the will of nature in its drive toward something new, toward acquiring the power to move toward a new and distant humanity. But this power is not acquired without first surrendering to a common ideal, and the plot line of *Demian* is the succession of tribulations that bring Sinclair along the difficult path to self-awareness, which for him is the awareness that he wears the mark of Cain and is in tune with the will of nature.

Oddly enough, in order to achieve the ultimate independence and self-awareness necessary to fulfill his destiny, Sinclair must first submerge his identity in the collective identity of the coterie surrounding the mysterious Frau Eva. In oblique homage to Christian mysticism, Hesse is echoing something very much akin to the Christian idea of spiritual rebirth that comes only with a total abnegation of self and total surrender to the will of God—what Hesse calls the "will of Nature." In yielding to a sense of inner direction that sets him above the herd, Sinclair is submitting to the cult that associates this special difference with the mark of Cain. Thus, a way out exists for readers who cherish the lonely journey but still long for brotherhood. They can anticipate Sinclair's joy when he is welcomed into Frau Eva's house and, after a long isolation, encounters the kind of companionship that to him is possible only between people who have tasted complete loneliness.

Before his entry into this world of warmth and light, however, Sinclair had enjoyed the vicissitudes of the dark night of the soul. The darkest nights were those suffered during his student days, which he passed in tortured debauchery. He tells of passing hours in "the lowest dives, among beer puddles and dirty tables" amusing his friends with "remarks of unprecedented cynicism." But even though he often succeeded in shocking these friends, he was inwardly tormented. "In my inmost heart," he confesses, "I was in awe of everything I belittled and lay weeping before my soul, my past, my mother, before God" (62–63).

His crude behavior makes him despise both himself and those who encourage him, thereby widening the gulf between himself and them. He refers to himself as a "barroom hero" with a cynicism honed to pander the most brutal tastes (63). Because he sees himself so clearly and judges himself so harshly, he is unable to become one with his companions. Thus, he feels more alone when he is among them, and he suffers greatly, the more so because not one of them suspects.

Although his degradation seems suicidal at times, Sinclair's most private opinion of himself never reaches the nadir of unmitigated contempt, partly because he does not really care what becomes of him. He is fully aware that he is often offensive, even obnoxious, but he excuses his behavior as his way of protesting. This is the boast of a person whose low opinion of himself is never so low as his opinion of the world. He admits that he is ruining himself in the process and he justifies himself in the manner of a petulant child who thumbs his nose at the world. "If the world had no use for people like me," he says, "if it did not have a better place and higher tasks for them, well, in that case, people like me would go to pot, and the loss would be the world's" (64–65).

Such boasting is music to the ears of cult readers eager to offend in the name of freedom.

Sinclair finally breaks with this life and these companions, as he must finally break with everyone on his difficult journey upward. He argues that everyone needs to undergo some "cruelly lonely experience," even if most people cannot endure loneliness for long and come crawling back to the banal security of the herd. Sinclair does not crawl back, but neither does he remain in splendid isolation. At the end of the lonely journey is the companionship of Frau Eva's clique, and it is in surrender to this clique that he finds that sense of power over life that he so brilliantly sums up in a passage curious for its mixture of singular and plural pronouns skillfully manipulated to balance separateness against unity, to preserve the one within the many.

Near the end of the book, Sinclair says that the only duty and destiny he and his kind acknowledge is that each of them should become utterly themselves by being totally faithful to the seed planted in them by Nature. Such a wish reveals the paradox at the core of *Demian* that allowed cult readers to have their cake and eat it too. The secret lies in the answer to the question: How can true individuals join together in a group and still be individuals? The answer lies in the term "collective individualism," an oxymoron that the Oriental mind might be capable of absorbing but that is alien to the Western mind. Thus, a cult in the West does more than absorb identities; it devours them. Many of Hesse's most devoted readers in the early thirties tried to persuade Hesse to remain in Germany and become its leader. They were ready to pool their wills in a mass movement, the very thing that Hesse reasoned against. That his message was easily misunderstood can be seen in the eagerness with which so many surrendered their will to Adolf Hitler, swallowed *Mein Kampf* whole, and then let both man and book literally devour them.

Those who rediscovered Hesse in the sixties had a familiarity with Oriental mysticism that Hesse's earlier readers had lacked. Interest in Zen Buddhism was high in the sixties and was influential in the revival of interest in Hesse. Thus, followers of Hesse did make the attempt to maintain the delicate balance between self and community. In *Demian* this balance results in a state of readiness, in a mind prepared to participate in destiny. Unprepared minds resist destiny and challenge fate, defend complacency and deny the inevitable. The ready mind patiently waits for the moment when it is needed to play its part in the unfolding of evolution.

Impatience is the nemesis of readiness. One might wait forever and never be needed, and this is too long a wait for Western temperaments. Even those schooled in Oriental mysticism could only recount the waiting in terms of a few years. They could bide their time in communes or crash in other people's pads only so long. Then something had to happen. And in the escalating turmoil of the sixties, that something could not be too far off. Sooner or later the balance had to tip in favor of community and one's involvement in its struggles. For this, however, Hesse had paved the way. At first Demian talks rather vaguely as if involvement will only be in a sort of spiritual way, not as leaders and lawgivers but rather as those prepared to "accomplish the incredible if their ideals are threatened." But then his speech becomes more strident as he talks again about being marked like Cain, about the need to "arouse fear and hatred," and to "drive men out of complacency" and into more "dangerous reaches" (124).

"Arouse" and "drive" are hardly weak verbs, and "dangerous reaches" does not suggest a spiritual harbor. When next he refers to men of the past who have driven other men into dangerous reaches, his list is not just of holy men like Moses and Buddha but of military men like Napoleon and Bismarck. With figures like this to follow, the next step is simply to find or create that cause. Demian says, "What particular movement one serves and what pole one is directed from are matters outside one's own choice" (124). Whose choice, then? The power to which one has surrendered? The movement one wishes to serve? This might not be what Hesse means, but it is easy to read it that way.

So the adjustment of one's mental patterns leads to modification of one's behavioral patterns. The mind is ready to seek out sympathetic minds, to band in groups, to join forces, to live a lifestyle that sets one apart. The sixties, with its revolutions in hair, clothing, and modes of living, its drug and rock culture, and its antiestablishment pose, provided the perfect setting for the transformation of Demian's readiness into physical preparedness.

A ready mind is no longer alert once it is fixed at ready stance. Like a satellite in orbit, once it has been thrust there, it jettisons its rockets and assumes a momentum not of its own powering. Cult followers are like multiple satellites in orbit, and once their minds are set, they are "ready" minds only in the sense that they are primed. Their control, however, has passed to external forces in the way satellites move at the whim of extraterrestrial forces and cosmic laws. In short, such minds become lazy.

At the end of *Demian*, Emil Sinclair's mind is in such a state. He has followed the path to the end, and there it has come to rest, ready, waiting, but no longer changing. He even refers to that state of readiness as if it were a locked chamber, deep inside himself, where as he gazes into a dark mirror, he sees his image, "now completely resembling him, my brother, my master" (141). These are the last words of the book, and no words could better express the static condition of the torpid mind. The image in the mirror is complete, unchanging, forever the final image of himself that is one with the image of Demian. He has lost himself in his mentor, his "master" to whom he has now become slave.

Cult followers could likewise put their minds at ease in this reflection. If they looked into their own dark mirror and saw Demian, they saw the mark of Cain on the impassive, "utterly remote" face, the mark that summed up their relationship to the world. Perhaps they oversimplified Hesse's mysticism, perhaps they were ignorant of his compassion; if so, he does little in *Demian* to mitigate the resultant smugness of their inferences. Difficult as he says it is, it all seems somehow much too easy.

FOR FURTHER READING

Knapp, Bettina L. "Abraxas: Light and Dark Sides of Divinity in Hermann Hesse's *Demian.*" *Symposium: A Quarterly Journal in Modern Foreign Literatures* (Spring 1984): 28–42.

Nelson, Donald F. "Hermann Hesse's *Demian* and the Resolution of the Mother-Complex." *Germanic Review* (Spring 1984): 57–62.

Neuer, Johanna. "Jungian Archetypes in Hermann Hesse's *Demian.*" *Germanic Review* (Winter 1982): 9–15.

Newton, Robert P. "Destiny and Hesse's *Demian.*" *German Quarterly* (Fall 1985): 519–39.

Ziefle, Helmut W. "God and Man in Hermann Hesse's *Demian.*" *Kosmas: Journal of Czechoslovak & Central European Studies* (Summer 1983): 43–58.

Dune

Frank Herbert
(1965)

The science-fiction genre is itself a cult genre, and among its prolific offerings are many titles that qualify as individual cult books. However, if one title were to head the list, it would have to be *Dune*—and for reasons that go beyond the routine components of cult fiction.

For one thing, *Dune* is as much admired by people who do not care that much for science fiction as it is by people who do, probably because first and foremost it is a cracking good yarn that owes as much to King Arthur and the *Arabian Nights* as it does to H. G. Wells and Jules Verne. For another, *Dune* has as many fierce detractors as it has fanatic devotees. This may seem like an odd asset, but whereas most books that are disliked are passively dismissed, *Dune* is passionately disputed. Cult books have always inspired controversy, but in the case of *Dune,* the dissenters amount almost to a cult following in themselves.

It would be helpful, therefore, to consider the points of contention before going on to examine the case for the enthusiasts. For one thing, detractors find its sheer size as offensive as the gigantic sandworms that torment its characters. They argue that such bulk merely enlarges the book's flaws, that going to such extremes to realize so fully a totally banal civilization amounts finally to supreme parody. The story is a tissue of clichés anyway, they maintain, and to dwell on them at such length simply magnifies their silliness. Thus, any attempt on the part of cult readers to argue the merits of the book's psychological and spiritual insights invites derision from opponents who see characters driven by jealousy, revenge, and fear—elemental motives that are fine for keeping the pot boiling but add nothing to the sum total of human awareness, except perhaps to those who have never read anything else.

Both admirers and detractors are unhappy about Herbert's apparent waffling on ecological matters. His ecological sensitivity is one of the things that made *Dune* so popular right from the start, particularly to the readers of the sixties who had just become environmentally aware. The Fremen's dream of turning the desert planet Arrakis into a garden found favor with readers who saw such dreams as incontestably good. But when the dream comes true, as it does in the sequels to *Dune,* the negative impact on the environment cannot be ignored. Water is anathema to the sandworms, and the sandworms are necessary to the production of *melange,* the unique spice so important to the inhabitants of all the planets.

When it first appeared, *Dune* was hailed as a bible of ecological awareness. Environmentalists saw as a dominant theme of the work the reminder that actions have consequences throughout the ecosystem. Thus, the idea of laboring for centuries to reform a whole planet seemed to offer the kind of vision so desperately needed in a nation just becoming aware of pollution and its problems. Although this vision survived relatively intact in *Dune.* It was in the sequels, *Dune Messiah* and *Children of Dune,* that the means used to get there were examined and found wanting.

Not only did readers feel betrayed when Herbert showed the liberated Fremen becoming barbarians themselves, they also had a hard time accepting the premise that the greening of the planet Dune was responsible for the degeneration of Fremen. What they seemed willing to ignore, of course, was the ease with which their hero, Paul Atreides, turns from bloodthirsty avenger to peace-loving savior. Before battle he is crying death to all Harkonnens. Afterwards he is welcoming in an era of peace. The truth is that slaves do become oppressors and that the downtrodden, once they have overthrown their rulers, inevitably end up taking their place, as in Orwell's *Animal Farm.* Herbert is being merely realistic, but his readers would have none of it, at least in the later books.

This reaction to the later books throws more light on the unique place that *Dune* occupies, for it points up the fact that when it comes to analyzing cult fiction, so much depends on the eye of the beholder. This is nowhere clearer perhaps than in cult readers' reception of the book's central myth, the coming of the prophesied Messiah. There is no doubt that this is an important—perhaps the most important—myth of Western civilization. Try as we might to evade it, the dream persists of an anointed leader, conceived under special circumstances, and destined to appear at a predetermined but unspecified time to rescue the world from evil and destruction.

There seems also to persist in the recesses of the mind—perhaps somewhere deep inside the Jungian collective unconscious—a reverence for some sort of hereditary authority that does not come from the will of the people but from the will of some transcendent power. *Dune* is by no means alone in presenting authority in this manner. Paul, like King Arthur, is clearly a supernatural being; notice how all before him who have taken the water of life have died. This is only one of many tests of a character forged in an Olympian crucible.

"Each age devises and believes its own fantasies," says Malcolm Muggeridge (*Jesus*, 49), and *Dune* is one of our age's most influential and enduring. Although it is an international favorite, its special appeal to American audiences may well owe something to its use of many of the familiar conventions of the traditional western. The fact that most of the action is played out in what looks a lot like Death Valley is only a superficial example of the similarity. Like Clay Blaisedell in Oakley Hall's *Warlock*, Paul Atreides is the unyielding redeemer who is above the law and who is welcomed as a savior by people held hostage by marauders. In *Warlock* it is the infamous McQuown gang, notorious for running deputy sheriffs out of town and then tearing the place up. The townspeople of Warlock, like the Fremen on Arrakis, are rescued by a superior leader who then vows to annihilate all traces of the enemy. From that point on, the story lines diverge, but whether Blaisedell shoots it out with McQuown in the streets of Warlock at high noon or Paul duels Feyd-Rautha Harkonnen to the death on Arrakis, the confrontations are essentially the same. It is the good guys and the bad guys locking horns in a power struggle, except that in Warlock, once the good guys win, they send their redeemer packing, afraid of any power—good or evil—that is above the law.

Dune is an odd blend of the vulgar and the sublime, a rich and complex mixture of depravity and nobility, of sword play and ceremony, of gore and glory. Its intrigues, both noble and nefarious, are Byzantine, and its enormities are Grand Guignol. It is in every way a *tour de force*, as seductive to the sophisticated as to the naive. Again, detractors find this sort of indiscriminate mixture ultimately cloying, rather like the spice *melange* harvested on Arrakis, disregarding, of course, its ability to expand the consciousness. They maintain sardonically that readers need to swallow something in order to make it through *Dune* whereas enthusiasts welcome the approval and use of mind-altering drugs as part of *Dune*'s essential appeal.

Since *Dune* is so obviously a pastiche of many myths, it would be redundant to argue its mythical appeal to cult readers. What needs to be pointed out, however, is the range and diversity of the myths the book contains. Paul Astreides, the young hero of the novel, has in him elements of Aeneas and Alexander, of Siegfried and Parsifal, of Buddha and Mohammed and, of course, Christ. And the detailed rites of passage that constitute his initiation are those that go into the making of every hero in cult literature from Werther to Emil Sinclair and from Holden Caulfield to Valentine Michael Smith. His mother, Jessica, later the Reverend Mother of the Fremen, is reminiscent of strong female figures from St. Augustine's mother, Monica, to Demian's mother, Eva, with more than a hint of Morgan Le Fey.

Incidental myths include the travail of the oppressed and the overthrow of the oppressors, the journey of the liberators from ignominy to victory, the quest for wisdom and power and love, the journey into exile, and the triumphant return. Overriding them all is the desire for revenge, a desire so insistent that it eclipses that most persistent of myths; namely the coming of the Messiah and the fulfillment of the prophecy heralding this sacred event.

Disciples of Carl Jung can rejoice in Herbert's testament to the collective unconscious in the form of a story that, while it takes place eight millennia hence, is as familiar as the legends of the past and as current as any headline from the Middle East. Just substitute oil for spice, Saddam Hussein for Vladimir Harkonnen, and Iraq for Arrakis, and you have a modern-day *Dune,* sand and all. Disciples of Sigmund Freud, of course, can have a field day analyzing the relationship between Paul and Jessica and Leto, for while Paul is the secret heir and prophesied Messiah, he is also dutiful son, protector of his mother and avenger of his father. Jessica is not only the mother of this Messiah but also a concubine and a witch who becomes Reverend Mother of the Fremen. Leto is the tragic father figure, a man of dignity and humanity who falls victim to the treachery of a trusted ally. The interaction among the three is complex; Jessica's delivery of Leto's daughter *after* she drinks the water of life and becomes Reverend Mother adds yet another twist to this intriguing puzzle.

The reality that Herbert creates in *Dune* is a surrealistic abstract of life lived constantly on the edge. Just as the stories about King Arthur or Robin Hood create the feeling that life back then was a neverending series of jousts and rousts and derring-do, so do *Dune*'s schemes and encounters engross the reader so that there is no time even to think of things like crab grass and compact discs and social security. Cult readers of this book are people for whom the word "vicarious" takes on new meaning; they don't just live the life of the Fremen and the Harkonnens secondhand, they are *there,* psychologically, emotionally, spiritually—everything but physically. But like the time travelers in *Dune,* they can travel without ever moving; for them space itself folds. And with its unmistakable debt to medieval romances, *Dune* invites readers to live in an eternal Middle Ages of the mind.

Western civilization may rest on the pillars of Christianity, but even Christians have never been entirely comfortable with the image of Jesus as common man, born in a stable, running around the desert in beard and sandals, consorting with low life, mingling with the masses, disdaining wealth, washing people's feet, and finally hanging ignominiously on a common cross between common thieves. Much as they may protest the opposite, deep in many hearts lurks a seed of disappointment that the promised Messiah did not measure up to expectations. The Jews have been much criticized for having expected a bit more show, some pomp and circumstance perhaps, maybe a fanfare or two, a blaze of glory, choirs of angels, a display of power, certainly some pretty unambiguous signs that he was who he said he was and that he meant business; but some of the criticism directed against this expectation stems from a Christian sense of guilt over sharing that expectation. Next time, we say, surely the Heavens will open wide their portals and, in robes of silk and wearing a crown of gold, Christ will descend an alabaster staircase and proclaim His second coming—and a chance to get it right this time.

That it is Paul Atreides who fulfills the expectation of the Messiah is one of the book's strongest appeals. When we see Paul survive superhuman tests of endurance and mature into a man of strength and wisdom and virtue, when we are privy to his keen intelligence and observe his self-assurance, we accept him as the leader he seems so obviously destined to be. At one point he wonders about his own lack of feeling for others (a feeling that does, fortunately, return later), and even then we accept this as a sign that he is above what could be a weakness of character; we believe that compassion must be deferred when there are matters of greater import at stake. This lack of feeling, even if temporary, is in striking contrast to the character of Christ, in whom compassion is uppermost, and was once called a "ruling passion." Christ died for His followers; Paul kills for his.

Of course, it is a convention of epic literature to present a hero in shining armor mounted on a white steed, a magic sword in his hand, around him a charmed circle. Some see in *Dune* a warning against the blind tendency of humans to follow a charismatic leader, but if this theme is present, it is one that is lost on most cult readers. If there is one thing a cult reader must have, it is someone to idealize, and that person can never be a villain. He may be an outcast or even an outlaw so long as we can take his side or follow safely in his footsteps. Where there are warnings against charismatic leaders, the message must be unmistakable, as it is in *Lord of the Flies*, where no one can admire Jack when all is said and done.

Throughout this work and others by Herbert there runs a distrust of anyone conceding responsibility and decision-making to another. It would seem that this distrust also extends to movie producers, for even such a cult figure as David Lynch, the creative intelligence behind such cult films as *Eraserhead, Blue Velvet,* and *Wild at Heart* and the offbeat television series *Twin Peaks,* failed miserably at making a film of *Dune,* for reasons only *Dune* freaks can fully appreciate. What these disappointed "doonies" recommend is watching the film with the sound off. The same thing could be said about the movie versions of most Stephen King books, especially *The Shining,* and for the same reason: Herbert and King are revered for their language more than anything else, and since no movie can do justice to the richness and diversity, the sheer virtuosity of the language, it is better not to try at all and simply go silent. That way the transformation from a literary to a cinematic experience is total.

Along with H. G. Wells's *The Time Machine,* Robert Heinlein's *Stranger in a Strange Land,* and Walter M. Miller's *A Canticle for Leibowitz,* Herbert's *Dune* defines the genre of classic science fiction. Epic in scope and complex in meaning, this extraordinary novel has been hailed as one of the major achievements of the human imagination. Arthur C. Clarke, author of *2001: A Space Odyssey,* has only the highest praise for this exceptional book, saying that he knows of nothing comparable to it with the possible exception of J.R.R. Tolkien's *The Lord of the Rings.*

FOR FURTHER READING

Cirasa, Robert. "An Epic Impression: Suspense and Prophetic Conventions in the Classical Epics and Frank Herbert's *Dune.*" *Classical and Modern Literature: A Quarterly* (Summer 1984): 195–213.

Collings, Michael R. "The Epic of *Dune*: Epic Traditions in Modern Science Fiction." In *Aspects of Fantasy: Selected Essays from the Second International Conference on the Fantastic in Literature and Film.* Westport, Conn.: Greenwood, 1986: 131–39.

Fjellman, Stephen M. "Prescience and Power: God Emperor of Dune and the Intellectuals." *Science-Fiction Studies* (March 1986): 50–63.

McLean, Susan. "A Psychological Approach to Fantasy in the *Dune* Series." *Extrapolation: A Journal of Science Fiction and Fantasy* (Summer 1982): 150–57.

Riggs, Don. "Future and 'Progress' in *Foundation* and *Dune.*" In *Spectrum of the Fantastic.* Westport, Conn.: Greenwood, 1988: 113–17.

Fear and Loathing in Las Vegas

Hunter S. Thompson
(1971)

Fear and Loathing in Las Vegas is such a product of its times that readers since have had trouble coming to terms with it. To a later generation scared straight by drug-awareness campaigns and trained to "just say no," the quantity and variety of drugs ingested by Hunter S. Thompson (alias Raoul Duke; a.k.a. Dr. Gonzo) and his Samoan attorney alone are no laughing matter. Where others see irrepressible free spirits, this audience sees irresponsible jerks. On the other hand, those who are attracted to the book only for its outrageous humor often fail to appreciate the bleakness of its moral landscape. *Fear and Loathing in Las Vegas* is both a jet-black comedy and a doomsday parable.

While most cult books survive their initial popularity and enter the mainstream of literature by dint of their universality, it is not uncommon for some cult books to fall into oblivion once the times have passed them by. One such book is *Jonathan Livingston Seagull*, which had an enthusiastic following in the early 1970s but then quickly and mercifully disappeared. *Fear and Loathing in Las Vegas* is unique among cult books in that it deserves universality mostly because it is such a perfect expression of its times. If it shares this fate with any other works, they would be *The Sorrows of Young Werther*, *The Great Gatsby*, or *Look Homeward, Angel*.

Fear and Loathing in Las Vegas is a deliberately offensive book. There is no doubt that Thompson is out to irritate. Playing the part of public gadfly has been a Hunter S. Thompson trademark, apparent in such early works as *The Great Shark Hunt* and *Fear and Loathing on the Campaign Trail '72*, and in a collection of abrasive articles that appeared in 1989 under the title *Songs of the Doomed: More Notes on the Death of the American Dream*. "Doctor" Hunter S. Thompson, as he is identified on the book jacket, is the self-styled journalist who invented, labeled, and defined "gonzo" journalism, the hallmark of which is its ability to see how far one can exceed what we shall call the Puke Factor (or PF). The Puke Factor is the degree to which a book can nauseate the reader, and the point of greatest nausea, the point at which the PF is highest, is what we would ordinarily call the climax.

The climax of this book is the scene in which the Hispanic maid unexpectedly enters the hotel room of Thompson and his attorney, a room that resembles "the site of some disastrous zoological experiment involving whiskey and gorillas," and startles the three-hundred pound Samoan attorney who is "kneeling, stark naked, in the closet, vomiting into his shoes" (180–91). The two men then proceed to reduce the woman to tears, first accusing her of spying on them, then enlisting her support with bribery and threats. This mixture of the unimaginable squalor of the room and their contemptible treatment of this poor woman really tests the reader's PF tolerance level, for this scene has been anticipated by earlier scenes of unspeakable grossness and abusive sexist behavior.

At this point even cult readers stop laughing, for they have the uneasy feeling that things have gone too far. It is the point at a particularly uninhibited party when what is happening is irreversible, the moment when rich rockers assure the management that all damages will be paid for, including the funeral of the teenage groupie who took a dive from the penthouse balcony. In *Fear and Loathing in Las Vegas,* it is a vision of the lowest circle of hell, but what makes it even more loathsome is that the perpetrators of this shambles get away with it. Operating parallel to the Puke Factor is the Thunderbolt Syndrome, a term that applies to behavior that can only be stopped by a bolt of lightning from God, behavior that recognizes no bounds other than physical impossibility, behavior that is based on ultimate risk taking.

Throughout this bleak black comedy Thompson and his attorney shake their fists in defiance at mortal limitations not only by ingesting incredible amounts of drugs but also by driving their cars as fast as they will go, by telling monumental untruths just for the fun of it, and by treating people and property with unabashed contempt. At every turn they are simply waiting for God to hurl that thunderbolt. About halfway through the novel, when he is barreling across Death Valley in his Great Red Shark full of six-hundred bars of Neutrogena soap, Thompson asks God for just "five more high-speed hours before you bring the hammer down. . . . Which is really not a hell of a lot to ask, Lord, because the final incredible truth is that I am not guilty. All I did was take your gibberish *seriously* . . . and you see where it got me? My primitive Christian instincts have made me a criminal" (86–87). And a few minutes later, when he has pushed his speed up to 120 miles an hour, his blasphemy reaches Thunderbolt Syndrome proportions. "You evil bastard!" he cries. "This is *your* work! You'd better take care of me, Lord . . . because if you don't you're going to have me *on your hands*'' (87).

Cult readers in the early 1970s were not in the least offended by Thompson's excesses in *Fear and Loathing in Las Vegas*. On the contrary, they rejoiced at the offense the book might give to readers ''over thirty,'' members of the establishment, and particularly parents. In their attempts to define a liberating lifestyle for themselves, these original readers felt it necessary to indulge in hyperbole wherever possible, and Thompson became, for them, the voice of excess. The unbridled vulgarity of his language itself was liberating, not to mention the highly unorthodox ideas it expressed and the behavior it promoted. It was as if Jack Kerouac and William S. Burroughs had joined in a *Totentanz*, both high on speed in every sense of the word. Thompson and his attorney are disciples of these two men in being both attracted to and repelled by the American Dream, driven as it were to get at the heart of it, yet sickened by the sight of it.

Already in the first chapter, Thompson announces that he and his attorney are off to Las Vegas to find the American Dream. What they find there, of course, is a nightmare, but it is as much a product of what they bring to it as what they find there. Thompson makes it clear from the start that Las Vegas is not a place you just find yourself in, a place you just happen to visit. Going there is a deliberate act, and once you are there, there can be no pretending that you are there by accident or that you do not know what you are doing there. Innocence, then, is not presumed as you enter the portals of the American Dream, nor is it in any way a desirable attribute for happiness there.

In equating Las Vegas with the myth of the American Dream, Thompson is not likely to find disagreement, except perhaps among those fervent disciples of Nathanael West who would prefer to give Hollywood (or the whole Los Angeles area) top billing. But what makes Las Vegas such an ideal setting for this myth is that it is such a haven for the bourgeois. Unlike Hollywood, which is a two-class town of haves and have-nots, Las Vegas is relentlessly middle-class, middle-income, and middle-aged. And while the dream everywhere is to get rich quick, here it is not motivated by power or ambition or the drive for success but by pure greed.

This is the place where the full dimension of the American Dream is explored, for that dream has always contained within it the risk of losing. And losers in Las Vegas cannot expect any handout but a one-way bus ticket to the border. This is the place where fantasy and reality are a heartbeat apart, where you either get what you came for or what you deserve; and while the former inspires only envy, the latter inspires only contempt. Inherent in the Las Vegas psychology is the American hypocrisy that favors the freedom to make a fortune, then insists that the fortune be shared. In Las Vegas you can despise the rich while you happily try to become one of them—and then when you lose,you can rejoice as others lose, too.

But there is much more to the American Dream as embodied in Las Vegas than just money, even though there is no doubt that the dream is lined with silver. Thompson finds the essence of the dream in the manager of the circus who dreamed as a kid of running away and joining the circus. "Now the bastard has his own circus, and a license to steal, too," says a jealous rival. Thompson replies, "It's pure Horatio Alger, all the way down to his attitude." Running a circus and stealing from the customers: this is Thompson's image of Las Vegas and of the way it embodies the American Dream. And, as "Raoul Duke" tells his attorney, "We'd be fools not to ride this strange torpedo all the way out to the end" (191).

There is also what Thompson calls the sociopsychic factor embedded in the American Dream, at least in its Las Vegas manifestation. "Horatio Alger gone mad on drugs in Las Vegas," relaxing, as it were, "in the womb of the desert sun" (12). For the dream, plainly stated, is to get away with murder: to con, to take advantage of, to outwit, outsmart, outrun, outlast anybody who can be suckered—and get away with it. "In a closed society where everybody's guilty," says Thompson, "the only crime is getting caught." And this total abandonment of responsibility becomes a sort of existential mandate, justified by living in a society that perpetrates horrors daily in the name of freedom and justice. "Against that heinous background," says Thompson, "my crimes were pale and meaningless" (72).

The "heinous background" Thompson refers to was, above all, the war in Vietnam, but it also included such countercultural concerns as the suppression of civil rights, threats to the environment, restrictions on freedom of speech, and the presence of Richard M. Nixon in the White House. Implied also, however, was a rejection of history. Anything that had got us into the mess we were in was by nature evil; therefore, when the older generation argued for a traditional sense of values, the young blamed those values for two world wars, a devastating depression, and all the heartache and human misery that went with them. "There was a fantastic universal sense that whatever we were doing was *right*, that we were winning," says Thompson. "And that . . . was the handle—that sense of inevitable victory over the forces of Old and Evil. Not in any mean or military sense; we didn't need that. Our energy would simply *prevail*. . . . We had all the momentum; we were riding the crest of a high and beautiful wave"(68).

As they ride the crest of that wave, Thompson and his grossly obese sidekick come to reveal, in their total disregard for the feelings of everyone around them, the essential heartlessness at the core of so much counterculture compassion. They terrorize hitchhikers and pedestrians with their reckless driving; bully women like Lucy, the artist, and Alice, the maid; vilify all authority; trash hotel rooms and rented cars; so that by the end of the book they have, by Thompson's own admission, "abused every rule Vegas lived by—burning the locals, abusing the tourists, terrifying the help" (173). In the process, of course, they have also abused every rule society lives by, but this is their point: Society deserves it, asks for it, has it coming.

One could argue that these rowdies are merely biting the hand that feeds them, but beneath this obvious truth lies a deeper one; namely, a testament of faith in America that would embarrass Thompson and his disciples were they forced to admit it. For theirs is not the nervous rebellion of those who fear reprisal; theirs is the rebellion of those who feel completely safe—even when they are in the midst of a National Conference of District Attorneys, purportedly covering a four-day seminar on narcotics and dangerous drugs.

Ultimately, *Fear and Loathing in Las Vegas* invites either total acceptance or total rejection. When it first appeared, cult followers liked the idea that the book would offend many; that was a big part of its attraction. But if the book were to speak *for* them, it had to come as close as a book could come to simulating a drug "trip" while maintaining an almost Kafkaesque lucidity. And this is a balancing act the book accomplishes brilliantly, which is why it succeeds as both black comedy and moral parable. The two drug-crazed main characters resemble the wildest of comedy teams—Laurel and Hardy, Abbott and Costello, Cheech and Chong—and their antics are hilarious.

The style, however, is so cold stone sober, so absolutely under control, that one is constantly reminded that a rational mind, in full possession of its faculties, is recounting a nightmarish experience in the full light of day. And this experience is no joke. Thus, it is this sobering second look, this objective assessment the book demands of the reader, that takes the edge off the book's smugness by letting nobody off the hook, neither offended nor offender, neither tourist-pilgrim to the Mecca of Las Vegas or Gonzo journalist there to make fun.

In *My Secret History*, Paul Theroux, one of the most literate products of the fear-and-loathing generation, says he believes comedy to be "the highest expression of truth," and calls it "the public version of a private darkness. The funnier it is," he says, "the more one must speculate on how much terror lies hidden" (407). Imagine, then,how much terror lies hidden beneath the fear and loathing Hunter S. Thompson conveys as he encounters the Vanity Fair of Las Vegas.

FOR FURTHER READING

Caron, James E. "Hunter S. Thompson's 'Gonzo' Journalism and the Tall Tale Tradition in America." *Studies in Popular Culture* 8.1 (1985):1–16.

Hellman, John. *The New Journalism as New Fiction*. Urbana: University of Illinois Press, 1981.

Smith, Kathy Anne. "Writing the Borderline: Journalism's Literary Contract." *DAI* 49 (1989): 3726A.

The Fountainhead

Ayn Rand
(1943)

Cult books are literary accidents. Usually the author is as surprised as anyone at the book's reception, and sometimes not a little embarrassed, as in the case of such cult classics as Johann Wolfgang von Goethe's *The Sorrows of Young Werther*, J. D. Salinger's *The Catcher in the Rye*, and Anthony Burgess's *A Clockwork Orange*. Cult books *happen*, and attempts to write one deliberately are doomed to fail—with, perhaps, one exception. If any author ever set out to write a book with the intention of rallying readers around a cause, that author was Ayn Rand, and that book is *The Fountainhead*.

The Fountainhead is a thesis novel. It illustrates a point. All the common fictional ingredients are there—strong narrative, well-defined characters, complex plot—but they are all subordinate to the idea that controls the novel: the absolute supremacy of the individual over the mob. Thus, the cult it inspired could be called the cult of sanctified selfishness, for Rand's individualists are totally convinced that they come first, that they know what is best for them, and that what is best for them is necessarily best for those beneath them. To continue to make this point throughout the novel, to keep the reader's mind constantly focused on it, and to make the idea stick, Rand manipulates all the techniques of fiction to that end.

Thus, situations are contrived in which the individual is pitted against the mob, characters make embarrassingly revealing speeches about their motivation, every plot device imaginable is employed—and the reader/convert is seduced into a more than willing suspension of disbelief. Rand's critics say that she cannot write, but one senses in such an indictment more of a political than a literary posture; for surely the enduring success of *The Fountainhead*—not to mention the enormously popular *Atlas Shrugged*—cannot be attributed to her philosophy alone. Her style may be somewhat overwrought and her characters cardboard, but she is a genius at plotting, and she knows how to tell a story.

Literary history is strewn with forgotten thesis novels that had their day and then became embalmed in literary history, such as Rousseau's *Emile*, Samuel Butler's *Erewohn*, or Edward Bellamy's *Looking Backward*. If *The Fountainhead* had been written by Upton Sinclair, for example, one doubts that it would still be on the shelves. Books like *The Jungle* become literary curiosities the moment the problems they confront are solved. *The Fountainhead* is a thesis novel that has become a curiosity largely because it has not suffered the fate of most thesis novels. Its detractors aside, part of the reason for the novel's enduring popularity must be attributed to its literary strengths. However, whatever literary strengths it has are not enough to account for the unique impact *The Fountainhead* has exerted on readers since its publication in 1943.

An analysis of the 1948 film version, can be quite helpful in understanding the mystery of the story's mythical appeal. Because Rand herself wrote the screenplay, it is a faithful adaptation (and condensation) of the novel and reveals clearly what an ingenious puppet master Rand really is. The essential melodrama of the book is played out against an art deco backdrop reminiscent of *Citizen Kane* and accompanied by a sonorous musical score by Max Steiner. Gary Cooper is the embodiment of the quiet strength of architectural genius Howard Roark, who would rather slave in a stone quarry than pander to the mob taste for fake Greek temples and phony Gothic facades. And Patricia Neal is seductively sinister as the neurotic purist, Dominique, who would rather destroy beauty than have it degraded at the hands of the Philistines.

Meanwhile, Rand puppets such as Gail Wynand, Peter Keating, and Ellsworth Toohey act out their variations on the themes of sellout and surrender and the vanity of artistic integrity, while ventriloquist Rand puts the appropriate words in their mouths. Ellsworth Toohey, the consummate hypocrite, mouths all those pious platitudes that are operative when the insolence of office meets the proud man's contumely. His is the forked tongue of the socialist who exalts people above individuals in public but who, in private, furthers his own cause at anybody's expense—especially Howard Roark's, for it is because of Toohey's campaign against Roark that Roark cannot find commissions.

One brief exchange between the two men illustrates how Rand manipulates dialogue to make a point. Toohey runs into Roark at the site of a new housing development that Roark has secretly designed for Peter Keating to save Keating from bankruptcy. Toohey, after gloating Iago-like over his own machinations, suddenly says, "Tell me what you think of me. Go ahead. I want to know." Roark stares at him for a moment and then says, "But I *don't* think of you." With one stroke Roark has the upper hand, Toohey is humiliated, and Rand makes her point: Socialists like Toohey live according to the Dow Jones average of public opinion. Individuals like Roark do not bother to even *have* an opinion of people who do not matter.

The focus of *The Fountainhead* is self-centeredness, the component of cult fiction most attractive to cult readers. That this self-centeredness, is embodied in the character of one of the few traditional heroes of modern literature, Howard Roark, makes for an irresistible combination. Roark personifies the sort of rugged individualism that is part of the folklore of the American myth from Natty Bumppo (*The Leather-stocking Tales*) to Captain Ahab (*Moby Dick*) to Huck Finn (*Tom Sawyer*). He is Henry Thoreau by the pond and Walt Whitman singing his "Song of Myself." He is the consummate loner,like so many heroes of cult fiction, but unlike most of them, he neither struts nor frets. He simply stands firm. Like Bartleby ("Bartleby the Scrivener") he does not give in, but unlike Bartleby he has no intention of giving up. What Roark says to cult readers is that any sacrifice is justified in the name of individual integrity and that no concession to please the mob is ever worth it. It is even all right to destroy what others have corrupted.

Perhaps the most audacious act in the novel is Roark's dynamiting of the housing development he has designed secretly for Peter Keating. Commissioned to design a building that is beyond his talents, Keating asks Roark, who has been blacklisted, to design the building for him. Roark agrees, but refuses any compensation, insisting only that Keating promise to respect the integrity of Roark's design. Keating, however, succumbs to pressure from the building's investors and allows alterations to the building that violate Roark's intentions. Roark cannot allow his work to be corrupted for any reason and decides that the building must be destroyed.

That the public good can be sacrificed in the name of artistic integrity is quite a tonic to the ego of readers who loathe the instincts of the herd. That Roark gets away with it may be the major flaw in the novel; certainly it is difficult for sensitive readers to accept emotionally even if they understand it intellectually. But it is the only message Rand dares send to any reader she hopes to convert. While defeat of the individual at the hands of the mob may appeal to a cult reader's self-pity, it is much more inspiring to see one's views exonerated. This is the kind of resolution that can lead to the formation of groups such as the Abraxas Society, inspired by Hermann Hesse's *Demian* or, as in the case of Ayn Rand, the Objectivist Society, a fully organized body with officers and newsletters that flourished during Rand's lifetime and continues to function today.

Ayn Rand usually casts her stories as myths, often setting them in the future when socialism has enslaved society, annihilating all vestiges of individuality, replacing names with social security numbers, and seeing to it that citizens devote most of their energy to the good of all. *The Fountainhead,* while closer to the reality of its times in terms of its architectural argument, actually takes place in a vague future, and the reality it depicts is a reality that has been so filtered through Rand's imagination as to become surrealistic. This is why the stylized movie sets of the film version work so well, with their blend of the art deco backdrops of the thirties and the famous Warner Brothers *film noir* moodiness of the forties, even though the picture preaches clearly of things to come.

In Rand's world the contours are sharp and the sides clearly drawn. On one side is a handful of men of genius—and the women who appreciate them. On the other is the crowd, the mob, the herd—ignorant, tasteless, gullible—eager to be led by the arch fiends of mind control, those power-hungry manipulators who preach humanitarianism in an effort to dupe the masses into following them. Rand's heroes, while they may be unabashed egoists, show their respect for people by refusing to patronize them with handouts and bad art. Her villains are the megalomaniacs who show contempt for the people by catering to the lowest common denominator as a cheap political ploy. But their motivation runs deeper than this, for it is not merely victory over the masses that appeals to them. This is too easily gained to be of much enduring satisfaction. What excites them is the opportunity to destroy the men of genius of whom they are insanely jealous.

In giving victory to the men of genius, Rand is assuring us that the masses are, after all, capable of being enlightened, that their eyes can be opened to the condescension that lurks behind endeavors to provide them with the things their benefactors think good for them—that behind the benign smile they can detect the snicker. The problem ordinary readers have with Roark's acquittal on charges of willful destruction of private property is that they find what he did indefensible and his justification for it smug. They would like to hang him for arrogance alone; thus, they cannot accept such a contrived conclusion. Cult readers, however, are willing to swallow Rand's optimism as an affirmation of their faith in the ultimate triumph of objectivism. While they may secretly wonder where such an enlightened jury might be found, they need to be told that it is worth holding out against the mob. For what good is the struggle without the hope of victory?

Thus what we have in the end is a parable rather than a myth, a story that places faith above reality. And after Howard Roark's acquittal, the plot moves swiftly to a vastly satisfying denouement. Remorseful for having sold out, Gail Wynand kills himself, thus freeing Dominique to marry Roark. However, before he dies, Wynand's last act is to commission Roark to build the "Wynand Building," both a monument to Gail Wynand and the tallest building in the world.

Adhering faithfully to both the spirit and the letter of the novel's conclusion, the movie ends with one of the most memorable scenes in film history. While Howard Roark stands atop this incredibly tall building, looking for all the world like an Olympian deity, Dominique is ascending to meet him in an outside hoist, just a "few planks with a rope for a railing, that rose up the side of the building." Higher and higher the hoist climbs as Rand describes the city receding before Dominique's excited gaze. "Skyscrapers raced her and were left behind. The planks under her feet shot past the antennae of radio stations. The hoist swung like a pendulum above the city. It sped against the side of the building," passing the line where the masonry ended and there was nothing behind her now but "steel ligaments and space. She felt the height pressing against her eardrums. The sun filled her eyes. The air beat against her raised chin" (687).

Then she sees him, "standing above her, on the top platform of the Wynand Building," and he waves to her. At this point the novel ends with a symbolic crescendo. "The line of the ocean cut the sky. The ocean mounted as the city descended. [Dominique] passed the pinnacles of bank buildings. She passed the crowns of courthouses. She rose above the spires of churches." Finance, law, religion have all been transcended. And now "there was only the ocean and the sky and the figure of Howard Roark" (687).

Since *The Fountainhead* is considered by many to be an overwritten tract extolling the virtues of ultraconservatism, its appeal has not been to those who have a taste for Richard Brautigan or Richard Fariña or Hunter S. Thompson. It was not a counterculture favorite, yet it did have its widest audience at about the same time. Thus, some of its appeal can be attributed to its stand against the prevailing forces of the time. However, the curious thing about this book is that beneath the surface politics and the right-wing posturing, there are kinships with counterculture cult books that might embarrass both sides.

One of these shared characteristics is the presence of a monomythical hero embodied here in the larger-than-life figure of Howard Roark. Certainly Roark is as much a strong-willed, independent, law-unto-himself leader as Max Demian (*Demian*), Valentine Michael Smith (*Stranger in a Strange Land*), or Larry Underwood (*The Stand*). Other similarities already referred to are the novel's reinvented reality and its solipsism. In its relationship to the real thing, Rand's New York is as selectively observed as Salinger's or F. Scott Fitzgerald's or Jack Finney's. And the hero as the self-discovered center of the universe is no less obvious in the character of Howard Roark than it is in the character of Clay Blaisedell

(*Warlock*), Werther (*The Sorrows of Young Werther*), or Meursault (*The Stranger*).

What sets *The Fountainhead* apart from most cult books is its unorthodox approach to familiar components of cult fiction particularly relevance, alienation, and suffering. Throughout the cold war, liberal sympathies were the most vocal ones and probably the most influential. In going against this particular grain, Rand was relevant to those who see in liberalism only a more insidious form of repression, who feared that guaranteeing the innumerable rights that liberals demand would require an authoritarian government of totalitarian dimensions, including a vast bureaucracy to sort out all the conflicting rights of all citizens, and a police force empowered to ensure that all rights were respected. This was not a popular view among students and intellectuals during the years of the cold war; therefore, those few who dared to adopt it felt the same revolutionary thrill as their liberal counterparts who were busily fighting "fascist oppression" by protesting against the establishment.

Both sides enjoyed a sense of alienation; both sides felt themselves to be out of step with the conformist silent majority. The only difference was that the Rand Objectivists felt doubly alienated because they were everybody's outcasts. When Ayn Rand appeared on the Phil Donahue show shortly before her death in 1982, she was met with hostility from all sides. Today there are more than a few universities that refuse to shelve her works in their libraries or even recognize her as a literary figure. Some claim that she cannot write decent prose, as if that ever stopped Theodore Dreiser or John Barth, for example; others frankly dislike her politics, while pretending that there was never anything political about Jean-Paul Sartre or John Steinbeck, Graham Greene or Gabriel García Márquez.

Objectivists admit to enjoying to a certain extent the special status of outcast assigned to them by their shrill opponents on the left. Like Howard Roark, they don't really suffer from the snubs and slights because they really don't care what others think. Rather than suffer from rejection or lack of understanding, they, like Roark, suffer self-imposed hardships that they prefer to anything remotely resembling compromise. Just as Roark worked in a stone quarry while he waited for the world to come to him, Objectivists relish obscurity if it means that they have not sold out to the Philistines. That such an attitude can lead to all sorts of self-delusion does not bear laboring. Unfortunately, Objectivists are susceptible to inflated opinions of themselves and a supercilious attitude that reeks of arrogance and greed. This is what happens when cults become institutionalized. The bad points get exaggerated into dogma while the good points reek of hypocrisy. Thus "enlightened self-interest," itself a slogan of the Eisenhower fifties, too easily degenerates into rationalized selfishness, at which point it is hard to distinguish the free-traders from the freeloaders.

There is a curious footnote to the Ayn Rand controversy. She is one of only four women writers included in this study of cult fiction, the other three being Mary Shelley, Sylvia Plath, and S. E. Hinton. (Unfortunately, Isak Dinesen did not make it onto the final list.) For reasons not at all clear, books by women, while they have enjoyed enormous popularity, have failed to inspire the sort of slavish devotion that qualifies them for cult status. One might expect, then, a more charitable reception of her works, but the truth is that her following among women is not great. Like Margaret Thatcher, she has not been accepted by the women one might expect to welcome a woman into the highest ranks of either politics or literature. And just as Margaret Thatcher was looked upon more as a Catherine the Great, surrounding herself with a male court and unashamedly enjoying the perks of power, all sorts of unsavory innuendoes have been made about the composition and character of Ayn Rand's mostly male entourage.

Mention must also be made of Ayn Rand's origins. She was born in Russia and came to America as a child. During her lifetime she became an outspoken enemy of the Soviet Union, a position many were uncomfortable with, seeing in the vehemence of her "defection" an element of treason against her fatherland, not to mention a generous dose of sour grapes. To them her attitude was reactionary, inspired by the Czarist Russia of her childhood and an abiding desire to undo all that has happened since 1917, regardless of its merit.

Alexander Solzhenitsyn found himself in a somewhat similar position when he arrived in the United States and began talking about gulags. It was one thing to find discreet fault with a country that could benefit from a little constructive criticism, but to accuse it of crimes more heinous than those of Nazi Germany was simply going too far. Thus, Ayn Rand found her followers among those who believed in an "evil empire," and as long as her message is obscured by those who see it only as anti-Communist, her appeal to the merits of good old American rugged individualism will continue to wane.

Meanwhile, objectivism is alive and well even though it has split into two bickering camps. While the Ayn Rand Institute flourishes and continues to release writings and tapes of previously unpublished or unreleased material, a breakaway movement spearheaded by David Kelley sprang up in the late eighties after Kelley was denounced by Leonard Peikoff, leader of the Ayn Rand Institute, for defending objectivism at the expense of Libertarianism. When Peikoff asked Kelley to leave objectivism, Kelley led a mass exodus from the Objectivist camp into his own organization and founded, along with philosopher George Walsh and others, the Institute for Objectivist Studies. Philosopher George Walsh, renowned for his scholarship and wit, has become a leading voice in the new movement, and he has joined with Kelley and others in trying to bring objectivism into the real world so that it might assume what they feel is its rightful place as a legitimate school of thought.

FOR FURTHER READING

Baker, James Thomas. *Ayn Rand*. Boston: Twayne, 1987.

Branden, Barbara. *The Passion of Ayn Rand*. New York: Doubleday, 1986.

Branden, Nathaniel. *Judgment Day: My Years With Ayn Rand*. New York: Houghton Mifflin, 1989.

Gladstein, Mimi Reisel. *The Ayn Rand Companion*. Westport, Conn.: Greenwood, 1984.

The Philosophical Thought of Ayn Rand. Carbondale: University of Illinois Press, 1984.

Frankenstein, or the Modern Prometheus

Mary Shelley
(1818)

When Mary Shelley's *Frankenstein* appeared in 1818, it was an immediate sensation, and a sensation it has remained. Several movies have been based on the book—rather loosely based, one might add, for to those weaned on Boris Karloff and Elsa Lanchester, a reading of the Mary Shelley classic comes as something of a shock. Where, for example, is the elaborate laboratory with all the machines and wires, the whirr of giant generators and the crackle of electric arcs infusing "life" into the twitching body of the monster? Where, indeed, since this is the stuff of Hollywood; Mary Shelley devotes only one vague paragraph to the creation of Dr. Frankenstein's notorious monster.

"After days and nights of incredible labour and fatigue," writes Dr. Frankenstein, "I succeeded in discovering the cause of generation and life; nay, more, I became myself capable of bestowing animation upon lifeless matter" (37). And except for a passage or two about spending "nights in vaults and charnel-houses" and dabbling "among the unhallowed damps of the grave," that is it. *Voilá!* The creature is made.

Also missing from the familiar film versions is much of the creature's humanity. While it is true that he is often portrayed as a victim, it is harder to feel sympathy for an eight-foot hulk with a boiler-plate face who stalks about tearing doors off jambs and walking through walls when you can actually *see* him than it is when you only read about him. Mary Shelley leaves his appearance almost entirely to the imagination of the reader, but since movies thrive on making the products of the imagination visible, Hollywood can hardly be blamed for playing Frankenstein itself by bringing the creature to life on the screen. And in the final analysis, no real harm has been done to the essential idea of the story contained in the subtitle "the Modern Prometheus." The idea of the relationship between creator and created and the responsibility one has to the other is still very much intact.

Frankenstein has become such a relevant metaphor for our times—the central myth of modern life, in fact—that its continuing popularity, regardless of the form it takes, is a testament to its enduring status as a cult book. If, over the years, emphasis has shifted from the creature as sympathetic offspring to the creature as demonic force, it only reflects our own increasing uncertainty and mounting fears about our ability to control the forces we unleash. We talk a lot about being at the mercy of our own inventions, helpless prey to a traffic gridlock, a power outage, a mechanical breakdown at a critical moment. Even more, when we think of something man has created only to have it threaten man's very existence, we think of nuclear power.

Although many wish it otherwise, there is no undoing what has been done, no *un*-creating Dr. Frankenstein's indestructible monster, no *un*-inventing the atom bomb. At the end of Mary Shelley's prophetic myth, after having killed Frankenstein's bride, his best friend, and finally the doctor himself, the griefstricken monster vanishes into the arctic night, "borne away by the waves and lost in darkness and distance," presumably to die. But does he die? The movies keep resurrecting him, and we may scoff, but Mary Shelley leaves us with an ambiguous ending. We know that the "demon," as she calls him, *wants* to die, but whether or not he *can* is something else. And that is one of the things about this novel that haunts cult readers.

Because *Frankenstein* has been made such a part of our popular culture, it is difficult to imagine it as the cult favorite it became in its own time, a time now halfway between Shakespeare's day and our own. Although the Gothic novel had been a popular genre for some time, its subject matter had usually been limited to fair maidens locked in towers by swarthy Lotharios. Today one or two of these novels—such as Anne Radcliffe's *The Mysteries of Udolpho*, and Horace Walpole's *The Castle of Otranto*—enjoy a sort of camp cult status, but even in their own day they were parodied by Jane Austen in *Northanger Abbey*, a satire written in 1797 but not published until 1818, the year *Frankenstein* appeared.

Thirty years after the appearance of *Frankenstein*, the publication of *Wuthering Heights* created quite a stir not only because of the demonic Heathcliff but also because its author, presumably a twisted man named Ellis Bell, turned out to be a tormented young woman named Emily Brontë. It is not hard to imagine, then, the astonishment with which *Frankenstein* must have been received, especially since the author was the daughter of the infamous feminist Mary Wollstonecraft and her equally infamous husband, William Godwin, and she was the wife of the notorious Percy Bysshe Shelley, who had married her shortly after his first wife had been driven to suicide by his heartlessness.

Mary Shelley was only nineteen when she wrote this novel, and sometimes it seems as if some mysterious force had guided her pen, for the circumstances surrounding the composition of the novel hardly indicate any larger purpose or meaning. It all began simply enough with Lord Byron's proposal that he and his friends join in a story contest to pass the time during the long days of a rainy Swiss summer. Having just gorged themselves on German ghost tales and romances, they elected to write of the macabre. Neither Byron nor Percy Shelley produced anything of consequence, but Byron's friend Dr. Polidori did manage to come up with a rather impressive vampire story. Mary, however, seemed inspired by the idea, and after a fitful night of bad dreams and wild imaginings, she felt herself possessed by an idea she knew she must write down in order to exorcise it.

In an introduction to the 1831 edition of the novel, she recalled her original intention: "I busied myself to *think of a story* . . . which would speak to the mysterious fears of our nature, and awaken thrilling horror—one to make the reader dread to look around, to curdle the blood and quicken the beatings of the heart" (xiii-xiv). Through a remarkable set of circumstances, that is exactly what she did. First and foremost, *Frankenstein* is a bloodcurdling thriller. And yet, in its theme and artistry Mary Shelley's novel proves more complex than most of its kind, and its very complexity suggests reasons for its having endured in popular taste long after the great Gothic novels of the time have been forgotten.

In his essay on Percy Shelley in *Intellectuals*, historian Paul Johnson comments on the popular misconception of *Frankenstein* as the work of a schoolgirl. He says of the group that gathered on the shores of Lake Geneva during the damp summer of 1816: "Yet if they were in a sense children, they were also adults rejecting the world's values and presenting alternative systems of their own, rather like the students of the 1960s. They did not think of themselves as too young for responsibilities or demand the indulgence due to youth—quite the contrary. Shelley in particular insisted on the high seriousness of his mission to the world" (41).

The popularity of *Frankenstein* even among her contemporaries cannot simply be attributed to the fad for Gothic horror stories. By the time Mary Shelley wrote her novel, those tales of medieval terror, full of darkness and mystery, rampant with bizarre occurrences in strange and haunted castles, had just about run their course. Although Byron and his friends might find momentary pleasure in reading them aloud, the Gothic novels and romances were about to become objects of ridicule in such parodies or humorous imitations as *Nightmare Abbey* by Thomas Love Peacock and *Northanger Abbey* by Austen. Had *Frankenstein* done no more than repeat the old formula, it would have been long since forgotten. Mary Shelley needed a different twist, something that would convey the horror of the old stories in a new and appealing way.

She found what she needed in the newly awakened scientific and humanitarian interests of her age. Mary Shelley did not invent the scientific romance but she was the first to combine it with the horror story to create what has been called variously the first of the "robot" books, a "pseudoscientific thriller," and a "philosophical romance." All of these labels accurately identify the novel's Gothic ancestors, but Mary Shelley was able to add her own inimitable inventions to the genre in a burst of genius that was never to be repeated in her later works. Although she exchanged the conventional medieval settings for a period closer to her own time, she retained the Gothic atmosphere by revealing Victor Frankenstein's passionate interest in the alchemists of the Middle Ages, a fervor that translates easily into his blind devotion to modern science. Moreover, Mary Shelley retains Gothic mood and atmosphere through her forebodings of evil, her descriptions of mist-shrouded mountains and craggy prospects, and her way of showing that Dr. Frankenstein's "project" requires him to work in secret recesses and seek his material amid the horror of cemeteries, the Gothic playgrounds of Mary Shelley's predecessors.

This blend of the old and new appealed to the nineteenth-century mind. The fact that the monster is created blameless, free of the taint of original sin, fascinated cult readers then even more than it does today. It was part of the Romantic rebellion to question the virtue of a God who could create beings whose innocence was compromised even before they had been given a chance to test it. In identifying with Frankenstein's monster, they could become the innocent outcast, the creature corrupted by his own creator.

While more detached readers can see part of themselves in Victor Frankenstein, the man tempted to compete with the gods, driven to unlock the mysteries of creation whatever the cost and then forced to suffer for it, cult readers identify exclusively with the creature, a miserable being, ill-used and put upon, his innate good nature shriveled up, his downfall the result of his creator's revenge on his own creation. For the monster has no wish to gain control, no desire whatsoever but to do good and be loved. But a superior moral stance, like an immaculate conception, is too much for fallible mortals to tolerate. They must destroy it, even if it is a child of their own loins.

Cult readers have little trouble identifying with outcasts of any kind and often feel most rejected by those who are responsible for bringing them into the world. Mary Shelley herself grew up thinking of herself as a monster because her mother had died in childbirth. It is said that she visited her mother's grave often, sitting for hours by the tombstone, punishing herself with guilt for having caused her mother's death. Yet it was something over which she had no control, and she knew it, and when she created the demon in *Frankenstein*, she was exorcising her own demon. Many readers joined her in that ritual.

In 1970 Brian Aldiss published *Frankenstein Unbound*, a provocative new look at circumstances surrounding Mary Shelley's writing of her book along with a fascinating conclusion to what Aldiss saw as her unfinished work. Aldiss's novel is a contemporary science-fiction thriller in which his narrator, Joe Bodenland, on a time trip from the twenty-first century, falls in with the Byron-Shelley-Polidori party on Lake Geneva during that cold, wet summer of 1816. There, in discussions with Byron and Percy Shelley, Bodenland is able to correct the errors in their optimistic, romantic predictions, especially those of Shelley, who sees machines as tools of liberation.

Bodenland argues that men will become adjuncts of machines, will become enslaved by them, and that human goodness will become increasingly irrelevant since it will be unable to operate effectively in such a system. "The greater the complexity of systems," he explains, "the more danger of something going wrong, and the less chance individual will has of operating on the systems for good. First the systems become impersonal. Then they seem to take on a mind of their own,then they become positively malignant." After a moment of meditation, Byron breaks the silence by saying, "Then we are heading for a world full of Frankenstein monsters, Mary!" (95).

In her reply, Mary Shelley speaks for cult readers, then and now, who feel that there is still time to take control. "Our generation must take on the task of thinking about the future," she says, "of assuming towards it the responsibility that we assume towards our children. There are changes in the world to which we must not be passive, or we shall be overwhelmed by them, like children by an illness of which they have no comprehension. When knowledge becomes formulated into a science, then it does take on a life of its own, often alien to the human spirit that conceived it" (96).

"Oh yes," replies Bodenland. "And always the pretense that the innovating spirit is so noble and good! Whereas the cellars of creativity are often stuffed with corpses" (96). Later, Bodenland tells Mary that, regardless of her hopes to the contrary, her tale is prophetic. "Man has the power to invent," he reminds her, "but not to control" (112). Aldiss's novel turns out to be more optimistic than Mary Shelley's and thus, perhaps, less realistic. He thinks that in the time since she lived, man's consciousness has been raised to the point where warnings are heeded and steps taken to avert enslavement to things meant to liberate.

What is missing from the Aldiss version, in spite of the author's reputation for ingenuity and frankness, is the unabashed blasphemy of

Mary Shelley's original. With the fieriest of the Romantics, she shakes her fist at Heaven and dares to call God's bluff, to blame him for creating paradise and then deliberately sabotaging it. And this was a generation before Catherine Earnshaw, madly in love with the Promethean Heathcliff in *Wuthering Heights*, proudly asserts that she dreamed of being in Heaven and while there, was overcome with such misery and homesickness that she was thrown out only to land laughing on top of Wuthering Heights.

Cult readers rejoiced at such audacity, and from that day to this, skepticism about the quality of God's mercy has surfaced in one cult book after another.

FOR FURTHER READING

Brennan, Matthew C. "The Landscape of Grief in Mary Shelley's *Frankenstein*." *Studies in the Humanities* (June 1988): 33–34.

Ellis, Reuben J. "Mary Shelley Reading Ludvig Holberg: A Subterranean Fantasy at the Outer Edge of *Frankenstein*" *Extrapolations* (Winter 1990): 317–25.

Freeman, Barbara. "Frankenstein with Kant: A Theory of Monstrosity, or the Monstrosity of Theory." *SubStance: A Review of Theory and Literary Criticism* 16.1 (1987): 21–31.

Hindle, Maurice. "Vital Matters: Mary Shelley's *Frankenstein* and Romantic Science." *Critical Survey* 2.1 (1990): 29–35.

The Great Gatsby

F. Scott Fitzgerald
(1925)

The Great Gatsby has become such a classic of American fiction that its avowed literary merits easily obscure those qualities that also made it (and continue to make it) a cult favorite. In a way, the early history of the book is a counterpoint to the history of J. D. Salinger's *The Catcher in the Rye,* with both books ending up as perennial favorites. The difference is that *Catcher* was a cult favorite first and then a critical success, whereas *The Great Gatsby* was praised by the critics long before it acquired a cult following.

Therefore, although *Gatsby* fits chronologically into an earlier time frame, one closer to Ernest Hemingway and Thomas Wolfe than to Salinger, it somehow caught the attention of a post–WW II audience and acquired a cult following that peaked in the early fifties but has by no means abated. In this respect it is like Hermann Hesse's *Steppenwolf, Demian,* and *Siddhartha,* books that originally appeared a generation before they gained the cult status that has made their titles household words since the 1960s.

Although critical reception of the novel has been kind, most critics have been quick to dismiss its thin plot and shallow characters as less important than Fitzgerald's brilliant depiction of the jazz age and his indictment of its shabby values. Cult readers take a different view, praising the book precisely because its plot *is* thin and its characters *are* shallow. To them this is Fitzgerald's point, that the age itself could do no better than to produce shallow people living superficial lives. Academic critics speculated about the probable causes of this phenomenon, attributing it to the disillusionment brought on by the first world war and the extreme measures taken to escape it. Cult readers concentrated on the effects and saw a culture wallowing in hedonism, high on jazz and bathtub gin, living life as if it were one long party and there was no tomorrow. But more particularly, they concentrated on one person, the sympathetic figure of Nick Carraway, the outside observer, a character straight out of Joseph Conrad or Henry James whose function it is to observe and report.

However, whereas Conrad's Marlow (*Heart of Darkness*) never becomes much more than a convenient narrative device, certainly not a character a reader can really identify with, Fitzgerald's Nick Carraway becomes very much a part of what he perceives, the sensitive young man that a host of sensitive young men have come to identify with. It is to him, then, that one must look to find the basic attraction of this novel as a cult book. To begin with, Nick has the sort of blessed innocence and shining ambition we associate with the monomythical hero. Although he is more a Telemachus than a Ulysses, there is a freshness about him, a basic goodness that appeals to that part of human nature that envies or craves or is irresistibly attracted to innocence. This is the quality one finds in well-mannered, unprepossessing heroes from Johann Wolfgang von Goethe's Werther (*The Sorrows of Young Werther*) to William Golding's Ralph (*Lord of the Flies*).

Beyond that, however, is the fact that, in the tradition of the hero, Nick goes forth into the world to encounter corruption and disillusionment and to come to terms with reality. He alone is able to see the essential worth of Jay Gatsby beneath the deceptive exterior. As he leaves Gatsby, Nick shouts to him across the lawn: "They're a rotten crowd. You're worth the whole damn bunch put together."

It is Nick's idealization of Gatsby that ennobles him in the minds of cult readers. Gatsby on his own is not an easy character for cult readers to sympathize with without the special insight of the young and sympathetic Nick. If Nick can see the good in Gatsby, then the reader can dismiss the corrupt side as Gatsby's victimization by the system and dwell on the charming side, that side made all the more intriguing by the mystery surrounding this handsome, rich, and devastatingly detached personality.

Perhaps the best way to describe the cult reader's perspective is to imagine Gatsby standing alone in the second-story bedroom of his palatial mansion in West Egg, looking out at the pool and the tent and the lavish party going on, at his expense, beneath his window; listening to the jazz band playing, seeing the shadows of the flappers against the sides of the tent, quietly watching, smoking a cigarette—aloof, detached, amused, powerful. And then imagine Nick Carraway, having received an invitation to one of Gatsby's parties, arriving on the scene and discovering his host in this pose: the observer watching the observer watching the observed.

In fact, Nick remembers vividly coming home from the Buchanans after his first visit and seeing Gatsby standing in front of his mansion, looking intently at East Egg across the bay. Both scenes spell alienation and ego-reinforcement tied up together with the sweet suffering of loneliness and the feeling of being privy to a special version of reality created by the wizardry of the enigmatic Gatsby, within whose magic circle one might feel threatened and secure at the same time.

It does not take long for the cult reader to be drawn in, even taken in, by Nick's own fascination with Gatsby, and by then the plot, whether thick or thin, takes on a special allure, for the reader is as eager to know more about Gatsby as Nick is. Nick has rented a summer cottage near Gatsby's place, and across the bay, in more fashionable East Egg, are Tom and Daisy Buchanan. Daisy is Nick's cousin, a lovely, exciting, but shallow young woman who had once had an affair with Gatsby before the war. While Gatsby was away in the war, she married Tom Buchanan. Handsome, wealthy, but cruel and insensitive, Tom is currently having an affair with a married woman named Myrtle Wilson. Gatsby wants Daisy back and thinks that his wealth, accumulated through shady transactions, will make Daisy admire him, but he overestimates her and underestimates himself.

Daisy is Gatsby's one dream, and the reason he bought his house and gives his parties is to get her back. He persuades Nick to bring him and Daisy together again, but he is unable to win her away from Tom. Nick can see this, but he is powerless to stop the chain of events that, for all their melodrama, seem necessary to act out the denouement of shallow lives lived recklessly, of shallow dreams shattered pointlessly. Daisy, driving Gatsby's car, runs over and kills Tom's mistress, Myrtle, unaware of her identity. Myrtle's husband traces the car and shoots Gatsby, who has remained silent in order to protect Daisy. Gatsby's friends and associates have all deserted him, and only Gatsby's father and one former guest attend the funeral.

Students of American literature are given to speculating about the American Dream—what it is, how ardently people pursue it, and how invariably they fail. The blame is usually laid rather vaguely at the feet of society, the convenient scapegoat for everybody's woes ever since the people seized control of the government from the privileged few. Cult readers enjoy indictments of society because such indictments reinforce their own sense of disaffection and protect them against taking blame for their own failures. However, there is more to it than that. Cult readers enjoy flirting with the demimonde, and if they can idealize a shady character, they will. It is part of the "gangster as hero" myth so popular in America, a myth that can be traced back to bigger-than-life outlaws from Jesse James to John Dillinger.

Jay Gatsby may be a bootlegger and a fraud, but he is only defrauding a system that is a bigger fraud, a system that advocates a farce like prohibition, that adores glittering surfaces, that cares only for the trappings of success and not for how the gains were got. But in the American tradition of trying to have your cake and eat it too, cult readers get to envy Gatsby while respecting Nick. Nick has his head on straight; Nick learns from what he sees; Nick acquires wisdom from his experiences and thus tells us a cautionary tale. Ah, but for one brief, shining moment, for no more than the time it took Werther to love and die, Meursault to murder and die, (*The Stranger*) Sinclair to fall under the spell of Demian, Gatsby illuminates the sky, and if his death is all a silly mistake, its sordidness is redeemed by his nobility. He dies, after all, for love, but it is a love that, like Werther's, is unrequited.

There is a particularly interesting parallel between *Gatsby* and Hesse's *Demian*. Like Jay Gatsby, Max Demian is a charismatic figure who holds a younger man, Emil Sinclair, in his thrall. The story is told through Sinclair's eyes, and we identify with him if only because he is more humanly frail and vulnerable. As Demian assumes mythical dimensions for Sinclair, he does for us, too, because we accept Sinclair's characterization of him, just as we feel the pull of Gatsby's magnetic personality through the perceptions of an admiring Nick.

Since Fitzgerald was such a product of his times, it is ironic that *The Great Gatsby* should have achieved its greatest popularity after his death. Most writers need the passage of time to give them a clearer perspective on their past experiences. Few have been able to record their own times with Fitzgerald's accuracy and detachment and at the same time be living those times to the hilt. Even D. H. Lawrence, a keen observer of his times, had to travel far from Nottingham before he could look back, see his life there whole, and then set it down in *Sons and Lovers*. But Fitzgerald mirrored his age so accurately that he was easily taken for granted. Only when the jazz age had passed could Fitzgerald be truly appreciated. It took the desolation of the Great Depression and the tragedy of World War II to provide the interlude needed to give readers the necessary perspective to penetrate beneath the glittering surface of Fitzgerald's work.

There is undeniably a certain amount of nostalgia mixed into the cult appeal of *Gatsby* and Fitzgerald's works in general. But it was not the ordinary nostalgia of older people for their lost youth. In this case it was the nostalgia of younger people based on a regret at having been born a generation too late. For to the youth who had grown up during the Depression and the war, the twenties were a paradise lost, a decade of fun and frenzy, of bootleg hooch and taxi dancers, of flappers with flat chests and rouged knees dancing the Charleston on tabletops in smoke-filled speakeasies. Gatsby's parties were Sodom and Gomorrah just before the fire and brimstone. It was a decade painted in primary colors as compared with the gray of the Depression and the olive drab of the war. Nick and Gatsby and Daisy and Jordan inhabited another world over which hung a smoky allure tinged with the melancholy of romantic tragedy.

For a while, especially in the fifties, there was a cult centering on the Paris of the twenties and the artists and beautiful people gathered there, on elegant songsmiths like Noel Coward and Cole Porter, socialites like Sara and Gerald Murphy, painters like Picasso and Miró, and writers like Gertrude Stein and Ernest Hemingway—but especially on Scott and Zelda Fitzgerald, and particularly on *The Great Gatsby*. For cult readers, *Gatsby* is the Lancelot of modern times, loyal to his friends, faithful in his promises, honorable in his fashion, a modern knight whose armor may be a bit tarnished but who stands head and shoulders above the tarnished souls of the avaricious Buchanans, the common Wilsons, and the deceitful Jordan Marsh.

Many have wondered about the unidentified guest at Gatsby's funeral, the strange frequenter of former Gatsby entertainments who was the only one who attended the funeral other than Nick, Gatsby's father, and the servants. Cult readers have no trouble identifying this lone soul, for he is their representative. They long to be at Gatsby's side as this tarnished and misunderstood hero is lowered into his grave. And they are there in spirit with Nick as he turns and walks away, his life forever changed, leaving a part of him behind with Gatsby, knowing that something has passed that will never come this way again.

It is a farewell of intense sentimentality, but Fitzgerald carries it off with impeccable style, and his cult followers know that only he can make them weep with dignity, make them happy to share the bittersweet memories of all his heroes, from Dexter Green of "Winter Dreams" to Dick Diver of *Tender is the Night*, heroes who will spend their lives fingering the scars of hopes safely misplaced and dreams pleasurably unfulfilled.

FOR FURTHER READING

Anderson, Hilton. "Weight and Balance in *The Great Gatsby*." *English Language Notes* (September 1989): 58–60.

———. "Synecdoche in *The Great Gatsby*." *North Dakota Quarterly* (Fall 1989): 162–68.

Green, Michael. "*The Great Gatsby*: The Structure of the Dream." *CRUX: A Journal on the Teaching of English* (April 1988): 51–60.

Magistrale, Tony, and Mary Jane Dickerson. "The Language of Time in *The Great Gatsby*." *College Literature* (Spring 1989): 117–28.

Overmyer, Janet. "Great Gatsby's Character: 'Daisy Fay Buchanan—Murderer?' " *Lost Generation Journal* (Spring 1987): 15.

The Hitchhiker's Guide to the Galaxy

Douglas Adams (1979)

After the reverential reception of such science-fiction masterpieces as *2001: A Space Odyssey* and *Stranger in a Strange Land* in the 1960s, it was inevitable that some sort of spoof of the genre would come along to create a cult following all its own. As it turned out, Douglas Adams was the right man at the right time, and *Hitchhiker's Guide to the Galaxy* was the perfect antidote to the glut of high-toned banalities that had held the flower children in thrall. Here was a sort of flip Anthony Burgess with a Woody Allen spin, having as much fun with his wildly imaginative universe as Steven Spielberg was to have on film with his.

For those who preferred their science fiction straight, Adams's book was a tough pill to swallow, for it refused, at least on the surface, to take either itself or its readers seriously. It was almost as if Adams were saying: "Look, science fiction is the biggest literary scam since the penny-dreadfuls. Ray Bradbury and Isaac Asimov may come across as latter-day literary saints, but they know as well as any true fan that it's all hokum but who cares? It's fairy tales for grownups with twice the malarky and half the depth."

Adams's message, in this book and others, is that too much thinking about things like the vastness of eternity and space and time can drive one mad. But instead of worrying about it, he takes control of it, for he realizes that as long as the human mind can *imagine* outer space, it is impervious to any threat from outer space. The universe acts in accordance with laws over which it has no control. It has no imagination. Man does. And this imagination allows him to laugh at the whole universe the way John Donne's brash young lover eclipses the sun with a simple wink.

The myth, then, that infuses *The Hitchhiker's Guide* is a parody of the myth of Prometheus, the Titan who dared bring fire to mankind and, in so doing, incurred the wrath of Zeus and was condemned to endless suffering. But Adams's Prometheus is no tragic hero. He is, rather, a clever politician named Zaphod Beeblebrox, an interstellar celebrity who has finagled his way into the highest office in the universe, that of president of the Imperial Galactic Government, just so that he could steal a prize spaceship called the Heart of Gold. When asked what is so important about the Heart of Gold, Zaphod is hard pressed to answer. He says that if he had consciously known what was so important about it and what he would need it for, it would probably have shown up on the brain screening tests, and he would never have passed. He suspects that he is carrying around secrets in his brain that he is unable to tap into. "I don't seem to be letting myself into any of my secrets," he says. "Still . . . I can understand that. I wouldn't trust myself further than I could spit a rat" (189).

Zaphod's confusion is mixed up with a mocking quest throughout the novel for the meaning of life. And the seriousness of this timeless metaphysical quest is constantly being undermined by the sort of silliness expressed above in Zaphod's comment about not trusting himself to let himself in on his own secrets. Adams makes great use of the absurdity of the non sequitur, and nowhere is this put to more hilarious, and at the same time satirical, purpose than in his spoof of the quest for the ultimate meaning of life.

To reach that point Adams transports the reader through a dizzying narrative beginning with the accidental (as it turns out) destruction of the earth and the escape of two people in one of the attacking spaceships. One of these people is Ford Prefect, the earth name for a galactic being who has been sojourning on Earth for years in anticipation of its imminent demise. Because he has become fast friends with Arthur Dent, a self-effacing young man with a dull job at a local radio station in an obscure English village, Ford Prefect stows him aboard the spaceship. Thus, Arthur Dent becomes the only earthling to survive the end of the world. The two men then proceed to have a series of incredible—and frequently hilarious—adventures as they get knocked about outer space.

To make their way, they have with them a copy of *The Hitchhiker's Guide to the Galaxy*, a sort of intergalactic Baedeker of the universe. However, they are frequently at the mercy of circumstances beyond their control. At times there is a Candide-like quality about the fixes they find themselves in and the nick-of-time escapes they make. And this seems to be another myth that Adams flirts with. If the best of all possible worlds is now only one man's memory, at least the universe remains, and it is not such a bad place after all, although frequently it resembles life on Earth. But aside from its idiotic wars and horrible blunders, it turns out to be a place where some of its inhabitants specialize in building new planets. There is even an effort afoot to rebuild Earth, once it is learned that its destruction was caused by a world-class blunder.

The figure in charge of such building, or in this case restoration, is an eccentric old man named Slartibartfast who tells Arthur that a being named Deep Thought actually designed the Earth and that Slartibartfast and his fellow designers built it ages ago but that the Vogons destroyed it five minutes before the program was completed. "Ten million years of planning and work gone just like that," he says. "Ten million years, Earthman, can you conceive of that kind of time span? . . . Gone." Then he adds a typical Adams punchline: "Well, that's bureaucracy for you" (191). This is a John Donne-like wink of the eye. But what follows is the almost throwaway essence of the novel, for Slartibartfast, who is at a loss to understand the meaning of life, finds consolation in helping design the continents that will appear on the rebuilt Earth.

Just after Slartibartfast throws up his hands and blames bureaucracy for the destruction of Earth, Arthur Dent says that he thinks what he has heard explains a lot of things. All through his life, he says, he has had a strange, unaccountable feeling that "something was going on in the world, something big, even sinister," and that no one would tell him what it was. But the old man pricks this balloon by assuring Arthur that it is "just perfectly normal paranoia" and that "everyone in the Universe has that" (191). However, once he has dismissed the idea of a secret meaning to life as mere paranoia, Slartibartfast finds he has acquired a new and curious kind of faith in the enigma of life. He says that maybe he is just old and tired, but he cannot help feeling that the chances of finding out what really is going on are so absurdly remote that the only thing to do is to stop trying to make sense of it and just keep oneself occupied. "Look at me," he says. "I design coastlines. I got an award for Norway." He is currently involved in the replacement Earth project for which he is busily designing a coastline for Africa that will be "all fjords again because I happen to like them, and I'm old-fashioned enough to think that they give a lovely baroque feel to a continent." When his detractors insist that fjords are not "equatorial enough," Slartibartfast gives a "hollow laugh" and says, "I'd far rather be happy than right any day" (192).

There is enough irony, satire, and high-spirited iconoclasm in this novel to inspire a cult of neo-absurdists impatient with the earnestness of *Dune*-style sci-fi. In fact, *The Hitchhiker's Guide to the Galaxy* is one of the first post-counterculture novels that dares to poke fun at a genre the flower children had appropriated as their own. When he wrote the book, Douglas Adams, who was born in 1952, was old enough to appreciate the irreverence of the sixties but young enough not to be overwhelmed by its rhetorical fustian. He was able, therefore, to turn irreverence against itself, and this surprise move attracted those whom the clannish flower children did not welcome among their number. And many of these were apostate flower children themselves.

At the heart of this nose-thumbing novel is a wicked satire on the search for ultimate meaning in the universe. Ford Prefect and Arthur Dent, along with assorted galactic weirdos such as a girl named Trillian, who hangs out with Zaphod, a dour robot named Marvin, whom Arthur describes as an "electronic sulking machine," and two mice named Frankie and Benjy, find themselves on the affluent planet of Magrathea whose inhabitants, after seven-and-a-half million years of waiting for the "Great and Hopefully Enlightening Day," have finally arrived at "The Day of the Answer." Never again will they have to wonder about such questions as "*Who am I? What is my purpose in life? Does it really, cosmically speaking,* matter *if I don't get up and go to work*?" On this day they are going to learn, finally and forever, the "simple answer to all these nagging little problems of Life, the Universe and Everything!" (176–77). Finally, from the depths of the elaborate communications system comes the voice of Deep Thought, who tells the people assembled and eager to hear the answer that he doesn't think they're going to like it. They persist, however, and finally, after considerable stalling, Deep Thought says that the answer is "Forty-two."

Consternation ensues until finally the computer itself says that the problem is not in the answer but in the question that has never been properly put. Deep Thought agrees, but admits that he cannot tell them what the Ultimate Question is. He can, however, tell them who can. "I speak of none but the computer that is to come after me" (182), he says, a computer that he shall design and that will be called Earth. As it turns out, the old planet Earth had, after millions of years, been on the verge of divulging the Ultimate Question when it was accidentally destroyed.

Now there is even greater incentive to come up with a question because of possible talk-show and lecture-circuit contracts. Therefore, even though it becomes clear that there is no Ultimate Question, Zaphod thinks it is important to come up with something in order to keep the show going. "We have to have something that *sounds* good," is the way Benjy, the mouse, puts it. And Frankie, the other mouse, justifies the idea by explaining that you finally reach a point in the pursuit of truth where you are plagued by the suspicion that if there is any real truth, "it's that the entire multidimensional infinity of the Universe is almost certainly being run by a bunch of maniacs." Forced to choose, therefore, between taking ten million more years to find that out or just "taking the money and running, then I for one," he says, "could do with the exercise" (200).

Benjy figures that the Ultimate Question is probably encoded in the structure of Arthur's brain, since Arthur is an Earthman, and offers to "buy" Arthur's brain, agreeing to replace it with an electronic one. However, Arthur is saved by the appearance of a hostile ship on the planet, and the mice conclude that they will have to "try and fake a question, invent one that will sound plausible" (203). After a few unsuccessful attempts, they come up with this one: "*How many roads must a man walk down*?" They like it. "Sounds very significant without actually tying you down to meaning anything at all," says Benjy (204).

And this is pretty much the way Adams leaves it as the novel ends, except to include in a one-page final chapter a tongue-in-cheek version of the three phases through which every major Galactic Civilization tends to pass, these three being "*Survival, Inquiry and Sophistication, otherwise known as the How, Why and Where phases*." These three phases, he says, are characterized by these three questions: "How can we eat?" "Why do we eat?" and "Where shall we have lunch?" (215) And Zaphod's puckish answer to the last question is "the Restaurant at the End of the Universe," which just happens to be the title of Adams's next book.

Because *The Hitchhiker's Guide to the Galaxy* is a spoof, it does not come with all the baggage common to most cult books. Its "hero" is not a role model, there is little sense of alienation or suffering, and the novel does not offer a value system or code of behavior to subscribe to, other than the example of surviving with grace and humor, the reliance on luck, and the virtue of not taking things too seriously. If a shadow falls across the novel's bright face, it is that this novel seems to herald an age of indifference to matters that many feel can be ignored only at great peril. One could argue that a comic novel is meant only to amuse, but there are two important factors that contradict this offhand assumption. One is that most comic novels worth their salt, from those of Peter de Vries to those of David Lodge, use humor to sugarcoat a message. The other is that one cannot easily dismiss as a mere diversion a novel that has achieved cult status, just as one cannot lump Woody Allen's dark comedies in with *Porky* or *The Revenge of the Nerds*.

Even so, it would be overstating the case to ascribe to this novel profundities that simply do not exist. Rather, it is more to the point to see, in the way Adams can make the reader dismiss the universe with a laugh and a shrug, how he can also lure the reader into looking into a dark mirror.

FOR FURTHER READING

Higdon, David Leon. "Into the Vast Unknown: Directions in the Post-Holocaust Novel." In *War and Peace: Perspectives in the Nuclear Age*, ed. by Ulrich Goebel and Otto Nelson. Lubbock: Texas University Press, 1988.

Kropf, Carl R. "Douglas Adams's 'Hitchhiker' Novels as Mock Science Fiction." *Science-Fiction Studies* (March 1988): 61–70.

The Killer Inside Me

Jim Thompson
(1952)

The Killer Inside Me is a different sort of cult book, almost in a class by itself. Whereas most cult books achieve cult status shortly after publication, this psychological thriller has grown steadily in popularity since it was published in 1952 to become an underground classic of long standing. While mainstream mystery readers hardly knew what to make of it, were even put off by its seemingly gratuitous violence, there were, among those early readers, many who sensed something special about Jim Thompson's use of the mystery story convention. Half a century later, in a world seemingly immune to violence no matter how graphically presented, *The Killer Inside Me* has the power to shock, not because it is graphic, but because it is all too real.

In the fifties it was easier to accept the protagonist, Lou Ford, as a Jekyll and Hyde cop-criminal because his character was so unfamiliar as to seem purely fictitious. That Ford told his own story was dismissed as an Agatha Christie gimmick (*The Murder of Roger Ackroyd*) that, in this case, seemed an excuse to let the murderer exaggerate his actions on the one hand while playing cat and mouse with authorities on the other. In the nineties, after decades of carefully detailed and pictorialized violence, we find characters like Lou Ford all too familiar. The hijacker has long since ceased to be a joke, and we have seen the disarming likeness of the serial murderer in the boyish grin of a Ted Bundy.

Later readers, therefore, are impressed with Thompson's chillingly realistic portrait of a murderer who is the charming dissembler on the outside and a cheerful killer on the inside. That the story is told by the killer himself now tends to disarm us completely and for two reasons. First, we realize that this is no gimmick, no last-page revelation that the one who "done" it is the one who wrote it. We know right from the start that the murderer is in control of the narrative, and this leads to the other reason why this novel unnerves us: the traditional bond between author and reader is broken, and we no longer feel safe in the author's hands. The killer has seized control of the narrative and is telling us how things *really* are—and we are not at all sure we want to know. We, who have become accustomed to accepting the word of experts on aberrant behavior, no longer trust them to understand the working of the criminal mind, no longer believe them when they warn us that the killer is only playing games with us when he speaks for himself. For now we have a killer who convinces us that he understands thoroughly not only what he has done but why he has done it. And what's worse, he knows that he will do it again, that he *wants* to do it again, that while there may be a way of stopping him, there is no way of curing him.

So far, this analysis helps only to explain the novel's continuing popularity, not its cult status. The difference between the novel's appeal to the general reader and its appeal to the cult reader lies in the way the reader perceives the protagonist. Whereas ordinary readers can remain sufficiently detached, cult readers get pulled in, even taken in, by something in the personality of the main character that gets to them with extraordinary intensity and blinds them to that character's flaws. One has only to remember Werther (*The Sorrows of Young Werther*) or Demian (*Demian*) or Holden Caulfield (*The Catcher in the Rye*)—or even Albert Camus's stranger, Meursault (*The Stranger*), another "killer" with whom cult readers could identify without bothering about the fine points of the law.

Identifying with a Lou Ford is another matter. Not that cult readers by any means view themselves as serial murderers or sadists or sociopaths or anything overtly menacing or downright deranged. But what they have acknowledged within themselves is the flicker of ecstatic horror with which they vicariously experience each violent episode. Fascinating criminals are nothing new, either in life or literature. From *Crime and Punishment* to *An American Tragedy*, from Jack the Ripper to Charles Manson, they have often taken on a sort of folk-heroic stature.

In popular entertainment, Alfred Hitchcock understood it and exploited it, even made it acceptable, if not exactly respectable. Take *Psycho*, for example, itself a cult film. Although essentially a black comedy, it bears much resemblance to *The Killer Inside Me*, particularly in terms of motivation and coldbloodedness, and helps explain the cult status of the Thompson book. Both Norman Bates and Lou Ford have known an overbearing parent who kept them in emotional bondage through contempt and guilt and the withholding of understanding or forgiveness. In Norman's case it leads to the murder of his widowed mother but not to the release from her bondage, since instead of being rid of her and her hold over him, he *becomes* her and is thus his own captive, with no hope of release. Thus he is driven by her spirit, so to speak, to kill evildoers.

In the case of Lou Ford, his father, a widower, never forgave him for having "known" the housekeeper. There was nothing he could say or do that would change anything, he says near the end of the story. "I had a burden of fear and shame put on me that I could never get shed of." Since he could not budge his father, he directed his hostility toward the housekeeper, but once the housekeeper had gone away, he could not "strike back at her, yes, kill her" for what he felt she had done to him. Since she was the first woman he had ever known, Ford says, "she *was* woman to me; and all womankind bore her face." He felt that he could strike back at any of them, any woman, especially "the ones it would be safest to strike at," and it would be the same thing as striking back at the housekeeper. "And so I did that, I started striking out," he says, and letting others take the blame (167). Knowing that no woman who shows him love is safe, he tries to keep at a safe distance the girl who grew up loving him. But it doesn't work, and it is her execution, so calmly planned, so ruthlessly carried out, so dispassionately related by Lou Ford in a tone of callous humor, that both thrills and disgusts the cult reader. In one sickening second, the civilized shell cracks, and the primordial slime oozes out.

As in a few other cult books, there comes a point in this one at which the author seems to be testing the reader's capacity to be offended. Whereas conventional authors might draw back discreetly from exceeding the boundaries—the way the Greek playwrights disdained on-stage violence—cult writers seem to arrive at the edge of the abyss and then, unlike Marlowe in *Heart of Darkness,* who gets a whiff of the stench and backs off, behave like the demon-possessed Kurtz instead and abandon all restraint. Again, as with the murder of the leading lady early in Hitchcock's *Psycho,* the pact between reader and writer is violated, and the reader is at the mercy of the author. Similar examples of this sort of stepping over the line occur in such cult works as *A Clockwork Orange, Lord of the Flies, Fear and Loathing in Las Vegas,* and *One Flew Over the Cuckoo's Nest.* In each of these, there seems to be a deliberate attempt to lose the reader—or, put another way, to test the reader's loyalty. Those who pass beyond this point willingly, even eagerly, are cult readers.

In *The Killer Inside Me,* that point is almost reached with the murder of Amy, Lou Ford's girl-next-door sweetheart. Loathsome as her murder is, however, it is by no means unexpected or gratuitous; rather, it is necessary to serve as the incident whereby Lou Ford's psychosis is fully revealed and explained. The incident that crosses the line is the one that occurs at the end of the book involving the surprise return of Joyce, the prostitute we thought Ford had brutally murdered earlier in the book. It turns out that she has been hospitalized for several months with injuries so severe that she is left crippled and disfigured. All along Ford has been led to believe that she is dead, the idea being that once she is released from the hospital, she will be able to accuse him to his face. But Lou Ford has had his doubts all along, and so he has one last trick up his sleeve—literally, for he has slipped a knife up one sleeve just in case—and as Joyce is led into the house and takes a few halting steps toward him, he stabs her.

What makes the scene even more harrowing is that, first of all, he is not all that surprised that she is still alive and, second, he realizes that she still loves him. Having suspected something all along, Ford has fixed it so that smoke will fill the house just as the police arrive with Joyce, giving him the moment he needs to stab her. The police are caught off guard, taken by surprise, says Ford, "because they hadn't got the point." Then he adds sardonically, "She'd got *that* between the ribs and the blade along with it." And then, as if this were not enough, he says, "And they all lived happily ever after, I guess, and I guess—that's—all" (188).

Ford concludes his narrative with a comment about "our kind" getting "another chance in the Next Place. Our kind. Us people . . . all of us that started the game with a crooked cue, that wanted so much and got so little, that meant so good and did so bad" (188). Cult readers identify with "our kind" and "us people," the ones who started the game with a crooked cue, the ones who are sensitive and intelligent, well-mannered and well-groomed but who, owing to circumstances they understand but cannot control, are walking time bombs. At one point, someone refers to Ford as a weed and defines a weed as "a plant out of place." There is no better definition of alienation, this feeling of being a plant so out of place that it becomes an expendable weed.

In the afterword to the 1986 edition of Thompson's *After Dark; My Sweet*, Geoffrey O'Brien wonders about those first readers who picked up *The Killer Inside Me* looking for escape only to find inescapable horror. "You begin to read, lured on by the compelling narrative vice with its folksy humor and jabbing emphases. Then—just as you thought you were on the verge of finding the truth about the killing, or the robbery, or the kidnapping—you fall through Thompson's trapdoor. You're down in the depths, all right: not just the depths of the city but the depths of a mind—and no return ticket is being offered. The enthralling voice turns out to be the voice of someone who doesn't know who he is, who's no longer sure which story he's telling, who may have been lying to you all along. By identifying with him—and Thompson's special gift is for making you do just that —you inherit his curse: a psychic hell which goes around and around without ever arriving anywhere" (133).

A good way to see Lou Ford through a cult reader's eyes is to listen to Ford philosophizing: "How can a man ever really know anything?" he muses. "We're living in a funny world . . . a peculiar civilization," and he talks about crooks and cops reversing roles, not to mention politicians and preachers. "It's a screwed up, bitched up world, and I'm afraid it's going to stay that way . . . because no one . . . sees anything wrong with it." As for himself, he straddles the fence. "I can't move either way and I can't jump," he says. "All I can do is wait until I split. Right down the middle. That's all I can do" (93–94). It may sound a bit folksy, with overtones of wisdom culled from experience. But it takes on a sinister tone once you realize that Ford is in a prison cell "comforting" a young man he has framed for murder, a young man he is about to kill and leave hanging to make it seem like suicide. But rather than negating his comments, this brutal act only serves to underscore their bitter truth. As Ford comments about a man who had a happy family and a happy mistress and killed them all, "He'd had everything, and somehow nothing was better."

"All any of us ever are [is] what we have to be" (143), he says, summing up his philosophy of life with grim irony, for by this time we know that what Lou Ford has to be is the kind of killer he is. It is not what he *wants* to be; it is what he *is*. This is the dark side of the "be the real you" injunction, a chilling reminder that the "real you" may not be the bright, positive, creative, moral person you like to think you are but rather a twisted, tortured psychopath given license to kill by a society urging you to "just be yourselves."

Cult readers are not about to take Lou Ford's example to heart and embark on killing sprees, but they may find that his abdication of responsibility fits in easily with the growing tendency to feel fatalistic about what is now casually excused as one's "genetic predisposition." If Lou Ford can't really help himself, why not sit back and enjoy watching him deal with those too dumb to figure him out in time?

Ultimately, cult readers are led to wonder if perhaps madness is not the price of wisdom, if indeed it has not been madmen (and women) like the Marquis de Sade and Fyodor Dostoevsky, Ezra Pound and Marcel Proust, Friedrich Nietzsche and Franz Kafka, Virginia Woolf and Sylvia Plath who have had to lose their minds in order to gain wisdom. To the trite axiom that says you get out of life only what you put into it, Lou Ford asks, "What's the percentage in that?" with exactly the kind of cynical logic that counterbalances a mind driven by illogical guilt and rage.

The "killer inside us" is a metaphor for anything we cannot help—or *think* we cannot help: addiction, guilt, anger, ambition—any obsession that leads us into temptation and abandons us to the forces of evil. For Thompson's killers, redemption is impossible since it depends on remorse, and Thompson knows that obsession stifles remorse. God's help, so the saying goes, is only for those who help themselves. Since Thompson's killers are beyond any kind of help, they are also beyond redemption. It is a bitter irony that has captured the mood of the nineties and revived Thompson's status as a cult favorite.

FOR FURTHER READING

McCauley, Michael J. *Jim Thompson: Sleep With the Devil*. New York: Mysterious Press, 1991.

O'Brien, Geoffrey. "Jim Thompson, Dimestore Dostoevsky." Afterword to *After Dark, My Sweet*. Jim Thompson. Berkeley: Creative Arts, 1986, 132–38.

Thorp, Roderick. Introduction to *Hard-Core*, 3 Novels by Jim Thompson. New York: Donald I. Fine, 1986, vii–x.

Lady Chatterley's Lover

D. H. *Lawrence*
(1928)

D. H. Lawrence has been a cult figure for most of the twentieth century, and his admirers draw upon a number of his works for inspiration. While two or three other Lawrence novels might also qualify for cult fiction status—*Sons and Lovers, The Rainbow, Women in Love*—there are three overriding reasons for selecting *Lady Chatterley's Lover*. First, it is the distillation of Lawrence's thinking, expressed in a story he dearly loved and told with the total abandon of the rebel who has nothing to lose. Second, the fact that it had been banned for thirty years before its timely release in 1959, endeared it to those who embrace anything that has been censored (thus the popularity of presses, such as Olympia and Grove, that specialized in controversial literature). Third, its equating of sexual freedom with spiritual salvation gave the sexual revolution the manifesto it needed.

Thus, Lawrence became a cultural event in the sixties, and while students grew excited about "blood consciousness" and "blood knowledge" and the search for our common humanity beneath the sooty veneer of industrialization, *Lady Chatterley's Lover* provided the missal whereby sexual liberation could be translated into a ritual of social and spiritual revitalization. It is hard to discuss this concept without irony, for today Lawrence seems quaint and even a bit cranky waxing philosophical about an activity that has since become both peremptory and perfunctory. But to young people coming of age in the sixties, there clung the hope (delusion perhaps) that the sexual freedom they sought would be more than just the opportunity to have a lot of sex with a lot of partners—that there might be a cosmic purpose behind it all, a release not just of frustrated sexual urges but of frustrated spirits too long enslaved by machines to respond to what their blood was trying to tell them.

To Lawrence's disciples, traditional morality was simply a tool of the industrialists to keep workers in check, a sort of Grundyesque gelding that ensured a docile, obedient work force ready to expend most of its energies on accumulating wealth for the owners and the state. Sir Clifford Chatterley's mines represented the sterile, antihuman mechanistic society that was strangling English society and the world, while Sir Clifford himself, crippled and confined to a wheelchair, was the perfect symbol of the spiritual impotence that was casting a blight upon the land. His wife, Constance, became the symbol of female submissive emptiness and yearning in this unabashedly sexist novel, and John Thomas Mellors, the virile gamekeeper, represented the answer: an earthy, sensitive, sensual man, in touch with blood and earth and all essentials, unsullied by machinery, unspoiled by a castrating civilization.

Mellors, then, is the monomythical hero of this novel, almost Wagnerian in the way he strides forth out of the forests to express the wisdom of his blood knowledge in deed as much as in word. But there is more action, more acting out of Lawrence's philosophy in this novel than in the others. Birkin may throw stones at the moon's reflection in *Women in Love*, and he may wrestle with Gerald Crich in a demonstration of male bonding in the same novel, but for the most part the characters are there to augment or argue Lawrence's ideas. In *Lady Chatterley's Lover*, while there is plenty of theory, there is even more action, and graphic action at that; hence, the reason the novel was banned. But Lawrence knew it would be banned—almost counted on it—and so instead of worrying about it as he had in the case of *The Rainbow* many years earlier, he decided he might as well be hanged for a sheep as a lamb and wrote exactly as he pleased—even overwrote in the sense that he was thumbing his nose at his detractors, giving them plenty of rope with which to hang him with.

The circumstances surrounding the publication of the novel, not to mention the scandalous reputation it acquired thereafter, made its author something of a martyr. And his death at 44, barely two years after the book's publication, added to the mystique of the young artist hounded by callous critics. Thus, readers who finally had uninhibited access to the book in the sixties could identify with both its persecuted author and its liberated hero and feel doubly alienated. Young readers, seeing the world through Lawrence's very special vision, were oblivious to his reactionary politics and thus vulnerable to his fascination with power. This fascination is a subtle but persistent element in most cult books, but in *Lady Chatterley's Lover* it is a more insidious influence because it lurks beneath a distractive layer of unbridled sensuality.

There is no doubt that Lawrence wanted to transform the world, or to see it transformed according to his vision. So much of his writing is preaching and polemic that most of his novels could properly be called thesis novels—with the acknowledgment, however, that they are also much more. Otherwise, his novels would have disappeared by now, although there has been an appreciable decline in their popularity in the latter years of the century as much of what he said sounds more and more dated and downright embarrassing. Someone once said that the novel as we once knew it, the novel of F. R. Leavis's "great tradition," died halfway through *Sons and Lovers*, a work that starts out as a novel of character and setting and ends up as a novel of issues and ideas. This might be why many readers prefer the Lawrence of the shorter works—the splendid novellas and short stories.

Cult readers, however, have a taste for novels that present an agenda, and *Lady Chatterley's Lover* presented just the right agenda for the sixties. Thus, its relevance owed much to the fact that both it and its readers shared a history of repression, and once both were liberated, there was no holding either back. That the book took place in an earlier age and among people of respectability only added to the pleasure of the young who could use this in their arsenal of weapons to be launched against their elders. In fact, the remoteness of the book not only in time but in place gave the book the very mythical quality so common to cult books, a quality enhanced by the presence of an aristocratic lady (like a fairy-tale princess) and a "man of nature" straight out of ancient folklore. With a somewhat different plot this would have been made into an operetta a decade or so earlier.

D. H. Lawrence has been called a "mystical materialist" who wanted to replace the shame surrounding sex with a sort of devout beauty. He even tried to ennoble certain degraded words, to remove the tarnish that had consigned them to the gutter and give them new lustre. But he labored in vain. These words have not only retained their tarnish, they have also lost most of their punch through overuse. He may have failed in his goal, but his intentions were noble. To wish to rescue sex from degradation and make it something exalted was hopelessly but admirably idealistic.

Lawrence pursued this idealism intensely in *Lady Chatterley's Lover*. In this novel more than anywhere else, Lawrence presents with absolute clarity the tension between the negative forces in society that obstruct human fulfillment and the positive forces that contribute to it. Clifford Chatterley, the impotent capitalist, represents the negative forces in society that threaten its well-being. Mellors, the lusty gamekeeper on the Chatterley estate who has turned his back on society, represents the positive life force that is society's only hope of rejuvenation and salvation.

The myth of rescuing a woman from a stultifying marriage and bringing her to a new kind of fulfillment can be described adequately only in religiomythical terms, and this Lawrence managed. It appealed especially to men of the counterculture who longed to drag their "old ladies" off to a commune where the women were supposed to find fulfillment raising children, performing humble domestic chores, and servicing the sexual needs of the men.

Lawrence hoped that the breakdown of class distinctions would lead ultimately to the breakdown of all other false distinctions and result in the emergence of true individuality. He believed that the individual must be totally free in order to function wholesomely. When Lady Chatterley and Mellors take off their clothes, they are shedding the artifice of civilization; and when they run naked through the woods in the rain, they symbolize total freedom. They have cast all trappings of repressive civilization aside in order to get in touch with what is whole and healthy and positive within them.

But where can these blissful creatures run to? Where can they live this liberated life? J. D. Salinger's followers dream of the wilderness, Hermann Hesse readers seek inner space, *Dune* readers seek outer space, J.R.R. Tolkien readers go back in time, *Space Odyssey* readers go forward. Mellors and Lady Chatterley hope to find their Shangri-la in Canada, to them a new and distant world. What a coincidence that during the Vietnam War, Canada became a haven for Americans seeking to avoid the draft.

Most of Lawrence is in *Lady Chatterley's Lover*, from the earnest yearnings of a prophet possessed to the embarrassing proposals of an obsessed fanatic. It is an easy book to poke fun at, for it is filled with errors he never got around to (or had no intention of) correcting. It is a brash book, a self-indulgent book, the book writers dream of writing when they feel they have nothing to lose. But best of all, it is a surprisingly good book, when all is said and done.

Later readers could sympathize with Lawrence's growing contempt for a society bent on self-destruction. England in the twenties was being torn apart by struggles between rich and poor, young and old, conservative and liberal. Unemployment reached staggering heights, disabled veterans begged and died on the streets, Bright Young Things drank and danced till dawn and scorned every value and virtue their parents held dear. There were strikes and lock-outs and threats of revolution. And overall there hovered greed and indifference and a frenzied sort of apocalyptic doom. Lawrence could only rail against it and call for the most radical sort of personal protest—Mellors and Constance uninhibited.

Lawrence knew it was an impossible dream, and it shows. As the British would say, maybe he's "having it on" with his readers, teasing them, taunting them, doing his level best to offend a good many of them. For beneath it all there is dark comedy in *Lady Chatterley's Lover*—the operetta quality, the hyperbolic characters, the outrageous plot, the overwritten descriptions. Lawrence is rubbing his readers noses in this brew and rubbing his hands at their predictable response. There is even a hint of literary humor here, as if the novel form itself were being parodied. However you cut it, what you get is the old story of the stableboy seducing the mistress of the manor, or vice versa. But that all of this is perpetrated at the expense of poor, old, wheelchair-ridden Clifford pushes it perilously close to a really sick joke.

Today the image of the bad capitalist versus the good peasant is almost too simplistic to take seriously, but Lawrence handles this melodrama with such innocent audacity that the story takes on the proportions of mythic truth. The man in tune with nature who is superior in every way to the dehumanized coal mine owner was a concept dear to the hearts of counterculturists who dreamed of getting in touch with themselves (and each other) in the rustic purity of the wilderness. Clifford Chatterley was such an easy target. He was mean father, unfeeling boss, overbearing teacher, unforgiving priest, repressive society; family, work, school, church, the establishment—all wrapped into one warped, dysfunctional, impotent little man.

"I am a passionately religious man, " Lawrence once said, "who tries to forge a new public wisdom out of a private revelation, a vision, purest intuition. I shall change the world for the next thousand years" (Schorer 4). His was a complete rejection of modern life and of the tradition behind it, of Christianity, industrialism, science, popular education, nationalism, romantic love; but it was also an affirmation, for his new consciousness involved him in an apotheosis of our instinctual life out of which he tried to construct a kind of inverted mysticism, a myth of what he called the "dark gods," the powers of the body and of the bloodstream that we have been civilized and educated into forgetting or denying for the sake of rationality and abstract mental process.

He demanded the total development of the self, of *being*, through a complete recognition of our primitive, pre-Christian selves, of our place in nature, our essential relation to the cosmos. From such a recognition would come true individual identity, a new oneness between the individual and others, the first real community in Western civilization. That was his affirmation. And that is all he wanted. Simply everything.

"Start with the sun," D. H. Lawrence wrote in the conclusion to his final book, *Apocalypse*, "and the rest will slowly, slowly happen." And for a while, back somewhere about the summer of 1968, it looked as if it just might.

FOR FURTHER READING

Efron, Arthur. "The Way Our Sympathy Flows and Recoils: Lawrence's Last Theory of the Novel." *Paunch* (December 1990): 71–84.

Gertzman, Jay A. "Legitimizing *Lady Chatterley's Lover*: The Grove Press Strategy." *Paunch* (December 1990): 1–14.

Jewinski, Ed. "The Phallus in D. H. Lawrence and Jacques Lacan." *The D. H. Lawrence Review* (Spring 1989): 7–24.

Rowley, Stephen. "The Sight-Touch Metaphor in *Lady Chatterley's Lover*." *Etudes Lawrenciennes* (May 1988): 179–88.

Whitehouse, Carol Sue. "D. H. Lawrence's 'The First Lady Chatterley': Conservation Treatment of a Twentieth-Century Bound Manuscript." *Library Chronicle of the University of Texas*, 1989, 40–55.

Lolita

Vladimir Nabokov
(1958)

Lolita is the only "camp" cult classic. From the minute it exploded on the staid literary scene of the late fifties, it attracted a devoted following that took delight in its breathless irreverence, its decadent detachment, and most of all, its calculated vulgarity—qualities that together make up what social critic Susan Sontag has labeled "camp." Sontag defines camp as the attempt of a dandy to stand out against the hyperbole of mass culture. The word connotes a mixture of excess, flamboyance, exaggeration, outrage, burlesque, and blasphemy carried off in deadly earnest but with a forked tongue in both cheeks.

While some earlier cult books now read like camp classics (*Werther, René, Axel, Against Nature*), *Lolita* is the only cult book that bore the stamp of camp right from the start. It would be misleading to say that writing a camp novel was Vladimir Nabokov's intention. Trying to be deliberately campy is as difficult and elusive a trick as trying to be deliberately cultish. What one can say about Nabokov and *Lolita* without missing the mark entirely, however, is that *Lolita* is a grand literary joke, as was *Pale Fire* a few years later. Nabokov is clearly poking fun at European intellectuals, American teenage girls, certain elements of American culture, the detective novel genre, the myths of the quest and the chase, and most particularly, the myth of American Puritanism.

Lolita appealed to those who take their prurience with a touch of class. Readers who would never admit to a taste for the James M. Cain or Erskine Caldwell brand of raunch felt safe with Nabokov. After all, here was a Russian émigré, a man of letters, a polyglot, and, above all, a European intellectual. In other words, it was possible to read *Lolita* without apology because its author was eminently respectable. *Lolita* was no *Fanny Hill*. It worked on the level of suggestion, not explicitness. It was not prurient, at least not in its presentation of the seduction of the middle-aged Humbert Humbert by the twelve-year-old nymphet Dolores (Lolita) Haze and their consequent odyssey across the United States, moving from motel to motel as the frantic Quilty relentlessly pursues them. At a deeper level, however, there is an appeal that is darkly prurient, for beneath the high comedy and sophistication there are echoes of incest, of child molesting, of the depravity of children and the moral vacuum of adults. Topping it all off is Nabokov's subtlest sleight-of-hand trick; namely, his ability to make a voyeur of the worst sort out of readers too hooked on the story to care. He makes them face the hypocrisy of their moral ambiguities and either wince or shrug. Cult readers shrugged. They were willing to accept guilt for such hypocrisy as long as they could point the finger at the "wincers," those who were unable to see or unwilling to admit their hypocrisy. But to leave it here would be to turn *Lolita* into a tract, and it is far from that.

To account for the cult status of the book, one must return to the idea of camp and realize that those who appreciated Nabokov's exposure of our moral hypocrisy also were beguiled by Nabokov's wizardry, by the dazzling ingenuity with which he tells his improbable story and the rich inventiveness of his characterization. The novel anticipates the zany impertinence of Hunter S. Thompson while retaining the tarnished charm of J. D. Salinger.

Some of the myths underlying *Lolita* have already been suggested: the myths of the quest and the chase, for example, and the myth of American Puritanism. But perhaps the most startlingly original mythical overtones resound from the perverse interlacing of the myths of Oedipus and Electra. Humbert Humbert marries Mrs. Haze in order to get to her daughter, Dolores. Mrs. Haze dies in an accident, thus freeing her husband to pursue her daughter, except that it is the daughter who seduces her stepfather—over her mother's dead body, one might say.

As the curiously ingenuous object of Lolita's erotic pursuit, Humbert Humbert is another in a line of antiheroes, of glorious innocents, who are really more sinned upon than sinning, from Meursault to Yossarian and from Holden Caulfield to Billy Pilgrim. By portraying the lecherous Humbert Humbert as the victim of Lolita's lust, Nabokov parodies the Victorian assumption, so popular with Henry James in novels like *The Portrait of a Lady* and *Daisy Miller*, that it is the innocent little American heiress who is easy prey for the rapacious European blackguard out to trade a title for a fortune. America has now become the villain, the sinister seducer capable of corrupting the European lulled into vulnerability by what seems to be a gum-chewing bubble-head.

Lolita is Humbert Humbert's own account of his misadventures with the wily nymphet Lolita. As such it is a combination confession, deposition, and apologia, written both to explain his actions and, in its own strange way, to convince Lolita of his real affection for her. He tries to justify his sexual misconduct with Lolita as well as the murder of Clare Quilty, who had urged Lolita to make pornographic films.

In his inimitably droll manner, Humbert Humbert recalls traveling to New England on scholarly business where he rents a room in the home of Charlotte Haze, apparently in order to get closer to her daughter, Dolores, who turns twelve on January 1, 1947. A month after the marriage, Charlotte is struck by a car and killed, and Humbert Humbert is obliged to break the news to Lolita and bring her home from summer camp. Before he has had a chance to tell her of her mother's death, Humbert Humbert finds himself the object of Lolita's fervent affections, and no sooner have they registered at a motel called the Enchanted Hunters than she reveals how sexually knowledgeable she is by actively seducing him. Afterwards, Humbert Humbert tells her about her mother and proceeds to "comfort" her with gifts he has brought and with the announcement that she will henceforth be in his care.

Knowing that legally he is in a precarious position, Humbert Humbert takes Lolita on a yearlong, 27,000 mile jaunt across the United States lasting from August 1947 to August 1948, hoping to continue his relationship with her as long as possible. When they return to New England, Lolita re-enters school, and Humbert Humbert finds himself insanely jealous of her school friends.

Later, when Lolita runs off with, or is kidnaped by, Quilty, Humbert takes up with Rita, an alcoholic divorcée. Lolita (Dolly) marries Richard F. Schiller, becomes pregnant, and dies in childbirth. In the meantime, however, Humbert Humbert tracks her down, gives her four thousand dollars, and gains enough information to embark on a manhunt for Quilty with the intention of murdering him. Humbert finds him in a sort of neo-Gothic castle where, after chesslike sparring, Humbert shoots Quilty with a borrowed gun. Then, relieved and feeling strangely free, he drives off down the wrong side of the road, hoping to attract the attention of the police.

The fun of the story lies largely in its spirit of inspired nonsense that coats like a fanciful frosting a number of social realities not generally acknowledged back then, like conspicuous consumerism, embalmed adolescence, institutionalized tackiness, false innocence, false pride, false modesty, and a whole array of questionable values. Lolita herself embodies the cheap taste that characterizes the stereotypical American, and Humbert Humbert is the phony intellectual and master deceiver, not only of those who fall for his continental manner but ultimately of himself. *Lolita* also flirts with issues that have only recently become the object of national attention: incest, child abuse, voyeurism, and the possibility that some children may simply be "bad seeds."

Cult readers shared a perception of Lolita as a symbol of all that was cheap and vulgar and crass about American culture. Lolita is certainly shallow. She loves comics, soda, and chewing gum, speaks in the most debased adolescent jargon of exaggeration and scorn (early "Valspeak"), and has virtually no interest in the sophistication that Humbert possesses. She is perfectly willing to be used sexually as long as she can be plied with cheap, entertaining material goods: "Mentally, I found her to be a disgustingly conventional little girl. Sweet hot jazz, square dancing, gooey fudge sundaes, musicals, movie magazines. . . . She it was to whom ads were dedicated: the ideal consumer, the subject and object of every foul poster" (136). Although she does eventually grow up, even marry and conceive, she never really grows up culturally or aesthetically.

To the young readers at the time, *Lolita* was an uninhibited story that mocked all institutions, overturned all conventional concepts of behavior and morality, violated the assumption of adult responsibility, and reversed classic roles (adult/child: seducer/seduced: innocent American vs. sly European). Humbert Humbert was Mr. Belvedere without inhibitions. James Mason played the part in the movie version of *Lolita* and was perfect in the part because there had always been a quality in Mason's voice and stance that suggested a parody of the idea of the English gentleman—well-spoken, polished, droll, yet tinged with cynicism and subtle mockery. And the casting of Peter Sellers as Quilty and Shelley Winters as Charlotte Haze was inspired, for Winters has always camped it up and Sellers was the cult comedian of his day.

Finally, *Lolita* pleased cult readers because it made fun of other readers who saw it as a dirty book. *Lolita* is not a dirty book. If anything, it is a parody of a dirty book, almost as if Nabokov set out deliberately to lay a trap for the unsuspecting hypocrite who derides pornography while secretly copping a peek. Those who read the book hoping to find salacious passages to condemn will find themselves being mocked for even looking. But if the mockery evades them and they read on with unselfconscious, lip-smacking fascination at the erotic antics of Humbert and Lolita, then it is only the cult reader who is left to enjoy the irony of catching a hypocrite in the act.

FOR FURTHER READING

Centerwall, Brandon S. "Hiding in Plain Sight: Nabokov and Pedophilia." *Texas Studies in Literature and Language* (Fall 1990): 468–84.

Giblett, Rodney. "Writing Sexuality, Reading Pleasure." *Paragraph: A Journal of Modern Critical Theory* (November 1989): 229–38.

Masinton, Charles G. "What Lolita Is Really About?" *New Mexico Humanities Review* 31 (1989): 71–76.

McNeely, Trevor. "Lo and Behold: Solving the Lolita Riddle." *Studies in the Novel* (Summer 1989): 182–99.

O'Connor, Katherine Tiernan. "Rereading *Lolita*, Reconsidering Nabokov's Relationship with Dostoevskij." *Slavic and East European Journal* (Spring 1989): 64–77.

Look Homeward, Angel

Thomas Wolfe
(1929)

Look Homeward, Angel is an intensely autobiographical novel that, despite a great deal of critical abuse, continued to hold readers spellbound for many years after its publication in 1929. Perhaps because it had the misfortune to be published just as the stock market crashed and the Great Depression began, this novel was met with derision by those who deplored what they called its lack of a social conscience. How, they asked, could any self-respecting author, writing at this critical time in American history, totally ignore the great problems afflicting this beleaguered nation? As if this were not bad enough, critics accused Thomas Wolfe of writing reams of romantic nonsense, most of it about himself.

Unsympathetic critics wondered who cared. But apparently there were enough young readers who did, for they turned *Look Homeward, Angel* into a cult classic, a status that has survived the ups and downs of the book's mercurial reputation. The book has fluctuated all over the literary stock market since its initial cautious reception, reaching a peak shortly after World War II and then sliding gradually into a literary twilight, hovering somewhere between oblivion and benign neglect. In the sixties one English critic called Wolfe "an obsessional neurotic" who admittedly had a gift for words but who was incapable of writing about anything or anybody but himself. The most frequent charges leveled against him are that he is guilty of "sprawling profusion," that he is "monstrously rhetorical and oratorical," and that he constructs formless pseudo-narratives that he then calls "novels."

Wolfe's defense was that there were two types of novelists: those who were selective, who "took out," and those who were inclusive, who "put in." In the former camp he put writers like Gustave Flaubert; in the latter, writers like Leo Tolstoy—and himself. All this controversy aside, what annoyed the critics is surely what has attracted and held captive a youthful audience over several generations, namely, the autobiographical nature of the novel. A taste for first-person accounts by young men of their coming of age, their initiation into the world, had been growing ever since Charles Dickens turned David Copperfield into every young man's story. In the early twentieth century, D. H. Lawrence had captured an eager audience with *Sons and Lovers*, and James Joyce with *A Portrait of the Artist as a Young Man*. And after them came Nick Carraway in F. Scott Fitzgerald's *The Great Gatsby* and Jake Barnes in *The Sun Also Rises*.

Now at last here was unabashed Romanticism rooted in the rich American soil of the South, a region in the process of becoming a land of mystery and legend, a storied land in which a literary renaissance was beginning to flower. Wolfe taps the mystique of the South, the earthy life of the soil and the soul that, because of new southern voices like his, was beginning to seem to many Americans more and more like the real thing—a rich, lusty counterpoint to their own pale imitation of life. Onto the shabby stage of drab, depressed America, a stage soon to resemble the bleakness of John Steinbeck's *Grapes of Wrath*, strides Eugene Gant, dark and brooding, tormented and vulnerable, a modern Heathcliff roaming the wooded hills and fertile valleys of North Carolina, part poet, part redneck, part mystic: one of the first of a line of American heroes to raise adolescent angst to the level of mystic experience.

Look Homeward, Angel is clearly an account of the author's own struggle for independence and integrity. Early readers identified with that struggle. They experienced the novel with a force and directness that made negative criticism largely irrelevant. Wolfe's editor, the legendary Maxwell E. Perkins, said in an introduction to a later edition of this unique work that although he knew that *Look Homeward, Angel* was autobiographical (Wolfe had said as much in his preface), he was expecting something along the lines of *David Copperfield* or *War and Peace* or *Pendennis*. "But when we were working together," he said, "I suddenly saw that it was often almost literally autobiographical—that these people in it were his people" (Skillion 160).

This intensity, this immediacy makes this a book that is still able to arouse, to revitalize, to liberate the latent yearnings of the Romantic spirit. In the thirties, it did achieve some measure of success in spite of its unpopularity with the critics, partly because it provided, at least for enthusiasts, an escape from the social realities about them that was justified by the seriousness and authenticity of the hero's struggle. This was far from the flight from reality others were finding in such contemporary bestsellers as *Anthony Adverse* or *The Prisoner of Zenda*. On the contrary, for those who felt they truly understood what Thomas Wolfe was up to, *Look Homeward, Angel* was an escape *into* reality.

The novel is rich in mythical allusion. The sprawling family—the house of Gant—is Greek in its tragic proportions. First there is Oliver Gant, the father, a huge, haunted man driven by undefined longings, a stonemason given to drinking sprees and denunciations of his second wife in madly inflated rhetoric. This second wife, Eliza, is consumed with greed and will stop at nothing to increase her fortunes, even to the point of alienating her children. So ruthless does she become that Ben, one of the twins, denounces her on his deathbed and will not let her approach him. Each of the seven children is nearly allegorical in character. The eldest son, Steve, is swaggering and dishonest; the eldest daughter, Daisy, is dutiful and subservient. Helen is temperamental, Grove otherworldly, and Ben proud.

Eugene Gant, the youngest, is a brooding dreamer, hungry for life, love, beauty. He resembles the monomythical hero in that he is the conscience of his family, sojourning in the world, going off to the university to study and to Richmond to work. It is he who returns with wisdom gained from his experiences and made manifest in a vision he has of his beloved brother, the dead Ben. Ben tells him that there is only one voyage, that there is no happy land, that the world is always within—that there is no more to be found in life than Eugene has found so far. But Eugene, standing on the brink, filled with hope, looks forward to the great voyage of discovery he is about to take, the voyage that is life.

The prepossessing figure of Thomas Wolfe adds to his appeal as a cult writer, especially to those fascinated by the eccentricities of artists. Wolfe was six-and-a-half feet tall, too tall, he said, to write comfortably at an ordinary desk. So he wrote standing up, using the top of the refrigerator as a writing surface. In this way, he turned out stacks of manuscripts that his devoted editors cut and pasted into fat, sprawling books that defied classification. He looked, someone said, like a visitor from Mars, a towering figure with a head too small for his body, emaciated from overwork and undernourishment. The fact that *Look Homeward, Angel* was met with hostility in his hometown only enhanced his reputation among his avid fans, for the image of the author as outcast, as prophet without honor in his own land, seemed only fitting given the rebellious, fiercely individualistic nature of the novel's protagonist.

Eugene Gant is typical of the cult hero who does not go out of his way to be different but even tries to conform, only to find out that he *is* different and that he cannot be other than what he is. The truly alienated hero is the one who cannot help being estranged from the world around him and wants only to locate that part of it that suits him. Gant is estranged because his eyes are open to the sins of his parents, sins that parallel those of society at large and that are responsible for the mess the world is in. Cult readers, reading the book just after the stock market crash of 1929, could see the novel as darkly prophetic and Eugene's parents as symbolic: the haunted, drunken father and callous, money-hungry mother representing the sickness that precipitated the collapse of the system and the punishment of the Depression. It has about it the aura of Greek tragedy: the excessive pride, the tragic flaw, the sins of the fathers being visited upon the sons.

If he could have, Thomas Wolfe would have recorded every syllable of every experience in an effort to absorb the totality of life, to fix it permanently in art. He was obsessed with a monumental desire to "get it all down," and while he may not have succeeded in accomplishing this impossible task, he did succeed in transmitting the emotional intensity of his own response to every facet of living. Thus, the reality he renders is truly reinvented, for it is imbued with the deep, rich colors and textures of a vividly romantic imagination that transforms the minutiae of reality into an endless stream of heightened moments, giving that reality the color and clarity of a landscape illuminated by intermittent flashes of brilliant, metallic lightning.

Like Joseph Conrad, Wolfe retrains the eyes to perceive reality through intensified perception, giving the reader the ability to see the ordinary in an extraordinary way. It is an effect more likely to work on young, impressionable minds already fevered by romantic longings, but when it does work, it is hypnotic. Cult readers become so immersed in Eugene Gant's North Carolina that the rest of the world looks unreal in comparison. And Eugene himself seems to be so alive that one can almost hear the blood sing as it courses through his veins. All this is done by means of a prose that is so lyrical, so soaring, so vibrant that it often rolls with the cadences of poetry.

As a matter of fact, Wolfe saw himself as a modern Walt Whitman, and there is a great similarity between Whitman's poetry and Wolfe's prose. Someone once defined good poetry as poetry struggling to be prose, and good prose as prose struggling to be poetry. The definition certainly fits Whitman and Wolfe. Modern readers have less patience with poetic prose, however, and this may account in part for the eclipse of Wolfe's reputation in recent times.

Nevertheless, it is the prose that overwhelms the cult reader and makes a journey into Gant's world a journey into a heightened reality. So personal is this journey and so central is Eugene Gant to this reality that the cult reader is irresistibly drawn to share a vision in which Gant (and thereby the reader) is the center of the universe, the sole vantage point from which everything else can be seen and grasped and made meaningful. Few books have this power to isolate readers, to draw them upward to a position from which they can only look down on the rest of the world.

Wolfe's own nature was restless and impatient—what today we would call "hyper." He chafed at his imprisonment in the mountain-ringed town of Asheville, North Carolina, and dreamed of the country at large, a country that took on the wondrous, fabulous quality he gave it in all his books. Wolfe has been described as a "Titan battling against odds," but that was the stance from which it pleased him to write, and it is a stance that cult readers admire and even adopt, feeling grateful for having been given the opportunity to view the world from such a privileged perch.

Like other cult heroes, Wolfe's Eugene Gant embodies the quality of loyalty—to family, to principles, to causes—a quality especially attractive to readers hungry for virtues they can aspire to unashamed. In a country where loyalty has come to be associated with everything from blind faith to naive respect, Eugene's loyalty to his family is like a beacon of goodness in an evil world. The theme is repeated in *The Grapes of Wrath,* something of a cult book in its own right, in which loyalty to family transcends all other commitments and becomes, ultimately, all that is worth living or fighting for. In the early thirties especially, Wolfe's own loyalty to his art, as expressed in Eugene's fierce idealism, was a shining affirmation of the power of the human spirit to produce something fine and ennobling in a world that seemed capable of producing nothing but war, chaos, and economic disaster.

Probably more than any other author who has inadvertently produced a cult classic, Thomas Wolfe stands as the consummate American romantic. Rather than the melancholy cynicism of Fitzgerald or the stoic surrender of Ernest Hemingway, Wolfe's voice is the voice of the visionary whose faith in the land and in the people who have roots in it is unshaken by the transient events in the world at large. Eugene Gant is unswerving and undefeated, bloody but unbowed, burning with purpose, as ready as Stephen Dedalus (*Portrait of the Artist*) to forge in the smithy of his soul the uncreated conscience of his race. Joyce and Wolfe are blood brothers in the noble aspirations of their heroes and in the similarity of their appeal to eager cult readers.

FOR FURTHER READING

Idol, John L. *A Thomas Wolfe Companion*. Westport, Conn.: Greenwood, 1987.
Johnston, Carol. *Thomas Wolfe: A Descriptive Bibliography*. Pittsburgh, Penn.: University of Pittsburgh Press, 1987.
Phillipson, John St. *Critical Essays on Thomas Wolfe*. New York: G. K. Hall, 1985.
———. *Thomas Wolfe: A Reference Guide*. New York: G. K. Hall, 1977.
Thomas Wolfe. New York: Chelsea House Publishers, 1987.

Lord of the Flies

William Golding
(1955)

Lord of the Flies focused attention on the concept of cult literature as a campus phenomenon. *Time* magazine called it "Lord of the Campus" and identified it as one in a series of underground literary favorites that were challenging the required reading lists of the traditional humanities curriculum. Up until William Golding's surprise bestseller, it had been common knowledge that students were reading "unauthorized books," especially J. D. Salinger's *The Catcher in the Rye*, in spite of (and frequently because of) their condemnation by "the establishment." But the existence of a serious sub-literature with an intelligent, dedicated readership flourishing in the midst of the conventional curriculum was something unprecedented on college campuses.

During the twenties and thirties, the novels of F. Scott Fitzgerald, Ernest Hemingway, and Thomas Wolfe had quickly been welcomed into the ranks of mainstream, respectable writers and labeled literature. While a few critics might choose to ignore these newcomers, there was nothing particularly subversive about what they wrote. Following the success of *The Catcher in the Rye*, however, no literary observer could be quite sure that the tastes of young readers could be trusted. After all, there were certain attitudes in Salinger that threatened the established order, and when Golding wrote *Lord of the Flies*, there was apprehension afoot that young readers might find Jack more interesting than Ralph—as indeed many of them did.

What nervous detractors overlooked was the obvious lesson in this Golding classic: that traits like naked aggression and gratuitous cruelty, selfishness, idolatry, superstition, and a taste for violence are not restricted to any particular nationality or race but are inherent in human nature and inhabit the mentality of every human being. If there was anything subversive about this idea, it was that no longer could evil be considered peculiar to the Japanese or the German character. In fact, those who had recently fought against them had waged war with equal relish.

When Golding saw the ecstasy on the faces of his fellow sailors in the North Atlantic as they returned the fire of the enemy or launched an attack he felt the shock of recognition that the beast was within us all, just waiting to break through that fragile veneer we call civilization. What he clearly intended as a reminder to his readers (after all, man's aggressive nature was not a new philosophical position by any means) became for cult readers another weapon to use against those who argued that atrocities such as those committed by the Germans and the Japanese could never be committed by the Allies who had struggled against them. "We" were good people who treated others with kindness and generosity and fought those who attacked us with the greatest reluctance and the utmost disdain. Even to suggest that we might enjoy the slaughter was to malign the honor and integrity of the Allied forces.

Regardless of how his theme was interpreted, however, Golding's thesis had firm mythological precedents. There are many myths underlying *Lord of the Flies,* but the basic description of reality is of a world inhabited by men of an evil nature restrained only by voluntary adherence to a pragmatic pact of nonaggression. Such a pact passes for civilization, but because it is maintained only through fear, it is constantly threatened by that fear. The defensive fear that keeps one man from his neighbor's throat can also incite him to cut that throat before his own gets cut.

Golding tells us that man's reason is subservient to his depraved instincts and that the moment he forgets why he has constructed a rational social structure to protect himself, these instincts will clamor for release and destroy that structure. At that point one dominant order arises that demands total fidelity. Once this order becomes oppressive, however, or fails to nourish the depraved instincts of the loyal, loyalty falters, restlessness takes root, and reason limps forth to offer at least temporary balance.

On Golding's island, order lasts only until the boys become aware that there is no one to enforce it but themselves. But because they have never known the reason behind it, they have no reason to respect its function. What they feel is a sense of freedom, freedom from restraint, from discipline, from rules they never understood and that seemed to be imposed only to keep them from enjoying whatever they wanted to enjoy. Freedom for them, as for many, is freedom *from* reason, therefore, freedom to indulge the instincts.

And these instincts, according to Golding, are aggressive. The boys kill primarily for the sake of killing and after that for sacrifice. Killing for food runs a poor third. Their killing is mixed up with power and sex and fear. They are driven by the desire to dominate, to violate, and to feel threatened by mysterious forces. Their feelings are, of course, the basic impulses behind political, social, and religious institutions. And their recrudescence is to the earliest known manifestation of these impulses, the primitive hunting society, led by a fierce oligarchy, circumscribed by a rigid code of social obligation, and dedicated to the pacification through worship and sacrifice of a mysterious threatening force.

According to Carl Jung, our "collective unconscious" retains primordial images, or archetypes, of essential forces and patterns of behavior from which we can never escape and to which we repeatedly return, regardless of whatever thin veneer of civilization may temporarily conceal them. For better or for worse, these inescapable archetypes are the forces that shape the institutions by which all societies have lived and died. Wise men and tyrants, artists and barbarians, slave masters and slaves: such are the immutable, irreducible elements of life on earth. About them one can truly say that the more they change, the more they stay the same. What happens on Golding's island would happen anywhere that civilization's fragile veneer is stripped away and man's essential nature is set free.

When Golding tips the scale in favor of the forces of darkness and evil, he is also drawing upon traditional religious mythology, especially the mythology of the Judeo-Christian tradition. The island is a paradise from which Golding has carefully excluded external threats such as predatory beasts, disease, or starvation. The dead parachutist arrives like the serpent to give the boys an excuse to indulge their instincts—to fall, as it were. The Lord of the Flies is, of course, Beelzebub or Satan, and Golding has not hesitated to use a figure from familiar religious literature. Nor has he obscured the inescapable parallel between Simon and Christ especially in the way Simon suffers the fate of all saviors who bring the word.

There are echoes of Greek mythology in the theft of the fire and the ritual orgies of the hunt, as well as in the victory celebrations. In fact, the Greek concern for the blindness of man to his own fate underlies Golding's assertion that man's nature is inimical. That the boys burn down their own paradise is only the most obvious example of this self-destructive tendency.

For dedicated admirers of this book, the most accessible myth is the conservative myth that exalts reason and restraint as the difficult but necessary means of survival, the means not to ecstasy or bliss but at least to a measure of contentment. To the conservative, liberalism is not faith in human nature but ignorance of it.

Readers who were attracted to this book in the fifties were at odds with a world that was sinking into complacency as a reaction to half a century of economic and political upheaval punctuated by wars of unprecedented horror. They saw a world that they feared was recycling itself for more disaster. They were concerned about social inequalities that festered because they were ignored, and they were worried about the atomic bomb. Golding's book gave them the explanations they were looking for. It made man's selfishness and indifference a cold fact of human nature. And it made the metaphor of the burning island only too relevant to their fears of a world in radioactive flames.

The book also spoke to their confusion about the world's shifting and baffling political alliances. Americans who had once been convinced that the Germans and the Japanese were less than human were beginning to suspect that these people were not really monsters. They were even more puzzled by the Russian bear who was suddenly chasing about the world gobbling up the defenseless and threatening his former keepers. Whom could you trust? No one, said Golding, and especially not yourself. However, a knowledge of the human heart of darkness, cold comfort as it might be, was at least some defense against dread. If we could admit our common beastliness, maybe we could do something to contain it.

This book acted also as an antidote to Salinger's "softness." Holden Caulfield would have fared very badly on Golding's island. Even as a Ralph, he would be of little comfort, since Ralph participates in Simon's death, then erases it from his mind, and probably retains what shreds of civilization he does only because he is the victim. At any rate, Salinger's belief in the essential goodness of man struck Golding's readers as a naive, even grudging evasion made possible only by the support of the phony society that permitted Holden the luxury of attack. They saw Holden as the precocious adolescent who merely bites the hand that feeds him. Golding stood outside the ruins of that society and took what his admirers saw as a cold, sober view of something immensely worse than mere phoniness. The effect, however, was oddly similar: run and enjoy while you can, or sit back and wait.

Golding postulates a future time and an imaginary island. What he tells us of that time in terms of planes, warships, and atomic bombs is an extension of the very real present. He does not suggest weapons or machines or circumstances that are still in the fantasy stage. His threats are real even if his setting is not. However, it is the very deceptiveness of the setting that gives his tale a turn of the screw. What could be farther removed from the threat of death and devastation than an exotic tropical island, the sort of paradise that holiday dreams are made of, a lotus-land of love and sweet indulgence? Instead, his island becomes a grim microcosm of the monstrous world that surrounds it and that introduces evil to it.

Golding is carefully selective of details, but those he provides are not the trappings of a fairy-tale world. The island at first seems as innocent as any island one might find in the Caribbean or the South Pacific. It has palm trees and fruit trees, sunshine and sandy shores, peace and quiet. At first the boys behave the way you would expect children to behave who are temporarily without adult supervision. They horse around and tease each other, insulting each other in the language of the playground, neglectful of their appearance, unaware that as the sun burns their faces and the saltwater bleaches their hair, their clothes are disintegrating and they are looking (and acting) more and more like savages.

The scene grows even more ominous as it dawns on the boys that there are no adults around to intervene, nor are there likely to be, and it is at this point that their play takes on sinister overtones. When at the end of the book adults do return "just in time," it comes more as a shock than as a relief, for we know that the boys' warfare has been interrupted by adults who are participating in a deadlier warfare of their own, and on a much larger scale. But it is not until the naval officer smiles indulgently at the little rascals and mutters something about "fun and games" that the full extent of the horror of what is happening really hits us. Although the boys have been temporarily halted in their regression to barbarianism, the sleek cruiser lying peacefully at anchor out there on the horizon is merely waiting to transport them back to a world that, like their island, is already going up in flames.

Lord of the Flies is a case study in alienation. Gradually, with horrifying inevitability, against a backdrop of paradise, the numbers of those who remember their humanity and still cling to the threads of civilization are reduced until there is but one solitary figure left, and just before the ironic rescue, we see him—become him—as he flees his savage pursuers, the backdrop itself reflecting the degradation of those pursuers as the island of paradise burns and smokes and is reduced to char and ashes.

First we see the whole group splitting and taking sides, but the balance, at least for a while, remains on the side of Ralph. Then slowly but irresistibly, Ralph's supporters are drawn toward the charismatic Jack and his choir, until finally there are only four holding out against them: the twins, Piggy, and Ralph himself. Then the twins are captured and Piggy is killed. Ralph is alone, civilized man alone against the powers of darkness. But we are left with the awful suspicion that he remains "civilized" only because Jack must have an enemy and Ralph must be that enemy. Excluded forever from Jack's group, Ralph encourages exaggerated sympathy because he is so terribly alone. A victim always seems somehow more civilized than his tormentors. Nevertheless, much of the power of this book derives from the fact that our sympathies can only be with Ralph and that we, therefore, can feel the vulnerability, the awful weakness, of flimsy rationality at the mercy of a world gone mad. There is no place to run, no place to hide, no exit. And rescue is only temporary and perhaps ultimately more horrible than quick and early death.

Golding stubbornly appeals to the remnants of reason that he firmly believes still reside in the modern mind, modern history to the contrary. Therefore, what he offers is the slim hope that the fire of reason can be restored to the mind or at least kept alive and that the eyeglasses of vision can be recovered in time to defend ourselves from the slime of our own minds and possibly even to combat its threat.

To be convinced that man is essentially depraved is to run the risk of becoming depraved oneself. One can either submit to that depravity as the only reality or insist on seeing it in everyone but oneself. Although Golding tries to tell us that we all carry the seeds of our own destruction within us, it is tempting to feel superior to that general condemnation and to believe that one has got hold of a truth in time to exclude oneself from it.

Nevertheless, in the world of the fifties, a world that had blotted out the recent past and was busily indulging itself in the accumulation of consumer goods, it was tempting to those who agreed with Golding to throw up their hands and join the world's downward slide. Man's essential depravity was a convenient explanation for the otherwise inexplicable myopia that seemed to possess almost everyone. Korea was unreal, McCarthy very real. War was boring, especially a war in which the stakes were so low and the action so restricted, but witch hunts in Washington fed an appetite for domestic corruption that, once whetted, has continued unchecked.

The fifties witnessed the first rumblings of social protest. But to those who felt threatened, this outrage seemed feeble and doomed to failure. And in many instances it was difficult to know who was guilty and who was innocent. Is a slave who beats his master righteously indignant or equally depraved? To threaten a social order simply to correct a few inequities was, to many, like burning the house down to get rid of the termites.

Golding appealed to conservatives who were deeply suspicious of humanity and who believed that people required constant restraint. However, to exclude oneself from this need was to assume the kind of lofty attitude that this book unfortunately encouraged. But then, Golding's thesis is an absolute that allows no room for balanced judgment. Either you accept your own depravity or else you deny it and wait for it to ruin you.

The discomfort that the boys willingly endure in *Lord of the Flies* is exceeded only by the pain they enjoy inflicting on each other. It is the politics of pain at its most basic: One is either a giver or receiver of pain. Bread and circuses is merely a euphemism for bread and brutality. The most powerful governments have always been those that know how much pain the people want and can take, just as the most powerful religions are based not only on the physical anguish of hair shirts and mortification of the flesh but even more so on the mental anguish of guilt and fear and deadly doubt. The boys in *Lord of the Flies* accept Jack's tyranny because it excuses their own licentiousness (It is a short step from "He made me" to "I was only following orders"). Their minds are possessed by fear, and by the handmaidens of fear, which are hate, lust, and anger.

Those who took Golding's thesis to heart were able to torture themselves by searching out their own depravity and either exaggerating it or capitulating to it—or both. To them this unalterable truth about their own natures soured every deed and thought. They grew suspicious of their own intentions and found in everything they did a selfish motive. To them civilization was a fraud—an artfully constructed facade designed to deceive both oneself and others while the forces of self-aggrandizement were doing their dirty work. Smiles, cooperation, united goals were also masks for the advancement of the self, and this advancement meant nothing more than self-gratification.

Those who saw depravity everywhere trusted no one. Behind every word anyone spoke, they heard a lie, and they saw in every action someone's attempt to gratify a voracious ego. They were surrounded by corruption, distrustful of everyone, believing in nothing except their own pronouncements. They fixed their eyes on doomsday, preached its imminence at every opportunity, and seemed to be deliberately hastening its arrival.

William Golding's most ardent followers turned reactionary. Since man's depravity had been revealed to the world most horribly and visibly in the two world wars of the first half of the twentieth century, there was every reason to believe that it was necessary to retreat to the safer ground of an earlier order, if only to postpone the inevitable Armageddon. Power was too diffuse, society too open, religion too ineffectual, education too liberal to decelerate the decline.

Governments had to be stronger, and there was even an upsurge of interest in the machinations of recent dictators, not to rejoice over their failures but to learn where they went wrong. If the world gave in to leaders like Jack, the world deserved them. How could Jack be blamed if others submitted so willingly? Where they might be called depraved, Jack was simply shrewd. At worst he was the one-eyed king in the land of the blind; at best he was a model of the man responsible only unto himself and not to those who chose to follow him instead of his example.

FOR FURTHER READING

Carey, John, ed. *William Golding: the Man and His Books*. New York: Farrar, Straus & Giroux, 1987.

Devkota, Padma Prasad. "The Darkness Motif in the 'Primitive' Novels of William Golding." *DAI* 51 (1990): 860A.

Monteith, Charles. "Strangers from Within into 'Lord of the Flies.' " (London) *Times Literary Supplement* (September 19, 1986): 1030.

Tanzman, Leo. "The Murder of Simon in Golding's *Lord of the Flies*." *Notes on Contemporary Literature* (Nov. 1987): 2–3.

Watson, George. "The Coronation of Realism." *The Georgia Review* (Spring 1987): 5–16.

The Lord of the Rings

J.R.R. *Tolkien*
(1954–56)

The Lord of the Rings is unique in modern fiction. Although *Dune* and its sequels rival it for scope and *The Stand* rivals it for size, it stands alone in terms of depth and diversity and ultimately sheer inventiveness. While it owes much to the tradition of the English novel, it has resonances of the Icelandic Eddas, of Nordic myths and folklore, of ancient tales and epic sagas, as if J.R.R. Tolkien contained within the crucible of his own genius the whole collective unconscious of the human race, or at least that part of it peculiar to the Western mind since prehistoric times. Clearly, then, much of the appeal of *The Lord of the Rings* is on the level of fairy tale, an appeal to a childlike fascination with wizards and witchcraft, kings and princes, sorcery and derring-do, all wrapped up in a spellbinding narrative.

The Lord of the Rings contains all the mystery and color and charm of a Nordic myth. It is a vast compendium of elves, dwarfs, trolls, orcs, hobbits, and men all inhabiting Middle Earth, which has its own history, languages, geography, and mythology. It is a vast, three-volume work that can really be appreciated only as myth and not as a novel or even a children's fantasy. And this is precisely the way cult followers do approach this work, as a mythical alternative to the way the twentieth century defines reality. They see in Tolkien a figure who challenges modern definitions of greatness, and they see in *The Lord of the Rings* an alternative to our blind loyalty to the questionable values of a world we just happen to inhabit, a loyalty that threatens to replace the traditional allegiance to country, family, or religious faith. Tolkien evokes a hierarchical order of values in which the battle against what he sees as real evil in the world draws on the ancient virtues of discipline and obedience and, above all, honor.

Critics of *The Lord of the Rings* argue that it is all too easy to lose one's way in it, to become distracted by the geography of Gondor or by the significance of the twenty Elven rings of Middle Earth. Tolkien himself called his creation an "unserious game," and Edmund Wilson claimed that its basic appeal was to readers with a "lifelong appetite for juvenile trash." Cult readers might just be inclined to agree, making sure to add, however, that it is only in juvenile fiction that we can still find a respect for moral stability, for set values, for a clear distinction between good and evil—for, in fact, a simple recognition that evil does exist in spite of modern attempts to explain it away as aberrant behavior, the product of a repressive society.

Children's stories present worlds in which such things as justice and loyalty and honor triumph over injustice, treachery, and dishonor. Children respond to these worlds spontaneously. No critic persuades them to like one book and dislike another. Cult readers respond in much the same way. Their intuition has not been corrupted by sophistry. This same innocent spontaneity accounts for the phenomenal popularity in the movies of the succession of adult cartoons from *Star Wars* to *Batman* to *Dick Tracy*—all made without the R rating ordinarily considered indispensable to box-office success. For what these movies have in common is the timeless myth of good versus evil presented as black and white issues with no murky middle ground.

The response to this "juvenile trash" reminds us of how much our notion of good and evil and our power to resist temptation depend, not upon reason and will, but upon the kind of family and society into which we happen to have been born and by which we have been educated. At any given time in history, some families and some societies are in a better state of moral health than others. In *The Lord of the Rings,* full justice is done to this fact. Like all classic myths, this one can persuade us to face life neither with despair nor with false hopes.

The reality that Tolkien has reinvented with such clarity and detail greatly resembles medieval Europe. No one knows exactly what the Middle Ages really felt like, but readers of *The Lord of the Rings* have the illusion of being in an ancient world that is somehow familiar, that is, in some mysterious way, part of the history of their own world. They feel at home there, yet they are never sure exactly why. One reason they feel comfortable, of course, has to do with their familiarity with the conventions of the epic tradition. According to this tradition, they can reasonably expect the story to follow the movements of a particular person who is of heroic stature (physically and mentally) and who embodies the ideals and values of a particular people. They know that the hero will, like the heroes of *The Odyssey* and *Beowulf,* go on a journey and survive many adventures, overcome many obstacles, and endure many hardships, after which he will return home in triumph bearing the wisdom acquired from his experiences.

Although *The Lord of the Rings* satisfies its readers' expectations by conforming to the conventions of the epic genre, it also contains many imaginative variations on the epic's traditional pattern. The role of the hero and the nature of his quest are presented with greater clarity and detail. Much attention is given to the special qualities necessary to the hero if his particular quest is to be successful. The adventures in which the hero is involved are clearly meant to provide situations in which he can be tested not only in skill and courage but also in spirit and heart. There is, in fact, much emphasis on the hero's worthiness even to undertake the quest, which is itself perceived as a sacred task laid on him by higher powers. Moreover, as if to emphasize that the quest is more than merely a personal one, the hero receives help not only from other persons, but often from other creatures or even nonhuman sources, both natural and supernatural.

The Odyssey and *Beowulf* presumed an audience who believed that evil could be dealt with effectively by a single, nearly invincible hero. If epic writing is at all possible in the twentieth century, it is quite unlikely that twentieth-century audiences will believe that single-handed acts of heroism will set things right—or are even possible. Middle Earth must be saved through the efforts of quite ordinary and even humble people. Yet genuine heroes do have a place in the great struggles of Middle Earth. Aragorn, son of Arathorn, is a hero cut from the great traditions, the main difference being that, unlike Odysseus and Beowulf, he does not seek his own glory. He does, in fact, subordinate his own will to the needs of people who neither know him nor appreciate his protection. The glory that comes to him comes as an unsought reward and in recognition of his essential humility.

Even though Tolkien maintained that his work was neither topical nor allegorical, most Tolkien admirers have understood the story to have very strong implications for human life in general and for our own age in particular. Tolkien creates a whole world that in its own peculiar way is a reflection of our own, in much the same way that historian Barbara Tuchman drew parallels between the fourteenth and twentieth centuries in *A Distant Mirror*. Middle Earth is a "distant mirror" of contemporary times, a world that exists only as a reflection in the mirror of modern times. But who is to say which period is the reflection of which, for does not the world around us look vastly different once we have seen it through the eyes of the inhabitants of Middle Earth?

A curious footnote to this exceptional book and its phenomenal reception is the fact that when it was being written and published, there gathered around Tolkien an informal group of Oxford men known as the Inklings, men who shared Tolkien's Christian commitment, his dislike of modern life, and his distaste for modernism in the arts. The Inklings seem to have been Tolkien's first cult following, for they were warmly enthusiastic about *The Hobbit* when it appeared in the thirties, and they encouraged him to develop his inspiration into the full-fledged epic that became *The Lord of the Rings*. The things they liked were the same things that accounted for the trilogy's success in the sixties, and it offered an alternative to young people disenchanted with society but unwilling to go the route of sex, drugs, and rock 'n roll that the counterculture was taking. Later, it appealed to the born-again religious element now in open revolt against the excess and emptiness of the counterculture.

Dyed-in-the-wool cult readers would like nothing better than to be able to move to Middle Earth and stay there, much as Dick Kilmarth, the hero of Daphne du Maurier's 1968 time-warp novel, *The House on the Strand*, becomes addicted to his drug-induced trips back to the fourteenth century and, when forced to choose, opts to return for good. This same syndrome is present in Jack Finney's cult novel *Time and Again* in which the hero, Si Morley, returns to the New York City of a century ago as part of a government experiment and ends up going back to stay.

The desire to stop the world and get off is not new to modern times. It is, in fact, literature's main reason for being. Like the world in Matthew Arnold's "Dover Beach," our world, too, which "seems to lie before us like a land of dreams, /So various, so beautiful, so new," is not very much to our liking. Instead of pleasing us with its variety and abundance, it can offer "neither joy, nor love, nor light, /Nor certitude, nor peace, nor help for pain," and consequently we yearn to escape.

For those who wish to travel back in time rather than ahead, *The Lord of the Rings* continues to attract passengers who would prefer a one-way ticket.

FOR FURTHER READING

Abbott, Joe. "Tolkien's Monsters: Concept and Function in *The Lord of the Rings* (Part II): *Sauron*." *Mythlore: A Journal of J.R.R. Tolkien, C. S. Lewis, Charles Williams, General Fantasy and Mythic Studies* (Spring 1990): 51–59.

Bettridge, William Edwin. "Tolkien's 'New' Mythology." *Mythlore: A Journal of J.R.R. Tolkien, C. S. Lewis, Charles Williams, General Fantasy and Mythic Studies* (Summer 1990): 27–31.

Kubinski, Wojciech. "Comprehending the Incomprehensible: On the Pragmatic Analysis of Elvish Texts in *The Lord of the Rings*." *Inklings: Jahrbuch für Literatur und Ästhetik* 7 (1989): 63–81.

Lindsay, Sean. "The Dream System in *The Lord of the Rings*." *Mythlore: A Journal of J.R.R. Tolkien, C. S. Lewis, Charles Williams, General Fantasy and Mythic Studies* (Spring 1987): 7–14.

Sammons, Martha C. *"A Better Country": The World of Religious Fantasy and Science Fiction*. Westport, Conn.: Greenwood, 1988.

Lost Horizon

James Hilton
(1933)

Lost Horizon was the first paperback novel ever published. It appeared in paperback in 1939, six years after its original hardcover publication, and it has remained in print ever since. One reason for its enduring popularity is James Hilton's engaging way of telling a story. His style is reminiscent of Somerset Maugham, and he shares with Maugham the technique of making the extraordinary believable without sacrificing its essential mystery. *Lost Horizon* is similar in spirit to Maugham's *The Razor's Edge* (1946). In addition to sharing an underlying pessimism about the future of Western civilization, both novels lean heavily toward Oriental philosophies, a leaning, incidentally, that anticipates the 1960s counterculture interest in Zen Buddhism, in Hermann Hesse's *Siddhartha*, and in eastern religious thought in general.

Aside from Hilton's ability to tell a good story in the tradition of Joseph Conrad and Maugham, however, probably the basic reason for the enduring appeal of *Lost Horizon* lies in the combination of ingredients peculiar to this particular story, ingredients not found in his other works, even though all of them were bestsellers in their day. In fact, *Goodbye, Mr. Chips* has remained a perennial favorite, better known, perhaps, than *Lost Horizon*, but whereas the appeal of *Chips* is primarily sentimental and nostalgic, the appeal of *Lost Horizon* is mythical and utopian. Everyone has heard of Shangri-La; the word has become a part of our vocabulary. People who have never heard of *Lost Horizon* use it everyday to identify a never-never land where all is harmony and peace, and time is not an enemy.

But *Lost Horizon* offers more to a cult reader than the concept of escape and leisure. In Hilton's Shangri-La, the holy men who inhabit the lamasery engage in intellectual and physical pursuits that have a positive and often quite practical purpose. These pursuits range in importance from something as trivial as the reappraisal of the Brontë parsonage to something as significant as a breakthrough in mathematics—or even to something as beneficial to the public good as an improvement in plumbing. The High Lama of Shangri-La has dedicated his order to the preservation of the world's culture in the hope that something may be left after the strong nations have destroyed the world outside. Writing in 1933, Hilton anticipated not only World War II but also the threat of nuclear holocaust.

Lost Horizon has all the classic elements of the frame-tale, the story-within-a-story told by an utterly reliable narrator to an incredulous audience. The story opens at Tempelhof airport in Berlin in 1932, where three English gentlemen and former schoolmates are sitting around after dinner, smoking cigars and talking about old times. Mention of another of their schoolmates, Robert "Glory" Conway, prompts one of the men, now a famous novelist, to give the narrator of the book a manuscript describing Conway's incredible adventures in a remote area of Tibet. The novelist, whose name is Rutherford, had run into Conway in China and had been so overwhelmed by Conway's story that he wrote it down.

It is Rutherford's account, then, that becomes the central narrative of the novel. While Conway and three other passengers are attempting to fly out of Baskul, a city under siege, the plane they are flying in is hijacked and flown to a remote spot high in an impassable mountain range presumably on the China-Tibet border. Although the plane is forced down on a desolate windswept plateau and the pilot dies soon thereafter, the passengers are rescued by a delegation from the nearby lamasery of Shangri-La. Eventually Conway learns he and the others are really victims of a plot to replenish the members of the lamasery and that they will not be allowed to leave Shangri-La. Conway has no objections to this; in fact, he is so attuned to the Shangri-La way of life that he eventually agrees to succeed the High Lama and take control of the lamasery of Shangri-La and of the valley of the Blue Moon far below. Two of the others are also quite happy to remain, but one young Englishman, Mallinson, rebels, and it is his attempt to escape that brings the story to a climax.

Unaware that the aging process at Shangri-La is delayed because of the difference in air and diet, Mallinson falls in love with Lo-Tsen, a Chinese woman he takes to be eighteen but who is really closer to one hundred. With her help, Mallison bribes some visiting porters to help him escape, but he needs Conway to help him through the treacherous mountain pass that is the only egress. Prevailing upon Conway's compassion and common sense, Mallinson convinces him to leave, and the three of them attempt the impossible. We are never told what happens to Mallinson, but we do know that Conway shows up at a remote mission hospital in China, his memory gone, and we are told that he was brought there by a very old Chinese woman.

Conway does eventually regain his memory and manages to tell most of his story to Rutherford before suddenly disappearing. Although Rutherford tries valiantly to track Conway down, Conway continues to elude him, but from the direction the trail leads, we can only conclude that Conway has returned—or died trying to return—to Shangri-La.

In *Lost Horizon,* Hilton combines several myths, the foremost being the myth of utopia, a never-never land known variously as El Dorado, Atlantis, Erewhon, Middle Earth, Islandia, and of course the place Thomas More first named Utopia. Utopia (which means "nowhere") is supposed to be an ideal spot where sorrow is banished and evil does not exist. In Hilton's Shangri-La there is no evil because the causes of evil have been removed, among them that favorite one commonly used to explain the existence of evil—envy brought on by the lack of something one wants, the not having what someone else has, the absence of one's fair share. In Shangri-La, there is plenty to go around and no one wants for anything. Thus, so goes the conventional wisdom, no one needs to steal anything. When Conway asks if this extends to love and the desire for a woman who belongs to someone else, he is told that if the love is strong enough, the man who possesses the woman should (nay, *would*!) yield his claim.

Lost Horizon also evokes the myth of renewal in the sense that a purgative experience can give one a new lease on life. Barnard, the American swindler who is running away from the law, finds his true calling as plumber and chooses to stay on in Shangri-La just so that he can modernize the facilities for those who live in the valley of the Blue Moon.

Along with the quest for spiritual salvation, for the elixir of youth, and for riches, there is also the pervasive appeal of the myth of the search for the father or mentor. Conway, who is described as pretty much of a loner, is favored by the High Lama to the extent that the High Lama breaks with tradition in holding frequent and long conversations with Conway. During these conversations, the High Lama (who turns out to be the original founder of the lamasery, Father Perrault, now nearly two hundred years old), tells Conway the history of Shangri-La, expounds on its philosophy and its purpose, and finally selects Conway as his successor. Conway responds in the spirit of a dutiful son or respectful protegé and in the process finds his cynicism being slowly replaced by hope. This is why, in the end, after the temporary lapse that led him to leave Shangri-La, he feels honor-bound to return there and fulfill the duties that were assigned and accepted in good faith. This is not to say that he would not have returned anyway, but his devotion to the High Lama makes his choice to return unarguable.

It is as a monomythical hero that Conway has tremendous appeal to cult readers. To begin with, it is clear even before we meet him that he was idealized at school by both classmates and teachers, that it was there, in fact, that he had acquired the nickname "Glory" after his exploits had been described to a headmaster as "glorious." He is described as the sort of person others remember vividly even after meeting him only briefly. The narrator describes him as "tall and extremely good looking," a remarkable young man who "not only excelled at games but walked off with every conceivable kind of school prize." There was "something rather Elizabethan about him—his casual versatility, his good looks, that effervescent combination of mental with physical activities," he says, adding that "our civilization doesn't often breed people like that nowadays"(7).

Although his friends still praise him for his exploits, especially for his heroism at Baskul, they call him a dilettante and think of him as "clever but slack." However, Chang, his guide in Shangri-La, finds it odd that the English regard slackness as a vice. He tells Conway that the people of Shangri-La prefer slackness to tension, arguing that there is too much tension already in the world and that the world might be better off if there were more slackers.

Conway himself attributes his avowed heroism to a certain indifference that keeps him cool under fire and notes that he is only admired because he is misunderstood. During his first days at Shangri-La, enough of his skepticism clings to make him an intelligent listener and observer and to make his eventual alliance with the lamasery come about so subtly as to seem not only inevitable but utterly logical. He is Ulysses, who may get sidetracked temporarily but who is never deceived or misled, not even by Mallinson when he knowingly lets his heart overrule his head.

Although right from the start it is clear that Conway's temperament is amenable to the philosophy of the tenants of Shangri-La, it is awhile before he completely dispels the doubts that make him wonder about the state of the world and the whole purpose of life. It seems to him that you could explain most things by blaming them on either "the will of God or the lunacy of man," or is it, he wonders, "the will of man and the lunacy of God"? At first most of his thinking is negative. He can only find fault with the world he is being removed from. He finds its taste for superlatives vulgar and does not care for "excessive striving." Hilton describes him as "always an onlooker," a man who refuses to be "fussed into deciding" at moments when others are losing their heads.

Enviable as this unflappable quality may seem to others, Conway does not deceive himself into thinking of it as bravery or coolness or "any especially sublime confidence in his own power to make decisions on the spur of the moment." Rather, he sees it as a kind of indolence, "an unwillingness to interrupt his mere spectator's interest in what was happening" (56). As they traverse the precipitous pass into Shangri-La, not knowing what is in store for them, Mallinson complains about what is happening to them, and Conway tells him that, cynical as it may sound, what they have left behind them is just as nightmarish as anything they are going through. In arriving there, he says, "the worst that can have happened is that we've exchanged one form of lunacy for another" (66).

Conway refers to the world outside Shangri-La as "a world of increasing noise and hugeness" and finds himself echoing a phrase of Barnard's—"the whole game's going to pieces." Thus, he responds enthusiastically to a culture that has concentrated on preserving the best in art, music, and literature at the expense of such modern intrusions as newspapers, radios, and movies. It is the High Lama, however, who detects the quality in Conway that sets him apart from the rest and makes him the sort of hero cult followers like to idealize. After expounding on the principle of moderation and expressing faith in Conway's acceptance of it, he tells Conway that Conway has an odd quality he has never met in any other visitors to Shangri-La, describing it as "not quite cynicism, still less bitterness," but made up partly of disillusionment. "It is also a clarity of mind that I should not have expected in anyone younger than—say, a century or so," he says, then adds that if he had to put a single word to it, that word would be "passionlessness" (157).

The High Lama makes his remark about passionlessness in the course of explaining to Conway the secret of longevity in Shangri-La, and it gives Conway the chance to express what even at this point continues to be his essential skepticism. For him to care anything about its length, he says, life must have meaning (something he sometimes doubts); otherwise long life would be pointless. Nowhere in modern literature is there a simpler expression of modern man's dilemma. While the world attributes heroism to a belief that life has meaning, the "hero" knows that he can remain cool and act brave precisely because it does not. In more ways than one Conway is a foreshadowing of cult literature's other "passionless" hero, Meursault, in Albert Camus's *The Stranger*.

It is here that the High Lama (in reality Father Perrault, who is old enough to remember the French Revolution) offers Conway his superior vision born of greater perspective and vaster experience. And what he offers is not the chance to redeem civilization or spare it a horrible destiny, nor the chance to reverse the course of destiny or breathe new life into moribund cultures. What Father Perrault offers is a chance "to outlive the doom that gathers around on every side." It is a dream of survival, a dream of performing the same service for the future that the church performed during the so-called dark ages, to keep the flame of art and learning, of love and compassion, of simple courtesy from going out. (Walter M. Miller's cult classic, *A Canticle for Leibowitz,* projects this dream into a post-nuclear world in which the church provides this same sort of sanctuary for artifacts from the pre-nuclear past, most of which are beyond the understanding of the priests who guard them.)

Father Perrault's prophesy of what will happen to the world is apocalyptic, but his greater vision is of a sort of kingdom on Earth. It is secular humanism at its most seductive, a hope too powerful to dismiss. At this point, Conway feels renewed. The long talk leaves him feeling empty but satisfied, his mind and spirit and emotions in harmony, his doubts resolved.

"Perhaps the exhaustion of the passions is the beginning of wisdom," Conway says to the High Lama after telling him that during the war he had felt "excited and suicidal and scared and reckless and sometimes in a tearing rage." "That also, my son, is the doctrine of Shangri-La," the High Lama tells him, to which Conway replies, "I know. It makes me feel quite at home" (178).

Hilton suggests that we are born into this world the way the refugees find themselves in Shangri-La—mysteriously, accidentally, irrationally. Even Barnard, ordinarily so practical, senses the mystery of it when he talks about not understanding "all the ins and outs of it, and why we've been landed here," adding "but then, isn't that the usual way of things? Do we know why we're in the world at all, for that matter?" (192)

The High Lama expresses the fears that most readers harbored during the uneasy thirties when the world, already deep in economic chaos, trembled on the brink of global war and holocaust. He predicts that there will be no safety from upheaval either by arms, from authority, or in science. "It will rage till every flower of culture is trampled, and all human things are leveled in a vast chaos" (198). It was not this prophesy that cult leaders clung to; they preferred to think that even the High Lama could be wrong or, barring that, that Shangri-La could remain a haven, a place of peace and harmony, a treasure house, remote, hidden, untouched, the only hope that the triumphs of the past would survive the chaos.

FOR FURTHER READING

Crawford, John W. "The Utopian Dream: Alive and Well." *Cuyahoga Review* (Spring-Summer 1984): 27–33.

Heck, Francis S. "The Domain as a Symbol of a Paradise Lost: *Lost Horizon* and *Brideshead Revisited.*" *The Nassau Review: The Journal of Nassau Community College Devoted to Arts, Letters, and Sciences* 4.3 (1982): 24–29.

Van Eeden, Janet. "The Monastery Months." *CRUX: A Journal on the Teaching of English* (February 1987): 22–25.

Lucky Jim

Kingsley Amis
(1954)

Kingsley Amis was one of a group of novelists and playwrights in England in the early fifties who acquired the label "angry young men." The label gained currency in connection with John Osborne's Jimmy Porter in his 1956 play *Look Back in Anger*, but it had appeared as early as 1951 in the title of Leslie Allen Paul's autobiography, *Angry Young Man*. Even though both Osborne and Amis disclaimed the label, it stuck, especially with the success of *Lucky Jim*.

Critics who attacked the movement seemed to do so more out of fear than loathing. They were usually older men who had watched England barely survive two world wars, who had stood by helplessly as the empire crumbled, and who were now disturbed by a postwar depression from which Britain seemed unable to recover. While England's wartime enemies were experiencing miraculous economic recoveries, the English seemed to lurch from one austerity program to another while their economy teetered on the verge of collapse.

Thus, critics of the new unrest feared any threat to an already precarious social order. The last thing Britain needed, in their opinion, was a gang of hotheads who could not see beyond their own selfishness. Unfortunately, these critics failed to assess the mood correctly and see it as symptomatic of a worldwide postwar shift in attitude. For what the angry young men saw beyond the economic backslide was a Britain insidiously retreating into her old ways, regardless of who was in power. They were convinced that if the future was not to be a devastating repetition of the past, Britain had to undergo a fundamental change in values and attitude. It was a determination that dominated the mentality of the postwar generation and contributed significantly to the revolutionary social and economic reform that was to change the face of Britain in the last half of the twentieth century.

The critics claimed that these young men were not really angry but simply disgruntled. The truth is that they were both. The anger is what erupted after the disgruntlement had festered too long. The things the "angry young men" found depressing might seem trivial when laid out and inspected separately, but taken together they summed up what was wrong in the lives of these young people and the society they hoped to rescue. Their disgruntlement was with their social status, with their work, with their colleagues, with the shabbiness of daily life, with their frustrated aspirations for self-fulfillment, with the drudgery of daily survival and the tediousness of all the trivial activities that drained their energies. When, however, they got angry like Lucky Jim, theirs was an outcry heard round the world, and in little more than a decade after the publication of *Lucky Jim*, that solitary cry in the wilderness had become the howl of multitudes.

Jim Dixon, the charming antihero of this prophetic novel, is the prototype of a breed that took hold in universities, particularly in English departments, after the war when enrollments mushroomed and instructors were scarce. This breed consisted largely of untenured junior professors disabled by a graduate school mentality. Most of them had worked their way through graduate school as teaching assistants and had become accustomed to a routine of drudgery, procrastination, and communal commiseration that they were never quite able to outgrow. Thus, their professional lives were merely an extension of the limbo life of a graduate assistant.

They are still around, and they still read *Lucky Jim*. Two elements of graduate school life have left permanent scars. One is their status: They are both teachers and students, forced to switch roles several times within a single day. One hour they are lording it over a pack of "functional illiterates," teaching freshman English as if it were a graduate course. The next hour they sit craven at the feet of a senior professor, suffering the indignities of exposed ignorance. And the next hour they're taking their humiliation out on the freshmen again.

Meanwhile, the second paralyzing factor kicks in: the way they live. Since their slave wages permit them no more than a basement room somewhere, furnished with the obligatory bricks-and-boards bookshelves and army cot, they spend most of their time in their offices, better known as rabbit warrens, for they are usually no more than cubicles in one vast, noisy, littered subterranean room that is overheated in the winter (because it is next to the boilers) and damply chill in the summer. Thus, they are also always either just getting over a cold or just coming down with one.

An important psychological component of this lifestyle is the tendency to consider themselves as a subclass and to hold permanent grudges against the full-time faculty, even when they themselves become a part of that faculty. And later on, when they finally do become full professors themselves, they prefer the company of graduate assistants with whom they share a proletarian political identity. The breed has been superseded in recent times by the yuppie graduate assistants who, in ties and blazers and tasseled shoes and favoring a deadpan hauteur known as the Important Young Mind expression, seem ready to take charge before their time, while the remnants of the *Lucky Jim* generation, looking nervously over their shoulders, seem caught in a time warp.

Academics are fond of an antihero like Jim Dixon because they can see in his gentle, resentful, hesitant, yet sensitive nature the promise of something they admire but fear to emulate. The message he brings—and which they wish they had the courage to follow—is to resist the temptation to play along with those in power. Today such resistance is largely taken for granted, and professors routinely file grievances for one thing or another, but back then it was tantamount to treason, and protest was not a viable concept. Lucky Jim's dilemma, then, at least articulated the young scholar's ethical crisis: how to maintain one's integrity and still get tenure. Not only does Jim feel compelled to toady to his chairman and anybody else in authority, he also feels pressured to peddle worthless "scholarly" articles just to add items to his vita—to literally publish or perish.

The zeal for reform that *Lucky Jim* inspired in the fifties led many of Amis's generation to act as *agents provocateurs* during the riotous sixties when sympathies for the free-speech and antiwar movements clashed with concerns over job security. Thus, it was not uncommon for student protestors to have briefing sessions in some professor's office just before storming the administration building or taking over the library. It was also not uncommon for untenured professors of the Jim variety, upon learning that their contracts would not be renewed, to ask their followers to forget Vietnam and fight for the instructor's reinstatement, arguing, of course, that their academic freedom was being violated.

Academic satire is a peculiar literary genre, one that has almost no audience outside the groves of academe. Usually it is both written and read exclusively by academics who enjoy flogging themselves while biting the hand that feeds them. Amis is the exception, and this may account for the wider appeal of his academic satire. He knows his territory, but he does not annoy the reader with inside jokes. His protagonist is more than a struggling junior faculty member; he is anyone struggling to survive in a world of favoritism and discrimination. And the fact that he abandons teaching in the end makes him someone with whom those outside the university can identify, for his leavetaking is both a graduation and an escape from a world that many students privately find eccentric and anachronistic.

One image that Amis holds up for ridicule is the stereotype of the professor with the "ceramics and macramé" wife and a passel of precocious progeny, all living in genteel poverty in a rented cottage where the professor, when not practicing on the recorder, is trying to figure out how to assemble his harpsichord. What Amis does is to tap a vein of self-loathing that is part of the academic psyche. Readers can laugh at the image even as they find themselves conforming to it. This masochistic strain is not unlike the strain common to all cult readers who need to suffer as well as rejoice with a cult book's protagonist. It is not necessarily a hero's strengths that attract a reader but his weaknesses, his vulnerabilities, the "tragic flaw" that disables him but ultimately ennobles him. Jim Dixon may be craven before the authority that has hold over his future, but once he burns his bridges and flees, he has avoided a weakness worse than fear, and that is cowardice. He refuses finally to conform, thumbs his nose at Chairman Welch and all the others, and strikes out for greener pastures.

The iconoclastic humor of *Lucky Jim* (for it *is* a very funny novel) places it in the company of later cult books like *Catch–22, One Flew Over the Cuckoo's Nest, Another Roadside Attraction, A Hitchhiker's Guide to the Galaxy*, and *Fear and Loathing in Las Vegas*. Its humor has not diminished over the years even though some of the situations in the novel are somewhat dated. Academe remains an anachronistic institution in the modern world, resisting all efforts to modernize it. While universities struggle to be on the cutting edge by rushing to install computers and launch new "outreach" programs, the computers are merely new bottles for old wine, and the new programs are only old wine in new bottles. The university is a schizophrenic blend of medievalism and socialism, two incompatible systems, one based on foolish notions of rank and privilege, the other on false notions of equality. When the two are joined, as in the Catholic Church, for example, the seeds of political intrigue are sown and progress is stifled.

What Kingsley Amis presents in *Lucky Jim* is a picture of the stagnant fen of academe. Jim is lucky. He knows that nothing will ever change, and that is why he leaves. People like Jim do not stay, and that is why nothing ever changes. People like Michel, the pedantic student who hounds Jim, are the ones who stay on, and that is also why nothing ever changes. When La Rochefoucauld said, "The more things change, the more they stay the same," he must have had universities in mind, for his words describe universities in a nutshell.

FOR FURTHER READING

Brady, Mark. "Funny Jim." In *Four Fits of Anger: Essays on the Angry Young Men*. Udine, Italy: Campanotto, 1986: 70–79.

Bell, Robert H. "True Comic Edge in *Lucky Jim*." *American Humor: An Interdisciplinary Newsletter* (Fall 1981): 1–7.

Hague, Angela. "Picaresque Structure and the Angry Young Novel." *Twentieth Century Literature: A Scholarly and Critical Journal* (Summer 1986): 209–20.

Hatson, George. "The Coronation of Realism." *The Georgia Review* (Spring 1987): 5–16.

Wilson, Keith. "Jim, Jake and the Years Between: The Will to Stasis in the Contemporary British Novel." *Ariel: A Review of International English Literature* (January 1982): 55–69.

One Flew over the Cuckoo's Nest

Ken Kesey
(1962)

One Flew over the Cuckoo's Nest is a modern morality play. It has a savior, McMurphy, who must be sacrificed before his gospel can be spread. It has a disciple, Chief Bromden, who is inspired by McMurphy to escape and spread that gospel. And it has a story in which good triumphs over evil and the forces of darkness, at least temporarily, are subdued and put to rout. Ever since William Golding dared to remind us that, like it or not, there really is evil in the world and in our hearts, cult readers have been attracted to books that contain the same bold assertion.

Earlier in the century, in spite of the obvious example of Hitler and the horrors of Nazi Germany, the notion persisted that man's nature was basically good and that it was only corrupted by institutions, a romantic idea that not even two world wars managed to squelch. Part of the problem was that while those wars gave us ready-made villains in the enemy camp, they tended to give us whitewashed heroes on the winning side. Pearl Harbor, Auschwitz, Babi-Yar, "resettlement," "final solution," "genocide"—all signified monstrous crimes, the enormity of which put anyone who opposed them on the side of the angels.

Consequently, those who first attempted to expose the heart of darkness in all men were either ignored as cranks or shunned as traitors. A book like Sinclair Lewis's *It Can't Happen Here* (1935) gained some favor on the left at a time of grave national doubt, but most readers had a hard time seeing a serious threat at home, especially a few years later when they were faced with the atrocities of the Germans and the Japanese. A potential demagogue like Huey Long could be exposed in books like Robert Penn Warren's *All the King's Men* and Adria Locke Langley's *A Lion is in the Streets*, but these were cautionary tales written after the man's assassination, and the lesson they taught seemed isolated and remote. Meanwhile, the belief grew—and was reinforced by world events—that some people were inherently evil, and that meant that others were inherently good. Like cowboys and Indians, cops and robbers, Christians and Fuzzy-wuzzies, the lines were sharply drawn and the distinctions clear.

Then along came Ken Kesey with his *Cuckoo's Nest*, and nothing was ever quite the same thereafter, for nothing quite like it had ever been written before. It was a literary phenomenon that caught the imagination of readers who suspected not only that evil really did exist but that we were all symbolically imprisoned in a mental institution run by wicked keepers determined to keep us docile and obedient. This book verbalized a suspicion that the truly crazy in the world were the ones who craved power while the truly sane were those who rebelled against authority and sought to exert their individuality. From there the novel went on to demonstrate methods of survival, elaborate strategies for trying to beat these self-appointed rulers at their own game. It also strongly suggested that only the totally insane could seize and retain absolute power and wield it with unreflecting authority.

One Flew over the Cuckoo's Nest was Kesey's first published novel. It was acclaimed by both professional reviewers and scholarly critics, who called it brilliant, powerful, convincingly alive, glowing, authentic, a mythic confrontation, and a comic doomsday vision. Primarily a novelist of the 1960s, Kesey had close affiliations with the counterculture that dominated the decade. Tom Wolfe helped Kesey achieve the status of a cult figure when he detailed the antics of Kesey and his Merry Pranksters in *The Electric Kool-Aid Acid Test*.

The things that made *Cuckoo's Nest* a cult book are so embarrassingly obvious that they tend to contradict the book's saving graces. Almost in spite of its bold antiestablishment, antiphilistine posture and its boldfaced Christian symbolism, the book is a harrowing parable of creative individuality versus repressive conformity. In fact, in its own way, this book is the definitive twentieth-century Romantic manifesto, the ultimate post-Dostoevsky, post-Kafka lamentation for the death of the individual before such rebellion went out of fashion and individualism along with it. Maybe it is for this reason that the book has continued to attract readers, but later audiences seem to read it the way they read *Moby Dick*, as a literary curiosity rather than a call to arms. To them, this is the way hippies used to rap about squares before hippies became yuppies and square became hip.

As a cult book whose luster has not been diminished by time, *Cuckoo's Nest* deserves serious analysis to unravel the complex strands that contribute to its continued cult status. Some of those strands are purely literary in nature and include the book's articulate and energetic style, its well-drawn characters and their clear-cut conflicts, its graphically depicted action and fully realized sense of place, and its brilliant use of such conventions of the novel as foreshadowing, plot, suspense, and closure.

On a deeper level is the way many of these strands connect with the readers, especially cult readers. The character of McMurphy, for example, is particularly appealing as a charming, bright, raunchy kind of guy—the perfect match for Big Nurse's humorless, joyless, authoritarian rule. And the setting, a mental ward, appeals to cult readers who like to see the mental ward as a metaphor for the repressive world they inhabit, a world run by a vast bureaucracy of Big Nurses ever ready to crush the spirits of those they label crazy but who, as all cult readers know, are really the sanest of the lot.

Of course, the one to watch (and emulate) is Chief Bromden, who pretends to be deaf and dumb because this is the only way to survive the wrath of the organizational mentality that wants everything clean and orderly and by-the-numbers. By his pretense, the chief is beyond their reach, and thus he is left alone to enjoy his own private world. However, even he has to undergo shock treatments when he gets involved in a ward fracas, but the fact that he survives the treatment relatively unharmed is a testament to what is obviously an iron will.

On another level, however, there are those things about the book that appeal to sensibilities that are less than noble: an over-eagerness to identify Big Nurse with anyone who crosses one's path or stands in one's way, coupled with an over-eagerness to identify McMurphy with any free spirit who is brash and pushy enough to speak up, lash out, talk back—anyone who defies authority simply because it is authority and not necessarily because it is oppressive or wrong. McMurphy comes perilously close to being the clown who will do anything for a laugh and who enjoys defiance for its own sake, a guy who makes a profession out of being a nonconformist and who, ironically enough, inspires others to conform to his nonconformist image. Thus, McMurphy becomes the ideal cult hero, the loner whom vast numbers imitate.

The arrogance of this sort of easy identification is the price of admission to any cult. It is the mark of Cain that graces Demian's forehead telling the world that he is different; i.e., superior. Thus, the cult reader of *Cuckoo's Nest* becomes McMurphy, surrounded by a few pitiful nerds whom he patronizes shamelessly, pretending to fight for them against Big Nurse even against their own wishes. Of course, trying to get them to recognize their chains is the first trick the revolutionary pulls, but his motive is victory over his opponent, not the welfare of his sidekicks.

A man like McMurphy secretly admires an opponent like Big Nurse, and he will use anybody in his struggle to overpower her. That he betrays himself in the process as a male chauvinist pig hardly matters, to cult followers of either sex. Men see Big Nurse as a combination of Wicked Stepmother, Bitch Goddess, and Grendel's Dam. McMurphy prefers good time girls who do not mind helping boys like Billy Bibbit achieve manhood. Nurse Ratched is woman as castrator, and McMurphy flinches automatically in her presence. Female cult followers also identify with McMurphy, and they see Nurse Ratched as a traitor to her sex, the mother who stands in your way, the boyfriend's mother who thinks you're not good enough for her son, the bitchy boss who make it through the door and then slams it in your face.

There is a strain of pseudo-intellectualism that runs through cult fiction and its followers, a desire to acquire instant intellectual superiority by adopting superior attitudes. About the easiest way to do this is to renounce the bourgeoisie, to desert the middle-class and then rebuke it with scorn or indifference. The point is to declare oneself outside the establishment. The trick is to stay on the establishment's payroll. A book like *Cuckoo's Nest* allows you to accomplish this neat trick by telling you that you are a prisoner of the middle-class, an innocent victim who, although condemned to live under society's roof, can still rebel by breaking the house rules.

McMurphy stands for booze, babes, and baseball, so there is a gutsy, macho, good-old-boy appeal to him that satisfies the closet slob. But when you put a shock-treatment halo around his head or crucify him with a lobotomy, you have a regular guy elevated to sainthood. This image satisfies a certain craving among some cult readers not to be identified with bookworms, people who read Henry James and Margaret Atwood and Umberto Eco. McMurphy relies on instinct; he doesn't believe in going by the book the way Big Nurse does. Relying on instinct requires faith in the natural, faith in knowing in your heart what is right. Books, therefore, are confirmations of this romantic notion. Books do not instruct or intrude. Books, as Emerson said, "are for the scholar's idle time."

Cuckoo's Nest is a cult book that contains generous samples of all the components of cult fiction. To begin with, the underlying Christian mythology is shot through with images from popular culture, from Frankenstein and Dracula to Doc Holliday and Rooster Cogburn, along with echoes of Queequeeg, the Morlocks, Conan, Tarzan, Tonto, and Fu Manchu in the background. McMurphy as Redeemer confronts Nurse Ratched as the Wicked Witch of the West in a setting in which reality is reinvented as an insane asylum, reflecting what has become a modern cliché that says that the keepers are crazier than the inmates but that the whole world is a looney bin, a funny farm, a cuckoo's nest. Relevance to the relatively untroubled, relatively conformist early sixties is clear as

McMurphy battles what would have been described at the time as a society of minds as buttoned down as its collars and as narrow as its lapels.

The battle between McMurphy and Nurse Ratched is a power struggle between two enormous egos, a battle literally to the death over turf. The opponents define the world according to widely differing concepts, but both concepts are entirely self-centered; thus, no matter which side you are on, you are committed to the schematics of an overwhelming ego. Cult readers, of course, identify with McMurphy's definition of the world in which he calls the shots, and they enjoy his temporary victory over Big Nurse, even though it is more of a victory for his vanity than for his followers.

When McMurphy upsets the routine, cult followers may cheer, but his fellow inmates turn against him, and although we are supposed to ascribe this cowardice to fear of Big Nurse, it can also be seen as a disinclination to stir things up, to ruffle the waters. While those on the outside looking in stand safely on the sidelines egging the patients on, the patients themselves know how much they have to lose by rebelling. The fact that revolution is usually a Pyrrhic victory is an irony that history itself manages to gloss over.

Most of what McMurphy "accomplishes" for his fellow patients results in disorder and unrest. Even their bacchanal ends on a sour note with their frolic seemingly forced and their endurance obviously exaggerated. Like the kid who incites the class to riot, McMurphy enjoys exercising power no matter what retaliation his cohorts suffer. This is not to say that his resistance does not have its heroic dimensions. Although too many are willing to pay the price of docility in exchange for order and stability, it is not something that comes naturally to human beings. The voluntary inmates in the ward bear this out; they have committed themselves only after an unsuccessful attempt at bringing their lives under control on the outside. But this very idea of control seems to bother Kesey most, as if he would rather celebrate man's tendency to anarchy than risk the possibility of control turning into conformity.

There can be no redemption without revolution. Before a new order can be established, say most redeemers, the old order must go, and its passing is always attended by chaos and upheaval. McMurphy preaches rebellion from within, peaceful rebellion in the spirit of Christ, and like Christ he must die before he has a chance to see his inspiration take hold. In the way in which he handles McMurphy's death, Kesey makes a final powerful appeal to cult readers. McMurphy's enemies have already symbolically killed him by performing a lobotomy on him and thus turning him into a vegetable. But it is left up to his most faithful servant, Chief Bromden, to spare McMurphy the humiliation of leading a zombie-like existence by smothering him and thus removing him forever from the hands of his enemies.

Performing such a service for a friend touched a sympathetic nerve in many cult readers of the sixties, readers who had spent countless hours talking friends down from a drug trip or talking them out of killing themselves. The idea of the "noble savage" as bodyguard had an irresistible appeal to streetwise young readers who fancied themselves caught in a subsidized trap and who longed for somebody as basic and self-possessed and freakish as this Indian chief to look after them, a Native American, symbol of the original victims of civilized repression. How fitting, then, that it should be Chief Bromden who finally escapes the asylum, feeling, as he hurries away, as if he is literally flying, thus making it true at last that, indeed, at least one flew over the cuckoo's nest.

FOR FURTHER READING

Adams, Michael Vannoy. "Sex as Metaphor, Fantasy as Reality: An Imaginal Re-Encounter with Ken Kesey and the Counter-Culture." *Indian Journal of American Studies* (Summer 1985): 83–95.

Hays, Peter L. "Kesey's *One Flew over the Cuckoo's Nest* and Dante's *La vita nuova*." *Explicator* (Summer 1988): 49–50.

Larson, Janet. "Stories Scared and Profane: Narrative in *One Flew over the Cuckoo's Nest*." *Religion and Literature* (Summer 1984): 25–42.

Madden, Fred. "Sanity and Responsibility: Big Chief as Narrator and Executioner." *Modern Fiction Studies* (Summer 1986): 203–17.

Slater, Thomas J. "*One Flew over the Cuckoo's Nest*: A Tale of Two Decades." In *Film and Literature: A Comparative Approach to Adaptation*, ed. by Wendell Aycock and Michael Schoenecke. Lubbock: Texas Tech UP, 1988: 45–58.

Whelan, Brent. "Further: Reflections on Counter-Culture and the Postmodern." *Cultural Critique* (Winter 1988–89): 63–86.

On the Road

Jack Kerouac
(1957)

His detractors have called him little more than a footnote to Thomas Wolfe, but Jack Kerouac captured a crucial element of postwar sensibility in his cult classic *On the Road*. Although not published until 1957, *On the Road* was written in 1951, at a time when it was assumed that such epics as *From Here to Eternity*, *The Young Lions*, and *The Naked and the Dead* had already made the definitive statement about the World War II generation. But Kerouac was to have the last word, for he sensed something fugitive and implacable in the generation that had known only depression and war, something ready to burst, something ready to lay claim to a purloined adolescence. So he put depression and war behind him and took to the open road and looked to the uncharted future, glimmering and vast and full of promise.

Thus, by the time *On the Road* appeared, it found a ready audience in a society increasingly worried about conformism and a faceless social order with a vision of freedom and restless movement, individualism, and the renewed possibility of transcending the self through jazz, drugs, and sex. In keeping with the anarchic spirit beneath this restlessness, Kerouac offered a prose style that was energetically sloppy. In fact, his exaltation of energy came to be, for many, his most endearing quality.

The characters in *On the Road*, especially those inseparable "buddies" Sal Paradise and Dean Moriarty, never seem to suffer from fatigue or indigestion or ennui. They are in too much of a hurry to sleep, too impatient to let illness stop them, too mobile to be bored for long. There is a whole country out there to get in touch with, and they try to touch base with it at every possible point. In their borrowed and battered cars they zoom across deserts and around mountains, their imaginations competing with their headlights for a glimpse into the dark wonders ahead.

And as they move, Dean Moriarty is constantly alert for signs of his father, that elusive figure whose path he follows but whose footprints he never finds; for he does not really want to discover his father in that figure huddled by the railroad track, eating beans out of a tin can, or in that panhandler shuffling past the penny arcade, or in that ghostly eminence just beyond the neon glare of Times Square. The apparition he seeks is the mirror of his own soul, an affirmation of his worth that will save him from being what Sal Paradise sees as a "holy goof." But to Sal this "holy goof" is somehow sainted. Sal worships Dean uncritically and would follow him to the ends of the earth. Dean is a knight and Sal his willing page, Don Quixote and Sancho Panza.

On the Road is played out against the backdrop of the overlapping myths that have accrued to the concept of America: America as land of unlimited opportunity, America as the land of the free and the home of the brave, America as refuge, as haven, as Promised Land. The West lures Sal and his friends, and the West disappoints them, but each time they return east, they turn around and head west again. The Pacific Ocean is the frontier, the outer limit, but when they reach it, all they can do is shift into reverse and backtrack. Just the retracing of the pioneer path is enough—or almost enough. Ultimately, the safe spot comes to be Denver, the hub of America, the only sizable city at the heart of the country and about as far as you can get from an ocean or a border. From Denver you can head in any direction and drive for hundreds of miles and still be in the United States. When at last Dean and his friends head south into Mexico, we detect the first hint of disenchantment with the American Dream.

At the end of the book the dream is still intact but the dreamer has awakened. Sal Paradise sits alone and thinks and wonders, but there is no bitterness in his melancholy, only vague regret and the stirrings of an uneasiness that is the beginning of fear.

Like Thomas Wolfe, Jack Kerouac wanted to record everything he saw and did and felt. To the extent that he succeeded, we have a vivid catalog of his firsthand impressions, told with such relentless detail that they form a tapestry of American life that seems to register its heartbeat. But it only seems to, for like all tapestries, it is highly stylized. This one, in fact, gets closer to the soul of a subculture than to the heart of America.

The photographic accuracy beneath Kerouac's observations is filtered through a vision clouded with emotional intensity. Every description is coated with the patina of Kerouac's emotional reaction. Thus, the image we are given is not of what America was really like in the fifties but of what it felt like to be "beat" and live at the edge. It is this image, of course, that helped make the book a cult book. As affluence spread through the stifling subdivisions of suburbia, Kerouac held out the hope that there was still room at the bottom.

In *On the Road* and elsewhere, Kerouac does not even attempt to deal with any segment of society above the lower class. There is almost a Dickensian flavor to his idealization of the underprivileged. Nor is he the first to lump revolutionaries, Bohemians, and poor people together in the same class. If any other class exists at all, it exists by implication, as some amorphous mass blindly carrying on the functions necessary to supply aid and comfort to the beats. He neither attacks nor rejects them. He simply ignores them and writes as if they do not exist. This attitude is based not on the unspoken acceptance of superior social levels but on "status inversion," the unspoken assumption that all those who think they are better than you are really inferior to you. There was a lot of talk in the fifties about intellectual class structure. While the beats liked to think of themselves as outcasts barely hanging on to the bottom rung of the social ladder, as intellectuals they were at the top of the heap.

Kerouac's *On the Road* was to the restless youth of the fifties what Johann Wolfgang von Goethe's *The Sorrows of Young Werther* had been to the restless youth of the late eighteenth century. Early in the book, Sal Paradise reminisces about the night Dean Moriarty met Carlo Marx. "They rushed down the street together, digging everything in the early way they had, which later became so much sadder and perceptive and blank. But then they danced down the streets like dingledodies, and I shambled after as I've been doing all my life after people who interest me, because the only people for me are the mad ones, the ones who are mad to live, mad to talk, mad to be saved, desirous of everything at the same time, the ones who never yawn or say a commonplace thing, but burn, burn, burn like fabulous yellow roman candles exploding like spiders across the stars and in the middle you see the blue centerlight pop and everybody goes 'Awww!' What did they call such young people in Goethe's Germany?"(9)

They called them, of course, "Werthers." And a century later in England they called them "aesthetes," those decadent young misfits who were also mad to live, mad to talk, mad to be saved, desirous of everything at the same time, who took as their creed this line from Walter Pater: "To burn always with this hard, gemlike flame, to maintain this ecstasy, is success in life."

In comparison with earlier cult novels of the fifties, there is a more aggressive tone in this book, a tone that foreshadows the revolutionary spirit of the sixties. Although Sal Paradise, Dean Moriarty, and the other beats in this Kerouac chronicle do not aim to overthrow society, they do find release in action from the despair that paralyzed readers of both

Salinger and Golding. For the first time, the cult readers have an identity. They are "beats" (or, as they later came to be called, "beatniks"), a subculture that was to gain momentum throughout the sixties.

Kerouac's instincts were right. They told him there was an audience out there just ripe for his type of message. His characters might be loners, but unlike Holden Caulfield, they were no longer alone. If the surface of the times reflected the slickness of a lethargic, affluent society, the feelings of undefined discontent had at last found release through companionship and action. *On the Road* is one of the few cult books to reflect and inspire a basically literary cult. The beats, like their English counterparts, the angry young men, were writers or would-be writers, and their leaders were Alan Ginsberg in poetry and Jack Kerouac in fiction. They gathered in coffee houses and read their works or talked about writing. They were quieter than their successors, the "hips," but in a way they were less welcome, probably because they were something new on the American social scene, possibly because they did write and, therefore, advertised themselves and made their dangerous ideas public.

The alienation of a literary cult is different from that of other cults in that it partakes of the flavor and tradition of the artist in solitude. Whereas most cult books appeal to the emotionally alienated, a book like *On the Road* appeals to the artist and the intellectual, outsiders who have always felt apart from society and who have usually preferred solitude to the company of ordinary people. Occasionally, the climate is such that these outsiders are able to enjoy each other's company. When this occurs and is productive, we have a literary movement. When it occurs and productivity fizzles, as it did, unfortunately, with the beats who were "mad to talk" but not mad enough to write, we have a cult.

A preoccupation with self is, of course, not uncommon among cult heroes or their admirers. In *On the Road*, Kerouac redefined egocentricity in a way that anticipated the self-indulgence of the sixties, the "me-ism" of the seventies, and the greed of the eighties. Dean Moriarty and his cohorts care for nothing but themselves and their own pleasure. They do as they please and let the chips fall where they may in a manner reminiscent of the "vast carelessness" of F. Scott Fitzgerald's thoughtless hedonists. But Sal and Dean are not latter-day Jay Gatsbys; rather, they are Nick Carraways, blessed with a special vision because they are special people. Sal even refers to Dean as an angel at one point and considers himself and the other members of the circle at a level only "a little below."

The act of surrender to the Kerouac cult was, for many with literary ambitions, a surrender of talent because they imitated Kerouac in the same way the previous generation had imitated Hemingway. Thus, there were those who went "on the road" via Kerouac's book and wrote stories about experiences they either never had or never had "that way." The main problem was that Kerouac had no formula to follow. Even he could not repeat himself, could not recapture the magnetic core around which the rogue elements of his sprawling style clustered. Kerouac himself called his writing "spontaneous prose," defined as a rapid outpouring of words and ideas onto paper with little or no editing, the idea being that the mind's unconscious selection and structuring would create a truer, purer, and richer discourse. Though the idea and material for *On the Road* had been bouncing around in Kerouac's head for several years, he wrote the bulk of the novel in the space of three weeks—apparently on a single roll of perforated paper. Truman Capote might have been unkind, but he was not necessarily unjust when he said about *On the Road*, "[This] is not writing—it's typing."

Whatever form the surrender to the Kerouac cult took, to become beat was to put on a mask, to assume an identity no longer exclusively one's own. It guaranteed entry to the coffee house where one was entitled to sit in dark corners and listen to "cool" jazz and pontificate about art. To be beat was to be, as Kerouac put it, "the root, the soul of Beatific."

Although nobody was ever quite able to define "beat," nobody really cared. It meant whatever you wanted it to mean, whatever you felt it meant: downtroden, depressed, crushed; excluded, exempted, exalted; downbeat, upbeat, offbeat. Never was it used in the sense of a game or a punishment, because the beats did not really think of themselves as losers or victims. Unlike their successors, they did not play games with society or set about punishing it, but they did join Ginsberg in his "howl" at society's shallowness. They maintained the distinction between artist and activist, but their snobbery was to become the stick the militants used to beat society with.

The restless mobility of Americans in the fifties is pitched at fever level in *On the Road*. The legendary westward migrations, which had slowed to a trickle during the dark years of depression and war, revived and gained momentum. By the thousands they poured into California and Arizona and Colorado, and cities like Los Angeles, Phoenix, and Denver burgeoned beyond belief. Most of these migrants had some purpose, however vague, in leaving one place and moving to another. The characters in *On the Road*, however, had no real motive at all for their travels except the raw, essential urge that was really at the heart of the whole shifting population. True, they invented excuses to head for one place instead of another, but it was the going there that mattered. If they never found what they thought they were after, it was partly because they were not really after anything except the experience of the search. They were like people who walk down the street and forget where they are going in the sheer joy of walking.

The excitement of movement for its own sake touched a nerve in many young readers and translated into action—and into a plan of action—their own evanescent longings and fantasies. In this book Kerouac makes movement function as both symbol and purger of the hungry mind. It is a book of bodies in motion, bodies whose motion is thought, impulse, craving made physical. It gave willing readers something to do and made the doing of it as important as the thinking about it. What it really gave them was a drama with parts for everybody and a script outline that left room for endless improvisation.

The behavioral model, of course, is Dean Moriarty—clown, guru, mimic, fornicator, crazy driver, boozer, friend of freaks and enemy of order, wild man. His charisma holds everything together even though he never seems to be able to put anything together himself. Imitators appeared everywhere, complete with their own hangers-on, idolators, and detractors. The fate of most of these imitators, however, was to perpetuate the motion of the beats without the meaning. Like Elvis look-alikes, they were never more than impersonators.

A cult book has the power to make an alternative lifestyle seem like the only alternative, and therein lies its smugness. Many great novels have offered compelling alternatives, but these alternatives are always tempered with irony or charm or true humor. They are vacations from which we return refreshed, enlightened, and relieved. In cult books the alternatives are presented in a tone of high seriousness. Against the drab, plastic backdrop of the fifties, Kerouac's *On the Road* offered an escape that had all the overtones of a pilgrimage. Either you joined the pilgrimage or you remained in Squaresville. The beats erected a fence and invited you to take sides. This fence became the dividing (and the wailing) wall of the sixties when society split into hostile camps and the opposing sides closed ranks. There were no other choices, nor was there any allowance made for the innocent bystander. "With us or against us" was the battle cry of the opposing team as it has always been with cults, and it is the challenge that a cult book flings at its readers.

On the Road glamorized poverty. Its characters had no money, so they made a life without it seem superior to a life with it, and cultists, most of whom were equally indigent, found their lack of means the best means of acquiring experience and wisdom. The most interesting people were the social rejects, the bums and runaways and criminals that populate the freight trains and alleys and cold-water walk-ups of the land. They are the only people worth knowing because they have been around, have been pushed around, have felt life, have really lived. Much of this attitude is based on total ignorance of higher levels of society and on a rejection of the middle-class from which the beats were retreating. It was a slap in the face of bourgeois affluence that offended these defectors even as it subsidized their defection. Their attitude could obviously not tolerate alternatives, and the lifestyles they affected had to symbolize this intolerance.

The paradox of *On the Road* lies in the fact that its characters are committed to one idea while they seem to be in pursuit of other ideas. They are committed to the idea of the search for "it," yet "it" is the search itself. This is either verification or mockery of Alexis de Tocqueville's analysis of the restless spirit of Americans who try to do everything at once. What he saw was people with the freedom and opportunity to try as many things as they could squeeze into—or out of—life. Let loose in the supermarket of possibilities, they could try as many brands of as many things as they could manage. Lurking in the backs of their minds, of course, is the hope that around the corner they are going to run into "it." They do not know what "it" is, but they are sure they will recognize it when they see it. Perhaps that is, after all, what de Tocqueville really saw, for certainly he was aware of the frenzy and disappointment that accompany the restlessness.

If this is so, then *On the Road* becomes an allegory of democratic ambivalence. While the trip lasts, it seems to be a joyful answer to the question of what do you settle for, for you do not have to settle for anything as long as the trip lasts. The trip did not last, of course, but even when it ended, the beats still would not settle for anything. Kerouac and the others on whom he based the characters in this *roman á clef* never recovered from the giddiness of their frenzied but ultimately futile race around the country, and one by one they died in confusion and despair.

Cult literature since *The Sorrows of Young Werther* has been concerned with the tension in human nature between limitations that cannot be transcended and the inherent impulse to transcend them. Why, they continually ask, are we troubled with dreams we cannot fulfill, desires we cannot satisfy? How real are these limitations? Why must we be a slave to them? Are not these dreams and desires the pointers toward finding meaning in life and the proof that meaning exists? Even though cult heroes may resent their limitations, cult followers often find meaning within those very limitations.

On the Road reversed this trend by arguing against the retreat into acceptance of limitations. If there have been ecstatic moments before, there will be more of them to come, it predicts. Life will be embraced and forced to yield its secrets. Cultists will expand the drug dabbling in the book to experimentation with hallucinogens of every variety in their determination to prove the unreality of limitations. They will take to the road again and again, assaulting life, demanding of it more than it seems willing to give. There can be no backsliding, they declare, even as the ground is slipping away beneath their feet. More was gained than lost, they will swear, but the task of containing this gain and finding victory in it will have to wait for others.

On the Road was the work that gave America its picture of the beat generation in the same way Fitzgerald left indelible images of the jazz age. It was Kerouac's only popularly successful work, although devoted readers cherish all his works and continue to exchange newsletters about them. At last count there were no fewer than five Kerouac newsletters in existence around the world. Apparently, whatever his literary faults, he continues to speak to—and even for—a sizable body of readers and thus to sustain a cult following that rivals that of J. D. Salinger.

FOR FURTHER READING

Boyle, James. "It! It!—*On the Road* as Religion." *Recovering Literature: A Journal of Contextualist Criticism* (Summer 1987): 19–36.

Coolidge, Clark. "A First Reading of *On the Road* and Later." *Talisman: A Journal of Contemporary Poetry and Poetics* (Fall 1989): 100–2.

Moody Street Irregulars: A Jack Kerouac Newsletter. Clarence Center, N.Y.

Poteet, Maurice. "On the (Written) Road." In *Un Homme grand: Jack Kerouac at the Crossroads of Many Cultures*," ed. by Pierre Anctil et al. Ottawa: Carleton UP, 1990, 85–92.

Ruppersburg, Hugh. "*On the Road* and the American Literary Tradition." *Post-script* 4 (1987): 31–37.

Wheeler, Elizabeth Patricia. "The Frontier Sensibility in Novels of Jack Kerouac, Richard Brautigan and Tom Robbins." *DAI* 46 (1985): 985A.

The Outsider

Colin Wilson
(1956)

Colin Wilson's *The Outsider* is one of the most influential cult books of the last half of the twentieth century. It is not itself fiction, but it deals with fiction in a way that gives readers direct access to the heart of a number of books that have themselves become cult classics. In other words, it is entirely possible to read what Wilson has to say *about* the works of Ernest Hemingway or Albert Camus or Hermann Hesse and feel that one has experienced something of the power of the originals.

In some respects, *The Outsider* is uncannily close to being a treatise on cult fiction itself. If it is not, it is because Wilson's interests stretch far beyond literature and his motive is to establish a cult of his own. He does not put it this way in the book, of course, but in the postscript to a later edition of *The Outsider*, Wilson writes: "I have taken more than ten years to create my 'new existentialism,' and it seems to me that I am working upon the most interesting problem in the world, the *only* interesting problem" (302).

Colin Wilson and Ayn Rand are probably the only two writers who deliberately set out to attract a cult following and succeeded. Ordinarily, such literary occurrences are random and inexplicable. The thing about Wilson's book is that, in spite of his intentions, it has paralleled the history of other phenomena in the canon of cult literature. For one thing, it is clear just from reading the book that Wilson *discovered* his intentions as he wrote. Thus the book has the spontaneity of a cult book. For another thing, it has remained the book by which Colin Wilson is known, in spite of the five books on "new existentialism" that followed, not to mention several novels and books of essays.

The Outsider swept the campuses of the mid-fifties and seized the imagination of a generation weaned on Hemingway and F. Scott Fitzgerald and Thomas Wolfe, gripped by Camus, inspired by J. D. Salinger, stirred by William Golding, ready for Jack Kerouac, and ripe for a work that would address their own specialness, their own ineffable feelings of alienation in a world of plastic and hairspray and picture windows. They saw the Outsider as an individual engaged in intense self-exploration, living at the edge, challenging cultural values—a person who "stands for Truth." Born into a world without perspective where others simply drift through life, the Outsider creates his own set of rules and lives by them in an unsympathetic environment.

By the mid-sixties, alienation had become a buzzword for the young and disaffected, the outcasts of the establishment, the misfits who were out of sync with a society that they felt was suffocating them. It was in 1967, the year that S. E. Hinton's *The Outsiders* became such a success and went on to become a classic of teenage rebel literature. But in the mid-fifties, when Colin Wilson appeared on the scene, terms like alienation, estrangement, outsider were labels few dared apply openly to themselves. To be different meant to wear a greasy ducktail and studded leather jacket and ride a motorcycle. It was okay for Marlon Brando or James Dean, but it lacked intellectual integrity. It was merely being a "rebel without a cause." Wilson supplied the cause and thus gave the term "outsider" and its associate abstraction, alienation, the respectability they needed to make them attractive to campus intellectuals.

Before this, except for a sort of sentimental attachment to Holden Caulfield, about all the disaffected campus intellectual of the fifties could do was to take comfort in Ralph Waldo Emerson's comment that"foolish consistency is the hobgoblin of little minds" and his assertion that "to be great is to be misunderstood." Reversing the premise, all those who felt misunderstood (and most did) became immediately great (whatever *that* meant). For all their fuzziness, these sentiments paved the way for Wilson's articulate examination and, in spite of himself, celebration of the Outsider. And the fact that Wilson was just twenty-four when the book came out helped matters considerably. He was a new voice, a young voice, an *angry* voice—one of the "angry young men" like John Osborne and Kingsley Amis and Alan Sillitoe who spoke passionately for a new generation longing for the liberation of the spirit from the threat of encroaching conformity.

It is important to understand that there is quite a difference between what Wilson really says in *The Outsider* and how cult readers interpret what he says. Throughout the book Wilson scrupulously examines the Outsider objectively and without sentiment. He does not really argue a case *for* him, at least not in the sense of setting him up as a role model. If anything, he seems to argue *against* him, insisting at every turn that the Outsider is not a figure anyone would willingly want to become. However, even as he protests, it is all too tempting for the cult reader to feel that such objections only increase the attraction of the Outsider, in the way that Marc Antony whetted the appetite of the Romans at Julius Caesar's funeral by telling them that they surely did not want to hear the terms of Caesar's will and learn how much he loved them.

As objective as he tries to be, Wilson betrays his enthusiasm for his subject—and thus his affinity for the Outsider—in every line. And once his early readers learned of Wilson's own poor upbringing and of his taste for asceticism, they were even more sympathetic, for here was an Outsider himself, independent, self-taught, poor, struggling, committed. There is a great appeal to cult readers generally in accounts of travail along the rocky road to salvation. The fear of not being able to measure up is an irresistible lure.

The Outsider's main desire is for control. "Freedom of response," says Wilson, "is the only authentic freedom" (xii). If this means descending, like Harry Haller in *Steppenwolf*, ever deeper into the "human life," so be it. Everything must be tried if the Outsider is to achieve his chief desire, which is to be unified. In a culture that has crippled itself by divorcing reason from feeling, the Outsider seeks to regain the unity that was present before the split occurred, before this schism in the Western soul separated action and thought from instinct and intuition.

The Outsider remains a valuable contribution to the understanding of the psychology of modern Western culture, especially in its identification of a type of character who goes beyond the terms "hero" or "antihero" to become a recognizable phenomenon in the literature of the twentieth century. However, to see it as a cult book, we have to focus on those perceptions, distorted as they may be, that turn the book into what followers want it to be.

The basic connection, of course, is between those readers who feel alienated and the status Wilson seems to be giving them, beginning with the simple act of capitalizing the word Outsider. The connection here with myth is fairly apparent. The Outsider becomes comparable to the Warrior, the Prophet, the Avenger, the Redeemer—a unique presence, a special being. "To the objection that he is unhealthy and neurotic," says Wilson, "he replies: 'In the country of the blind, the one-eyed man is king' " (20).

Supporting his special status, Wilson says, for example, that the Outsider is the only one in a sick civilization who knows he is sick, the only man not susceptible to the general enthusiasm, an island unto himself; that the vitality of the ordinary members of the society is dependent on him, that he has immense powers of surrender and suffering, that only he knows the loneliness of the garden of Gethsemane. We have no communication with other human beings, he says, not even with those we love the most. To this he adds that man is a useless passion, too stupid to know that he is never free, that the distinction between being and nothingness is the only important distinction, and that ideas are valueless; only life has value.

The Outsider's problem, says Wilson, is the problem of denial of self-expression. He cannot accept life as it is, cannot consider his own existence or anyone else's as necessary. Yet he wants to be integrated as a human being, to achieve a fusion between mind and heart, and in pursuit of this union he seeks vivid sense perception in an attempt to understand the soul and its workings. In a society that trivializes everything, he longs to get beyond the trivial, to express himself so that he can better understand himself. And the only way he sees out is by means of intense extremes of experience.

The search for "vivid perception," for "understanding the soul and its workings," the desire to "get beyond the trivial," and especially the desire for "intense, extremes of experience" characterize the cult reader who had found, at last, a book that gave utterance to his innermost yearnings. The way was cleared for opening the doors of perception by whatever means necessary and for stretching experience to its limits regardless of what conventions must be ignored, what taboos violated.

Such searchers came to be called the "inner-directed," and they described themselves as more interested in self-fulfillment and self-expression than in mere economic rewards. However, the atmosphere of conformity they rebelled against in the fifties and sixties and that made them feel different from their peers now came under attack from the mainstream. Once the Outsider's sensibility becomes the norm, the Outsider will no longer want to be an Outsider, or so Wilson maintains. Thus, some would argue that Wilson's Outsiders of the fifties and sixties have become the thirtysomething yuppies of the eighties and nineties.

When *The Outsider* first appeared, however, its attraction was pure and noble. Wilson tells of spending Christmas of 1954 "alone in my room, feeling totally cut off from the rest of society," and that "an inner compulsion had forced me into this position of isolation." Out of this intense isolation came the idea for a work that exudes the atmosphere of its origins, filled as it is with anguished Outsiders for whom there is no way out, or round, or through, loners in the grips of a sense of unreality, accepting this unreality, tormented figures caught in the "tragedy of unrealized freedom," as he describes Jake Barnes's wound in Ernest Hemingway's *The Sun Also Rises* (33).

"The Outsider's sense of unreality cuts off his freedom at the root," says Wilson. "It is as impossible to exercise freedom in an unreal world as it is to jump while you're falling" (39). This is an apt metaphor for the feeling the Outsider has when he catches a glimpse of the real world but is powerless to retain that glimpse. It is amazing how well Wilson himself manages to capture the mood of alienation in the fifties with his own vivid glimpses, for the world did indeed seem to stall somewhere in the early years of that decade, especially in "austerity-ridden" Britain, where the grip of the past was reluctant to give way to the pull of the future.

Although Wilson is quite sincere in his belief that the true Outsider wants to cease being an Outsider, there is an inescapable feeling throughout the book that, in spite of this, he is glorifying the Outsider, celebrating the splendid isolation of all those whose histories he recounts. In this respect he is conceding, albeit reluctantly, to that part of an Outsider that wants to remain an Outsider, that glories in being an Outsider just for the sake of being different.

Certainly impressionable readers relished being in the company of Hemingway and Camus, Vincent van Gogh and Vaslav Nijinsky, and Lawrence of Arabia. Usually, those less likely to qualify as genuine Outsiders are the first to include themselves in the ranks, for if they can do nothing else in life, they can pretend not to be part of it. Knowing this is probably what motivated Wilson to show outsiderism as a temporary but inescapable posture, something unavoidable in a world of mindless conformity but destined to diminish as the individual gains control of his destiny and respect for the expression of his freedom.

For some time now there has been a Colin Wilson Society, but Wilson himself seems to have mixed feelings about his status as a cult figure. He has come to sound like a prophet without sufficient honor in his own land, suggesting that he may be taking himself too seriously. While he has a great deal to say that is sane and perceptive, there is reason to suspect that he is in the thrall of his own designs—or even, as it were, his own delusions. He concludes the latest edition of *The Outsider* on a self-congratulatory note to the effect that his many years of work on his "new existentialism," while virtually unrecognized in England (which he calls an intellectually backward country) and Europe (which he says has little to offer "besides the dead philosophy of Sartre and Heidegger"), may yet flourish in the United States, a country not yet immune to the virus of new ideas.

He ends by saying that "we are on the brink of some discovery that will make our century a turning point in human history" (302), rather an ambitious claim, some might say, for a spin-off philosophy that has not really gained a lot of ground. One is left wondering if Wilson himself is not the deluded victim of his own seductive philosophy—the ultimate Outsider with a persecution complex.

Wilson's reputation went into decline immediately following the phenomenal success of *The Outsider*. He thinks that the unkind (and often unfair) critical attacks had a lot to do with resentment—and envy—of his youth. Be that as it may, such a roller coaster reputation also bespeaks the vagaries of democratic ambivalence, the syndrome in free societies that offers consumers a succession of faddish philosophies to which they can afford to devote only so much time.

While Colin Wilson has not suffered the oblivion of many contemporary prophets, *The Outsider* was, in its early days, a fad that, like much of its competition, did go out of fashion only to resurface as a scholarly tome rather than a philosophical treatise. Without it, Hermann Hesse might never have been translated or become the cult figure he did, Camus might not have been quite so popular, and Dostoevsky might not have enjoyed such a successful revival. Whatever else he did, Colin Wilson changed the shape and direction of fiction studies.

FOR FURTHER READING

La Bossiere, Camille R. "Marcel Ayme and Colin Wilson on the Bourgeois, the Outlaw, and Poetry." *Dalhouse Review* (Spring 1981): 104–12.

Wilson, Colin. *Autobiographical Reflections*. New York: Pauper's Press, 188.

———. *Beyond the Occult*. New York: Bantam, 1989.

———. *Beyond the Outsider*. New York: Houghton Mifflin, 1965.

———. *The Bicameral Critic*. New York: Ashgrove, 1985.

———. *An Essay on the 'New' Existentialism*. New York: Pauper's Press, 1986.

———. *Existentially Speaking: Essays on Philosophy and Literature*. New York: Borgo Press, 1989.

The Outsiders

S. E. Hinton
(1967)

By the late sixties, rebellion had become institutionalized as an expected and accepted way of behavior among normal, healthy, restless youth. Holden Caulfield planted the first seeds in *The Catcher in the Rye*, and during the next twenty years—after the beats, the mods, the rockers, not to mention the romanticizing of youthful rebellion in *West Side Story* and *Rebel Without a Cause*—young people were ready for S. E. Hinton's *The Outsiders*, the first novel of teenage angst actually written by a teenager.

S. E. Hinton was sixteen when she wrote *The Outsiders*, and for all its literary flaws—and there are many—the book has an unmistakable authenticity that transcends those flaws and makes the book a genuine expression of the confusion and fear, and even more so, the idealism, that mix so explosively in the troubled soul of an adolescent on the threshold of life. There are also, as one might well expect, generous portions of embarrassing romanticism, exaggerated altruism, and maudlin self-pity. But whereas older writers cannot escape leavening nostalgia with irony, S. E. Hinton is saved by pure ingenuousness.

In *The Outsiders*, nostalgia is missing, except for Ponyboy's occasional memory of his parents who died in a car crash eight months earlier. And as for irony, although a cynic could find it between the lines, its effect is dissipated by the upbeat tone of the book. Instead of whining about the unfairness of life and welcoming its bitter burdens, Hinton's characters are unbelievably mature in their understanding of worldly injustice and unbelievably positive in their ability to take others for what they are and still maintain their faith in human nature. To paraphrase

William Faulkner, they seem determined to prove that mankind will not only survive but prevail.

The Outsiders is told through the eyes of Ponyboy Curtis, a fourteen-year-old orphan who lives with his two older brothers, Sodapop and Darry, somewhere in the Southwest. The Curtis brothers are Greasers, a gang of underprivileged kids who grease their long hair and try to act "tuff." They are the sworn enemies of the "Socs" (short for Sociables), a rival gang made up of affluent kids who wear Madras shirts and drive fancy cars. Ponyboy, a late-sixties version of Holden Caulfield (smart, slight, independent, sentimental) pals around with Johnny (sometimes known as Johnnycake), a pint-sized, dark, and brooding Greaser who still carries scars from a beating he suffered at the hands of the Socs. When a gang of Socs attacks the two boys, and their leader, Bob, tries to drown Ponyboy in a playground fountain, Johnny stabs Bob to save Ponyboy's life.

When Bob's wound proves fatal, Ponyboy and Johnny fulfill the teenage paranoid fantasy of being pursued, of running away, of having to survive as fugitives even though they are in the right. They hop a freight train, then hide out in an abandoned church somewhere in the middle of nowhere, living on baloney and cigarettes and reading to each other from a paperback copy of *Gone With the Wind*. Johnny decides to turn himself in, but before he has a chance to, the church catches fire, and he is fatally injured while rescuing some small children who have wandered inside and become trapped.

Johnny's death conveniently resolves the problem of the murder of the Soc and is followed within hours by the death of Dally, an unregenerate Greaser whose violent end fulfills the American fantasy of the gangster as hero. Dally is made into a tragic antihero. He "fought for Johnny," and when Johnny dies, Dally, too, must die. And what he dies for is the absence of fairness in the world, for as all teenagers know, life is anything but fair. Again, though, where adults may guffaw at the sentimental silliness of Dally's way of death, Hinton makes it all quite credible—even moving.

Ponyboy is the one who understands best the meaning of these experiences, and this understanding prompts him to use his experiences as the basis for an English theme he has been asked to write. Ponyboy speculates near the end that there are "hundreds of boys who maybe watched sunsets and looked at stars and ached for something better. I could see boys going down under street lights because they were mean and tough and hated the world, and it was too late to tell them that there was still good in it, and they wouldn't believe you if you did" (155). However, when he realizes that his English assignment is his chance to warn them, he seizes the opportunity to become the "catcher in the rye" to *his* generation. "And I decided I could tell people," he says, "beginning with my English teacher" (155).

The story that Ponyboy tells is a boy's story, and boys continue to identify with its narrator and his buddies. But the story also holds a powerful fascination for girls who can wax ecstatic about the way this book is their voice. That the book can exert this kind of hold over readers of both sexes seems to have little or nothing to do with the author's sex. At the time of its publication, Hinton concealed both her sex and her age from the public, apparently to reach a larger, unbiased audience, since boys are not likely to read a book about gangs written by a girl who could be their sister.

However, knowledge of Hinton's sex soon became irrelevant, and has certainly not inhibited sales of later books or stopped Hollywood from filming them. What young people cared about was that one of their own was writing *for* them, not just *about* them. Here was a person who was actually going through what they were, not just remembering it, as J. D. Salinger and John Knowles had done in *Catcher in the Rye* and *A Separate Peace*.

Although the book does not appeal to both boys and girls for precisely the same reasons, their responses have more in common than one might expect. What they share are those things that are present in most cult books: a strong sense of myth, a heightened sense of reality, relevance, a hero-figure, a fierce self-centeredness (tempered, of course, with sentimentality), a strong sense of alienation, a high degree of suffering, a distinctive lifestyle, and a simplistic sense of reality.

The very title of the book, *The Outsiders*, is an indication of its underlying myth as well as its sense of estrangement. All the Greasers are outsiders, alienated from the rest of the world by virtue of their hardships and deprivations and because the rest of the world (read "The Sociables") looks down on them. It is a convention of teenage literature that these two extremes are always present, are always pitted against each other, and that the stories always take the side of the poorer, "hoodier" elements, portraying them as projecting a toughness that conceals a basic goodness.

What is curious is that readers, who come from all walks of teenage life, always identify with the "Greaser" element, leaving one with the impression that the "Sociables" do not really exist since no one claims to belong to them. If the reception of *The Outsiders* is any indication, just about all teenagers see themselves as Greasers. Obviously, there is a deep-seated wish to feel put upon, to identify with the underdog, to feel that one has to battle one's way out of an extremely disadvantageous position.

This desire to suffer finds its release in the suffering of several of the sympathetic characters in *The Outsiders*. Poor little Johnnycake is everybody's pet, and when we read of the way he had been beaten and bruised and nearly killed by the swaggering Socs with their fancy rings, we are given a picture of a defenseless little Daniel at the mercy of the sleek and pampered lions. Later, when he valiantly defends Ponyboy against drowning by stabbing a hot-tempered Soc, we sympathize with his plight. And since we cannot possibly imagine Johnnycake behind bars, we know he has to die. And to have him die from wounds and burns received while rescuing little children from the flames of a burning church, of all things, is to give readers a tear-jerker death scene worthy of Charles Dickens or Harriet Beecher Stowe. But Hinton is not content to leave it there.

At the end of the story, when everything is just about wrapped up, Ponyboy discovers a note that Johnny wrote on his deathbed. The note makes reference to a Robert Frost poem that Ponyboy had once recited, spontaneously, at a particularly sentimental point in the story. The poem calls the early spring green of nature (youth) "nature's gold" and makes the point that just as the green will fade, so then does the "gold" not last. "When you're a kid everything's new, dawn," says Johnny. "It's just when you get used to everything that it's day. Like the way you dig sunsets, Pony. That's gold. Keep it that way, it's a good way to be" (154).

Along with the note is Johnny's copy of *Gone With the Wind*. He had read it only up to the point where the gallant Southern gentlemen are going off to war. Back at the church, while they were in hiding, Ponyboy and Johnny had watched the sunrise dispel the autumn mist and talked of "gallantry," a concept almost as quaint in the modern world as "chivalry" or "honor."

The reality of the streets and of street gangs is not the reality that most teenagers live in, but street life has become a powerful metaphor for the way many of them view their lives. Ponyboy and his brothers have a decent home life, all things considered, but they find on the streets and among the Greasers the toughness that helps them survive in a world bereft of parents who, as all teenagers fear, can be here today and gone tomorrow, through either death, desertion, or divorce. Mixed in with this fear is also a deep-seated conflict between fear of being orphaned and a guilty desire to experience its pangs.

Perhaps it is a vestigial apprehension, but teenagers seem to feel that they are living on the brink of disaster, that the world is fraught with dangers to their well-being, that tragedy looms at every turn. This is one reason they love to torture themselves with horror films and why they devour Stephen King novels. Something inside tells them to be prepared for the worst. This is why the more secure the home, the more they don't trust it. It's all well and good while it lasts. But how long will that be? How long before a parent dies or disappears? How long before you get thrown out? How long before you have to take to the streets to avoid the abuse at home?

When Cherry Valance, the Soc who serves as a sort of liaison between the warring gangs, sighs and says that Socs have it rough, too, that "things are tough all over," there is not a trace of irony in her mouthing of this cliché. And those who echo this sentiment are merely comforting themselves with the reminder that everybody is hurting. Teenagers seem to need melodrama, and if they don't have enough of it in their daily routines, they will invent it, or turn to *The Outsiders* and read about it. Shakespeare understood this perfectly when he told the story of *Romeo and Juliet*.

Although there are stronger characters in the book, Ponyboy serves as the book's conscience as well as its heroic center. He is the one who translates experience into understanding, who goes out into the world, learns from it, and returns with a message for others to profit by. He is also the sentient center of the book, functioning much as Holden Caulfield does to draw in the lonely reader, for Ponyboy describes himself right off the bat as a loner who "digs" movies and books in a special way: "For a while there, I thought I was the only person in the world that did" (5). He likes walking and poetry and gazing at sunsets. In fact, when he discovers that Cherry Valance watches sunsets, too, he thinks, "Maybe the two different worlds we lived in weren't so different. We saw the same sunset" (38).

Ponyboy is a character with whom both sexes can easily identify. For boys he is the kid brother they either are or have, and his puppy-dog devotion and kiddishness mix comfortably with his aggressiveness, for he does not back off from a fight or take insults lying down. He also is young enough to get away with being respectful of girls without feeling obliged to come on to them. He is everybody's friend or brother.

For girls he performs a subtler function, for he allows them to indulge in subconscious erotic fantasies. Ponyboy's loving description of his brother, Soda, could be a junior high school girl's dream: "Soda is handsomer than anyone else I know. Not like Darry—Soda's movie-star kind of handsome, the kind that people stop on the street to watch go by. . . . He has a finely drawn, sensitive face that somehow manages to be reckless and thoughtful at the same time. He's got dark-gold hair that he combs back—long and silky and straight—and in the summer the sun bleaches it to a shining wheat-gold. His eyes are dark brown—lively, dancing, recklessly laughing eyes that can be gentle and sympathetic one moment and blazing with anger the next" (10). His good looks are mentioned repeatedly throughout the novel, and Ponyboy can only sleep well when he is literally sieeping in Soda's arms. (Later there is a similar scene between him and Johnny in the abandoned church.)

Such scenes also speak to the longing of pre-pubescent boys for the comfort of older "pals," but the physical appeal of Ponyboy—and of many others—is perhaps Hinton's way of revealing her own fascination with such people. The girls in this novel (and there is really only Cherry Valance) are bland and unremarkable, but the boys are all lovingly described and just a little larger than life.

The blue jeans and T-shirts, the leather jackets and the greasy hair are all part of the uniform that teenagers have always worn in one variation or another, and in this case, except for the hair, the uniform has not changed much since the time in which the novel takes place. Later on the jeans might sport designer labels and the hair might be "designed" by a stylist, but the urge to adhere to a dress code (while adamantly denying it) is a part of teenage life, a part that *The Outsiders* speaks to, especially when Ponyboy is forced to cut and bleach his hair and worries that he might get his picture in the paper looking this way. Such vanity is indicative of the self-centeredness that is inevitably at the heart of this novel. For all its avowed concern for others, its sympathies are only superficially for others—even close friends and relatives—and ultimately for oneself.

But this, too, is an essential phase of the maturing process, and in early adolescence, when egotism is at its most overwhelming, it is important to feel kinship with a character who shares your feelings; for it is in fostering this subconscious recognition of a "shared loneliness" that *The Outsiders* makes its contribution, in the same way *The Catcher in the Rye* and *On the Road* and other cult books have made theirs.

The Outsiders may present an even more simplistic way of looking at life than many cult books do, but that is not surprising in a book written not to exorcise a haunting adolescent memory but to speak directly from the heart. What sets this book apart from something like *The Sorrows of Young Werther* and its successors is the novel's refusal to surrender to defeat or to perpetuate the sentimentality of suffering. Ponyboy emerges from his pain with a message of encouragement. Ultimately, what has happened is that he has broken free of the shackles of ego and moved on to a position of selflessness. This, too, is an easily overly sentimentalized position, but its extremes must also be tested before Ponyboy reaches the maturity we are sure he will one day attain.

In the meantime, cult readers continue to consider Ponyboy their Werther (*The Sorrows of Young Werther*), their Axel (*Axel*), their Nick Carraway (*The Great Gatsby*), their Holden Caulfield (*The Catcher in the Rye*), their Sal Paradise (*On the Road*). And rather than fulfilling their parents' prophecy that they, too, will take to the streets in gangs and commit antisocial acts, it is more likely that they will continue to find in the good-hearted, nondrinking, good student Ponyboy Curtis a role model who can be a nice guy without necessarily being a wimp. So what if he smokes too much. A girl like Cherry Valance could put a stop to that in a hurry!

FOR FURTHER READING

Daly, Jay. *Presenting S. E. Hinton*. Boston: Twayne, 1987.

Stanek, Lou Willett. *A Teacher's Guide to the Novels of S. E. Hinton*. New York: Dell, 1975.

A Portrait of the Artist as a Young Man

James Joyce
(1916)

A Portrait of the Artist as a Young Man is a largely autobiographical novel that portrays the childhood, school days, adolescence, and early manhood of Stephen Dedalus, later one of the leading characters in James Joyce's *Ulysses*. The narrative is a series of significant incidents from various stages of Stephen's life with the emphasis on the spiritual, emotional, and artistic growth of Stephen away from family, Church, and politics and toward a state of exalted creative isolation in which his dedication to art transcends all other loyalties.

Stephen finds everything in his environment antagonistic, from his childhood amid poverty and sordidness through his schooldays of ridicule and discipline. After struggling to free himself from the hysteria of religion and the compromises of love, Stephen reaches the point at which he throws off all human ties and faces life alienated from society and committed solely to his art.

Novels about artists have become a genre in their own right with the flowering of Romanticism and its emphasis on genius and inspiration, solitude and suffering. The *Künstlerroman,* as it is known critically, is extremely popular among aspiring artists and others with natures bordering on the neurotic, since such novels invariably nurse the wounds of children who have suffered at the hands of insensitive fathers, wicked stepmothers, or playground bullies. Aldous Huxley once satirized such novels by suggesting that the opening line of any one of them could be: "Little Percy was not good at games." Huxley had a right to tease since he suffered himself as a schoolboy. It is easy to see, though, how quickly such novels could become unintentional parodies: They are all too frequently predictable, turgid, self-pitying.

A Portrait of the Artist as a Young Man is also a *Bildungsroman*, a novel of initiation, of growing up, of being introduced to life. As such it has been ranked with such distinguished works as Thomas Mann's *Buddenbrooks*, Samuel Butler's *The Way of All Flesh*, and W. Somerset Maugham's *Of Human Bondage*. However, while these novels never achieved cult status, Joyce's slim volume attracted the kind of following that made cult books of such popular novels of initiation as J. D. Salinger's *The Catcher in the Rye* and John Knowles's *A Separate Peace*.

One could argue that the cult appeal of *Portrait* might have something to do with its imaginative use of symbols, its psychological depth, and its heightened artistic sensibility, yet the presence of these elements alone would not tell the whole story behind this novel's uncanny ability to do what cult novels have to do to become cult novels: speak not only *to* but *for* the reader. And no novel seems to speak *for* the artist as tellingly as this one. Aspiring artists have been known to have strong reactions to this book, ranging from the predictable to the bizarre. Some renew their flagging dedication to art by deciding *not* to sell out and write that trashy bestseller; others swear that the ending of the book brought them to their feet, that they finished the book standing up, and that they can disgorge whole passages from memory after just one reading. Most can recite the book's stirring last lines with an absolutely straight face: "Welcome, O life!" they declaim, echoing Stephen's final diary entry. "I go to encounter for the millionth time the reality of experience and to forge in the smithy of my soul the uncreated conscience of my race" (252–53).

This is the sort of hyperbolic pledge that is just vague enough—and ultimately just altruistic enough—to stir the emotions of any artist who thinks of art not as a job but as a calling. The phrase "for the millionth time" identifies one with the faceless multitudes (the anonymous stonemasons who built the Pyramids, Stonehenge, the Gothic cathedrals), artisans who sacrifice anonymously for the greater glory of God. Cult followers of *Portrait* are the sort who prefer either splendid isolation or the sort of identification with the nameless masses that does not entail actual rubbing elbows with them. Like the unknown soldier, the anonymous artist has a tomb all to himself. A phrase like "the reality of experience" is cryptic enough to mean anything from actually getting your hands dirty to appreciating abstractly what experience signifies.

But it is the final phrase that stirs the heart of the dedicated reader. "To forge in the smithy of my soul" is a poetic image so graphic yet so unreal that it mixes echoes of the myth of Vulcan with romantic images of the village blacksmith. And if in that smithy of my soul I am forging the "uncreated conscience of my race," then I am assigning to my soul the highest, the noblest, the most exalted purpose it could have: to take upon itself the awesome responsibility of carrying the burden within it of the conscience of all my fellow men. What higher calling could there be for an artist? How much closer to sainthood can an artist get? At one stroke art has been rescued from debasement and restored to the supreme level to which the Romantics had striven to elevate it.

It is such a movingly idealistic summons to the highest aspirations of the artistic temperament that it is well nigh irresistible to all who claim to have a shred of conscience left in their souls. In recreating the myth of the hero whose reach exceeds his grasp, the myth of Dædalus, who dared to fly too high, regardless of the risks, and died for his defiance, Joyce provided a powerful lure to the disenchanted young of the early twentieth century and after. He told them that life might be a painful, bitter, solitary struggle but that the struggle was worth it if what came out of it was art. Nothing else mattered. What he succeeded in doing was infusing his exhortation to dedicate oneself to art, to accept on faith the creed of "art for art's sake," with the sort of Messianic fervor that wins converts.

More so than many cult heroes, Stephen Dedalus confronts head-on the religious, political, and domestic demons that he must slay before he acquires the vision that becomes the book's message. The fact that he does not physically leave his immediate area only makes his experiences more meaningful to cult readers. It tells them that the idea of actually traveling in search of experience is merely a symbolic way of accounting for any struggle in which the hero may become involved. As long as he is aware of who his enemies are and what they are up to, he can emerge victorious and enlightened. One does not have to go beyond the playing fields to experience this sort of challenge.

What makes Stephen's experiences peculiarly meaningful in terms of cult followers is that at the conclusion, when he symbolically "returns" full of wisdom, his message is not one of reconciliation but of rejection. He tells his followers that they must leave home, church, family, and country and become wholly responsible unto themselves. They must withdraw physically and mentally from all previous allegiances for the sake of art. The appeal is so much like the call to the cloth that it is not difficult to see how easily some cult readers could be influenced. Even the hack writer has harbored the dream of becoming a "true" artist. The idealistic young artist probably does not even know that it *is* a dream. He knows only that Joyce did become successful as a true artist, which goes to show that total dedication does pay off.

It is the dream, of course, that justifies all the suffering, for without suffering there would be no dream worth fulfilling. Therefore, Stephen's earlier suffering is looked upon almost wistfully by cult readers who either see their own miseries reflected or, more likely, secretly envy Stephen the luxury of being treated harshly and unjustly. The myth about suffering and the soul is one that all cult books unabashedly exploit, and this one goes farther than most in ennobling suffering and presenting it as something indispensable to artistic achievement. In fact, in comparison, happiness in the ordinary sense seems almost sinful, and whenever Stephen experiences it, as he does when he sticks up for what he believes or wins prizes or runs his little loan service, it is always tinged with melancholy, as if the sun has only peeped out temporarily between the ominous and ever-threatening rain clouds.

When he is put upon and singled out, as is the case when he breaks his glasses, Stephen's suffering is bad enough, but when he does something to bring remorse upon himself, his suffering knows no depths. No sooner has he succumbed to the temptations of the flesh and visited the Dublin prostitute than he is plagued with guilt; and the punishments of the damned, which are described so vividly at chapel, only twist the rack of torment another notch or two. When a kindly old priest gives him absolution and relieves his mind, he sets about mortifying his flesh by seeking out disagreeable experiences in order to see if he can rise above them. He even tries to control his dreams, but since dreams are beyond human control, he backslides and then suffers doubly for it.

One by one the institutions that were to serve as his supports let Stephen down, and he feels compelled to abandon them. Studying church dogma only raises doubts in his mind; the more he knows of Irish politics, the more put off he is by their narrow nationalism; and since his family itself is split over these same issues, he becomes increasingly independent and estranged. He finds it odd that he no longer feels at home in his own homeland and can only attribute the feeling to his growing commitment to living the life of an artist.

A situation like this begs the question. Is it the artistic temperament that alienates the man, or is he bound to be alienated because of his artistic temperament? Cult followers take comfort in either proposition in the way some might read Ralph Waldo Emerson's statement "to be great is to be misunderstood" as proving that those who are misunderstood are, *ipso facto*, great. Although many artists feel alienated, not all who are alienated are artists. This distinction is easily lost on the naive, who need a better reason than a bad complexion to explain why they feel so psychologically dislocated. Thus, *Portrait* also fuels the fires of the ego and makes it easier for cult readers with alienation anxieties to move from feeling inferior to most people to feeling vastly superior to just about everybody—and especially those who do not appreciate Joyce.

The artist is a lonely being to begin with, necessarily so, since art is a solitary endeavor. Therefore, it is not surprising that *Portrait* is more self-conscious than many other cult books. Werther can feel alone in his suffering, but he is constantly seeking the company of others as both witnesses and contributors to his misery. Holden Caulfield is unlike anybody around him, yet he manages to surround himself with people, if only to see himself in their reflection. Stephen Dedalus seems truly at home, if not at ease, in his own skin. If he is Joyce, then we know that he is an authentic artist, a writer who spends most of his time by himself, in his own company, spinning tales from the stuff of his own psyche the way a spider spins a web.

The difference between the authentic artist and the ardent cult reader is that the true artist is spared, at least in his art, from being solipsistic. True, he may have an enormous ego in real life, but in his art, he is, as Joyce is in *Portrait*, detached enough to be ruthlessly objective. In fact, it is Joyce's supreme objectivity, his ability to see Stephen's faults as clearly as his virtues, that raises the novel above the level of the ordinary autobiographical ego trip. A cult reader who is not a sympathetic artist, however, may absorb all the hype without absorbing any of the humility. All too often cult readers become cult readers in order to boost their self-esteem. Therefore, when they encounter ego-reinforcement, they do not want it watered down with reservations.

A Portrait of the Artist as a Young Man seems to have lost some of its original power to move, especially since the sixties. Much of this has to do with the changing ways in which we now look at church and family and at national politics. In Ireland the situation may not have changed much over the years, but elsewhere in the Western world, the impact of church and family has lessened drastically, and disenchantment with national politics has become the conventional attitude. And certainly Stephen's episode with the prostitute would hardly warrant a second thought among contemporary artists unless the warning were changed from fire and brimstone to the threat of AIDS.

However, it is the attitude toward the artist himself that has changed the most in the course of the twentieth century. From being a respected arbiter of taste and dispenser of wisdom, the artist has sunk to the level of a scandal-scarred celebrity, capable of entertaining us now and then, but whose views on serious matters are taken lightly. Could it be that the fire has gone out in the smithy of our soul, leaving the conscience of our race still uncreated?

FOR FURTHER READING

Calvin, Thomas. "Stephen in Process/Stephen on Trial: The Anxiety of Production in Joyce's *Portrait*." *Novel: A Forum on Fiction* (Spring 1990): 282–302.

Finney, Brian. "Suture in Literary Analysis." *Lit: Literature Interpretation Theory* (November 1990): 131–44.

Harper, Margaret Mills. *The Aristocracy of Art in Joyce and Wolfe*. Baton Rouge: Louisiana State University Press, 1990.

Kittay, Jeffrey. "On Notation." *Language and Communication: An Interdisciplinary Journal* 10 (1990): 149–65.

O'Shea, Michael J. "Raiders and Cinemen Too: Joyce on Video." *James Joyce Literary Supplement* (Spring 1990): 21–23.

René

François-René de Chateaubriand (1802)

"With me began the so-called Romantic school, a revolution in literature," François-René de Chateaubriand boasted in his *Memoirs from Beyond the Grave*. Although there would be enough critics around to question this statement, there were also enough devoted readers to support it, or at least its Romantic and revolutionary spirit. This did not mean that these readers agreed with Chateaubriand's avowed intention, which was to prove in modern terms the validity of Christianity. Instead, the readers of *René* discovered in the character of René the incarnation of their own spiritual malaise and tended to ignore Chateaubriand's theology entirely. As with most books that achieve cult status, the author may aim at one target but as far as his readers are concerned, he hits quite another.

René came to be for the youth of France in the early nineteenth century what Johann Wolfgang von Goethe's *The Sorrows of Young Werther* (1774) had been for the youth of Germany (and the whole world) a generation earlier. In each case social and philosophical upheavals had produced a temperament to which these books were uniquely suited, for they expressed sentiments that their readers harbored but had trouble articulating. The books are similar in many ways. For one thing, they both challenge the tyranny of reason and demonstrate a preference for emotional over spiritual experience. "I read *René*, and I shuddered," said Charles Sainte-Beuve. George Sand said, "It seemed that René was myself." And Maurice de Guérin confided to his *Journal*, "This reading [of *René*] soaked my soul like rain from a storm" (Mack 1183).

René also shares with *Werther* a number of Romantic themes: the hero who starts out as a sensitive child, unhappy because he is misunderstood by others and thus a candidate for an attack of profound melancholy; a melancholy that is reflected in nature as it responds to the sufferer's moods with appropriate weather and scenery; an unattainable—and thus tragic—love that distinguishes him from his carefree but dull contemporaries.

Although both Werther and René have tragic love experiences, they are tragic for different reasons. Whereas Werther is in love with another man's wife, René finds himself in love with his sister, Amelia. He declares that Amelia is the only person in the world he has ever loved, that she is like a mother but "something more tender." Almost as in a Greek tragedy, the enormity of his feelings gradually overwhelms him, and he finds himself hoping that some calamity would strike him so that at least he might have some tangible reason for suffering. Then Amelia falls ill and decides to enter a convent. She urges René to consider the church, for she is convinced that he, too, would find solace in a religious retreat far from a world that she insists has nothing to offer that is worthy of him. She makes him promise to go on living, however, even as she reminds him how easy it would be for a man of his character to die. "Believe me," she tells him, "it is far more difficult to live." Her final piece of advice to him is "to resemble ordinary men a little more and be a little less miserable" (1349). But of course that is impossible, and he suffers all the more for knowing it.

Amelia takes the vows, and René attends the ceremony as a surrogate father. During the ceremony, he becomes so overwrought that at one point he is tempted to disrupt what he looks upon more as a sacrifice than a sacrament. "Hell even goaded me on with the thought of stabbing myself in the church and mingling my last sighs with the vows tearing my sister away from me," he says, "[but] instead of blasphemy and threats, I could find in my heart only profound adoration and sighs of humility" (1352).

Amelia has to pass symbolically "through the tomb" in order to die for the world and then pronounce her vows. From under the shroud she says, in tones audible only to René: "Merciful God, let me never again rise from this deathbed, and may Thy blessings be lavished on my brother, who has never shared my forbidden passion!" With "these words escaping from the bier the horrible truth suddenly grew clear" (1353). René loses control, falls across the death sheet, and clasps his sister in his arms, then faints and is carried away unconscious.

The incestuous feelings of brother and sister clash with Amelia's Christian decision to enter a convent, and René is made to feel the full horror of his illicit passion. But even in his horror he finds a peculiar pleasure, "a kind of unexpected satisfaction" in the fullness of his anguish, and he becomes aware, with a barely concealed joy, that unlike pleasure, sorrow does not consume itself but is endlessly renewable. He concludes that God had sent Amelia to him not only to save him but to punish him.

These exquisite feelings exalt him as a hero of sensibility above his coarse fellow men. He has purified his soul in the fires of remorse and renunciation. He is ready now to embark on an odyssey of spiritual regeneration.

To assuage his grief and purge his soul, René travels to the United States, then a new country filled with all the things so dear to the heart of a Romantic: unspoiled nature, noble savages, and innocence. It is not uncommon for the monomythical hero to travel in search of a better world. In traveling from Europe to the New World, and particularly to the bayous of Louisiana, René moves from civilization and the company of insensitive fellow beings to an unknown, exotic, mysterious land where there is always the promise—though rarely the fulfillment—that the jaded soul will discover peace.

In some ways René recalls his countryman Candide, who journeyed to the New World and even found a utopia in El Dorado, but with similarly lamentable results. He also recalls the frantic journeys of the beats in Jack Kerouac's *On the Road*, but ultimately the Romantic journey becomes a voyage of the imagination, the form it is most likely to take in cult fiction. This was especially true for Des Esseintes, the decadent centerpiece of Joris-Karl Huysmans' *Against Nature*, who is probably the first character in cult fiction (and possibly in literature) to argue the superiority of mental traveling.

René is so clearly an ideal cult hero that he could stand as a model as easily as Werther. He is intensely emotional, and he monitors his own emotions with unabashed fascination as he alternates between fits of frenzy and bouts of pathological boredom. Conscious of his superiority to the world, contemptuous of religion, he sees no recourse but suicide. Today we would label him manic-depressive and hustle him into therapy, but in his own time, René represented the superior young man's dream-picture of himself. It became fashionable to confront the world with loathing and despair, to wander along lonely cliffs on dark and stormy nights, to be a misanthropic recluse one moment and a volcano of passion the next. This attitude, or affliction, became known as *le mal de René*, and later as *le mal du siècle* (the sickness of the century).

In an earlier age young men like René would have found peace in a monastery. In fact, René is tempted to retire to one forever, but after the damage inflicted on the whole idea of religious life by the skepticism and sophistry of the eighteenth century, monastic life was no longer an option. Young men were preached to about responsibility to society, and when they found the idea of duty and dedication withering to their spirits, they had nowhere to turn except to madness or the muzzle of a gun. Chateaubriand argued that he was teaching the young not to withdraw from their duties toward society, but by showing them the evil results of eighteenth-century skepticism, he undermined that sense of responsibility, leaving them only René's fate as an alternative.

As he drifts toward suicide, René writes: "Alas! I was alone, alone in the world. A mysterious apathy gradually took hold of my body. My aversion for life, which I had felt as a child, was returning with renewed intensity. Soon my heart supplied no more nourishment for my thought, and I was aware of my existence only in a deep sense of weariness." He talks of struggling against this malady, but admits that it is only a halfhearted struggle "with no firm will to conquer it." Finally, unable to find any cure for ache in his heart, which he cannot locate and yet which seems to be everywhere at once, he makes up his mind to take his own life. Once he has reached this decision, he resolves to apply his full consciousness to committing this desperate act. However, he sees no reason for haste. "I did not set a definite time for my death," he says, "so that I might savor the final moments of my existence in long, full draughts and gather all my strength, like the men of antiquity, to feel my soul escaping" (1346–47).

In pioneer America, René manages somehow to miss out entirely on the momentum that was driving a new nation in all directions. The way Chateaubriand describes René once he has exiled himself to America is like anything but a young man accepting his duty toward society. René's melancholy nature was more inclined to draw him away from society and into the woods where he would spend entire days in solitude, "a savage among the savages" (1336).

When René receives a letter from the convent telling him of Amelia's death, the sad news prompts him to tell his story to the elders of the Natchez tribe. But the story he tells is not of what he has done but how he has felt. It is not the adventures of his life he recounts (not that he really has had any), but the innermost feelings of his soul. He describes himself to the Indians as a young man full of passion, sitting at the mouth of a volcano and weeping over mortal men whose dwellings he could barely distinguish far off below him. He knows that his story will elicit only pity from his listeners even though he insists that he is presenting them with a true picture of himself, one that reveals his real character. Nevertheless, he perceives an unbreachable gap between them, a gap made all the more sad because it has been foretold in the visions of his childhood.

Like other cult heroes, he first accuses himself, then feels sorry for himself, and ends up exalting himself. His friend Chactas reacts like a cult follower: "My young friend," he says, "a heart such as yours cannot be placid . . . you suffer more than others from the experiences of life; a great soul necessarily holds more sorrow than a little one" (1342). But the elders hear something else. What they hear is the story of a young man, with neither strength nor moral courage, who finds the source of his torments within himself and can hardly lament any misfortunes save those he has brought on himself.

When René has finished with his emotional autobiography, Father Souël sizes him up with unexpected perception and frankness. He begins by telling René that there is nothing in his story that merits the pity he is currently being shown. He tells him he is a young man "infatuated with illusions, satisfied with nothing, withdrawn from the burdens of society, and wrapped up in idle dreams." He then takes René to task for his arrogant cynicism. "A man is not superior, sir, because he sees the world in a dismal light," he scolds. "Only those of limited vision can hate men and life" (1357). He tells him that if he looks a little farther, he will soon be convinced that there is absolutely nothing to the griefs that René complains about.

When René argues that saints have often retired to the wilderness for spiritual renourishing, Father Souël points out to him that "they were there weeping and subduing their passions, while you seem to be wasting your time inflaming your own." He challenges some cherished Romantic assumptions when he calls René presumptuous for thinking that man is sufficient unto himself. "Know now that solitude is bad for the man who does not live with God," he warns, but René does not really want to hear this. However, the good father presses on, telling René that anyone who has been gifted with talent is obliged to devote that talent to serving his fellow men. If he does not, the priest warns, "he is first punished by an inner misery, and sooner or later Heaven visits on him a fearful retribution" (1357).

René is disturbed and humiliated by these words, but to cult readers such chastisement fell on deaf ears. Soon after telling his story, René, Chactas, and Father Souël, perish in the massacres of the French and Natchez in Louisiana.

Chateaubriand, like Goethe and other leading figures of the Romantic movement, was taken in by the hoax of the *Poems of Ossian*, epic poems allegedly written by an ancient bard and found in a cave by a Scotsman named James Macpherson in the eighteenth century. Given the enduring influence that these brilliant fakes had on the Romantics and their disciples, one is tempted to call them the *Ur-text* of cult fiction. The very mystery of their origin lends an aura of authority to the excesses of their content similar to the reception of the Book of Mormon or the Dead Sea Scrolls, documents that seem to have acquired authenticity by virtue of the obscurity of their provenance.

Atala, a "prequel" to *René*, appeared in 1801, and in some minds it should at least share equal billing with *René* as a cult classic by virtue of its sheer intensity. True, it is heralded as the novel that introduced Romanticism to France, but it lacks the depth of the Romantic agony so exquisitely rendered in *René*, and much about it was as preposterous then as it is now (e.g., tigers prowling the banks of the Mississippi). In their day, however, it was both works that elevated Chateaubriand to cult status, and today they are usually published together and frequently read as companion pieces. (*Atala* is included in the extended bibliography of cult classics at the end of this volume.)

FOR FURTHER READING

Bishop, Lloyd. *The Romantic Hero and His Heirs in French Literature*. New York: Lang, 1984.

Call, Michael. "René in the Garden." *Constructions* (1984): 43–53.

Gans, Eric. "*René* and the Romantic Model of Self-Centralization." *Studies in Romanticism* (Fall 1983): 421–35.

Hamilton, James F. "The Anxious Hero in Chateaubriand's *René*." *Romance Quarterly* (November 1987): 415–24.

Knight, Diana. "The Readability of René's Secret." *French Studies: A Quarterly Review* (Jan. 1983): 35–46.

A Separate Peace

John Knowles
(1960)

A Separate Peace may not be in a class by itself, but within the genre of novels about adolescent male friendships, it stands out from the others for reasons that are not immediately apparent. Like J. D. Salinger's *The Catcher in the Rye*, its popularity has not diminished since its original publication; it has never gone out of print, and it continues to sell at a steady pace. But more than that, it continues to exert a powerful influence on the young people who read it. The reasons for the success of this type of story are fairly predictable, but the singular success of this particular version of a familiar conflict bears closer scrutiny.

One possible reason for its special status in the United States is that it is easily the best version of this story written by an American. For this reason, young American readers can identify more closely with it than they can with the conventional English "public school" version, or with such foreign classics of the genre as Thomas Mann's *Tonio Kröger* or Hermann Hesse's *Narcissus and Goldmund*. Although the latter is familiar to many American readers, much of its popularity is owing to the cult status of its author, whose best-known books, namely *Steppenwolf*, *Demian*, and *Siddhartha*, have become such classics in themselves that his other works are relegated to a lower tier.

As with *The Catcher in the Rye*, *A Separate Peace* reveals the loneliness of an adolescent boy attempting to come to terms with the world and with himself. Although both novels deal with prep school life and take place at about the same time, the differences are more significant than the similarities. Holden Caulfield may be a child of the forties, but there is no mention in his story of war or of anything going on outside the small, stifling world Holden inhabits. In *A Separate Peace*, Gene Forrester's inner turmoil is set within the framework of the turmoil of World War II.

It is difficult enough to grow up during ordinary times when society is relatively stable, but when this maturing process takes place during a time of war, the instability of society only aggravates the insecurities that torment the adolescent mind. Gene Forrester is fighting his own private war. He is torn between remaining within the safety and seclusion of Devon School or abandoning this security for the confusion of the adult world. At the same time he is struggling to resist the influence of his best friend, Finny, and his undisciplined approach to life. Throughout the novel, Gene is tormented by the tensions within himself, by the conflict between him and Finny, and by the growing awareness of the unreal world of Devon School in contrast to a world at war.

Gene Forrester is a character whose worst enemy is himself. Although he is a capable athlete and an excellent student, Forrester is unable to prevent the dark side of his inner self from perverting and distorting his enjoyment of the world and the people around him. Like Holden Caulfield, Forrester always finds something bad in the things around him, and if he does not find it, he invents it. It is a paranoid proclivity that speaks to the reader—especially the young, impressionable reader—whose trust in those around him has been shaken or even shattered.

At one point in the novel, Gene is convinced that Finny is out to get him, that he is deliberately trying to destroy Gene's scholastic success. Since in reality Finny is totally indifferent to Gene's academic ambitions, there is no foundation for this suspicion; but Gene harbors it anyway because he would rather imagine Finny as a rival than accept that he really does not care. Like an abused child who prefers being beaten to being ignored, Gene prefers Finny's rivalry (even if imaginary) to his indifference. This is a feeling cult readers respond to completely, for if there is one fear that is common to most adolescents, it is the fear of being ignored. Recognition they crave, of course; rejection they can handle; but to be treated as if they did not exist, especially by someone they admire or love, is torment beyond endurance.

Once he has convinced himself of Finny's perfidy, Gene decides that he must somehow get even. He does this by causing Finny to fall from a tree and break a leg. The tree is no ordinary tree; it is a special tree that the schoolboys like to climb to jump into the river. Gene and Finny are the youngest ever to try this feat, and once they succeed, Finny organizes the Summer Suicide Society, whose sole purpose is to initiate new members by having them jump into the river. At each initiation, Gene and Finny jump first, but Gene never loses his fear of jumping. Near the end of summer, under pressure of exams and the growing conviction that Finny is undermining his scholastic endeavors, Gene jumps up and down on a limb, causing Finny to fall and break a leg.

As it turns out, the leg is so shattered that Finny may not walk again, let alone participate in any sport.

At first Finny refuses to think that Gene had anything to do with the accident, even after Gene confesses. Eventually, there is an inquiry into the matter, and as he sees Gene being accused, Finny leaves the assembly room in a state of extreme agitation. He is so upset that he falls down the stairs and breaks the same leg again. When Gene appears at his bedside the following day, Finny has come to realize that Gene did indeed cause him to fall from the tree, and he asks Gene why. Gene is powerless to explain, blaming it on some mysterious blind impulse. But cult readers know, and their anguish is for the feeling between the two boys that cannot be expressed. And when, a short time later, marrow gets into Finny's bloodstream and he dies suddenly, Gene grieves but does not cry, for he feels that he, too, has died and that it is not fitting to cry over one's own death.

The loss of a friend through one's own excessive feeling is a common adolescent misfortune. It is fraught with irony, for the ultimate loss is precipitated by the fear of loss. How, one asks, do I hang on to this friend whom I love more than he loves me? If he should die, then he would never leave, and I could carry with me the melancholy memory of a friendship frozen in time. To be responsible for the death of that friend is closer to suicide than to murder—at least in the mind of the tormented one. Like some sort of weird reworking of *Romeo and Juliet*, the two star-crossed friends find peace in the permanence of death. In this case, however, the one responsible for the accident lives on, unpunished except by his own guilt, a guilt he aggravates into an abiding pain that sustains him the way mortification of the flesh sustains the flagellant.

The relationship between Gene and Finny is representative of the sort of symbiotic relationship to be found in much modern literature including many cult novels. Mann deals with it definitively in *Tonio Kröger*, and it is prominent in several of the Hesse novels mentioned earlier. There are reminders of it in the contrasting personalities to be found within the gangs in S. E. Hinton's *The Outsiders*, in Anthony Burgess's *A Clockwork Orange*, and in Oakley Hall's *Warlock*. There is even a hint of it in the teacher/learner relationship in Carlos Castaneda's *The Teaching of Don Juan*, and more than a hint of it in the mutually destructive relationship between Hunter Thompson and his Samoan lawyer in *Fear and Loathing in Las Vegas*.

In these relationships, one person usually symbolizes what the other person wants to be. Emil Sinclair wants to be Demian, Tonio Kröger wants to be Hans Hansen, and Gene Forrester wants to be Finny. In mythology, the object of idealization is a god, and the only way to become that god is to overcome him, sacrifice him, devour him, symbolically cannibalize him. Christ on the cross is an enormously pathetic figure, but He is also a comforting one, for now the tables are turned, the Savior needs *our* protection, and at last we can unburden ourselves of an obligation too great to bear. This interpretation may seem extreme, but it is the only one that gets at the heart of a story in which one friend kills another out of love.

Gene loves Finny so much that he must either become him or get rid of him. And since he cannot nail him to a cross and then partake of his flesh and blood, he must do away with him. Gene's suppressed homoerotic feelings only intensify his extreme idealization of the god Phineas. Finny is the guy who can do everything, can construct a world all his own out of his imagination. It is Finny who invents new games to play, and it is even Finny's idea to jump from the tree into the river. Finny is all spontaneity.

His one flaw—his tragic flaw, as it were—is that he cannot face unpleasant realities. It is the fate of most tragic heroes that they are blind to an essential truth, the very truth that eventually leads to their downfall. At the end of *A Separate Peace*, Finny is forced to confront the truth about Gene's perfidy, and he runs away from it. Dealing with this reality seems to break Finny's will at the novel's end. Of course, then, he must die. How could Gene stand it if Finny were to remain alive, remembering? Would Finny accuse him, forgive him, or, more likely, ignore him?

Finny's death is necessary to the novel, but it is also a dead giveaway. Beyond resolving the plot and concluding the story, it betrays a homosexual fantasy in which the beloved dies a young and tragic death, leaving the lover with a memory that is more secure than reality. This, then, is the separate peace that appeals to dreamy young readers half in love with the captain of the soccer team.

The finishing touch to this unsettling study in the labyrinths of adolescent psychology occurs at Finny's burial when Gene cannot cry because he has the feeling that part of himself is being buried with his friend. What is being buried, of course, is not just his guilt over Finny's death but the guilt he feels about those dark impulses that brought on his actions in the first place. When, later, Gene enlists and goes off to war, he does so without any strong feelings, almost as if his emotions have been anesthetized. In symbolically killing the enemy inside himself, he has effectually excised his capacity to feel anything at all. It is a curiously merciless resolution to the problem, as if the penitent, through pain and tribulation, has driven not only the devils into exile but the angels as well.

It is bitterly ironic that Gene's torment will be the awful torment of indifference, the very thing he most feared from Finny. For, as John Donne says, "When God's hand is bent to strike, 'it is a fearful thing to fall into the hands of the living God'; but to fall out of the hands of the living God is a horror beyond our expression, beyond our imagination."

FOR FURTHER READING

Bryant, H. B. "Phineas's Pink Shirt in John Knowles's *A Separate Peace*." *Notes on Contemporary Literature* (November 1984): 5–6.

Bryant, Hallman B. "Symbolic Names in Knowles's *A Separate Peace*." *Names: Journal of the American Name Society* (March 1986): 83–88.

Reed, W. Michael. "*A Separate Peace*: A Novel Worth Teaching." *Virginia English Bulletin* (Winter 1986): 95–105.

Slethaug, Gorden E. "The Play of the Double in *A Separate Peace*." *Canadian Review of American Studies* (Fall 1984): 259–70.

Siddhartha

Hermann Hesse
(1922)

Hermann Hesse, who died in 1962, would certainly have felt a mixture of flattery, bewilderment, and dismay, had he known that within two or three years of his death his name would be on the lips of every counterculture intellectual. And the book they would all mention first would inevitably be *Siddhartha*. Hesse seemed to touch all the right nerves with novels that appealed to most of the major concerns of the age. *Demian* catered to an appetite for adolescent angst whetted by such cult books as *The Catcher in the Rye* and *A Separate Peace*; *Steppenwolf* explored the same dark regions William Golding had penetrated in *The Lord of the Flies*. Even Hesse's magnum opus, *The Glass Bead Game*, attracted readers interested in science fiction with a metaphysical twist.

But *Siddhartha* topped the list, primarily because of the growing interest in Oriental religions, particularly Zen Buddhism. Students en masse were converting to Zen during the sixties and early seventies for a variety of reasons, many of them suspect. Naturally there were honest zealots among the converts, serious seekers, some who traveled to the East as Hesse had done. There were even some who actually spent time in lamaseries and monasteries, experiencing Buddhism or Hinduism firsthand the way Robert Conroy had done in James Hilton's cult novel, *Lost Horizon*, or Larry Darrell in Somerset Maugham's *The Razor's Edge*.

However, other converts to Buddhism or some other Oriental religion often did so simply to be different, to upset their parents or impress their friends, often in the hope of finding an excuse to gain spiritual ecstasy through sex and drugs. Whatever their motivation, most experienced the restlessness and impatience characteristic of the Western mind—and particularly the American mind—and soon tired of the effort.

All that aside, there was and remains a solid core of enthusiasts who find in *Siddhartha* the spiritual solace and intellectual satisfaction that Hesse had sought in his own journey to the East and his quest for peace and understanding. Fortunately, in reading Hesse, these people were in good hands, for Hesse's own interest had been a lifelong one, and his research into Oriental philosophy was extremely thorough. His grandfather had been a missionary in India for thirty years and had brought back objects as well as stories. "From the time I was a child I breathed in and absorbed the spiritual side of India just as deeply as Christianity," Hesse once wrote, adding that for over half his life he had been concerned with Indian and Chinese studies and accustomed to "breathing the air of Indian and Chinese poetry and piety" (Otten 72).

It was only natural, then, that Hesse should want to visit the lands that had so long filled his imagination. Fortunately, when he got to India, he found there the land he had dreamed of. Unfortunately, he came to the bitter realization that, as an Occidental, he would never be able to penetrate entirely the mysteries of the East or partake of what he envisioned as an Oriental paradise. This would be the same sad conclusion so many of his readers would reach in spite of the sincerest efforts to cross the line that divides West from East.

However, the wisest of them take from *Siddhartha* what Hesse brought back from his trip, "a deep reverence for the spirit of the East." They feel that they can profit greatly from an encounter with Oriental mysticism even though they realize that Western man can never hope to return to that state of primitive innocence necessary for total immersion. Something like this point is also made in *Lost Horizon*, where even the best attempt by Westerners to absorb Eastern thought falls short of the mark.

Hesse once stated his credo in a letter to André Gide, and it is the message of all his works: "There is no duty, no duty whatever, for awakened humanity except the one duty to seek one's self, to become firm within oneself, to grope one's way forward no matter where the road may lead" (*Briefe* 265–66). No call was more insistent in the sixties than the call to find oneself, get in touch with oneself, trust oneself, be oneself, express oneself, even exalt oneself. Individualism no longer meant silent rebellion or secret guilt; neither did it mean the shame of being different, of not fitting in, of not conforming.

Individualism, even though it sometimes struck onlookers as an orgy of conformity, now took the direction of assertion and aggression, of turning the spotlight on one's differences and flaunting them. And for all its inescapable hypocrisy, there was a great deal of necessary clearing of the air. For what was good about it, Hesse can take a fair share of credit. No author is responsible for those who misread him, but he may take credit for inspiring his readers, just as he must take the blame if that inspiration leads them astray.

Throughout Hesse's works there runs the reminder that one can learn how to live only from life itself, not from books or teachers. Thus, Siddhartha, the eternal seeker, goes his own way, bowing to no one. He must disregard the wishes of his father, the advice of his friend Govinda, and finally even the counsel of the great Buddha. Only thus can he find his way to his true self. This, then, is the heart of the matter, the essential appeal of Hesse to his readers, especially to those who made a cult figure of him and a cult book of *Siddhartha*.

Thus, the alienated take comfort in following the example of the monomythical hero Siddhartha, and as they share his journey inward, their faith in themselves is restored and their self-esteem reinforced. Should the journey require some sacrifice, some suffering, then so be it, for the path to spiritual enlightenment lies through the mortification as well as the gratification of the flesh. Unlike Christianity, which separates body from soul and achieves the purity of the latter at the expense of the former, Oriental religions teach that body and soul are one and that to deny either is to injure both.

Wise readers also realize that at some point they must part from Siddhartha and follow their own path as he has followed his. This lesson is reinforced in the novel at the point where Siddhartha's son runs away and Siddhartha realizes that he must let him go. His love for the boy is like a wound, but he knows that this wound will heal. Eventually, of course, it does, but not until after Siddhartha has learned to be more understanding of human frailty and more sympathetic to fellow sufferers whose travails he once dismissed as weaknesses.

The story of Siddhartha is told with the simplicity of a biblical parable, and it is important to the understanding of the book as a leading cult favorite to know something of the provocative nature of its narrative. The myth of the quest is certainly among the few elemental myths common to all civilizations. In the case of Siddhartha, the quest begins when he feels that the teachings of Brahmanism do not lead to salvation and decides to try other paths. He leaves home with his friend Govinda to join the ascetic Samanas, with whom he spends three years. But gradually realizing that asceticism and yoga are only leading him further away from himself, he goes with Govinda to hear the teachings of Guatama the Buddha. Govinda remains with the great teacher, but Siddhartha perceives that all must find their own way. Departing from Buddha, Govinda, and a life of the spirit alone, Siddhartha determines to immerse himself in the world of the senses.

He crosses a river on a ferry and reaches a large city where he meets and falls in love with Kamala, a famous courtesan. With her help, Siddhartha becomes wealthy and is able to afford anything he wants, including Kamala herself. After a while, however, he realizes that this life of indulgence is just as pointless as a life of denial, that both luxury and asceticism are extremes that clutter rather than clear the path to spiritual illumination. He decides, therefore, to turn his back on the world of Sansara and illusion. Unaware that Kamala is now pregnant with his child, Siddhartha flees the city and returns to the river where, in despair, he almost commits suicide. But at the last moment, something from his old self stirs inside him, and he realizes that suicide is an evasion, not an answer.

He decides to stay by the river and try to understand himself. He looks upon the contrary experiences of asceticism and profligacy as necessary opposites that define and neutralize each other, leaving him once again in his original state of innocence but with a knowledge of good and evil. Living with the wise ferryman Vasudeva, Siddhartha learns many secrets from the river, the most important ones being that time is an illusion, that all being is one, and that for knowledge to be significant, it must be conditioned by love.

After twelve years have passed, Kamala comes to the river with her son in search of Buddha. She dies from a snake bite, and Siddhartha begins to care for the boy. He loves his son desperately, but the boy longs to get away from the two old boatmen and return to life in the city. Eventually he escapes, and as Siddhartha realizes how deeply he loves his son, he also realizes that loving him means letting him go. Soon thereafter, Vasudeva dies, and Siddhartha takes his place. Govinda appears one day and is struck by the change that has come over Siddhartha, for it is clear to him that Siddhartha, like Buddha, has at last achieved absolute peace and harmony.

When Hesse talks of peace and harmony, he means the perfect balance of opposites. Every truth is made up of equally true opposites, but this truth can only be *known*, not articulated. An idea can be expressed in words only if it is one-sided, but then it is only a half-truth. It cannot become truth until it achieves totality, completeness, unity.

In order for Buddha to teach about the world, he had to divide it into Sansara and Nirvana, illusion and truth, suffering and salvation. But the world itself is never one-sided. A deed is never wholly Sansara or wholly Nirvana, just as a man is never wholly a saint or a sinner. These absolutes persist because we are under the illusion that time is real. Time is not real. And if time is not real, then the dividing line between this world and eternity, between suffering and bliss, between good and evil, is also an illusion.

The message that Siddhartha brings to cult readers is that the world is perfect at every moment, that every sin carries the flake of grace within it. During deep meditation it is possible to dispel time, to see simultaneously all the past, present, and future, and then everything is good, everything is perfect, everything is Brahman. Thus, everything that exists is good—death as well as life, sin as well as holiness, wisdom as well as folly. Everything is necessary; it needs only the concurrence of true believers. Then all will be well with them and nothing can harm them.

"I learned through his body and soul that it was necessary for me to sin," Siddhartha tells Govinda, "that I needed lust, that I had to strive for property and experience nausea and the depths of despair in order to learn not to resist them, in order to learn to love the world, and no longer compare it with some kind of desired imaginary world, some imaginary vision of perfection, but to leave it as it is, to love it and be glad to belong to it" (146).

Siddhartha's conclusion is that love is the most important thing in the world, a sentiment that had great appeal to the flower children of the sixties. "It may be important to great thinkers to examine the world, to explain and despise it," he says. "But I think it is only important to love the world, not to despise it, not for us to hate each other, but to be able to regard the world and ourselves and all beings with love, admiration, and respect" (148–49).

Siddhartha admits that his emphasis on brotherly love and love of the world may seem in contradiction to the mystic teachings of the Buddha, but he blames this misconception on the necessity of using words to express the ineffable. "That is just why I distrust words so much," he says, "for I know that this contradiction is an illusion. I know that I am at one with Gotama. . . . His deeds and life are more important to me than his opinions. Not in speech or thought do I regard him as a great man, but in his deeds and life" (149).

The irony of *Siddhartha* lies in its ultimate failure as a substitute for the real experience, as any book must. And since its wisdom is from a totally foreign culture, Western readers are twice removed from the source and thus have twice the difficulty crossing cultural barriers. Nevertheless, the book continues to work as a sort of Buddhist Baedeker, a provocative guide (and lure) to the unraveling of the tantalizing mysteries of Oriental philosophy. Siddhartha's ultimate message, however, that wisdom is not communicable, remains both the key and the obstacle to penetrating those mysteries.

FOR FURTHER READING

Bischoff, Howard W. "Hesse's Philosophy of Timelessness and the Western *Modus Vivendi*." *Journal of Evolutionary Psychology* (February 1980): 69–74.

Grislis, Karen, and Adrian Hsia. "Siddhartha's Journey to Brahma/Tao." *Par Rapport: A Journal of the Humanities* 5–6 (1982–1983): 59–66.

Narasimhaiah, Sanday. "Hermann Hesse's *Siddhartha*: Between the Rebellion and the Regeneration." *The Literary Criterion* 16 (1981): 50–66.

Rao, R. Raj. "God-Consciousness in *The Guide* and *Siddhartha*." *The Literary Endeavour: A Quarterly Journal Devoted to English Studies* (January–June 1982): 87–91.

Verma, Kamal D. "The Nature and Perception of Reality in Hermann Hesse's *Siddhartha*." *South Asian Review* (July 1988): 1–10.

Slaughterhouse-Five or the Children's Crusade: A Duty-Dance with Death

Kurt Vonnegut, Jr.
(1969)

Kurt Vonnegut, Jr., has been called *the* novelist for the sixties. More than any other writer of the decade, Vonnegut articulated the fears of a generation determined to change America's course. His novels preached the folly of war. They warned of a future ruled by machines, not men. They advocated sex. ("Make love when you can. It's good for you," is the way he ends the introduction to "Mother Night.") And throughout, his point of view was invariably that of an innocent looking out with a mixture of horror and resignation at a world gone mad.

If his pacifist stance was not enough to attract the antiwar protesters whose voices were at their loudest at about the time *Slaughterhouse-Five* appeared, his philosophy of life was sure to pull them in. The aim of life, as he stated it in *Slaughterhouse-Five,* was to live a life in which "everything was beautiful and nothing hurt." "Beautiful" was a buzz-word of the sixties, while seeing to it that "nothing hurt" was the main reason for taking drugs. Summing it all up was a philosophic, almost stoic phrase of Vonnegut's that still rings in the minds of aging counterculturists, the gentle-but-cynical words that followed each of the numerous references to death in *Slaughterhouse-Five*: "So be it."

Slaughterhouse-Five or the Children's Crusade: A Duty-Dance with Death is a framed narrative that begins with Kurt Vonnegut, Jr., apparently in his own voice, telling of his lifelong desire to write a book about his experiences as a prisoner of war in Dresden at the time of the fire-bombing that destroyed most of the city in 1945 . He ends his novel with references to the year of its completion, 1968, that disastrous year that witnessed the assassinations of Robert Kennedy and Martin

Luther King, Jr., race riots in the inner cities, violent peace demonstrations at the Democratic convention in Chicago, and escalating losses in Vietnam.

Inside this frame is the story of Billy Pilgrim, who has lived two lives. In one life, Billy is an ordinary, quiet American who graduates from high school in 1940, just in time to be drafted. At the Battle of the Bulge in 1944, he is captured and transported to forced labor in Dresden. Billy feels relatively safe there because Dresden is an open city of no military importance. In fact, he actually finds life rather pleasant in this historic, eighteenth-century city of legendary charm and beauty.

Soon after Billy's arrival, however, allied bombers create a fire storm that incinerates the heart of the city. Such an incident was grist for the mill to cult readers eager to find any evidence to prove that Americans could be just as bad as Germans, or even worse. After all, there was no good reason to bomb Dresden (as if there had been good reason to bomb Warsaw or Coventry or Leningrad). Billy survives because he is working underground in the meat locker of "Slaughterhouse-Five" when the bombing occurs.

Billy had been a chaplain's assistant in the army. When he returns from the war, he becomes a successful optometrist, marries happily, survives a plane crash, loses his wife in a strange auto accident, becomes the prophet of a kind of stoicism, and dies of an assassin's bullet in a baseball park in 1976 while speaking of flying saucers and the nature of time.

But there is much more to Billy Pilgrim than a brief biography discloses. Shortly before he was captured by the Germans, Billy began to "come unstuck in time." Without warning, he might be transported either backward or forward in his own life. One moment he might be under sedation in a prison camp, the next he might find himself in bed with the gorgeous Montana Wildhack in a zoo on the planet Tralfamadore. But it was not until 1967, when he was kidnapped and taken to Tralfamadore, that he really began to understand the nature of this extraordinary sort of time travel. Because Tralfamadore is outside time and Tralfamadorians see time as a dimension, like distance, Billy is never really absent from the Earth. In 1968, after his near fatal plane crash and the death of his wife, he comes to the conclusion that he must tell the world what he has learned about time from the Tralfamadorians. Thus, he becomes the prophet of a new brand of stoicism.

The Tralfamadorians teach him that all time is coexistent, that it is not something that is created or something that passes away. Like space, it has always been there, has always existed, with all periods of time coexistent with all others. This is why Billy is able to shift back and forth between his two lives, moving, as it were, in a sort of "stream of consciousness," to use the phrase coined in the late nineteenth century by

Henri Bergson, the first person to propound the theory of coexistent time.

Paradoxically, Billy learns that this view of time leads both to fatalism and compassion. Since all events have already happened, one is powerless to change them. But since one goes on reliving one's life, it matters that one lives it well. As Vonnegut, the narrator, says in the last chapter, "If I am going to spend eternity visiting this moment and that, I'm grateful that so many of those moments are nice" (183). Billy, of course, enjoys the best of both worlds. When life on earth gets rough, he can escape to the pleasures of life on Tralfamadore.

Because Billy is unstuck in time and leads two lives, the organization of the novel is quite complex. Billy moves back and forth within his two lives almost arbitrarily, though frequently there are colors, sounds, and other sense experiences that cause the moves. Sandwiched between these jumps through time are glimpses of his sojourns on Tralfamadore, his stays in a mental hospital, his wedding night, his daughter's wedding night, his son's troubled youth, and many other events, including the crucial moment in Dresden when Edgar Derby is executed for looting during the clean-up after the fire storm. Vonnegut makes much of the irony that Derby should survive such a disaster only to die for a petty theft.

Billy Pilgrim is an unlikely hero but an ideal antihero. He is tall but physically weak. He is not ambitious, yet he becomes rich by marrying the daughter of the owner of the optometry school he once attended. Billy is not particularly courageous, yet when he grasps the meaning of the Tralfamadorian philosophy, he is determined to teach it to the world, whatever the consequences. Once he learns that he must do what he must do, he can face life with courage and some joy. He is living proof that even an average guy can become a "pilgrim" in the right crusade. He is the ordinary little man who, when put into extraordinary situations, rises to the occasion with unexpected eloquence and determination.

Vonnegut, as narrator, is clearly skeptical of the truth of Billy's revelation, worrying that while such deterministic stoicism may help one to bear life's minor troubles, it offers no way of dealing with the major ones. Cult readers, though, were well aware that Vonnegut was having fun with Billy, and it did not bother them that Vonnegut could tease his own protagonist. They saw Billy as naive in a hostile world, and they appreciated his Candide-like attitude, an attitude that was particularly endearing to counterculturists. It was easy for them to identify with a cockeyed optimist who tried to believe that it was the best of all possible worlds while suspecting (maybe even knowing?) all along that it was not.

This attitude appealed to those cult readers who did not really want to grow up. ("Don't trust anybody over thirty," they warned, while Vonnegut, who was forty-seven when *Slaughterhouse-Five* came out, smiled and kept on writing.) Nothing characterized the counterculturists more than their contempt for age and their attempts to stop the clock, from their long, unkempt hair to that peculiar bouncing walk that simulated the carefree stride of reckless adolescents out on a spree. Age equaled corruption and boredom and war; youth was the hope of the world. Make love, not war. Kids don't start wars, old people do—old men taking their revenge on youth. Kids just wanted to "tune in, turn on, and drop out." But this did not mean they were totally oblivious to what was going on. Why else behave that way?

In *Slaughterhouse-Five,* Vonnegut reveals some of the circumstances surrounding the writing of the book and some of his high hopes for it. He admits that he wanted to write an antiwar book even though he knew how futile it was to dream of stopping wars. At least, he says, he could write a war novel in which there would be no film parts for John Wayne or Frank Sinatra, two icons of a time the new generation wanted to relegate to oblivion.

One reason for the novel's commercial success was that Vonnegut's concern with peace coincided with his growing popularity among young-adult readers and that audience's mounting opposition to the war in Vietnam. In wrapping the firebombing of Dresden in irony and fantasy, Vonnegut had the perfect conduit to the conscience of the times. With joyful wrath, his readers pounced on the sins of their fathers that they saw being repeated in Vietnam at Hue and in the Mekong Delta.

The wrath of self-righteousness is a destructive and sometimes evil force. In the case of *Slaughterhouse-Five,* it blinded readers to the Pied Piper in Vonnegut who, like Dr. Spock or Timothy Leary, gleefully led his dedicated followers down the poppy-strewn path. Vonnegut had constructed a fiction that, while pretending not to be deeply engaged in moral problems, did nevertheless arouse indignation not only against war but also against all the ways by which humans justify depriving one another of life and dignity. And to his fans, these ways were myriad.

Vonnegut appeals to those who already believe what he has to say. He appeals to younger readers because, like Stephen King, his own spiritual age seems to be late adolescence, a time when a flip manner often disguises priggishness, and skepticism is just a defense against vulnerability. It is also a time when prejudice obstructs the search for truth and lack of experience means a lack of imagination, as well as a time when confidence in one's superiority reveals itself in false modesty, and the herding instinct is hidden beneath a cry for independence.

Kurt Vonnegut remains a prolific writer, and his books continue to attract readers with a taste for zanines and a twisted sense of humor.

There can be no doubt that he found the right voice to speak to—and frequently for—a generation. One suspects, though, that all along he has been just as interested in entertaining as in instructing and that he has never worn the mantle of cult figure or guru comfortably. After all, he is one of our great humorists, and when the dust finally settles, it may turn out that there he is closer to Voltaire than he is to Ghandi.

FOR FURTHER READING

Cooley, John. "The Garden in the Machine: Three Postmodern Pastorals." *Michigan Academician: Papers of the Michigan Academy of Science, Arts, and Letters* (Spring 1981): 405–20.

Dhar, T. N. "Vonnegut's Leap Within: *Slaughterhouse-Five* to *Slapstick*." *Indian Journal of American Studies* (Winter 1985): 57–73.

Dimeo, Stephen. "Novel into Film: So It Goes." Festschrift article in *AN*. (1979): 282–92.

Mayer, Peter C. "Film, Ontology and the Structure of a Novel." *Literature/Film Quarterly* 8 (1980): 204–8.

The Sorrows of Young Werther (Die Leiden des Jungen Werthers)

Johann Wolfgang von Goethe (1774)

The Sorrows of Young Werther is the original cult book in Western fiction. Johann Wolfgang von Goethe wrote it when he was just twenty-four, and its notoriety caused him great embarrassment as he grew older. Eventually he came to regret, even denounce, its excesses and would have disowned the book if he could have. Nevertheless, the book captured the restless spirit of the age, the spirit that was soon to revolutionize Europe and America, the spirit that was to dethrone reason and exalt passion.

Translations appeared promptly in France and then in England, where twenty-six separate editions (of a translation from the French) were published before 1800. It is said that Napoleon admitted to reading the novel seven times and even to carrying it into battle, and it is known that he discussed it with Goethe when the two men met in 1808. In Germany the work created a tremendous sensation. Within twelve years after its publication, twenty unauthorized editions had been issued.

The fevered reception of this book set off a wave of "Wertherism" throughout Europe and spread even to China, where dolls were fashioned in Werther's image. The "Werther costume," consisting of blue tailed coat, yellow waist-coat and trousers, and high boots, was adopted everywhere and was already being worn at Weimar by the court when Goethe went there in 1775. Everywhere Werther impersonators were falling hopelessly in love, writing passionate letters (*Werther* is an epistolary novel), even committing suicide.

Werther, therefore, is the obvious source book for the study of cult literature because it contains, unadulterated, all the ingredients that have appeared in varying degrees in cult books ever since. However, its most immediate and significant contribution to the study of cult literature lies in the fact that it is the first full-fledged expression of the Romantic temper in novel form. Its colors are primary, its chords dominant. It is not a work that could suffer—or bear—repeating. Modern-day counterparts are muted variations of its bold themes. But these themes are always present, and they are always fired by the energy of young Werther's Romantic spirit.

The story is simple. Werther, a young man in love with love, plummets from ecstasy to despair as he sees his beloved Lotte being drawn into the arms of his rival, Albert. There is little doubt that he relishes his despair almost more than his ecstasy as he records, in letter after tormented letter, his drift toward suicide. The irony is that he is too idealistic to succeed in his pursuit, for like all Romantic heroes, his idealism dooms him to failure. "It is the fate of a man like myself to be misunderstood," he says at one point, expressing for the first time a sentiment that was destined to become the slogan of cult heroes ever after (10).

Most myths are accounts of disobedience and its consequences, and the myth of Werther follows the classic pattern. His Romantic temperament incites him to disobedience, and his democratic spirit prompts him to exercise that freedom; but this same spirit counsels obedience to the rule of law. Thus, it is the tension between contradictory impulses that aggravates Werther's "sorrows." His counterpart in mythology is Prometheus, the favorite god of the Romantics. Because he was free to disobey, yet was punished for his disobedience, his rage and pain held more appeal for them than did the respectable disgrace of conformity. Better to defy and suffer than to surrender and sulk.

Disobedience to God means obedience to oneself: Thy will versus my will. There is no middle ground. Great artists like Goethe find submission to their own wills to be but temporary and unsatisfactory waystations on their path towards greater wisdom and full creative expression. Goethe's Faust learns the bitter lesson of preoccupation with self. But cult literature has no Fausts. Its heroes are never humble. Their courage may fail them, but never their self-confidence. They are arrogant, self-serving, and inevitably destructive. But it is not the gods who destroy them; they destroy themselves.

In a letter composed on Christmas Eve, 1771, Werther writes that he is so preoccupied with himself, that his heart is in such turmoil, that he would gladly let others go their own way if they would only let him go his. His self-absorption, his wish to go his own way, was a revolutionary note in a revolutionary age. It was the cry of the individual for identity as a unique being, at whatever cost. It signaled a retreat inward from the sweetly reasoned, intellectual consensus that was the legacy of the Enlightenment—a retreat into a private world of limitless fantasy and longing, morbidity and despair, the extremes of dream and nightmare, an intensely personal world in which self and only self mattered. Such rebellion was an inevitable reaction to the previous age that had come close to refining itself out of existence. As the Neoclassicists closed one door of inquiry after another by presuming to have uttered the last word on art, drama, history, politics, and morality—in short, as they constricted the arena in which the mind must thrive—rebellion was bound to erupt. And when it did, it released energies that have not yet dissipated.

Goethe's Werther begins in rebellion against those forces beyond his control that keep him from his beloved Lotte, and when those forces win, he takes his life rather than accept his fate. His frenzied letters are a record of his resentment of what he suspects to be true: that the laws of the universe can never accommodate his desperation. As far as he is concerned, his heightened emotions and tortured sensibilities are the highest virtue. He thinks of himself as a superior being (as *wert*-er: worthier), and while he knows that the universe will not tolerate pride, to him it is the universe that is wrong, not he.

His suicide is a symbolic act of defiance, his way of removing himself from the universe before it has a chance to crush him. Suicide is the consummate act, possibly the only real act of rebellion against a universe one disapproves of. It cheats the universe of its prerogative of settling the matter of one's death in its own way. It is a way of punishing God for not ordering the universe to one's own liking.

But if suicide is the consummate act of rebellion, it is also the paramount expression of submission, for it is an admission that the laws of the universe are peremptory and inviolate, including the law that says that all that lives must die. Those of the Werther cult lamented, as did he, the injustice of a universe that disregarded their commandments and punished their excesses. Werther's tragic flaw is the deadly sin of pride (*hubris*) and its consequences, but the effect of the story is not to purge this sin but to provoke it.

Although Werther's preoccupation with himself may strike one initially as self-pitying and his attitude petulant, he really has great resilience of soul and certainly the courage of his convictions. Anyone at odds with life is apt to sound—and even be—vacuously cynical, forever whining that the world is not made up the way one would like it and distributing blame all over the place so as to excuse oneself from responsibility. But Werther, even though he complains bitterly about God, does so in defense of man and, ultimately, in defense of his own sensitive soul, which he insists ought to triumph and for which he takes full responsibility, even to the point of risking its damnation. His lament is not that he has been given extraordinary sensitivity but that he must suffer so much to express it.

That part of him that he rejects is not his imagination but his feeble reason. "O you rational people," he exclaims in one letter. "You stand there so complacently, without any real sympathy, you moralists, condemning the drunkard, detesting the madman, passing by like the Levite, and thanking God that you are not made as one of these. . . . Shame on you sober ones! Shame on you sages!" (58). And in another letter, he expresses amazement that anyone can derive comfort from rational answers, calling such comfort merely "a dreamlike kind of resignation in which we paint our prison walls with gaily colored figures and luminous prospects." It "leaves me speechless," he says, and "I withdraw into my inner self and there discover a world" that he admits is made up more of "vague perceptions and dim desires than of creative power and vital force." But at this point, "everything swims before my senses," he admits, almost boastingly, "and I go on smiling at the outer world like someone in a dream" (11–12).

By descending into the depths of feeling and imagination, he is making contact with, to use Carl Jung's phrase, the "collective memory" of mankind; he is voyaging in the world of dream and the unconscious, the realm that dwells within all men but to which only the hero has access and from which he returns with the symbols to which all men respond automatically.

That Werther senses the possibility of coming in contact with the ultimate forces of eternity, the essential energy of creation, the "ubiquitous powers," is apparent when he says how often he has yearned to drink from "the foaming cup of infinity that effervescent rapture of life" and to feel, if only for a moment, "a drop of the bliss of that Being who creates all things in and through Himself" (65).

Book One of *Werther* is largely the story of his separation, stage one in the rite of passage. Gradually the bliss of his early letters gives way to melancholy as Werther becomes disappointed with society, alienated from the world order, and rejected by Lotte. Inequality and human meanness frustrate his associations with people except for those occasional encounters with unhappy wayfarers. He finds most people "unsympathetic" and castigates the human race for its "base stupidity." Even when he declares that he won't let class differences stand in his way "toward experiencing a little joy, a gleam of happiness, on this earth," he says in the same breath, "I'll gladly let the others go their own way if only they will let me go mine" (81). Cut off from those of lower social rank and snubbed by those above, he finds solace in grieving over the sad fates of innocent strangers brought low by the callousness of others.

More agonizing for Werther than social separation is the broken promise of metaphysical illumination. The future recedes before his grasp. He talks of surrendering his entire being into "one great well of blissful feeling," only to be frustrated at the last moment "when There has become Here," when nothing after all has changed, when all is as it was and his soul longs for the solace that remains so tantalizingly elusive. Ultimately, it is the separation from Lotte that becomes the crucible of his initiation, the second stage in the rite of passage that leads finally to his symbolic, if not actual, return.

Each encounter with Lotte, with Albert, and with their domestic bliss determines that day's particular emotional drift for Werther. Every action is a reaction to her, and every thought is colored by her behavior to him. The cult hero, like the monomythical hero, does not remove himself from the contest until he has been tested by all that the experience has to yield. Once he disengages himself, he knows his own powers and foresees the curve of his own destiny. If the hero does not necessarily come to terms with man and God, he at least understands what the terms are, and he proceeds accordingly. Werther sees suicide as his destiny, but for him it is an act of sacrifice, not despair.

"It is decided, Lotte, that I shall die," he writes in a letter to be delivered after his death. He boasts that he is calm on this morning of the day during which he will see Lotte for the last time. He insists that he is "without any romantic exaltation" (140), but a few lines later he is again in the throes of a "terrible revolt," with "everything rushing into my heart" and, falling on his knees he thanks her for a "last consolation of bitter tears!" No, "it is not despair;" he insists, "it is the certainty that I have suffered enough, and that I am sacrificing myself for you. Yes, Lotte!" (141). Although he carries out his sacrifice with Christian symbolism (his last supper consists of bread and wine), he glories in the sin that is motivating his death, and it is in this "heresy" that he appeals to the cult enthusiast. He tells Lotte that he knows it is a sin to love her, at least in this world, a sin to wish to snatch her from Albert's arms, but if it is a sin, he writes, then certainly "I am punishing myself for it; for this sin, which I have tasted in all its rapture, which gave me life-giving balm and strength" (157).

Werther's claim, then, that he is one of a few noble souls allowed to shed their blood for someone they love seems a less convincing reason for his suicide than the fear that anything less would be anticlimactic after all his grandstanding. But all that aside, the idea of sacrificing oneself by an act of magnificent blasphemy after exhausting every possible emotion and doing one's utmost to frustrate fate is intoxicatingly seductive to cult followers. And it is in this subversion of the monomyth that the paradox of the cult hero becomes apparent. He acts as if he feels condemned rather than privileged to relive the myth, and, therefore, his rite of passage pits him not against the vicissitudes of worldly fortune but against the very myth he is recreating. He feels tyrannized rather than liberated by it, and although he cannot escape it, he offers the only conceivable alternative to it—the commitment to render it inimical to itself, to use the myth to destroy the myth.

If Werther's lamentations have a hollow ring today, it is probably because we laminate our self-pity with a thick coat of irony. Instead of crying over our fate, we make fun of ourselves, even hold ourselves up to public ridicule. The stand-up comedian has become the symbol of modern man mourning the tragicomedy of his inconsequential fate. Hunter S. Thompson's "Raoul Duke" punishes himself as severely with drugs and disgrace as Goethe's Werther punishes himself with self-pity. But both are arrogant and unrepentant. Inherent in Werther is the making of a modern antihero, the professional loser, as if failure in life were the only decent comment one could make on God's botched job.

But Werther was only recreating the part of Prometheus, the rebel angel so dear to the hearts of the Romantics, a hero who might lose in his struggle against authority but whose every torment was a moral victory for the indomitable spirit of denial. Werther says "No!" in thunder to his unhappy lot, and it is a cry that has echoed through cult literature ever since.

FOR FURTHER READING

McCormick, E. Allen. "Poema Pictura Loquens: Literary Pictorialism and the Psychology of Landscape." *Comparative Literature Studies* 13 (1976): 196–213.

Wellbery, Caroline. "From Mirrors to Images: The Transformation of Sentimental Paradigms in Goethe's *The Sorrows of Young Werther*." *Studies in Romanticism* (Summer 1986): 231–49.

The Stand

Stephen King
(1978)

Stephen King's novels are so enormously popular and have attracted such a devoted following that almost any one of his books could contend for the distinction of cult classic. From *Carrie* onward, avid readers have taken to each work as if it were holy writ, making King's reputation one of the most controversial in modern times. Those who adore him are passionate in their defense of him, while those who detest him (many of whom have never read him) find him impossibly vulgar and, worse yet, unforgivably popular. King's curse is that he gives new meaning to that overworked adjective "riveting." Whether you like his stories or not, he certainly knows how to make you turn a page.

Those who are writers themselves would like to think that *Misery* is King's best claim to cult status because of the spellbinding way in which it penetrates the mind of the writer and the art of storytelling. Those doomed to enjoy a place in the sun find *Misery* a lament for the agonies of the harassed celebrity. *The Shining*, an equally well-controlled novel for a writer known best for unedited sprawl, also has its dedicated following, but its readers admit, too, that it is the brilliantly manipulated horror that appeals to them, not any depth of character or theme.

However, there is only one Stephen King novel that has really gone beyond mere popularity to achieve cult status, and that is *The Stand*. Although *The Stand* meets all the criteria of a cult book, it takes something more than this to give it the stamp of cult classic, since many books with similar criteria have never achieved cult status. One argument is that, whenever Stephen King novels are discussed, his most ardent admirers invariably put *The Stand* in a class by itself outside, and usually above, all other King novels, claiming for it special properties that indeed do set it apart.

Probably the best proof of the book's claim to cult status, however, is to be found in its unique publishing history. When *The Stand* first appeared in 1978, it was a "king-size" book even by Stephen King standards—823 pages of fine print. In addition to its discouraging length, it was confusing to read, disjointed, diffuse, and seemingly unedited. It had the feel of a sprawling rough draft, overflowing with possibilities but out of focus and virtually out of control, just crying out for the practiced hand of a legendary editor like Maxwell Perkins to do with it what he had done with Thomas Wolfe's stacks of shapeless narrative.

Nevertheless, in spite of the book's bulk, the faithful loved it, even praised its unevenness as a sign of something special, almost as if it had been dictated to King by some superior force. Whenever King was discussed, *The Stand* was singled out for special adoration. Yes, *Salem's Lot* was a first-rate piece of gothic horror, *Firestarter* and *The Dead Zone* were scary stories with scary themes, and *Christine* and *Pet Sematary* were spine-tinglers with bizarre twists. But only *The Stand* had both epic narrative and something important to say. Only *The Stand* had a message, a vision, and perhaps an answer to what had gone wrong with the world and how to set it right.

What is unique about the publishing history of *The Stand* is that when the book was reissued in 1990—with 500 pages added!—it outsold the 1978 edition, climbing up the bestseller list faster than before and staying there longer. The first time around, King's publishers feared that even King's name might not be enough to lure readers into paying twelve or fifteen dollars for such a long book. Curiously enough, in 1990, readers, most of whom had read the first edition, gladly paid twice that amount for a book that now runs to 1,153 pages. The restoration of the 500 pages King had been forced to cut from the original manuscript, a revised beginning and ending, and a great deal of judicious editing in between have combined to make the new edition a vastly improved work.

However, it was not this that cult readers were excited about. What drew them to the second edition was the hope that (a) they would learn more about their favorite characters, that (b) the conflict between good and evil would be even more explicit and, above all, that (c) the book's message would be amplified. In other words, they seized the newer work in the same way biblical scholars seized upon the Dead Sea Scrolls in the fervent hope of more questions answered and more prophesies made. Stephen King admits in his preface to the new edition that he is "republishing *The Stand* as it was originally written not to serve [himself] or any individual reader, but to serve a body of readers who have asked to have it" (x). King says that while it is not his favorite novel, "it is the one people who like my books seem to like the most," the one they always speak to him about and whose characters they discuss as if they were living people (xii).

The story of *The Stand* combines elements of science-fiction, horror, myth, epic, and the apocalyptic. Beginning with the frighteningly contemporary threat of a deadly epidemic and concluding with a decisive showdown between the forces of darkness and the forces of light, this novel presses all the buttons calculated to enthrall the fearful inhabitants of beleaguered planet Earth at the twilight of the twentieth century. The deadly epidemic of the novel is a highly contagious flu virus that is accidentally released at an air force base in California in July 1985. Before the base is sealed, a panicked employee escapes, spreading this "super-flu" across the Southwest and then across the nation where, in a four-week period, it kills 99 percent of the population.

The only survivors are those who inexplicably have a natural immunity to the disease. These survivors quickly divide into two groups according to the nature of the dreams that come to them, telling them of two opposing forces. One force is heralded by Mother Abigail, a pious old woman who has received messages to prepare a meal for unknown guests. The other force is represented by Randall Flagg, an evil man known alternately as either "walkin' dude" or "creeping Judas." Flagg's first convert is Lloyd Henreid, a convicted murderer found starving to death in a jail cell in a prison where all others have died. Just when Henreid is about to resort to cannibalism, he is mysteriously released, whereupon he bows down and worships Flagg, and the two of them set out across the country.

Meanwhile in New England, Harold Lauder and Frannie Goldsmith set out on a journey to find a cure for the super-flu, leaving a sign on the roof of their barn informing any survivors who may be looking for them where they have gone. In their dreams Mother Abigail calls them west, and on the way they meet Stuart Redman. Harold immediately becomes jealous of Redman, and begins to turn toward the dark force. Meanwhile, Larry Underwood, the novel's hero, is traveling west following the signs left by Lauder. Others are mysteriously lured westward; some of them, under the influence of Mother Abigail, end up in Boulder, Colorado, a city mysteriously free of dead bodies, while the rest, under the spell of Randall Flagg, gather in Las Vegas, Nevada.

Flagg establishes a dictatorship and immediately begins stockpiling weapons and training fighter pilots, while the people in Boulder organize a democracy under the direction of Nick Andros. Flagg's plans deteriorate, however, and eventually Underwood and others from the Boulder community go west at God's command and witness Flagg's destruction by the wrath of God. The survivors of the climactic events then return to Boulder to revive civilization.

King calls *The Stand* his "long tale of dark Christianity" (xii), and

Mother Abigail is his Christ figure in this version of the Apocalypse. Mother Abigail, who is 108 at the time of the story, often reflects on the meaning of her life. As a young woman, she had been a guitarist and singer and had inherited money and land. Later, the land was taken away, bit by bit, to pay her taxes. In spite of all her troubles, Mother Abigail has always relied on the Lord to save her and support her in her time of need, and she continues to do so throughout the course of the novel.

Randall Flagg, the antichrist figure, can pass for either a black or a white man. He is not clearly of one race or the other, and his evil is such that he is against all that is good and participates in all that is evil. In the past he has participated in Ku Klux Klan burnings, carried pamphlets by Lee Harvey Oswald, and conspired with revolutionaries. Randall Flagg is also a creation of contemporary fear, especially the fear that satanic power lies behind the evil that we see on television or read about in the newspapers.

When confronted with the reality of Lee Harvey Oswald's assassination of President John F. Kennedy, or a gang of racists wearing sheets of their own design to frighten and torture blacks, many people can find an explanation only in the agency of some superhuman evil. Flagg is presented as a source of such evil. He walks the land, and a great darkness is with him. His action in commanding Lloyd Henreid to fall down and worship him is the first time that the viewer sees Flagg in motion. Later in Las Vegas, where he sets up his kingdom, Flagg shows more of his power as he draws the weak (such as Harold Lauder, eaten up by jealousy) to his side. At this point, he seems too strong to be defeated under any circumstances, but he is gradually weakened by his own evil emotions and his uncontrollable temper.

Larry Underwood is a rock musician who, after years of struggle and one-night stands in seedy bars, finally makes it in the music world. As his wealth increases beyond his wildest dreams, he begins to throw lavish parties, take drugs, and in general go downhill. Finally, realizing that the people at his parties do not care about him, he leaves Hollywood one night to drive to New York. His mother still lives there in the same little walk-up apartment in which Underwood grew up. When the super-flu strikes, Larry is one of the survivors and endures the horror of seeing New York filled with the bodies of the dead. Larry and another survivor, a woman he picks up, travel west together. Larry's irresponsibility is demonstrated after his companion dies: He leaves her body to the scavenger birds because he does not like the thought of handling her dead body.

Frannie Goldsmith, the pregnant college girl from New England who joins Harold Lauder on his trip west, is one of King's more realistically drawn female characters. Although unmarried, Frannie decides that she will carry the child and refuses to consider abortion. Frannie's gentleness and love add some tenderness to this bleak novel. When she meets Lauder, he is an overweight, clumsy teenager who has a crush on her. Because of her encouragement, he begins to grow and mature; though he is ultimately drawn to evil, he has known what it is to love and care for someone else.

Stephen King is very popular with people who came of age in the sixties, but mostly with those who remember the decade with nostalgia, not hostility. King's car radio is stuck at 1965, and his language is salted with the slang of the day (including its casual but always comic profanities) and with the rhythms of the sentences in which that slang appeared. For example, in the preface to *The Stand,* King tries to explain why he thinks the expanded version is better than the shorter one by presenting a skeletal version of "Hansel and Gretel," leaving out the "nonessential" parts about the rabbits' hearts and the bread crumbs. He calls this version a loser, saying that while the story is there, it is not elegant. "It's like a Cadillac with the chrome stripped off and the paint sanded down to dull metal. It goes somewhere, but it ain't, you know, *boss*" (xi). His style is inimitable, and it is a great part of what endears him to cult readers who feel that whatever world King plunges them into, they are safe as long as he is at the wheel of the Impala and Neil Diamond is on the radio.

In the last chapter of *Danse Macabre,* King's treatise on horror fiction, he talks about writing *The Stand.* He admits that there were times he hated the book but that regardless of his feelings toward it, he was drawn to it irresistibly, that he could not wait to get to it each morning, to sink back into that world and find out what Randall Flagg or Larry Underwood might be up to. He talks, too, about the climate of the times during which he wrote the book, the mid-seventies, a time when the country was reeling from the bruises of Vietnam and Watergate and the whole cultural upheaval that came in the wake of the revolutionary sixties.

King says there were times when he was writing *The Stand* that he felt as if he were tap dancing on the country's grave, an apt expression when one considers how easily events of the time might have followed any number of worst-case scenarios from toxic plague to widespread terrorism to bitter and destructive ideological confrontation. Today it reads as a fate narrowly escaped but still threatening, maybe inevitable. However, instead of the gloomy fatalism of most doomsday books, *The Stand* reaffirms the dignity and resilience of the human spirit, the spirit in which William Faulkner placed so much faith when he talked about mankind not only surviving but prevailing.

FOR FURTHER READING

Cheever, Leonard. "Apocalypse and the Popular Imagination: Stephen King's *The Stand.*" *RE: Artes Liberales* (Fall 1981): 1–10.

Collings, Michael R. "*The Stand*: Science Fiction into Fantasy." In *Discovering Modern Horror Fiction, 1*. Mercer Island, Wash.: Starmont, 1985: 83–90.

Indick, Ben P. "Stephen King as an Epic Writer." In *Discovering Modern Horror Fiction, 1*. Mercer Island, Wash.: Starmont, 1985: 56–67.

Somtow, S. P. "A Certain Slant of 'I': Stand by Stephen King." *Fantasy Review* (October 1986): 11, 16.

Spignesi, Stephen J. *The Shape Under the Sheet: The Complete Stephen King Encyclopedia*. New York: Popular Culture, 1991.

Steppenwolf

Hermann Hesse
(1927)

Since the day of its initial publication, *Steppenwolf* has been a cult favorite among intellectuals who find its expression of the moral ambiguities of modern times to be the clearest statement of their own moral crisis. This experimental novel bombards the reader with a sequence of vivid images and scenes that document the spiritual and intellectual journey of Harry Haller, the aging cynic torn between the pious side of his nature and what he refers to as "the wolf" in himself. Only after a radical change, after wildly embracing all the vices of the senses, including alcoholism, sexual aberration, and narcotic intoxication, does he finally reach a new platform of humor and irony that makes life bearable.

As a social outsider, a "lonely wolf of the steppes," Haller becomes increasingly aware of the dualism of the human personality as manifested in the split between reason and emotion, the flesh and the spirit, the mind and the subconscious. His transfiguration is brought about by Hermine and Maria, two girls who reveal to him the ultimate innocence of sexuality, and finally by the "Magic Theatre," which enables him to see the different "souls" of his split personality.

As is true of other Hermann Hesse novels in which the reader is challenged to take sides (*Demian, Narcissus and Goldmund*), *Steppenwolf* is a novel few readers can read objectively or passively. Haller is filled with so much anguish, is torn so between the opposite sides of his nature, that one is forced either to reject the idea of the novel entirely or to embrace it with uncritical enthusiasm. Cult followers fall into the latter category, even though the book is good enough to satisfy the most rigorous critical standards. What critics like about the book is that, although it is experimental in nature, it is written with extraordinary restraint. And, although it is written in the first person from the point of view of the protagonist, it is presented in the form of Harry Haller's abandoned diary, which is being edited by the author, whose identity is only dimly disguised.

Alienation is a theme that runs through all of Hesse's works, and there is no clearer statement of its effect on the artist than in *Steppenwolf*. Like Stephen Dedalus (*Portrait of the Artist*) and Eugene Gant (*Look Homeward, Angel*), Harry Haller is an outsider, torn between his own frustrated artistic idealism and the inhuman nature of modern reality that, in his eyes, is characterized entirely by philistinism and technology. It is his inability to be a part of the world and the resulting loneliness and desolation of his existence that causes him to think of himself as a "Steppenwolf."

The divided self, especially in the soul of the artist, has been a recurrent concern in modern literature, particularly since the days of Romanticism when William Wordsworth wrote of "two voices" and Johann Wolfgang von Goethe of "two souls." The presence of the double, the alter ego, the Doppelgänger in modern literature, has created something of a subgenre, but whereas one side is usually triumphant because it is traditionally "good," Hesse makes the choice more difficult, opting ultimately not for the simplistic good but for the "bad" that has been transmuted into something higher than either ordinary good or bad. In *Demian*, for example, those with the mark of Cain, traditionally a symbol of evil, are elevated above all others by virtue of their fearless assertion of the dual nature of man and the necessity to recognize the dark as well as the bright side.

Popular as this book has always been, it reached new and unexpected heights in the sixties when it became the favorite of the youth of the counterculture who felt oppressed by their middle-class backgrounds and tortured by the "wolf" within them that was panting to be released. Given the climate of the times—a generation gap on a grand scale, a sexual revolution whose shock waves have not yet subsided, open rebellion against authority of a kind most people thought possible only on the cobblestone barricades of European capitals—this was the dose of European angst the American cultural revolutionaries needed. *Steppenwolf* had everything the counterculture valued: sex, drugs, and martyrdom.

Hermann Hesse was a mild-mannered man who died just as his books were about to become the underground cult favorites of a new generation of readers. Hesse scholars were appalled at the new audience and at what seemed a distorted perception of what Hesse was all about. Even though many cult enthusiasts were sincere enough about their pacifism and their spirituality to have gladdened Hesse's heart, others took to him for what Hesse critics thought were all the wrong reasons, misinterpreting his politics, misunderstanding his religious leanings, and totally ignoring his ironic sense of humor.

Whether these accusations are true or not, the fact remains that Hesse, more than any other cult author, has suffered the fate of the writer whose books have taken on a life of their own, a life far beyond what the author could ever have imagined. Whereas most authors are lucky (or unlucky, depending on how you look at it) to have one of their books become a cult favorite, at least three of Hesse's have achieved that status (*Demian, Siddhartha, Steppenwolf*) and some would include the very popular *Narcissus and Goldmund* and maybe even *The Glass-Bead Game*, the book that capped Hesse's illustrious career and did much to win him the Nobel Prize in 1946.

The components of cult literature that account for a book's inclusion in this category are so subtly pervasive in *Steppenwolf* that only a closer look at what is going on in the novel can truly reveal them. *Steppenwolf* is not a novel of action or character in the ordinary sense but a novel of ideas in which philosophical and psychological truths are presented dramatically and symbolically. Since the main action is internal, dreams and hallucinations are as significant as "real" happenings. Hesse creates a new myth in the act of reinterpreting an ancient one. The twin sides of human nature, the warring factions that split the soul in two, the clash and fusion of opposites: this tension provides the conflict for much of traditional mythology. However, the dual nature of man has become the prevailing myth of modern times (Faust, don Juan, Jekyll and Hyde, Dorian Gray), and in so becoming, it has taken on new shapes and forms that require reinventions of the myth.

This conflict between reason and emotion, flesh and spirit, duty and inclination appears frequently in European literature as a conflict between the artist and what the author of the "Treatise on the *Steppenwolf*" calls the "Bürger," which may be translated as "citizen" or "bourgeois." Restless young Americans of the sixties saw in Hesse's presentation of this conflict a mirror of what would come to be known as the generation gap. They saw themselves as sensitive, misunderstood, alienated artists and their parents as narrow-minded, intolerant Bürgers, ready to conform and easily led, eager to achieve self-preservation at the cost of all intensity of feeling. In this bourgeois world the Steppenwolf is a perpetual outsider, the man who is potentially both a saint and a profligate, the man who longs for absolutes and responds to the claim of the unconditioned. Nevertheless, because of inertia or cowardice, he cannot break completely with the world, but makes some kind of uneasy compromise with it. Consequently he never rises to the dignity of tragedy. His destiny is more ignoble: to live in an atmosphere where he cannot flourish and to penetrate all the disguises of the world without any compensatory counter-revelation.

Harry may seem a bit too old for cult readers to relate to, but it is not Harry they see at the center of things but the "immortals," those few beyond the Bürger and the Steppenwolf who have risen to a state of unified life in which the polar opposites of this world are no longer reciprocally exclusive, a state in which it is possible to affirm all aspects of life, flesh, mind, and spirit without compromising any. Such men no longer cling to their personal egos. They are beyond self-affirmation. Instead, they have expanded and multiplied themselves until they have merged in the All. They include the saints and also the great artists like Goethe and Mozart. These men have discovered the secret of cosmic laughter, of an eternal gaiety that both affirms and transcends the world.

Likewise, it is not so much with Harry himself as with Harry's quest that cult readers identify. For Harry to rise to the condition of the immortals, he must learn to accept the part of himself that he has hitherto denied: the sensual and nonintellectual. In this his guides are Hermine and her friends. Another man might have found wholeness of spirit by other roads and other mentors. Harry's act in symbolically killing Hermine is an attempt on the part of the old, unliberated Harry to crush his own sensual nature. It is proof that he has only partly learned his lesson.

Most cult books have a socially responsible dimension that speaks to the social consciences of their readers. They are usually more than private romantic indulgences or, in the parlance of the sixties, "ego-trips." However, whereas many cult books are only superficially concerned with humanity and its spiritual health, *Steppenwolf* is one of the few cult books that can truly claim to care about the condition of modern man and the future of civilization. Harry Haller's misery is not just private misery. It is a true expression of the spiritual malaise of the times, the alienated and fragmented quality of modern life.

Someone once remarked that in a world gone sane, madness is one's only defense. On the surface, a bourgeois world is a world of sanity. There is order in the streets and domestic tranquility at home. God's in His Heaven and all's right with the world. Harry Haller looks about him at the comfortable routine of domestic existence, and although he feels nostalgia for it, he can no longer accept it. Thus, when he sees a sign that says MAGIC THEATRE; ENTRANCE NOT FOR EVERYBODY; FOR MADMEN ONLY, he tries to enter, because only madmen can make any sense out of a bourgeois world. Cult readers responded to this idea enthusiastically.

In the sixties, when middle America was a society of "button-down minds," the young Steppenwolves, wearing serapes and headbands, their hair long and unwashed, a fanatic gleam in their bloodshot eyes, longed to escape the bondage of the bourgeois, and it was through Harry Haller's redemption that they found a way. Until Haller reads the pamphlet titled "Treatise on the Steppenwolf," he has always thought of himself as a double personality: man and wolf, the civilized human being and the freedom-loving outlaw from society. So great is this inner tension that Haller has often been on the point of taking his life, and indeed is able to keep on living only because he has promised himself the luxury of committing suicide on his fiftieth birthday. This suffering, nevertheless, marks him as a superior being set apart from the ordinary run of human beings; he is the type from which spring artists, intellectuals, and social critics.

After reading the treatise, however, Haller realizes that he is wrong in supposing that he is a twofold person. All men, he learns, have manifold personalities, and the common notion that each of us is a single ego is quite false. The road to enlightenment, or the "way of the immortals," is to surrender the idea of a central ego, to accept the multiplicity within us, and to expand the soul until it includes nothing less than everything. The best way to this condition is through laughter, the one force that embraces all the polarities of life and at the same time transcends them.

It is to be assumed that this treatise could only have been written by one of the "immortals" themselves, since no one else could assume such a lofty point of view. In the novel, this treatise reads like holy writ, and it is no trouble at all for cult readers to make the leap of faith required to deem it so. This done, there is no obstacle to prevent them from becoming one of the immortals. To do so, however, requires certain symbolic rites of passage that will remove them from the clutches of the bourgeois.

Harry Haller has such an experience when he runs into an old acquaintance, a professor of comparative folklore with whom he once studied. What happens is a confrontation that spoke directly to the disaffected students of the sixties. Harry accepts an invitation to dine with the professor and his wife, but the meal is painful. Harry is forced to behave courteously and exchange social lies with his host and hostess. Worse still, the professor, who is a right-wing nationalist, proceeds to attack a newspaper article denouncing the Kaiser that Haller wrote under a pseudonym. Never dreaming that his guest is the author, the professor holds the article up to ridicule. Haller can stand it no longer; he declares angrily that he is tired of keeping up a polite pretense, that he is the author of the offending article, that he cares nothing for the professor, his scholarship, or his politics. Calling himself a schizophrenic who is no longer fit for human society, Haller storms out, relieved; the lone wolf in him has decisively triumphed over the bourgeois. One can still hear the cries of exultation that arose from the throats of devoted readers eager to throw off the yoke of a stultifying professoriat.

Cult readers also respond to the way Hermine gets Harry to loosen up and enjoy the pleasures of the flesh and of contemporary music. He meets a girl named Maria, who becomes his mistress, and a saxophonist named Pablo, a handsome young man with a languorous, caressing manner and no morals, a versatile sensualist with extensive experience in both sex and drugs, who generously puts himself at Harry's disposal for either purpose. Pablo's ideas about music are of special interest to modern cult readers because they place all music on the same plane, distinguishing only between good and bad performances. His sole object, says Pablo, is to play as well as he can and to give pleasure to his hearers, whatever their taste.

But it is the psychedelic climax of the novel that removes the last vestiges of doubt from the minds of any would-be cult readers. It begins with a fancy-dress ball and continues on to the magic theater, and it contains everything from cross-dressing and sexual ambiguity to drug-induced, "mind-blowing" hallucinations. After the dance, Pablo invites Harry and Hermine to his quarters for a little entertainment. It is, he explains, for madmen only, and the price of admission is Harry's mind. At last, Haller is to enter the magic theater that he has repeatedly heard of. The ticket of admission is one of Pablo's narcotic preparations: opium or hashish.

When all three have come under its influence, Pablo holds up to Haller's gaze a small mirror in which Haller sees himself in a double vision, as a man whose features blend with those of a shy, beautiful, dazed wolf with smoldering, frightened eyes. This is Haller as he has hitherto known himself. Next Pablo leads him into a theater corridor where there is a full-length wall mirror. Standing before it, Harry sees himself in a hundred forms: as child, adolescent, mature man, and oldster, solemn and merry, variously dressed, and quite naked. One form, an elegant young man, embraces Pablo. Turning from the mirror, Haller walks down the corridor, off which there open dozens of doors, each with an inscription like a penny peep show, promising a different diversion within.

Each of these doors offers the fulfillment of a thwarted or unrecognized aspect of Haller's personality. Harry goes through a sequence of bizarre experiences climaxing in the symbolic murder of Hermine and culminating in his appearance before a dozen robed judges who, instead of sentencing him to death, as he expects, condemn him to "eternal life." Then all but Harry laugh, and Harry is left feeling he still has much to learn about how to live but promising himself that he will work at it and one day even learn to laugh.

No wonder Hesse's hypnotic novel lent its name to a popular sixties rock group!

FOR FURTHER READING

Costa, Richard Hauer. "The Man Who Would Be Steppenwolf." *South Central Bulletin* (Winter 1982): 125–27.

Delphendahl, Renate. "Narcissism and the Double in Hermann Hesse's *Steppenwolf. Journal of Evolutionary Psychology* (March 1988): 141–53; (August 1988): 208–17.

Shear, Walter. "*Steppenwolf* and *Seize the Day*." *Saul Bellow Journal* (Fall 1981): 32–34.

Spoerl, Linda Bell. *The Methods of Madness: Insanity as Metaphor in Five Modern Novels. DAI* 4 (1984): 3379a.

Tusken, Lewis W. "The Question of Perspective in Hesse's *Steppenwolf*." *Journal of Evolutionary Psychology* (March 1989): 157–65.

The Stranger

Albert Camus
(1942)

In *The Closing of the American Mind,* Allan Bloom maintains that *The Stranger* is possibly the only novel in recent times that modern students can relate to. He attributes this phenomenon to the fact that the book's antihero, Meursault, has freed himself of the obligation to care about others, to feel anything, to do more than sustain himself in a series of small pleasures. He has no large appetites, makes no large demands on others, asks nothing but to be left alone. Even though Meursault's impulsive murder of an Arab sounds like the hysterical outburst of a repressed personality, this act of violence is treated like a temporary aberration to cult readers who prefer the side of Meursault that is utterly indifferent to whatever is going on around him. What they admire is his "cool," his detachment, his aloofness, his attitude that says "No big deal" to the things that bother most people.

Modernism has been defined as neither a continuation of the past nor a rebellion against it but rather an attitude of total indifference to it. This could be a description of Meursault's personality. He lives totally in the present, blissfully unaware of the past and completely unconcerned about the future. What cult readers admire in this attitude is Meursault's perception of history as nothing but bad news. Santayana's injunction to know the past in order not to repeat its mistakes is ludicrous to those who suspect that knowledge is temptation and that the repetition of history is not a matter of ignorance but of instinct.

When *The Stranger* appeared in English in 1946, readers could only look back with anger at nearly two decades of depression and war—and before that more war and more poverty and more repression, slavery, sweat shops, disease, madness, and early death. History seemed to be nothing less than a record of man's immense foolishness, and since up until then knowing it seemed only to make matters worse, the lesson was clear: Ignore it. And as for the future, it was pretty clear to anyone that the less you bothered with it, the less you tempted fate. The less you tried to change things, it seemed, the better off you were. The idea was to take life a day at a time and live it without asking too much of it.

It sounded pretty good to all who were listening, except for that sour note when Meursault snapped and in the twinkling of an eye changed from a laid-back, easy-going, nice guy, aloof but eager to please, to an overwrought murderer firing five bullets into the body of an Arab on a deserted stretch of beach under a blinding sun. Conveniently for the reader, Camus makes it possible to downplay the actual murder in favor of the travesty of justice that sends Meursault to the guillotine.

By making a mockery of the trial in which more questions are asked about Meursault's callousness at his mother's funeral than about the murder itself, readers can interpret the murder as merely a device to get Meursault into court in order to expose the corruption of a system that convicts on character rather than on evidence. The fact that Meursault happens to be guilty only makes the whole procedure more ludicrous. Of course, it also makes the existential point that because death is inevitable, it really does not matter how we die or what we die for.

Although *The Stranger* has overtones of such enduring myths as that of the lotus-eater or the alien, both of whom want to be left alone, and while it also echoes the Oblomov myth of the superfluous man, it comes closest to drawing upon the modern myth of the man who is mysteriously driven to commit a "gratuitous act." The concept of the gratuitous act (*acte gratuit*) was advanced by André Gide who writes of it so chillingly in *Lafcadio's Adventures* (*Les Caves du Vatican*). Gide concludes that the gratuitous act is not traceable to common motives such as love, hate, or self-interest, but is motivated solely by a personal need to assert one's individuality, and is thus the only human act that reveals one's essential character. There is a morbid purity to such an act that appeals, at least in the abstract, to cult readers bored with the inexorable laws of cause and effect.

While ordinary readers may see Meursault as something of a manic-depressive, too unemotional early in the novel, too emotional later, cult readers see him as a victim of a repressive society that would rather convict him for bad manners than for murder. Because he does not cry at his mother's funeral, because he is not sure of her age or even what day she died, because he put her in a nursing home in the first place, he is guilty of insensitivity and of disrespect for society. And these transgressions are compounded by the fact that when he returns home after his mother's funeral, it is no time at all before he is going to the movies—and then to bed—with his girlfriend, Marie.

At his trial, Meursault remains indifferent to what is going on around him, even chastising himself at times for not taking more interest. He seems not to care what will happen to him, although he confesses in moments of weakness to feeling a rush of joy at the prospect of an acquittal. Nevertheless, his attitude continues to be largely one of amused detachment. What, he asks, do these people think they are up to, condemning me to death as if they themselves are going to live forever? Don't they realize that we are all under sentence of death, that it is merely a matter of time before we must die? "I could see," he says, "that it makes little difference whether one dies at the age of thirty or threescore and ten [for] whether I died now or forty years hence, this business of dying had to be got through, inevitably." Why then, he wonders, do some gloat and others despair when death occurs, daring to feel sorry when their sorrow is ultimately only for themselves? "Once you're up against it," he concludes, "the precise manner of your death has obviously small importance" (143).

Meursault's pleasures are largely passive ones. There is nothing he enjoys more than just sitting on the balcony of his apartment, smoking cigarettes and watching the life of the neighborhood pass before him. When others make demands on him, he acquiesces as far as possible, less out of charity than out of indifference. He avoids involvement, unable to understand why people make such a fuss about trivial matters.

Critics of the book find his attitude deplorable, calling it unfeeling and self-centered, even cruel. Actually, however, he is caught between the religious attitude that places no value on earthly life, other than as a testing ground for eternity, and his own suspicion that life has pleasures enough if one's demands are modest. It is obvious that he enjoys his daily routine, that he expects little of life and enjoys what he gets. But it also seems as if he holds back, not because he really does not care, but because he is afraid to care too much. For when you care too much, when you give in to your emotions, you lose control, as he most certainly does when he shoots the Arab or loses his temper with the prison chaplain.

Camus is considered a leading voice among existentialist writers, for much of his work reflects the existential insistence on self-discovered values based on personal experience over secondhand values taken from vicarious experience. However, Camus himself refuted much of the existential platform, and it diminishes him, or any other writer of great vision, to interpret him so narrowly. That he appealed to the fashion for existentialism in the fifties is indisputable, and that he continues to speak to those who prefer to forge their own morality is one reason for his continuing popularity. But Meursault touches a deeper nerve, one more representative of the *Zeitgeist* of the latter half of the twentieth century.

What Meursault appeals to, in the final analysis, is the rich vein of narcissism that has come to characterize the dark side of the modern psyche. Whereas it is only harmlessly self-indulgent to like to swim and go to movies and make love to Marie, it is narcissistic to commit murder with only the slightest provocation and then jeer at those who demand your life in exchange, accusing them of convicting you for the wrong reasons when the world would call it only fair. Unless the killing of the Arab can be justified, the magnitude of the act refutes all that has preceded it in terms of an enviable lifestyle. Obviously, Meursault is *not* cool, *not* in control, *not* charmingly indifferent. Rather, he is an emotional time bomb, symptomatic of a syndrome that has become almost commonplace.

Cult readers, however, brush Meursault's outburst aside or dismiss it as "temporary insanity." What they respond to is his sublime detachment. In a world in which honor students go "wilding" through Central Park, clubbing joggers with lead pipes, a world in which tourists get mugged and murdered in subway stations so that gang members may go dancing, Meursault's detachment is a very attractive stance, indeed. How tempting is the life of small pleasures and no strong commitments. How nice to sit on the sidelines and watch, or look the other way. How comforting not to feel too intensely, not to care too much, not to put oneself at the risk of being hurt. And, ultimately, how gratifying to feel superior to all those people out there who are slavishly following other people's rules, living secondhand lives, obeying meaningless rules, all those people who think they are immortal and that death is a punishment they have the right to inflict, blindly unaware that their turn is coming, all those people who with both their mockery and their tears are really only laughing at or crying for themselves.

Because Meursault tells his own story in *The Stranger*, all we know about him or about what happens to him is what he tells us. It is probably a violation of literary manners to wonder why he bothers to tell his story at all when nothing seems to matter much to him, but we certainly can wonder about the sort of reality he invents and how much he leaves out. If someone else were telling his story, it is highly unlikely that we would become so quickly sympathetic to Meursault's eccentric personality once we are into the story—or that we would ever be sympathetic at all, for that matter.

However, because it is the nature of soft-spoken confessors to ingratiate themselves easily as long as they display no signs of self-pity, we are more likely to identify with Meursault at, say, his mother's funeral, than with those who later condemn him. In the sense that the narrator's story is our story, we are on his side until he alienates us. Many readers of this novel find Meursault attractive until he shoots the Arab. At that point they are immediately distanced and find themselves siding with his detractors.

Many women, in fact, find Meursault difficult to like from the very start, especially when his response to Marie's overtures is so unfeeling. When Marie asks him if he loves her, he tells her the question is meaningless but that he supposes he doesn't. And when she asks him why he would agree to marry her anyway, he says it is because "it would give her pleasure." Women find this selfish altruism offensive, although Meursault is more naive than calculating about it. Far from thinking of himself as "God's gift to women," he does not really think about himself at all. In fact, he is almost totally unself-reflective, and this failing alienates him from those who might otherwise come to his rescue.

Among those are the bourgeois who require only a trace of contrition, even if it is forced, in order to forgive him his seeming callousness. They feel that in the absence of true emotion, Meursault owes it to society to pretend. It is only those few who champion Meursault's cause to the end, then, who constitute a true cult following, and if Allan Bloom is right, their numbers are legion.

Another strong appeal to fans of this novel is Meursault's estrangement from those around him and from the mainstream of life in general. Regardless of what he might become guilty of later, those who identify with Meursault see him as a unique expression of alienation. Instead of being obviously different—weird, outrageous, eccentric, wild—or even an outsider in terms of race or handicap, talent, or sexual preference, Meursault is everyman. True, he lives in an Arab country, but this fact has no appreciable significance in terms of the story's theme.

Since Camus was born and raised in Algeria, setting his novels in Algeria need not be construed as a statement, and in *The Stranger* there is no hard evidence of a political or social agenda, regardless of what wishful thinkers have found. Some have tried to make something out of the suggestion of racial tension in the novel. Meursault's friend Raymond, the pimp, deals drugs with the Arabs, and Meursault's killing of an Arab seems indirectly related to this, but once the killing has taken place, Camus drops the matter entirely. In fact, he seems to take pains to show us how ordinary Meursault's life really is, how commonplace, how routine. Meursault walks through the streets, goes to the beach, rides the trolleys, and does his job without being remarkable in any way.

How then is he alienated? We can get a clearer answer to this if we look at his life from a perspective other than his own. To do this we have to sift through Meursault's testimony, as it were, to find what clues we can. What we learn is that others, when they have reason to notice, find his unemotional behavior odd, even menacing. That he cannot cry, cannot grieve, cannot care, cannot love bothers them. And the fact that he tells us this himself suggests that his inability to display emotion has less to do with any rebellion against conformity and more to do with shallowness of soul. When he boils over at the chaplain and flies into a rage in defense of his view of the world as godless and meaningless, his very anger dilutes his credibility. It is not very convincing to be passionate about passionlessness.

Meursault, then, is a stranger in a familiar rather than a strange land, a situation made all the more disturbing because he seems on the surface to fit so comfortably into his environment. But a closer examination shows him to be apart from or even at odds with just about everything around him: old Salamano, who abuses his dog; Raymond, whose friendship he finds tedious; Marie, whose love he cannot truly requite; an uninteresting job, repetitious pastimes, the indistinguishable Arabs. By using passivity to protect himself from reality, Meursault becomes the role model for people who feel safer living life at a distance. To them, Meursault's fate is not a summons to get involved while there is still time but a warning to disencumber oneself before it is too late.

Few cult books have withstood the passage of time as well as *The Stranger*. While others still have their following, often their continuing popularity can be attributed either to nostalgia or curiosity. As times change, *The Stranger* continues to have something meaningful to say to readers, continues to speak not just to them but for them. In its early days, *The Stranger* was read as a primer of existentialism regardless of whatever Camus might have intended. In the aggressive sixties, when such passivity as Meursault's would ordinarily have been anathema to counterculture revolutionaries, Meursault stood as a martyr from an earlier age of oppression, a man who became the helpless victim of a system dedicated to stifling its nonconformists, even eliminating them, given half a chance. Had he lived in the sixties, his prison would have been stormed like the Bastille.

Later, when the counterculture ardor congealed into self-indulgent consumerism, Meursault emerged as that favorite of the contemporary short story, the "minimalist moralist." He asks for too little to be called selfish, is too agreeable not to be called kind, and regardless of motive, gives of himself while others freely take. As the century lurches toward its unimaginable end, Meursault is closer to what he was at the beginning: a dispassionate man whose indifference is the true label for the uncaring attitude the world prefers to call tolerance.

FOR FURTHER READING

Makari, George J. "The Last Four Shots: Problems of Intention and Camus' *The Stranger*." *American Imago: A Psychoanalytic Journal for Culture, Science, and the Arts* (Winter 1988): 359–74.

McCarthy, Patrick. *Albert Camus*: The Stranger. Cambridge, England: Cambridge University Press, 1988.

Ohayon, Stephen. "Camus' *The Stranger*: The Sun-Metaphor and Patricidal Conflict." *American Imago: A Psychoanalytic Journal for Culture, Science, and the Arts* (Summer 1983): 189–205.

Sterling, Elwyn F. "Albert Camus: The Psychology of the Body and *The Stranger*." *The USF Language Quarterly* (Spring-Summer 1987): 11–20.

Stranger in a Strange Land

Robert Heinlein
(1961)

Science fiction historians point to the early 1960s as a period of growing acceptance of the science fiction novel as more than fantasy or speculative literature. The social criticism and astute observation of human behavior demonstrated in the best of this genre gained considerable respect during this decade, when the pulp science fiction writers were finding their voice in the longer novel. Probably the most outstanding example of the acceptance of this new voice is the cult status accorded Robert Heinlein's now legendary *Stranger in a Strange Land*. It stands with *Dune* and *A Canticle for Leibowitz* in the first rank of classic science fiction.

Heinlein's work achieved instant cult status. It was embraced enthusiastically by the frontrunners of the sexual revolution who saw it as something of a manifesto, and it contributed to the "flower child" phenomenon of the Vietnam years much as J. D. Salinger's *The Catcher in the Rye* had influenced the post–WW II generation in its discovery of universal adult "phoniness." If today *Stranger in a Strange Land* seems a bit silly, even irresponsible, it has much to do with our awareness of the tragic consequences of that sexual revolution and our consequent disillusionment with a gospel that promised unprecedented freedom and joy. However, Heinlein's landmark book, despite its overwriting and its self-conscious style, remains an important part of both the history of science fiction and the history of cult literature.

In *Stranger in a Strange Land*, Valentine Michael Smith, as a Martian, is totally alienated from life on Earth. Even when he learns the customs of the planet, he remains essentially alienated by virtue of his incredible mental powers. And when he becomes the leader of his own religious movement, he assumes the roles of teacher and prophet, and ultimately scapegoat. The possibility of the existence of someone so totally different, so wonderfully unique, encourages cult followers to see alienation as a sign of superiority and thus an attitude to be adopted.

Valentine Michael Smith's discovery of sex as a means to the full realization of brotherhood and understanding helped make *Stranger in a Strange Land* a cult favorite. Just as *Demian* gives permission to indulge in drinking and drugs, Heinlein's book gives the green light to sexual indulgence and promiscuity on one condition. The book places no restrictions on the varieties of sexual experience permissible as long as the participants are what Heinlein calls "water brothers." Water brothers are those who possess full understanding of themselves, each other, and the universe. They "grok," as Smith puts it. "God groks," he says, and adds, "All that groks is God." The upshot of this syllogism is "Thou art God." Being God puts any "water brother" (i.e., cult follower) above the law.

Believing this, cult followers are free to behave according to their own rules. It is easy to see how such thinking could lead to the anarchy that reverberated through the sixties. Modification of behavior according to the lifestyle advocated in *Stranger in a Strange Land* found its most extreme expression in the Charles Manson cult, where sexual license was rampant, regard for law nonexistent, and murder not only condoned but exalted.

Because he is culture-free, Smith is able to explore unorthodox sensuality and sexuality free of the inhibition and guilt that plague ordinary mortals. The joy of his discoveries is also powerful enough to free others from their hang-ups (even his mentor, Jubal Harshaw), so they create a mystical new religion. But Heinlein undermines his myth with the mocking cynicism of the Reverend Foster, a fraudulent evangelist given to saying, "Certainly 'Thou art God'—but who isn't?" The creed of the new religion is nothing special in the cosmic scheme of things. This self-mockery comes a little late to counter Mike's simplistic message of free love and the power to dispel all earthly problems simply by correct comprehension, but to cult readers Foster is the self-mocking voice of the establishment, a figure whose cynicism is seen as sour grapes.

As a rule, cult books avoid overtly sexual matters, their main characters being either sexless or sexually ambiguous. Even the relationship between Meursault and Marie in *The Stranger* is oddly functional and dispassionate, no more important to Meursault than any of his other simple pleasures. The only cult figure who glorifies sexuality is Valentine Michael Smith, and his case is extraordinary. To begin with, he is a human who was born on Mars into a culture that knows nothing of sexual matters. When Smith is brought to Earth, he is sexually innocent. When at last he does learn about sex, he discovers in it the one thing that had been missing in an otherwise perfect Martian society. To him, sex is the ultimate expression of brotherhood. For persons to become what he calls "water brothers," for them to "grok" (harmonize perfectly with) one another, they must know each other sexually.

The sex in *Stranger in a Strange Land* is heterosexual, but there are no limits to its variety, nor is deviant sexuality necessarily prohibited. The implication is that it is sexuality itself that matters, not the form it takes. Even so, Smith remains a curiously asexual person himself. Perhaps it has something to do with his original innocence, which seems to cling to him even after he has discovered and exalted sexuality. His sexuality is never like that of any other male character in the book. Maybe one simply can never quite imagine him engaged in ordinary sexual relations, especially when he assumes leadership of a religious group and takes on more and more the appearance of a god. Smith is described in terms of androgynous beauty. He is slim and fair and smooth-skinned, well-built but not muscular, good-looking but not pretty. Both men and women find him attractive, and he gets along with both equally well.

Much of Valentine Michael Smith's special attraction stems from his unique background and upbringing. Smith is the child of two astronauts whose expedition to Mars ends in disaster. Smith, the only survivor, is raised by Martians until soon after he has reached manhood, when another expedition from Earth "rescues" him. No sooner is he back on Earth than he finds himself mixed up in a complex legal battle over who "owns" Mars. The governments of Earth, having just recovered from World War III, have joined together in an uneasy federation whose secretary general, the Honorable Joseph Edgerton Douglas, keeps Smith sequestered in a hospital where he languishes in a comatose state. One day Jill Boardman, a nurse, brings Smith a glass of water, and since to Smith the sharing of water denotes a sacred bond of friendship, Smith tells Jill that the two of them are bound together for life. Jill then sneaks Smith out of the hospital and takes him to the secluded estate of Jubal E. Harshaw, described as "bon vivant, gourmet, sybarite, popular author extraordinary, and neo-pessimist philosopher."

Harshaw spends his days churning out potboilers from soap operas to screenplays, assisted by a trio of secretaries blessed with total recall who act as tape recorders as he dictates script after script with no apparent need to edit. When the sinister forces of the Federation try to recapture Smith, Harshaw's retreat provides reasonable protection, but his chief weapon against intruders is his ability to "discorporate" people, a process that removes a person totally from the face of the Earth and into an alternate time zone. Forced to negotiate, Douglas agrees to hold a conference with Harshaw, whose interest in Smith is solely humanitarian. This conference results in an agreement that allows Smith to explore the planet Earth without interference.

The exploration of Earth takes up most of the rest of the novel, during which there is a great deal of "water-sharing," particularly with one of Harshaw's stenographers who initiates Smith into sex. It is in this section that we learn about "grokking," a form of communication in which two people comprehend each other's meaning so completely that a psychic bonding occurs. At one point, Smith says to Jubal: "Thou art God," but Jubal refuses to accept the nomination.

"You can't refuse it," says Smith. "Thou art God and I am God and all that groks is God, and I am all that I have ever been or seen or felt or experienced. I am all that I grok. Father, I saw the horrible shape this planet is in and I grokked, though not in fullness, that I could change it. What I had to teach couldn't be taught in schools; I was forced to smuggle it in as a religion—which it is not—and con the marks into tasting it by appealing to their curiosity. . . . Male-femaleness is the greatest gift we have--romantic physical love may be unique to this planet. If it is, the universe is a poorer place than it could be . . . and I grok dimly that we-who-are-God will save this precious invention and spread it" (397).

Thus, the Harshaw estate becomes a utopian paradise of sexual initiation and spiritual joy, but the day comes when Smith, seduced by what he sees on television, decides that it is time for him to go out into the world.

When his time to leave the protective environment of Harshaw's estate arrives, Smith first joins a sideshow of carnival types for whom "bilking the mark" is a way of life—and a new lesson in human nature for Smith. He is particularly taken by the greatest confidence game of all, the Fosterite movement, an evangelical television enterprise organized by the Reverend Doctor Daniel Digby. This undertaking is so successful that even the prayer sessions are sponsored by commercial companies. The self-ordained Reverend Foster is described as having an instinct for the pulse of his times stronger than that of a skilled carnie sizing up a mark. His assessment of American culture was one that cult readers recognized. To him the culture known as "America" had a split personality throughout its history. Its laws were puritanical; its covert behavior tended to be Rabelaisian; its major religions were Apollonian; its revivals were almost Dionysian. In the twentieth century, nowhere on Earth was sex so vigorously suppressed, and nowhere was there such deep interest in it.

Impressed with the success of the Fosterites, Smith starts his own "religion" of free love, "grokking," and total abandonment of guilt—a movement that gradually draws converts from the Fosterites and precipitates a showdown. A violent confrontation occurs, but by this time Smith's followers have so completely mastered the telekinetic arts and the notions of immortality Smith has taught them that they happily assume that Smith has joined the Martian "Old Ones" and, like the archangel after whom he is named, will watch over human progress from above. They are right. The final scene finds Foster (the namesake of the Fosterite church), Digby, and Smith in a Martian "heaven," busily making plans for the preservation of Earth.

Throughout the novel there are references to Smith as godlike. One character calls Smith Prometheus, and Jubal finds the label fitting. "Prometheus paid a high price for bringing fire to mankind," he says. "Don't think that Mike doesn't! He pays with twenty-four hours of work every day, seven days a week, trying to teach us how to play with matches without getting burned" (369). What really sets him apart is simply the extraordinary circumstances of his upbringing. He can innocently watch the strange land of his adopted planet, a "stranger" to the motivations lying beneath the surface, because he is not a participant in the collective unconscious that brings characters together. "Alien" in outlook rather than biology, despite his organically human makeup, Smith goes through his experiences feeling very little of the emotions that move other characters forward and backward. As such he ultimately resists classification in any recognizable category. To him all lands would be strange, and he would always be a stranger in them.

Utopian literature, of which this is an example, automatically presents a series of ideals to which the human species should aspire. Inevitably these ideals include international peace, freedom from guilt and false accusation, understanding of all human impulses, and collective existence based on mutual respect for individual life within limited variety. By placing Smith on Mars during his formative years, however—literally alienating him—Heinlein is denying any opportunity to suggest that the utopian ideals are in fact attainable given human conditions as the reader knows them.

Heinlein is a pessimist in that he maintains that the necessary conditions for utopian life do not prevail on Earth but can only be imagined by a unique human being who has *not* been crushed by Earth experiences in his youth. The book's central theme does not advocate improvement, and certainly is not a call to action. Rather, it is an admission, even an accusation, that human beings are incapable of extricating themselves from the tangle of experiences that prevent true heroes from coming forward. If Smith had not learned his tricks of teleportation and discorporation, he would not have survived the cruelties of human society. Instead, he would have become another victim of the species' natural tendency to destroy all innocence.

As a result of Heinlein's decision to place the utopian possibilities in the realm of science fiction, none of the novel's strengths are derived from hope. In Ayn Rand's fiction, for example, the reader is introduced to possible heroic conduct, however slanted it may be toward the free enterprise system. In Heinlein's work, the hero is an impossibility; therefore, the "heaven" Heinlein constructs lies beyond the reader's grasp. Incidental themes, such as free love and universal brotherhood, are diluted because no amount of effort can achieve the ideals described.

The neopessimism of Harshaw is nothing more than the Heinleinian observation that 99 percent of the world is frittered away in the effort to survive its own chaos. To advance, human beings must be instructed from a distance. Since the solutions to the immoral world as depicted by Heinlein are no more accessible by human endeavor than Mars is accessible by rocket, the author is free to disregard any impediment to his plan, giving to Smith and his converts any powers he believes will drive home his major theme: that the world is drowning in its own folly.

Heinlein's work follows the traditions of every utopian writer since Sir Thomas More. So-called scientific utopias suggested in fictional form by H. G. Wells, Jules Verne, and Isaac Asimov either state or intimate that the advances of technology would eventually bring about the ideal social state. Heinlein's novel, in true neopessimistic fashion, warns that the habits of human behavior must also undergo drastic changes before technology can solve world problems. Prophetic in several respects, Heinlein's novel foresees the devastating power of television evangelism, a clear model of how high technology serves, rather than alters, human impulse. An example even more frightening is the case of Charles Manson, a mass-murderer who cited this novel as his model for building a cult of adoring servant women who shared his crimes. What appears in the novel as a bucolic "grokking" and sharing of pleasures is transformed by madness into bloody orgies and mindless obedience.

Perhaps the truth about the novel's influence lies in Jubal's reference to Jill's "invincible innocence that makes it impossible for her to be immoral" and his confession that the rest of us fall miserably short of such an idea. "Ben," he says, "I am afraid that you—and I, too—lack the angelic innocence to practice the perfect morality those people live by. . . . Yes, I think what those people—the entire Nest, not just our kids—are doing is moral. I haven't examined details but–*yes*, all of it. Bacchanalia, unashamed swapping, communal living and anarchistic code, everything" (345). Everything, in fact, that appealed to the liberated youth of the sixties.

FOR FURTHER READING

Franklin, H. Bruce. *Robert A. Heinlein: America as Science Fiction*. New York: Oxford University Press, 1980.

Pielke, Robert G. "Grokking the Stranger." In *Philosophers Look at Science Fiction*. Chicago: Nelson-Hall, 1982, 153–63.

Pringle, David. *Science Fiction: the 100 Best Novels*. New York: Carroll & Graf, 1985.

Smith, Curtis C., ed. *Twentieth Century Science-Fiction Writers*. New York: St. Martin's, 1981.

Stover, Leon E. *Robert A. Heinlein*. Boston: Twayne, 1987.

The Sun Also Rises

Ernest Hemingway
(1926)

Ernest Hemingway, like F. Scott Fitzgerald, became such a cult figure himself that it is sometimes difficult to separate the novels from the celebrity who wrote them and whose personality continues to overshadow them. *The Sun Also Rises*, Hemingway's first and many say his best novel, was an immediate success both critically and commercially. It was also an instant cult book, partly because it was taken to be the definitive statement about the legendary "lost generation."

Hemingway resented that label and refused to accept it as descriptive of the age or of the characters in his novels. Although it was certainly true that some of his characters had lost their moorings, Hemingway saw something steadfast, even heroic, in the stoicism of Jake Barnes and in the code of honor he quietly subscribed to. It was a code that bullfighters lived and fought by, and Hemingway saw it as the only way to live life with dignity and integrity in a world of chaos and disorder. This code could be summed up in Hemingway's definition of "guts": "grace under pressure."

However, as much as cult readers could appreciate the stoic virtues of Jake Barnes as opposed to the strident boorishness of Robert Cohn, the bigotry of Mike Campbell, or the irresponsibility of Lady Brett, they were more likely to respond to the quality of romantic doom that a phrase like "lost generation" suggests. This was as true in the fifties, when the book enjoyed an enthusiastic revival, as it had been in the twenties, when the book was new. To cult readers of the twenties, Jake Barnes was a symbol of the disillusionment brought on by the "war to end all wars." Although never one to complain about his lot, he suffers severe emotional and spiritual damage from the war wound that emasculated him. And when he weeps in the night, it is for a life forever diminished, a life made bearable only through the pain of endurance: in short, through suffering.

The only difference between Jake Barnes and Johann Wolfgang von Goethe's Werther is that Jake has better manners. Far from wearing his heart on his sleeve, he behaves with dignity and reserve, noble behavior that only made him more appealing to contemporary readers who had come to view displays of emotion with skepticism and suspicion. Impotence, disillusionment, occasional bouts of despair: these were the lot of those whose youth had been blighted in the trenches of the war ironically called "great." Their war wounds, both physical and psychological, were the badge of courage that separated them from the others.

It is not just Jake's war wound that makes him different from Robert and Mike and the rest of the crowd he runs around with in Europe. It is also his having been part of the war itself, part of the first generation of Americans ever to fight a European war, part of that generation of Americans and Europeans that was plunged from the golden innocence of the Edwardian twilight into the nightmare of the war and then asked to pick up the pieces and put the world back together. Men like Jake Barnes wondered where a man dehumanized and demoralized by war was supposed to find the courage and compassion with which to rebuild the world, to bring order out of chaos, to assure liberty and justice for all.

Those who survived World War II read *The Sun Also Rises* in much the same way and asked many of the same questions, and this helps to account for the novel's renewed popularity in the fifties. But this time around, it was more than the novel's philosophy of serene stoicism, of "grace under pressure" that attracted readers. To a new generation, Paris in the twenties was itself a heightened reality, and many of those who devoured the novel dreamed of reinventing that reality in the Paris of the fifties. As with *The Great Gatsby*, Hemingway's "moveable feast" exerted a powerful attraction on those who, looking back, saw the twenties as a golden age and longed to bring it back. Inevitably, all attempts to recreate the twenties in the fifties failed, but the dream of being an "American in Paris" refused to die. Young people, mostly artists, flocked there and, when the time came, crossed the Pyrenees into Spain to run with the bulls at Pamplona, drink wine from a *bota*, and search for the camaraderie they imagined had existed among the aimless dreamers who swarmed around Lady Brett.

Cult readers read for reasons that are peculiarly their own, with an utter disregard for the opinion of critics. Whereas critics may find, in a five-day fishing trip in the Pyrenees or a week-long *corrida* at Pamplona, existential answers to questions about the purpose of life, cult readers are more likely to view such excursions as escapes from the need to think about such questions. While critics analyze the dynamics of the bullfight, the fearlessness of the matadors, the blood lust of the spectators, the whole psychology of "death in the afternoon," cult readers prefer to immerse themselves in the experience for its own sake. To them, if there is "death in the afternoon," at least it has come after experiencing the most profound sense of being alive.

The post–WW I generation was existential in the most fundamental sense of the word. To them the meaning of life was to be found in the living of it. Living was meaning. And it was the reality of death, so palpably present in the bullring, that gave life its intensity. These survivors did not have to seek for meaning, for meaning was not something you could "find"; rather it was something you could only "feel," and the imminence of death only heightened that feeling.

Cult readers can stand back and admire Pedro Romero for killing three bulls after having had his face smashed in by Robert Cohn, for not only has he felt intensely and therefore really lived but he has also survived to fight another day. Outside the ring Romero is a foolish figure, so easily manipulated by Lady Brett and so easily overwhelmed by Cohn. Lady Brett tosses him back into the ring, as it were, after engaging him in a rather seedy erotic encounter. But in the bull ring, face to face with death, he assumes a grandeur that transcends the tawdriness of his escapade with Lady Brett. She might touch him, but she cannot tarnish the splendor of his lonely journey through the valley of the shadow of death, of his single-handed confrontation with the only reality, death, of his solitary "moment of truth." It is fairly heady stuff, romantic, exhilarating, and irresistible to cult readers who see through the eyes of Jake Barnes but secretly long to feel through the nerves of Pedro Romero.

Cult followers can take comfort in Jake because he provides them with an excuse for inaction, for resisting the pressure to do things they either cannot do or simply do not care to do. Jake is safely out of the fray, safely on the sidelines, involuntarily alienated and thus different from the rest whether he likes it or not. Jake seems not to like it; cult readers do. Of course, they experience his emasculation only vicariously, so the "pleasure" they take in his alienation is more an exercise in psychological masochism. At the same time it is symbolic admission of the truth that able-bodied people can come to envy disabled people the convenience of their excuse.

The concept of the *aficionado* is also something cult readers respond to in *The Sun Also Rises*. An *aficionado* is a follower whose enthusiasm surpasses admiration and approaches idolatry. A true *aficionado* understands the object of his admiration deeply and intuitively. The reason Jake is the only one of his group the Spaniards (and particularly the chauvinistic Basques) respect is that he is a true *aficionado*. Unlike most tourists—and too often American tourists–Jake does not intrude upon foreign customs, looking upon them as either "cute" or "quaint" and taking a lot of photographs or, worse, having a lot of photographs taken of himself frolicking with the natives or teasing the bulls.

Unfortunately, in spite of Jake's example, it is still possible to visit Pamplona and see the fake Jakes behaving more like Robert Cohns or even Mike Campbells, swilling cheap wine, joking loudly, gesturing crudely, and generally making pigs of themselves. (In the novel, incidentally, the scene in which Lady Brett is surrounded by drunken, loutish lechers owes much to the myth of Circe, the sorceress who turned Ulysses' men into swine.) Sometimes it is hard for Hemingway fans not to parody what they would like to emulate.

This confusion between emulation and parody extends also to the famous Hemingway style. Among cult followers there have always been a number of would-be writers who were lured into the trap of his deceptively simple style only to discover how difficult it really is to imitate successfully and how foolish it is for them to try. Precisely because it looks so easy, it is almost impossible for any writer to imitate his style without lapsing into parody. Even Hemingway himself was occasionally guilty of self-parody, especially in his later years, as in *Across the River and into the Trees*.

More recent readers would label Jake's air of detachment as "cool," in spite of his private agonies, and see him as an early expression of the benign indifference to life they find so endearing in someone like Meursault in Albert Camus's *The Stranger* or Conway in James Hilton's *Lost Horizon*. Like Meursault, Jake is struggling to maintain his emotional equilibrium in a world that has invaded his space. Both are victims, one of a fatal impulse, the other of a crippling wound, and both find solace within the privacy of their own souls, Meursault in a prison cell, Jake by a mountain stream. Finally, in the fishing scene and in the quiet resolution of the last section of the novel, Jake has everything under control. The pleasures he enjoys are not the ones calculated to incur misery, such as pleasures of the flesh invariably do, but are ones that refresh the spirit and restore the soul.

Conway in *Lost Horizon* also tolerates no claims from either his physical or emotional side. In fact, he seems to have successfully jettisoned both sides long ago and is glad to have been abducted to Shangri-La where he no longer has to pretend. As in Jake's case, it is loyalty that gets him involved where he would be better off not being involved, loyalty to others and to an unswerving code of honor. Meursault, too, does not let his friends down, even if it means getting himself into trouble. Cult readers see in all three men the sort of person they would like to have as a friend or ally or leader.

Cult literature seems to contain more than its share of men who manage to free themselves of obligations, especially obligations toward women. Werther claims he wants Lotte, yet he sets himself up for rejection and then seems to thrive on it. Conway has no passion left for anything and welcomes the chance to become the celibate High Lama of Shangri-La. Meursault makes love as if he is doing the girl a favor; a woman to him is a convenience to satisfy a biological urge. Jake is the most sympathetic, and yet his disability is a deliberate contrivance of the author's that, while it makes a strong symbolic statement, also manages to get Jake off the hook where women are concerned. Lady Brett can only spell trouble for any man; she is promiscuous and unfeeling. It takes Cohn's attack on Romero to shame her into dropping the bullfighter for his own good. She calls herself "such a bitch," and she is right. Jake knows he is better off without her; that is why it is easy to understand his reply to her at the end of the novel when she says they could have been so good together. "Yes. Isn't it pretty to think so?" he says.

This novel's underlying mythology is made so painfully obvious by Hemingway that it hardly seems worth mentioning except to say that it probably has less to do with the book's appeal to cult readers than the general sense of alienation and its accompanying self-centeredness. The occasional vague allusions to Homer's *Odyssey* do little more than tease the informed reader.

The key to the deeper myth behind this book is in the Old Testament passage from *Ecclesiastes* from which the title of the novel is taken: "Vanity of vanities; all is vanity. . . . The sun also ariseth, and the sun goeth down, and hasteneth to his place where he arose . . . and that which is done is that which shall be done: and there is no new thing under the sun." In the midst of a century of technological novelty and monumental upheaval, the reminder that nature repeats itself, that there is an endless cycle of life, and that "there is no new thing under the sun" is a powerful antidote to the frenzy, the blind ambition, and the moral bullying that thrive on chaos and disorder. To thumb one's nose at "progress" and get back to basics is heresy in a society devoted to technology and in danger of being enslaved by it. *The Sun Also Rises* had the audacity to introduce a spiritual reminder into a secular age, and with it to encourage readers to be cautious about embracing the new gods so eager to replace the old.

The characters in *The Sun Also Rises* never really change. They are powerless within the grips of their own moral stagnation, stultified by experiences that have robbed their lives of meaning or purpose. They have lost their way and are compelled to drift aimlessly like rudderless ships. What cult readers sense intuitively is the awful moral paradox that says that while war renders life meaningless, war is itself an immensely meaningful experience. It can act like a powerful drug, after which daily life seems intolerably bland. Veterans of both world wars could appreciate this and sympathize with the aimless wanderings of the characters in this novel for whom there is no substitute for the excitement they once knew and still crave.

FOR FURTHER READING

Balassi, William. "Hemingway's Iceberg: The Composition of *The Sun Also Rises*." In *Writing the American Classic*. Chapel Hill: University of North Carolina Press, 1990, 125–55.

Barnett, Louise K. "The Dialectic of Discourse in *The Sun Also Rises*." *University of Mississippi Studies in English* 8 (1990): 168–84.

Daiker, Donald. "The Affirmative Conclusion of *The Sun Also Rises*. In *Modern American Fiction: Form and Function*, ed. by Thomas Daniel Young. Baton Rouge: Louisiana State University Press, 1989, 39–56.

Lockridge, Ernest. "Primitive Emotions: A Tragedy of Revenge Called *The Sun Also Rises*." *Journal of Narrative Technique* (Winter 1990): 42–55.

Rudat, Wolfgang E. H. *A Rotten Way To Be Wounded: The Tragicomedy of* The Sun Also Rises. New York: Peter Lang, 1990.

The Teachings of Don Juan: A Yaqui Way of Knowledge

Carlos Castaneda
(1968)

Timing is an important factor in determining which books will achieve cult status, and certainly Carlos Castaneda's *The Teachings of Don Juan* was the right book at the right time. It is the first in a series of books having to do generally with Castaneda's experiences in Mexico, inducing in himself altered states of consciousness and practicing rigorous disciplines in order to achieve a heightened awareness of reality and a deeper perception of his own innermost self.

Specifically, it is the account of the five years Castaneda spent as a "sorcerer's apprentice" to don Juan, during which time don Juan taught him the uses of peyote, jimson weed, and other hallucinogenic plants to open the doors of perception. Don Juan's purpose was to initiate his pupil into the ways of achieving awareness and mastery of a world of "nonordinary reality" completely beyond the concepts of Western civilization and to start him on the strange and frightening journey one must undertake in order to become "a man of knowledge."

Followers of the cult of Castaneda devoured each book the moment it appeared, but this first one remains the most provocative, the one most likely to captivate readers and turn them into believers.

The timing was right because 1968 was the year when a succession of unpleasant world events gave flower children all the excuse they needed to follow the advice of Pied Piper Timothy Leary and "tune in, turn on, and drop out." Although experimentation with all sorts of drugs was already widespread, the experimenters were finding that without some sort of direction, the results ranged from disappointing to deadly. What they needed was someone who could lend authority to drug use, prescribe a regimen, lay down some laws, and even add some sweat to the effort so that it all seemed well earned and worth it once the result was achieved. Castaneda gave them all of this and more. The "more" included an exotic locale: the dry hilly wastes of Sonora in northwestern Mexico; the use of peyote, the legendary loco weed of cowboy legend; and, best of all, a real live authentic guru in the form of a wise and wizened Mexican Indian of the Yaqui tribe named, of all things, don Juan.

This venerable old white-haired Indian is described as a possessor of "secret knowledge," in Spanish a *brujo*, a word meaning medicine man, curer, witch, sorcerer. It connotes essentially a person who has extraordinary, usually evil, powers, but in the case of don Juan, the evil exists only if one "abuses" (in the old-fashioned sense) the peyote. At the time of his encounter with don Juan, Castaneda was a graduate student in anthropology at UCLA, gathering information on peyote and the medicinal herbs used by the Indians in Sonora. When he first went there, he had no idea that he would devote the next several years to an attempt to plumb the secrets of the teachings of this Yaqui Indian from Sonora, an old man in his seventies known to be a *brujo*.

As Castaneda describes it, it was never an easy process, for above all else it demanded monumental patience. Frequently, he was obliged to sit in one spot for several hours, oblivious to discomfort, or he might have to wait weeks or months before don Juan deigned to communicate with him. Explanations were rarely forthcoming, and when they were, they were usually as enigmatic as the pronouncements of the notorious oracle at Delphi. Castaneda says that he had known don Juan for a whole year before the old Indian took him into his confidence. On that momentous occasion, don Juan explained that he possessed a certain knowledge that he had learned from a teacher, or "benefactor" as he called him, who had directed him, in a kind of apprenticeship. Don Juan then explained that he had, in turn, chosen Castaneda to serve as *his* apprentice, warning him that he would have to make a very deep commitment and that the training was long and arduous.

On his way to a "separate reality," Carlos Castaneda submits himself to a great deal of suffering in order to purge his body and purify his soul and thereby acquire power over that reality. Cult readers respond enthusiastically to rigorous and painful self-discipline if it leads to control, and no other book matches the Castaneda books for self-inflicted pain. The most noticeable feature of all his books, particularly this first one, is Castaneda's repeated references to the excruciating discomfort he endures in order to attain higher levels of consciousness. He sits for hours in a cold, cramped position, he abuses his stomach with mysterious concoctions; he vomits, runs wild, soils himself.

And all this physical punishment is nothing compared to the way he torments his mind. Since suffering has commonly been associated with goodness in most religions, it is easy to conclude that the more one suffers, the more virtuous one is, or the closer to a virtuous state one gets. It is this same concept that motivates the "no pain, no gain" generation to strain for that "jogger's high."

Castaneda's "high," however, is of the old-fashioned variety, the effect of substances ingested—or as the next generation would say, "abused." Separately and on different occasions, don Juan used three hallucinogenic plants: peyote, Jimson weed, and a mushroom. Because of their special properties, these plants have been widely employed for healing, for witchcraft, and for attaining a state of ecstasy. In the specific context of his teachings, don Juan relates the use of Jimson weed and mushroom to the acquisition of power, a power he refers to as an "ally." The use of peyote he relates to the acquisition of wisdom, or what he calls the knowledge of the right way to live.

As far as don Juan is concerned, the importance of the plants lies in their capacity to produce stages of peculiar perception in a human being. Thus, for the purpose of unfolding and validating his knowledge, don Juan guides Castaneda into experiencing a sequence of these stages. Castaneda calls them "states of nonordinary reality," a phrase meaning unusual reality as opposed to the ordinary reality of everyday life. The distinction is based on the inherent meaning of the states of nonordinary reality. In the context of don Juan's knowledge, nonordinary is no less real than ordinary reality; it is just different.

Castaneda's own way of testing the validity of his excursions into nonordinary reality was to wait several days after the experience to set it down, thereby reducing the chance that what he had experienced was no more than a particularly vivid dream. He felt that if he could recollect it in tranquility, so to speak, treat it calmly and objectively, its reality would be more convincing.

Although Castaneda is impressed by his old Yaqui mentor and treats him with great deference, his interest seems to be more in the drugs than in the man. He values don Juan's instruction as a necessary entrance into this new world of experience, but he values even more the experience itself. What endeared Castaneda to cult readers was the seriousness with which he approached the ingestion of the drugs don Juan was supplying him. He was ostensibly not interested in simply getting high, an accusation that rankled serious drug takers in the sixties. What he wanted most was what his readers wanted most: to experience a higher level of perception, a heightened reality, to find out if drugs really could induce superior spiritual states and higher levels of wisdom and understanding.

Castaneda admits that he first became interested in don Juan because the old man was rumored to be "very learned about plants, especially peyote." The whole attempt to systematize the teachings and the experience, no matter how painstakingly done, reads like an attempt to rationalize a highly questionable experience. After four years, Castaneda says he is still a beginner! Even so, Castaneda persists in legitimatizing don Juan by devoting the entire last half of the book to a structural analysis of his teachings. Throughout, Castaneda insists that don Juan's teachings constitute a system of logical thought that makes sense when examined on its own terms rather than by a set of objective criteria, and that the system was devised to guide an apprentice to a level of conceptualization that explains the order of the phenomena he has experienced. There is a fair amount of circular reasoning here (it takes a drug trip to understand a drug trip, but the experience justifies the experience), but believers who had already sliced peyote buttons were in no condition to split hairs.

The concept of being one of "the chosen" has great appeal to cult readers, for it reinforces their egos to believe that they are above—or at least apart from—the common herd. In don Juan's scheme of things, a person who is singled out is called the *escogido*, "the one who was chosen." To be the *escogido* means more than to be a mere apprentice. The *escogido*, by the sheer act of being selected by a power, is considered already to be different from ordinary men in that he is the recipient of a minimum amount of power that is supposed to be augmented by learning.

The *escogido* has freedom to seek a path. Having the freedom to choose is not incongruous with the lack of freedom to innovate; these two ideas are not in opposition, nor do they interfere with each other. Freedom to seek a path refers to the liberty to choose among different possibilities of action that are equally effective and usable. The criterion for choosing is the advantage of one possibility over others based on one's preference. As a matter of fact, the freedom to choose a path imparts a sense of direction through the expression of personal inclinations.

The idea that the *escogido* has an ally is perhaps the single most important theme in don Juan's teachings, for it is the only one that is indispensable to explaining what a man of knowledge is. Having an ally makes a man of knowledge different from ordinary men. An ally is a power that allows one to transcend the realm of ordinary reality. Again, the question is begged, but this time the begging takes one of two forms: (a) a man of knowledge is one who has an ally, and one who has an ally is a man of knowledge, or (b) the goal of a man of knowledge is to know how to obtain an ally, but one has to obtain an ally in order to become a man of knowledge. However, since an ally is some sort of hallucinogen anyway, circular reasoning is the only way to rationalize its use.

There are two allies: *yerba del diablo* (devil's weed) contained in Jimson weed and *humo*, possibly *Psilocybe mexicana*, contained in a mushroom.

Yerba del diablo is considered to be woman-like and a giver of superfluous power. It makes one possessive, violent,and unpredictable and has deleterious side effects. The second ally, *humo*, is considered to be male-like and the giver of ecstasy. It makes one dispassionate, gentle, and predictable and has beneficial side effects. The ally contained in *yerba* is believed to be an extraordinary helper, but the ally contained in *humo* is considered to be an even more extraordinary helper.

The way the *escogido* can know whether or not he has experienced nonordinary reality is by means of "special consensus." In don Juan's teachings, special consensus means tacit or implicit agreement on the component elements of nonordinary reality that he, in his capacity as teacher, gives the *escogido* as the apprentice of his knowledge. This special consensus is not in any way fraudulent or spurious, such as the one two people might give each other in describing the component elements of their individual dreams. The special consensus don Juan supplies is systematic, and to provide it he must draw on all the knowledge he possesses.

Put another way, special consensus means that it is possible to have general agreement on what constitutes nonordinary reality, to be able to codify, as it were, the general outlines of nonordinary reality in the way we now codify the general outlines of ordinary reality; e.g., charting new seas or mapping new lands. Nonordinary reality would be like a newly discovered planet having its own rules and making sense only according to them. To make the breakthrough to another reality is the stuff of science fiction and has been vividly imagined and realized there, but to accomplish it on one's own, either through sheer will or with the help of drugs, is an experience that, at least for Castaneda, remains beyond his efforts. He feels unprepared to undergo the rigors himself, but he does not rule out the possibility of others doing it. The question arises as to whether his attempts to legitimize it actually work against its realization, since Castaneda never seems able to let go of either his notebook or himself long enough to find out unencumbered.

Putting it this way gives the experiencing of nonordinary reality a certain respectability, as if the rigors of attaining it give it value—like climbing to the top of Mt. Everest instead of being airlifted. However, if one wants to bypass all this and still experience nonordinary reality, it can be induced by *Lophophora williamsii*, a cactus that contains an entity called "Mescalito," purported to be a unique power similar to an ally in the sense that it allows one to transcend the boundaries of ordinary reality. Don Juan firmly believes that under certain conditions, such as a state of profound acquiescence to Mescalito, the simple act of being contiguous to the cactus would induce a state of nonordinary reality.

Mescalito is available to anyone without the necessity of a long apprenticeship or the commitment to manipulative techniques, as with an ally. And because it is accessible to anyone without any training, Mescalito is said to be a protector. However, although Mescalito is *accessible* to everyone, it is not *compatible* with everyone. With some individuals, Mescalito's "unbending morality" can come in conflict with that individual's own questionable character. Cult readers appreciated this property of moral exclusivity almost as much as they appreciated Mescalito's shortcut to a separate reality. Don Juan believed Mescalito taught simplification of behavior. Be that as it may, it certainly taught simplification of thought!

At the conclusion of the first two don Juan books, Castaneda insists that he cannot go on. Yet he does go on because, as he explains, he has too much invested to turn back. And he would sooner die than drop out. It is very likely that writing down his experiences became an expression of power for Castaneda himself. If the experiences he recounts so vividly strike some readers as fictitious, maybe it is because the experiences do not ring true. Too often they sound more like failures masquerading as successes than like legitimate triumphs over the restrictions of ordinary reality.

While the experiences themselves may very well be real ones, Castaneda's interpretation of them often lacks credibility. For cult readers, however, this posed no problem. On the contrary, they delighted in the mystery of these experiences the way Christians delight in miracles. And the hold that Castaneda has had over these readers is as strong as the power of faith. This is why it is so easy for those who believe unquestionably to surrender to his visions of a separate reality and to share his disdain for doubters.

FOR FURTHER READING

Carpenter, Lorene H. "Maps for the Journey: Shamanic Patterns in Anaya, Asturias, and Castaneda." *DAI* (February 1982): 3588A.

Murray, David. "Anthropology, Fiction, and the Occult: The Case of Carlos Castaneda." In *Literature of the Occult: A Collection of Critical Essays*. Englewood Cliffs: Prentice-Hall, 1981: 171–82.

Nieto, Margarita. "Border Aspects in the Works of Carlos Castaneda." *Tinta* (Spring 1987): 51–57.

Shaw, Mark. "An Exploration of a Phenomenological Approach to Understanding: An Analysis of the Conversation and Teachings of Don Juan." In *Phenomenology in Rhetoric and Communication*. Washington: University Press of America, 1981: 195–204.

This Side of Paradise

F. Scott Fitzgerald
(1920)

This Side of Paradise ushered in the roaring twenties. Its timing was flawless and its message irresistible. World War I, known then as the Great War, had ended in late 1918, and by 1920 the restless and disillusioned survivors of that "war to end all wars" were not about to let the world slip back into the absurdities and hypocrisies that had triggered it. The old order was dead, but the new was powerless to be born. Meanwhile, young people, stranded on this side of paradise, set about flouting the rules of propriety while down deep they tortured themselves with questions that not even bootleg hooch could silence.

Like Tom Wolfe a generation later, F. Scott Fitzgerald had the uncanny knack of seeing things whole even as they unfolded. Whereas most people, authors included, need time and distance to give them perspective, Fitzgerald seemed to be chronicling the events of the jazz age at the very moment they were happening. Although he was happily at the center of things, he could still draw back and watch himself from a distance, in the way people who have technically "died" describe out-of-body experiences. His vision was 20/20, but compassion softened the edges so that readers were spared the full brunt of his irony and could share in his "instant nostalgia" for an age that had not yet ended, yet could never last.

The composition of *This Side of Paradise* is clearly a quest for self-knowledge, a not uncommon ambition in a beginning writer, and a forgivable one where genius is present. However, because Fitzgerald is trying to find out about himself but lacks sufficient experience and maturity to succeed entirely, some of the ideas in the book remain vague, especially toward the end when the novel degenerates into long, rambling monologues.

Nevertheless, the novel helped Fitzgerald clarify for himself—and consequently for admiring readers—a number of issues. For one thing, he accepted his estrangement from the Catholicism into which he had been born, and readers for whom the times had induced a crisis of the spirit found solace in Amory Blaine's alienation from the Church. Fitzgerald also came to terms, however tentative, with his own life. In "The Rich Boy," one of his best stories, Fitzgerald remarks that most lives end as a compromise but that it was as a compromise that Anson Hunter, "the rich boy," began his. Fitzgerald learned the necessity of compromise from observing how the rich dealt with the disillusionment of "answered prayers," and since he restated this compromise in one way or another throughout his fiction, his readers were able to make it work for them, too.

For Fitzgerald, the key to this melancholy wisdom lay in the acceptance of a personality that was hopelessly divided against itself but that could only function when the tension was maintained. Any attempt to subdue the self-destructive side invariably translated into banalities on the creative side, just as any attempt to control the creative side led to excesses of indulgence on the wild side. That Fitzgerald could write three days a week and party four (those famous Thursday to Tuesday "weekends") is a perfect example of the interaction of these two sides to his nature. It is the same delicate balance that is expressed in the relationship between Amory and Rosalind, who resurface as Anthony Patch and Gloria Gilbert in *The Beautiful and Damned*, as Jay Gatsby and Daisy Buchanan in *The Great Gatsby*, and as Dick Diver and Nicole in *Tender is the Night*.

Fitzgerald hoped not only to clarify his ideas but also to make a large amount of money with this novel, and in both respects he succeeded. The book was certainly a financial success. "The presses were pounding out *This Side of Paradise* like they pound out extras in the movies," he later remarked. Between its publication in March 1920 and October 1921, it sold 49,000 copies. And for all its flaws, it spoke to the lost generation of the 1920s as no other book would. Glenway Wescott said that it "haunted the decade like a song." Fitzgerald was to write better novels than this one, but none more popular.

It remains the first and best record of the tastes and enthusiasms of a generation later to be called everything from "flappers" to "flaming youth" to "bright young things." Fitzgerald caught the cadence of their music and speech as much as he caught the spirit of their liberation from the shallow, stifling world of their elders. A young man struggling to find himself and his place in society is the essence of initiation literature, but Fitzgerald gave it his own special twist. Of course, there had not been a generation since the dawn of Romanticism that had broken so completely with the past, that was so determined to break the rules, and that wanted so desperately to cheat the hangman. When their descendants surfaced in the sixties, they blew in with a great deal of sound and fury, but they lacked what Fitzgerald understood instinctively: class.

The hero of this *Bildungsroman* is Amory Blaine, a rich boy who spends his early years traveling around the United States and Mexico in his father's private railroad car. At fifteen, he leaves his Midwestern home to attend St. Regis, a preparatory school in New Jersey, where he concentrates on football and popularity. Shortly after enrolling, he meets Monsignor Darcy, with whom he has a number of intellectual conversations and with whom he corresponds on important issues. Darcy serves as both confidant and mentor to the maturing youth.

From St. Regis, Amory goes on to Princeton, where he spends his first two years socializing rather than studying. He gets elected to the prestigious Cottage Club and begins writing for the *Daily Princetonian*, but poor grades keep him from becoming the editor, even though he wins a writing competition that makes him the most likely candidate.

Among the friends Amory makes at Princeton is Thomas Parke D'Invilliers, a young man whose poetry in the *Nassau Lit* Amory admires. D'Invilliers introduces Amory to many modern writers, among them William Butler Yeats, Oscar Wilde, and Algernon Charles Swinburne. Under D'Invilliers' influence, Amory begins writing poetry. Thus, at Princeton he begins his love affair with literature.

He also begins his love affair with love. He exchanges love letters with a girl he meets in Minneapolis during the Christmas holiday of his sophomore year, and he becomes infatuated with his widowed third cousin whom he almost marries. When he returns from military service in France, he falls in love with the sister of his rich Princeton friend Alec. She turns down his proposal of marriage, however, because Amory's family fortune has been squandered in bad investments, and Amory is now too poor.

On the rebound, Amory takes up with Eleanor Savage, an eighteen-year-old girl as wild as her name suggests. Together they write poetry and joyride through the countryside, and for six summer weeks they are passionately in love. Then one night Eleanor tries to kill herself, for no discernible reason, and the romance ends.

Amory suddenly finds himself adrift, out of work, out of money, alienated. Restlessly, he haunts the scenes of his earlier life, drifting from Atlantic City to New York to Princeton. However, in spite of setbacks and disillusionments, Amory believes that he has learned something about himself and that he can face the future with hope. "I know myself," he proclaims in the last chapter, and the novel ends on a note of wistful hope, a fragile compromise delicately balanced between stoicism and self-pity.

Cult readers at the time adopted Fitzgerald as their spokesman. And indeed, his reputation as spokesman for the jazz age has never waned. He chronicled the changing mores of the children of Victorian parents, children who indulged in petting parties, flirted shamelessly, and kissed promiscuously. He celebrated the liberating effects of the automobile. He also pointed out the demoralizing effects of World War I and Prohibition, two moral crusades that he felt had not made the world better. Cult readers agreed wholeheartedly. It was the beginning of an attitude that was to prevail for the rest of the century: that there was something hypocritical about a society that could justify war but condemn drinking. Before Gertrude Stein made her pronouncement about the "lost generation," Fitzgerald wrote prophetically in this famous passage of the novel: "Here was a new generation, . . . dedicated more than the last to the fear of poverty and the worship of success, grown up to find all Gods dead, all wars fought, all faiths in man shaken" (282).

At the same time that Fitzgerald is attacking the emotional and intellectual wasteland of twentieth-century America, he is expressing a yearning for financial success. Amory is poor but loathes poverty. He advocates socialism, not because he seeks a more just social order, but because he hopes that a revolution might advance him. He attacks ownership of property while clinging desperately to the family estate. In his contradictions as in his college experiences, Amory is Fitzgerald, who wrote the novel to achieve the financial success he criticized in order to win the girl he recognized as unworthy of him. There is a humanity in this innocent hypocrisy that endears itself to readers who pursue goals they know they cannot reach in order to have things they know are not good for them.

It is this pervasive humanity that keeps *This Side of Paradise* from becoming judgmental. Fitzgerald looks back with nostalgia, not rancor, turning splintered, painful reality into a lovely mosaic. Along with other sensitive spirits of the 1920s, Fitzgerald believed that they and their world had lost something precious. In an uncanny way, although he is only at the beginning of the decade, he seems to be standing at the end of it, surveying it from the perspective of the grimness of 1929, regretting what was over before it had even happened.

Certainly one of the most appealing ideas in this book, especially to a later generation dedicated to the pursuit of eternal youth, is Fitzgerald's sentimental suggestion that one's first age is the best, that one is happiest in youth and innocence. Amory has not reached the splendid aloofness of "the rich boy," but the ingredients are there for the kind of charming arrogance that characterizes so many of Fitzgerald's heroes. It is easy to idealize all of Fitzgerald's heroes, but none more than Amory Blaine, for he has all the folly and intensity of any young man who has set his sights high and made promises to himself that he intends to keep but suspects he never can. He is "of his age" in a way every young person longs to be but seldom is.

This Side of Paradise remains an excellent chronicle of a bygone day that even the faint odor of mothballs cannot sully. Reading it today is like finding in the attic the old tuxedo that your grandfather wore to the 1922 cotillion. You ache to try it on and return, as in a time warp, to the days of speak-easies and rouged knees, of dolls in ermine and daddies in tails. So what if the wool is too heavy, the grosgrain too worn, the pants too baggy for modern taste. For a fleeting moment you can hear Paul Whiteman playing "Avalon," see the flappers dancing the Charleston, and taste the rawness of bootleg hooch right out of the flask. Twenty-three, skidoo!

FOR FURTHER READING

Donaldson, Scott. "The Political Development of F. Scott Fitzgerald." *Prospects: An Annual Journal of American Cultural Studies* 6 (1981): 313–55.

Haywood, Lynn. "Historical Notes for *This Side of Paradise*." *Resources for American Literary Study* (Autumn 1980): 191–208.

Hendriksen, John Oscar. "*This Side of Paradise* as a Bildungsroman." *DAI* (September 1990): 851A.

Hook, Andrew. "Cases for Reconsideration: Fitzgerald's *This Side of Paradise* and *The Beautiful and Damned*." In *Scott Fitzgerald: The Promises of Life*. New York: St. Martin's, 1989, 17–36.

Moreland, Kim. "The Education of Scott Fitzgerald: Lessons in the Theory of History." *Southern Humanities Review* (Winter 1985): 25–38.

Rusch, Frederik L. "Marble Men and Maidens, the Necrophilous People of F. Scott Fitzgerald: A Psychoanalytic Approach in Terms of Erich Fromm." *Journal of Evolutionary Psychology* (April 1982): 28–40.

Time and Again

Jack Finney
(1970)

Examples of cult fiction that come under the heading of fantasy usually take place in the future (*2001: A Space Odyssey*), in the present (*Lost Horizon*), or in some timeless world of the author's own imagining (*Lord of the Rings*). There has been an interest for some time, though, in fiction that places modern characters in a historical setting. In Daphne du Maurier's *The House on the Strand*, Dick Kilmarth is transported back to the fourteenth century by means of a hallucinogenic drug, and in Brian Aldiss's *Frankenstein Unbound*, a timeslip takes Joe Bodenland back in time from the twenty-first century to the early nineteenth century at the time Mary Shelley is completing her classic tale.

The only novel of this sort to acquire cult status, however, is *Time and Again* by Jack Finney, author of *Sleep No More*, the novel on which the 1956 cult movie *Invasion of the Body Snatchers* was based. In *Time and Again* Finney is again concerned with government attempts to interfere in the private lives of its citizens. In this case, it is a plot to alter the course of history by sending selected people back in time to perform nefarious deeds. Simon Morley, the hero of the story, is a bored young advertising artist who is approached by a man named Ruben Prien with an offer to participate in this secret government project. He describes the person he's looking for as someone who has to be physically, psychologically, and temperamentally right. It must be someone who has a special way of looking at things, says Prien, someone with the rare ability "to see things as they are and at the same time as they might have been" (11). What he means by this is someone with the eye of an artist. He says there are other requirements, but these alone have eliminated most of the population. In fact, he has narrowed the list down to five men and two women. This is enough bait already to hook any cult reader who longs to be among the chosen.

Without giving him any details, Prien piques Si's interest, promising him the greatest adventure any human being has ever had. Si agrees to undergo a battery of tests, and he becomes increasingly fascinated by the extraordinary nature of the experiments he witnesses, experiments in what looks to him like time travel. But to his amazement, this is not time travel to some imaginary future but travel back to a very real past of nineteenth-century New York City. Although Si is initially reluctant, he finds himself becoming increasingly intrigued by Prien's subtle comparisons between then and now as the two men tour famous landmarks of New York.

Of particular interest to him and to the people who are recruiting him is the old Dakota Hotel, now a legend and something of a historic site but new back then—or almost. Finney admits in a footnote that although his efforts at accuracy became compulsive, he did not let accuracy interfere with the story. "If I needed a fine old Dakota apartment building in 1882, and found it wasn't finished till 1885, I just moved it back a little; sue me" (399). It is clear as the two men tour the New York City of the 1970s that Si is disenchanted with the modern world and suspects that there was more quality to life in the New York City of a century earlier.

Dr. Danziger, the brains behind the whole operation, tells Si only of plans to reverse the destructive course of history: return grazing grounds to the buffalo, restore a New England village to its pristine past, things like that. He also makes it clear that these restorations and recreations are intended to give selected inhabitants (like Si) a chance to return to the past and relive it exactly as life was lived then. Of course,he doesn't tell him that his ulterior motive is to alter history in a serious, political way.

Dr. Danziger wants to send Si back to pre-earthquake San Francisco, but Si opts for 1882 New York City, because he has an ulterior motive. His girlfriend, Kate Carmody, has a letter dated January 23, 1882. The slightly charred envelope is addressed to Andrew W. Carmody, Esq., 589 Fifth Avenue, City. Inside is a message that ends with a sentence made cryptic by the absence of a word where the paper had been burned: "That the sending of this should cause the Destruction by Fire of the entire World . . ." (72).

Kate is eager to learn what happened to this relative of hers, and Si is both intrigued by the mystery and just plain curious. Kate was adopted by Andrew's son, and all Kate knows of her grandfather is that he had been a fairly well-known financier and political figure in New York City, and later a minor adviser to President Grover Cleveland during Cleveland's second term in the nineties. Andrew went bankrupt. Then suddenly and mysteriously he moved to Montana, where he committed suicide and was buried with a strange nine-pointed star on his tombstone. All she knows about the letter is the rumor that Andrew's wife had found him, the envelope still burning on his desk, and had extinguished the flames and saved the letter. Now Kate wants to know just what happened, and Si thinks he can find out if only he can return to the New York of 1882 and watch the mailing of this letter on January 23.

Danziger agrees without putting up a fuss, but not purely out of sympathy for Si's curiosity about his girlfriend's family. It turns out that Danziger's parents met accidentally in the lobby of Wallack's Theatre on the evening of February 6, 1882, on his mother's sixteenth birthday. Danziger would dearly love for Si to witness the momentous occasion and return with all the details.

In early January Si is installed in a suite at the Dakota overlooking Central Park. After two weeks of somewhat frustrating anticipation, he becomes aware one afternoon of a deep silence outside and of some subtle changes in his room. The silence is the result of six inches of snow that have blanketed the city and brought traffic to a standstill. Except that when he looks out, the traffic, which is barely crawling, consists of horsedrawn carriages and omnibuses. Si is back in 1882, and the subtle changes in the room are true to that time.

But it is not until Si goes for a walk in the park and realizes that he can see the Museum of Natural History without all the buildings in between that he realizes he is actually back in 1882. Within a day or two he returns to modern times long enough to persuade Kate to return with him to 1882 to watch the famous mailing of the letter. They see the mailing occur, but its consequences are not revealed to them until much later in the story. By then Si has become so infatuated with Julia, the young lady who helps run the boarding house in Gramercy Park where he takes up lodgings, that he would rather stay in the past with Julia than return to the present and Kate.

At a time when altered states of mind were in vogue and drug-induced time "trips" not uncommon, Finney's fantasy had great appeal. Young people who felt victimized by an immoral war, an exploitative society, hypocritical parents, and callous leaders longed to "tune in, turn on, and drop out"; and *Time and Again* was one of the more imaginative ways to do it. It also reminded Americans that values such as respect for the environment and consideration for other human beings had once existed. And it catered to a national nostalgia for a simpler age, even on the part of people reluctant to sacrifice even one modern convenience. Finney gives himself away in a charming episode in which Si brings Julia to the New York of the seventies and then cannot keep from enjoying her wide-eyed acceptance of the wonders of modern technology.

Even so, Si has some telling comments to make about what he thinks has been lost in the bargain. "*Today's faces are different*," he says, "they are much more alike and much less alive." Although he sees on the streets of the 1880s the same human misery that exists today, the same depravity, hopelessness, and greed, what he also sees is an "excitement in the streets of New York in 1882," an excitement that is missing in modern life. He sees this excitement in the faces of women moving along the Ladies' Mile and in and out of the legendary department stores. "Their faces were animated," he says, "and they were glad to be just where they were, alive in that moment and place." He says that he could see in their eyes as they passed how much pleasure they took in being outdoors in the winter in this city they clearly liked. "They weren't bored, for God's sake!" (218)

Just looking at them convinces him that the people back then never doubted that their being had a purpose, and he feels that such a conviction is something worth having, that to lose it is to lose something vital. "Faces don't have that look now; when alone they're blank, and closed in." Although he is convinced that nobody today takes any real pleasure in living in New York any more, he is confident—and not a little wistful—when he insists that "New York *was* once a different place, and in many many ways" (219).

In the New York of 1882, Si passes himself off as a "private detective," and as such he solves the mystery of the cryptic fragment in the charred letter, the sending of which "should cause the destruction by fire of the entire World . . . " The missing word turns out to be "building," for it is the building that once housed the newspaper known as the *World* that has burned in one of the most famous fires ever recorded. The fire actually did occur, and its origins remain a mystery, but for the sake of the story, Finney has Si figure it out. What he learns is that Andrew Carmody set fire to the World Building to destroy papers that would have caused a scandal and brought an end to the Carmody social dynasty.

Later that same evening, at a glittering ball, Si looks at Mrs. Carmody in amazement. She does not yet know how closely she has come to being completely ruined. Si relishes the high drama of the occasion. He tells Julia that he is more than fascinated, that he is, in fact, "illicitly thrilled," for he knows that the time will come when Mrs. Carmody's kind of face and person will cease to exist, when the kind of high drama that she is involved in will be the stuff of legends. It will all be "out of style," he tells her. Instead, in time to come, "evildoers will be tawdry, committing crimes of violence or bookkeeping in which any sense of drama will be nonexistent. And of the two kinds of people and evil," he declares, "I'll take those with a sense of style" (324–25).

Much of the "style" has to do with the cover-up that follows the fire.

To save Mrs. Carmody and the Carmody fortune, Pickering, the man who was blackmailing Carmody, survives to take Carmody's place and thus avert a scandal. He manages this because he is swathed in heavy bandages that cover his extensive burns. Rather than face ruin, Mrs. Carmody strikes a bargain with Pickering.

Meanwhile, Si and Julia are being pursued by the police for what looks like their implication in the death of Pickering. To escape detection, they spend the night in the right arm of the Statue of Liberty. The statue has not yet been erected, and until it is, the giant arm that will one day carry the torch, is resting in Madison Square, waiting to be hoisted into place. (Finney even includes an actual—and truly amazing—photograph of this in the text.) Si and Julia wake up in modern times, still in the right arm of the Statue, and have to take a ferryboat back to Manhattan. This is when Si, with all the enthusiasm of a dedicated tour guide, cannot resist showing off his home town, even if it is noisy, polluted, crime-ridden, dirty, and expensive.

Soon, though, he sees the city once more through the disillusioned eyes of a present-day inhabitant who wishes he could go back and start over and get it right this time. He realizes that there were horrors in Julia's time, "that the seeds of everything I hated in my own time were already planted and sprouting in hers. But they hadn't yet flowered." In Julia's New York he is enchanted by streets filled with sleighs on a moonlit night, by the sound of cheerful voices, calling to each other, laughing, singing. "Life still had meaning and purpose in people's minds; the great emptiness hadn't begun. Now the good times to be alive seemed to be gone, Julia's probably the last of them" (379).

Danziger and his people tell Si that they want him to return and do one thing: expose Pickering and discredit him, thus preventing Pickering (who they now know was passing as Carmody) from advising Grover Cleveland on Cuba. Their hope is that Cuba might become a permanent American possession in 1890 and thus avoid its turbulent (and to Danziger, distasteful) political future. Si dislikes the idea and is amazed at his own rebellion. It is totally unlike him to talk back. He has never had the nerve, never thought he had the right. Now he realizes that if he is no better than anybody else, nobody else is any better than he. How dare they alter the course of history? Thus, he resists; he refuses; and one can almost hear the howls of delight emanating from the happy throats of readers who have been waiting for Si Morley to assert himself.

They argue that a lot of men make far greater sacrifices for their country than Pickering would be making if he were to be quietly eliminated. The dialogue that ensues articulates the concerns of readers worried about being conscripted against their will into fighting a war they were conscientiously opposed to. When Si argues that Pickering would be making this sacrifice without being consulted about it, he is told that draftees likewise are not consulted. Si's angry retort is, "Well, maybe they should be asked, too. . . . Maybe it's wrong to force a man to join an army and kill other people against his own wishes" (388). And his last words are "No sir, gentlemen; I refuse" (389).

"No!" in thunder. This has always been the cry of the rebel, and it was certainly the cry heard round the world when the Vietnam War was raging and the draft was in effect.

Si wanders about in a state of agitation. He has never taken a stand before, and he finds the experience both exhilarating and not a little frightening. Suddenly he finds himself back in 1882, at the theater where Danziger's father and mother had met. Only this time they *don't* meet because Si is about to strike a blow for everyone who sees Danziger as the symbol of all that was anathema to youth: the war, the draft, and the superior attitude that sees nothing wrong with tampering with fate, with history, or with destiny.

For a split second, Si hesitates. After all, if he tampers with Danziger's destiny, won't he be guilty of the thing he deplores? But a moment later Si has made up his mind. He intercepts Danziger's "father" at the entrance to the lobby and asks him for a light from his cigar. In the time it takes Danziger to give Si a light, the girl and her family have disappeared up the staircase,the two never meet, and thus Dr. Danziger never gets born. It's an ironic twist on a man who had planned to alter the course of other people's lives. Si walks away, pleased with his small revenge and pleased with the world he plans to remain in. The only hint we get as to how he rationalizes doing the very thing he was against is implied in his statement about tolerating evildoers who have style. Apparently, he justifies pulling off this trick in the lobby of the Wallack Theatre because he did it with "style."

Or maybe the justification can be found in his concluding reflection: "This, too was an imperfect world," he thinks, "but—I drew a deep breath, sharply chill in my lungs—the air was still clean. The rivers flowed fresh, as they had since time began. And the first of the terrible corrupting wars still lay decades ahead" (398).

FOR FURTHER READING

Wolfe, Gary K. "Jack Finney." In *Twentieth Century Science-Fiction Writers,* ed. by Curtis C. Smith. New York: St. Martin's, 1981: 196.

Trout Fishing in America

Richard Brautigan
(1967)

Richard Brautigan wrote *Trout Fishing in America* in 1961, but it was not published until 1967, the year of the "summer of love," and by then it was seized upon by an audience that brought to it all the political, cultural, and emotional baggage that we associate with the term "hippie." In fact, to some it is *the* cult book of the sixties, possibly because it seems to require an "altered state of consciousness" to understand what it is all about. Reading it today gives meaning to the joke, "If you remember the sixties, you weren't there." *Trout Fishing in America* comes closer to being a literary high than any other book of its time with the possible exception of the novels of William S. Burroughs.

Written as early in the decade as it was, it also has much in common with the novels of the beat generation in its emotional and intellectual detachment, an attitude closer to the existential aloofness of the hipsters than to the idealistic involvement of the hippies. "Hippie" has an inescapably quaint sound to it now, like "dandy" or "flapper," but it meant something specific in the sixties; and it was as a "hippie writer" that Brautigan was received.

When we refer to the sixties, we usually mean the last half of the decade, not the first, for the two halves are as different as day and night. The first five years were the years of beehive hairdos and rhinestone glasses, button-down shirts and narrow ties, Audrey Hepburn movies and Henry Mancini music. Then came the assassination of John F. Kennedy and the start of the Vietnam War, and from 1964 on everything got turned upside down. It is from the latter half of the decade, then, that we get the image of the sixties as an era of long hair and granny glasses, headbands and serapes, bellbottoms and muumuus; of strung-out flower children clustered in communes, strumming dulcimers against a psychedelic backdrop of dope, sex, and hard rock. And it was into this milieu that Richard Brautigan was wildly received.

The secret of the book's success is quite simple. *Trout Fishing in America* was the literary equivalent of the Grateful Dead—something instantly gratifying when one was high, something requiring no context, no frame of reference other than what one supplied at the moment. *Trout Fishing* was unlike anything these cult readers had ever seen before, totally unlike the structured, boring novels they had been forced to study and analyze in high school or college. Here was a novel that seemed to be—and for the most part was—totally without plot or narrative or sustained characterization. It was, rather, a series of psychedelic moments—like the succession of *frissons* so dear to Oscar Wilde and the decadents—that could only be indulged in fleetingly but that yielded an elusive kind of thrill that depended on nothing but the confluence of language, music, and dope.

Thus, *Trout Fishing* was blissfully immune to the claptrap of literary criticism. There was no analytical apparatus available to deliver this unique creation into the hands of pompous critics or patronizing professors. The book might seem disorganized and meaningless to them, but to the stoned it was an added high just to be able to open the book to any page and find something "mind blowing," something "far out," something silly you could get a kick out of without getting "heavy" about it. The only other book that even came close to it was William Burroughs's *Naked Lunch*, about which it was rumored that the chapters had been shuffled like a deck of cards and then published in whatever order resulted. The fact that these two books looked utterly chaotic was quite to the taste of a generation that condemned authority, reason, and order as enemies of all that was good.

But there was a curious contradiction in this high-handed condemnation of authority, for it was precisely authority, albeit of a different nature, that the counterculturists worshiped. One has only to think of the pantheon of counterculture gods and gurus, now mostly gone—Janis Joplin, Jimi Hendrix, John Lennon, Abbie Hoffman, Timothy Leary, Benjamin Spock, Daniel Berrigan, Mark Rudd—to realize how hungry the hippies were for someone to order them around, to tell them how to dress, what to listen to, what to smoke, when to make love and, of course, what to think. Books like *Do It* and *Steal This Book* do not begin to indicate how eager these so-called rebels were to follow some charismatic leader. (The word "charisma" came into common usage in 1960 with John F. Kennedy.) Both Hunter S. Thompson and Christopher Lasch have drawn attention to this clear and curious desire for authority that they claim reached into every corner of life and left little room for individual initiative.

Thus, Brautigan's first readers tended to let the immediacy of their reading experience blind them to his essential individualism. Here again one can see how much closer Brautigan was to the hipsters and the beats of the fifties, who cultivated a fierce individuality, than to the hippies, who cultivated communes. And in a commune there is little room for individual conviction when the good of all comes first.

One reason Brautigan went undetected for so long is that he did not assert his personality into this book the way Kerouac did. In Brautigan's prose, American people and things are seen as they are, observed and documented, as it were. Brautigan acts as witness, not judge. And like the "true witnesses" of Robert Heinlein's *Stranger in a Strange Land*, he makes neither more nor less of whatever he sees. He uses no conventional techniques to achieve a comic or a dramatic effect. He sees everything with cool, neutral detachment.

Because Brautigan does not intrude upon his story or impose on it any particular slang, the book lacks any sense of the didactic, any intimation that, regardless of how satiric and political it seems, it is supposed to instruct its readers in how to think or behave. Brautigan allows the satire to emerge from his unadorned reporting of America's own internal contradictions rather than from an implied criticism of its ability to measure up to the standards of some arbitrary ideological presumption. With *Trout Fishing in America*, the reader brings politics to the book. For cult readers, this was no problem. Finding what they wanted to find in the book made reading it all the more enjoyable, in the same way a mystic might find religious reinforcement in working out the numerological references in the Bible to prove some arcane hypothesis.

Brautigan's disengaged, thoroughly nonpolitical narrative voice is the subtle hook by which this book takes hold of its readers, for nothing is more convincing than the report of the disinterested journalist who just happens to uncover something about some governmental cover-up. Another hook, this one much more subtle and much more insidious, is the use of the disinterested voice that indiscriminately accepts evil as well as good. By documenting without judging, Brautigan sends the message that it is pointless to try to change anything, that decisive change is impossible, because the evil inevitably returns.

The acceptance of the immutability of a world divided between good and evil carries with it the tainted thrill of heresy. Emil Sinclair arrives at the same point in Hermann Hesse's *Demian*, and there is a longing for it that runs through Albert Camus's *The Stranger*. It is ultimately a deeply cynical attitude that only adds to the moral confusion in which good and evil are merely interchangeable options, menu items, equal choices. Evil is accepted, even condoned, as being as valuable a part of experience as good, and perhaps even preferable to it. This dispassionate, disembodied, impersonal narrator invites belief precisely because he seems so objective. A man with no score to settle has no reason not to tell the truth. Because Brautigan apparently has nothing to gain by portraying *America* one way and not another, we trust him implicitly.

Several things contributed to the phenomenal success of this extraordinary book. For one thing, the book is not at all about what it says it is about: trout fishing. Any angler who picked it up would be in for a shock. This kind of zaniness appealed to the age. Another attraction was the apparent absence of a traditional hero. Instead, in his place there is the absurd substitution of "trout fishing in America" used in every conceivable metaphorical sense. So ultimately, *it* becomes the center of attention, both message and messenger combined, and Brautigan can make the title mean anything or anyone he wants it to mean—or the reader wants it to mean.

Another explanation for the phenomenal popularity of *Trout Fishing in America* is that it is so unapologetically self-indulgent. By claiming no right to exist, it seems to earn that right. This is an impregnable, unimpeachable, nonassailable book. It seems to belong by itself and to itself, to have nothing to do with anything *but* itself. And within itself, all is delightful disorganization. It provides a fine escape from a world where everything is perceived as being altogether too regimented and logical.

Brautigan had no ax to grind. No ramparts are breached or causes advanced in this slim volume. Brautigan, like Meursault in *The Stranger*, is simply too passive to get involved—not because he agrees with the world as he finds it, but because he does not seem to feel that there are social revolutions worth fighting. It is no surprise, then, that this book has been called *The Great Gatsby* of its time. All wars fought. All Gods dead.

Naturally, the book had its detractors. Those who were mixed up in movements, involved in crusades, concerned about solving the problem instead of being part of the problem, tended to think that books without some obvious agenda were like people who stood on the sidelines and minded their own business: just taking up space. They found the book carelessly gross and its author/narrator preoccupied with a phony detached self, playing the role of this droll, poker-faced, seemingly disinterested third party, detachedly observing something that he never makes quite clear. How can you describe what you are observing, they asked, without having a basic opinion? If you talk about observing the follies or the inanities or even the peculiarities of Americans, aren't you already making a judgment?

What is probably closer to the truth—and closer to the book's central appeal—is the presence of a situation in which the observer is observing himself observing. This interpretation is congruent with the extreme self-consciousness of the age, the passion for keeping one's finger forever on one's own pulse, the obsessive preoccupation with how one was perceived and what image one projected. Brautigan, then, is looking in the mirror, watching himself showing off, pulling his tricks and performing his stunts with a "Who, me?" look on his face. But there was no way that a sixties cult figure could remain neutral, certainly not in the eyes of those who put the spin on what they read, regardless of what the author might have intended. Nobody straddled the fence, least of all Richard Brautigan—certainly not as far as his followers were concerned. And where cult books are concerned, it is the readers who have the last word.

One thing they glimpsed in Brautigan's vision was the bleakly pessimistic view that America, sooner or later, transforms even its finest things into salable commodities. This was the America of mindless restrictions and prohibitions, of broken promises and shattered dreams, the America the beats had rebelled against in the fifties. However true or false this image of America was historically, it fueled the disenchantment, anger, restlessness, and rebellion that found its way into all counterculture writing in the sixties, including Brautigan.

Brautigan's deceptive passivity is pure beat. Unlike the Marxists of the thirties or the New Left of the sixties, the beats did not set out to change the world but to change themselves, to reach beyond the limits and repressions of America and find a heightened personal awareness through whatever means promised fulfillment—mysticism, drugs, sex, "relentless motion." They were continually reaching out for something beyond America's metaphysical boundaries. It mattered little how vocal you were or how dedicated to changing the world, the truth was that the only person you could ultimately reform was yourself.

There is something sweet about such a gentle philosophy, and some of its acceptance had to do with the respect with which the flower children of the sixties welcomed their forerunners, the beats, into their midst. Brautigan came to be known as the "honorary kid" and "the last hippie in America." He was a little older than the rest, and so it was easy to look upon his books as charming but dated, as old-fashioned reminders of the way things were, the way the students of the fifties read F. Scott Fitzgerald, less as literature than as an excuse to wax nostalgic about a time they never knew. It is, in fact, the way today's students read Kurt Vonnegut and Burroughs and even Brautigan.

Brautigan's picture of America as oppressive and morally weak was commonplace among the beats, but unlike most beats, he displayed neither rage nor horror but almost a kind of contentment, neither smug nor approving, with America as it was. Anger and rational solutions were both irrelevant at this point, for America, as understood by the narrator, was dying. The book is filled with references to death, and the report on *Trout Fishing in America*'s autopsy is not entirely a joke. There was nothing to do now but sit back and watch.

Brautigan's deepest appeal, then, is to an almost Oriental passivity that some consider the ultimate wisdom: the true ability to "let go and let God." It is possible that he was the most deeply spiritual of all the writers of that period, for at the core of *Trout Fishing in America* is the legendary serenity of the fisherman at rest in the middle of the glassy-surfaced lake, a fine mist rising about him, the frost of his own breath before him, and a palpable peace surrounding and protecting him.

Tom Robbins once said that no matter how fervently a romantic might support a political movement, he must eventually withdraw from active participation in the movement because it means the supremacy of the organization over the individual and is, as such, an affront to intimacy, the principal ingredient with which this life is sweetened. Romantics do not want to limit themselves, to surrender their freedom to anyone or any group.

It is possible that if the generation of the sixties had read this book (the one they claimed to love so much) a lot more carefully, they would have realized that dreams such as theirs never have a chance. Brautigan's real message to them, one that has only later emerged with striking clarity, is that the man who does not go along with the dominant culture must, if he wants to survive, stand alone.

Or it may be that Brautigan is asking the ultimate question of the age, the one Hunter S. Thompson put this way: "Is there anyone tending the light at the end of the tunnel?"

FOR FURTHER READING

Cooley, John. "The Garden in the Machine: Three Postmodern Pastorals." *Michigan Academician: Papers of the Michigan Academy of Science, Arts, and Letters* (Spring 1981): 405–20.

Iftekharuddin, Farhat Mohammet. "Richard Brautigan: A Critical Look at *Trout Fishing in America, In Watermelon Sugar* and *The Abortion.*" *DAI* (March 1990): 2896A.

Kolin, Philip C. "Food for Thought in Richard Brautigan's *Trout Fishing in America.*" *Studies in Contemporary Satire: A Creative and Critical Journal* (Spring 1981): 9–20.

Stull, William L. "Richard Brautigan's *Trout Fishing in America:* Notes of a Native Son." *American Literature: A Journal of Literary History, Criticism, and Bibliography* (March 1984): 68–80.

Wheeler, Elizabeth Patricia. *The Frontier Sensibility in Novels of Jack Kerouac, Richard Brautigan and Tom Robbins. DAI* 46 (1985): 985A.

2001: A Space Odyssey

Arthur Clarke
(1968)

2001: A Space Odyssey is unique in that it was simultaneously a cult film and a cult book, the book having been written in conjunction with the making of the film. Since its release as a film and a book in 1968, two sequels have been made: *2010: A Space Odyssey* and *2061: A Space Odyssey*, but the original remains the cult classic for reasons peculiar to the times in which it appeared.

Making a religion of science has been inevitable since the days when scientific investigation first threatened the tenets of religious faith. In the 1960s, when 90 percent of all the scientists the world had ever known were living, when men had orbited the Earth in rockets and were about to walk on the moon, when life on Earth seemed to be getting more desperate and more hopeless, people everywhere—and especially young people—were ready for a prophet who would resolve the split between religion and science and usher in a new and brighter age.

At the core of the anarchic unrest of the sixties lay the bitterest disenchantment. The world seemed too sick to change, yet too tired to resist its drift into meaninglessness. To the young the world was like a cancer patient with only enough strength left to refuse the medicine that contains the cure. Much of this resistance was directed against the space program, which, to the young, seemed already to have gotten completely out of hand.

Even so, they were still young enough to be curious about what lay beyond the outer limits and to wonder if the meaning of life that eluded them on Earth might be found in outer space. Thus, when the Stanley Kubrick–Arthur Clarke film *2001: A Space Odyssey* appeared, these young people glimpsed in technology an escape from the banality and viciousness of earthly life. The film seemed to offer an explanation of human limitations and of the way they could be exceeded.

To the followers of this cult, the novel clarified many points that the film had left obscure. Furthermore, it was such a powerfully and beautifully written novel that it even appealed to many who had been baffled or bored by the film. Even though the film made the encounter with creation a visually thrilling experience, the book was able to make the triumph of mind over matter even more compelling. However, both media made the thrill of space travel overcome all fears. This was not a story to frighten you out of your wits with freakish extraterrestrials committed to the total destruction of "earthlings." Here were no "star wars," no intergalactic rivalries, no "aliens" running amok.

The closest thing the book has to a "monster" is HAL (Heuristically programmed ALgorithmic Computer), the computer that is "almost human," but even HAL cannot hold out against the mind of man. And the threats to the ship are less important in themselves than they are as events that signify the evolution of the hero, Frank Bowman. Once it is clear that Bowman can never expect to return to Earth, things like personal danger or discomfort cease to matter.

This book is a far cry from the scream-and-scare science-fiction stories and movies of the fifties. Perhaps the most important difference is that much of what happens in *2001: A Space Odyssey* is within the realm of possibility—had, in fact, already been accomplished. After the first moon walk, the only part of the book that remained in the realm of fantasy was the journey to distant planets and remote galaxies. Beyond that, the spiritual speculation is no more fantastic than any other explanation man has ever indulged in concerning the sources of life and intelligence on Earth and in the universe. Thus, the book had more immediate basis in reality than did *Stranger in a Strange Land*, and its eschatology was all the more convincing for that reason. The mind in the sixties needed a faith and it needed a future, and *2001: A Space Odyssey* gave it both and made them irresistible by placing them within the mind itself.

Through the eyes of Dr. Floyd, the scientist called to inspect the monolith just uncovered beneath the moon's surface, Arthur Clarke describes the state to which the Earth has degenerated by the year 2001. Two problems dominate the world, problems that, ironically, tend to cancel each other out: overpopulation and the threat of nuclear war. Birth control methods have come too late to do much good, and the human instinct for aggression has made the proliferation of nations' strike forces ever more threatening. To complicate matters, the Chinese, with the largest population in the world, are also the ones who are selling nuclear weapons systems to have-not nations for large sums of money, presumably to bolster their sagging economy.

Concern over the earth's survival had been on everyone's mind since

Hiroshima. The Cuban missile crisis made that fear felt, and the conflict in Vietnam kept that fear at fever pitch. For beneath all political and ideological concerns lay the cancerous worry about nuclear confrontation. Curiously enough, *2001: A Space Odyssey* did not allay that fear; what it did was to postpone it, to give cult readers hope that there might be time to get off the planet before the end came. Like "1984" the figure "2001" had the same effect on the mind as a stay of execution. If these dates were offered as deadlines, in the grimmest sense of the word, they suggested times *after which* anything could happen. It was as if things might get worse in the meantime, that signs might point toward disaster, but that nothing serious would really happen before the target date, that one had until then.

In an age of confusion and uncertainty, a "doomsday" offers a curious measure of comfort. Followers of the *2001* cult could not really expect to fly away from it all like David Bowman; they would be too old by then, anyway. But they could at least count on thirty-some years to get what they could out of life on Earth before it was all over. And when you are twenty, thirty more years is a lifetime. Thus the sequels, *2021* and *2061*, keep doomsday at a comfortable distance. So much for posterity!

2001 appealed to the more undemonstrative elements among the rebels of the sixties, those vaguely troubled youths who suffered inwardly and sought escape in fantasy. All it asked of them was passive acceptance of its creed. And all they had to do was watch and wait and take comfort in cosmic inevitability. There is a psychological phenomenon that is known popularly as the "not until but after which" syndrome. It describes the tendency to think that certain things will not happen "until after" something else has happened. These "things that will not happen until after" can be either good or bad. An example of a good thing might be the anticipation of happiness but not "until after the kids are gone" or "until after the mortgage is paid off" or "until after retirement." A bad thing might be the anticipation of disaster but "not until after 1984" or, as is the case with the *Space Odyssey*, "until after 2001." This probably accounts for the two sequels that have postponed the date to a time sufficiently remote to discourage worrying.

Passivity is an expression of alienation, and in *2001* it characterizes David Bowman, who is systematically estranged from all vestiges of the life he once knew. Even while his copilot, Frank Poole is still alive, the two men see little of each other and work mostly alone. Because they rotate shifts, they have only their own company, taped entertainment, or the electronic companionship of HAL, the computer. Later, with Poole dead and HAL deactivated, Bowman is more alone than any man has ever been. As he drifts through uncharted galaxies, he becomes a harrowing symbol of man utterly alone, utterly on his own. To readers who felt cut off from their fellow men, Bowman's loneliness became theirs.

Once Poole is gone and the three scientists are dead in their hibernacula, Bowman has lost final contact with anything human. When even HAL suffers human psychosis and must be dealt with, Bowman's alienation is complete and irrevocable. At first Bowman longs to hear a human voice and listens to tapes of famous works of literature. But he soon grows indifferent to that sort of distraction and turns to music, mostly romantic music played at earsplitting volume. Eventually even that sort of music ceases to interest him, and he ends up listening to nothing but the icy majesty, the "abstract architecture" of Bach.

Eventually, says Clarke, "Bowman [adapts] himself so completely to his solitary way of life that he [finds] it hard to remember any other existence." As one by one his emotions leave him, says Clarke, he passes "beyond despair and beyond hope," but he has not passed "beyond curiosity," and sometimes the thought of the goal toward which he is driving fills him "with a sense of exaltation—and a feeling of power" (174).

Bowman's "sense of exaltation" and "feeling of power" erase from his mind all concerns over his solitary state. Instead of feeling sorry for himself, he begins to have what might be called delusions of grandeur. He thinks of himself as the representative of the entire human race and realizes that whatever he does during the next few weeks will determine its very future. "In the whole history, there had never been a situation quite like this," he thinks boastfully. "He was an Ambassador Extraordinary—Plenipotentiary—for all mankind" (174).

There is always psychological readiness for even the most seemingly unavoidable capitulation, and this has already been noted in Bowman in such readiness as his curiosity, his sense of exaltation, and his feeling of power that makes him feel that he has been chosen to represent mankind in some unique historical event. Once he sees himself as an ambassador and believes that his actions might determine the human race's future, it cannot be said that he is just being carried along. He is participating, actively, willingly. In surrendering to this cosmic destiny, however, he is not so much giving up as acquiring.

Heretofore, we have known him as little more than a robot. His personality has been subordinated to his function as a part of the spaceship, a ship in which it seems for a while that his presence is superfluous. He asserts himself for the first time when he makes the decision to deactivate HAL, for this is more than an act of physical survival; it is an expression of power and the first indication of the tremendous force of the human ego.

Bowman wants more than just to survive; he wants to prevail. His mind, which we have reason to believe has never been occupied with metaphysical speculation, is now ripe for anything. It is uncluttered by philosophical and religious preoccupations, and it has been emptied of most of its emotional content. It is simply curious, exhilarated, and ready. It is also intelligent, and there can be no doubt that enthusiastic readers were equally intelligent and probably of similar mental bent. Clarke's imagination is the imagination of the scientist, unmuddled by the flesh-and-blood irrationality of artists and mystics. In a strange little chapter in which he recounts the history of creation, Clarke says: "The first explorers of Earth had long since come to the limits of flesh and blood; as soon as their machines were better than their bodies, it was time to move." Eventually, "they could become creatures of radiation, free at last from the tyranny of matter" (185). Part of that tyranny is the emotional baggage Bowman manages to discard, must discard before he is ready for the ultimate intellectual experience.

Ego reinforcement is an ingredient common to cult books, but in *2001* Clarke gives it an ironic twist. The computer, HAL 9000, the nervous system of the spaceship, has units on its panel labeled EGO-REINFORCEMENT, and these are among the first units Bowman disconnects when he sets about deactivating HAL. HAL is unique among computers and needs to be constantly reassured that it is tops and is doing its best. It undoubtedly reinforces Bowman's ego to know that he is still superior to HAL, and it certainly reinforced the egos of readers who shared his triumph over technology.

Bowman's regression and transformation amount to nothing less than surrender, but because everything happens so suddenly, this is scarcely noticed. If one is powerless to resist, the idea of surrender seems irrelevant. Much of what he surrenders is what we would call his "humanity," the emotional, caring, feeling side of him that generates compassion. The new world that Clarke envisions is not one in which human feeling has any place whatsoever. Clarke's Star-Child is not a thing toward which one can feel anything except, perhaps, awe. It is certainly no Christ of compassion and love. It is an abstraction capable of whatever is necessary to settle matters on Earth, a planet Clarke coldly describes as "a glittering toy no Star-Child could resist" (220). As this Star-Child thinks to himself, "Down there on that crowded globe history as men knew it would be drawing to a close" (221).

To help it draw more quickly to that close, the Star-Child wreaks what seems to be nuclear havoc on a major portion of that crowded globe. This occurs on the last page of the book and has puzzled many readers. "A thousand miles below, he became aware that a slumbering cargo of death had awoken, and was stirring sluggishly in its orbit. The feeble energies it contained were no possible menace to him; but he preferred a cleaner sky. He put forth his will, and the circling megatons flowered in a silent detonation that brought a brief, false dawn to half the sleeping globe."

Whatever he did, he was exercising the power that is the reward of surrender, power over those unready and unfit for the next level in man's eternal evolutionary climb. It is unlikely that admirers of this book would actively engage in such destruction. Like passive Christians, they await the flaming sword with patience, resignation, and hope. When and if such destruction threatens, they will find it fitting that the ignorant should be punished and the enlightened spared.

Central to the meaning of *2001: A Space Odyssey* is man's relationship to machines. Echoing warnings heard since the beginning of the Industrial Revolution, Clarke shows the dangers of overreliance on, and too high hopes placed in, machines. The aboriginal Moon-Watcher and his group would probably have starved into extinction without the intervention of the monolith. Yet in providing them with the means of survival, it also gave them the means to kill for reasons other than food, first as an act of self-defense against the leopard, then as deliberate murder.

On *Discovery*, the dangerous dependency of man on machine is almost complete. The astronauts rely on HAL for communication with Earth, for the success of the mission, and for their own life support. While man's increasingly complex machines have made it possible to travel the billions of miles to Saturn, it is also a machine that kills Poole and the three hibernating scientists. Indeed, it is only by donning his spacesuit, symbolically becoming a machine himself, that Bowman can "kill" HAL.

The book version of *2001: A Space Odyssey* is the much expanded and matured version of an earlier Clarke story called "The Sentinel." It is also the culmination of a long series of works in which the journey of man away from his primal past and toward a possibly terrifying future is a major concern. For all the book's virtues, it cannot capture the spirit and beauty of the film. The lack of dramatic tension, which is a flaw in the book, works to the film's advantage by allowing the mood and the pictorial beauty to control the momentum of the narrative. While Clarke is a master at creating a believable, meticulously detailed extraterrestrial world, Kubrick is a genius at making visible a world beyond all imagining.

Thus, *2001: A Space Odyssey* shares with a few other noteworthy titles the distinction of being both a cult book and a cult film. These titles include *A Clockwork Orange*, *Warlock*, *The Outsiders*, *One Flew over the Cuckoo's Nest*, and to a lesser extent *Lolita* and *Lost Horizon*. Other cult books have been made into films—*The Stranger*, *The Great Gatsby*, *Dune*, *Catch–22*, *Slaughterhouse-Five*—but they have fallen far short of the mark. Like cult books, cult films are dependent on too many factors beyond anybody's control. Even the sequels to the Clarke/Kubrick classic did not measure up.

The message to cult followers is clear: One can drift toward the year

2001 with one's eardrums pulsating with the frozen thoughts of brains dead or alive, heartless and practically mindless, ready for the next broadcast from the monolith, ready for the divine spark that will elevate one another evolutionary notch with nothing to pass through except the psychedelic eye of the needle.

So why bother to know anything else except whatever is necessary to get one to that point as comfortably and pleasantly as possible? What use is present knowledge when the future will bring awareness beyond belief—instantly, automatically, with no prerequisites except the willingness to receive? Faith without works equals knowledge without effort.

FOR FURTHER READING

Erlich, Richard D. "Moon-Watcher, Man, and Star-Child: *2001* as Paradigm." In *Patterns of the Fantastic*, ed. by Donald M. Hassler. Mercer Island, Wash.: Starmont House, 1983, 73–80.

Galbreath, Robert. "Ambiguous Apocalypse: Transcendental Versions of the End." In *The End of the World*. Carbondale: Southern Illinois University Press, 1983: 53–72.

Hellen, Richard A. J., and Philip M. Tucker. "The Alchemical Art of Arthur C. Clarke." *Foundation: The Review of Science Fiction* (Winter 1987): 30–41.

Sofia, Zoe. "Exterminating Fetuses: Abortion, Disarmament, and the Sexo-Semiotics of Extraterrestrialism." *Diacritics: A Review of Contemporary Criticism* (Summer 1984): 47–59.

Spector, Judith A. "Science Fiction and the Sex War: A Womb of One's Own." *Literature and Psychology* 31 (1981): 21–32.

Walden Two

B. F. *Skinner*
(1948)

Like Ayn Rand's *The Fountainhead* of a few years earlier, *Walden Two* has created such controversy that one could almost claim two cult followings for it: those who see it as the way to realize the Shangri-La of *Lost Horizon* and those who see it as hastening the horrors of *Brave New World*. It is seemingly impossible to remain neutral toward the image of life inside B. F. Skinner's behaviorally engineered society. On the one hand, Skinner projects a vision of what life could be inside utopia: happy, secure, productive, creative. On the other hand, there are those who see this utopia as a euphemism for a behavioral prison in which human beings are totally conditioned and controlled and ultimately reduced to automatons.

As usual, however, cult readers follow their own design or, to put it more accurately, find the design they prefer to follow in whatever book it is that speaks directly to them. One would expect a book like Skinner's *Walden Two* to be compared to *Brave New World* or *1984* and not taken seriously as a true picture of a viable utopia, at least not by the mainstream counterculturists of the sixties. But it was precisely to the commune crowd that this book had its greatest appeal, even to the point of motivating a group of followers to establish a real-life Twin Oaks and attempt an experiment in Walden Two living.

Although the concept of social utopia has diminished to an intellectual abstraction in the twentieth century, during the turbulent sixties there emerged a renewal of interest in social utopias among the counterculture movements: communes, hippie families, The Diggers, etc. Some of these were back-to-nature movements, but some were committed to qualitative changes in the future. What the cult readers found, in spite of the book's obvious defense of behavioral engineering, was enough reinforcement of their own attitudes to allow them to ignore the unpopular side of Skinner's argument. In short, they cracked the acorn and kept the shell but threw the nut away.

First of all, they liked Walden Two's emphasis on positive rather than negative reinforcement. In Skinner's utopia, techniques of aversive reinforcement such as coercion, threat, and punishment are eliminated in favor of techniques of positive reinforcement that promote happiness, tranquility, and contentment. In the world outside Walden Two, the educational system, the political system, and all other institutions function on the principle of aversive control that, according to its leader, T. E. Frazier, is in the hands of charlatans, demagogues, and salesmen who use these techniques for their own self-interest and personal gain in a competitive world. Not only are these techniques inefficient and wasteful of human energy, they also account for our atrocities in the past and our anxieties about the future. At this indictment of society, cult followers could only nod in absolute agreement.

Something else cult readers liked about *Walden Two* was its work system, a system designed to eliminate menial, debilitating labor through automation and technology. *Walden Two* tries to exploit the liberating potential of technology in order to maintain the general welfare. This preference for a technological utopia over a pastoral one marks a departure in utopian aspirations that appealed to readers who were already too dependent on the conveniences of modern life ever to want to abandon them completely. While it is true that modern commune living is well known for its organic gardening, potbellied stoves, and creative recreation, it is still unapologetically reliant on electric lights, running water, and pickup trucks.

Another antiestablishment facet of *Walden Two* that appealed to cult readers was its elimination of the negative aspects of a consumer-oriented society. At Walden Two there is no advertising industry that creates a desire for worthless products, no tasteless (and tainted) frozen food, no compulsion to buy useless gadgets. There is no affluence in Walden Two, but there is also no poverty or human depravity. If there was one thing above all else that many young people despised in their elders it was their infatuation with appliances. Since these children had grown up with, and thus grown used to, the easy conveniences of appliances, they could never share their parents' boundless enthusiasm for such things as washers and dryers, freezers and microwaves, big-screen TV and remote control—and later, trash compactors, tractor mowers, garage–door openers, and VCRs.

Historical memory is embarrassingly short. It did not take long for people to forget the drudgery of cooking on a coal stove in midsummer or of boiling clothes in brown soap, forcing them through a hand wringer, and hanging them out to dry in midwinter, not to mention starching them and ironing them, for there was no such thing as "wash and wear." And it took even less time to romanticize that drudgery as "good, honest work." Imagine, then, how dismayed the real-life residents of Twin Oaks were when they discovered that it was cheaper to buy frozen chicken at the supermarket than to raise chickens themselves. Nevertheless, thumbing one's nose at (most) appliances was, for more immature inhabitants, worth the look of total astonishment on the faces of one's elders.

Yet another element that appealed strongly to cult readers was Walden Two's ostensibly egalitarian society, a society that eliminates racial, sexual, and economic prejudices. Here there is no "some are more equal than others" hypocrisy, at least not in theory. Wealth is equally distributed, and there is complete sexual equality. While Walden Two does not promote sexual permissiveness, its communal conditions invite relaxed standards relative to sexual behavior. In fact, much of the allure of *Walden Two* for cult followers was the dream of a utopia much like James Hilton's Shangri-La in which moderation in all things—including virtue—would be practiced. If this meant sacrificing one's sexual partner to another for the sake of communal harmony, so be it. The intensity and variety of personal experience, so highly prized in the outside world, is subordinated in *Walden Two* to the general well-being.

Perhaps overriding all other attractions—or certainly absorbing them—was the appeal of a sense of community, of what some religions call "fellowship," a feeling of brotherhood that became a mystical ideal among counterculture youth who shared their space with soul brothers and sisters, who mingled at musical orgies like Woodstock, who strained to fulfill some inexplicable craving for communion with others. "If you're not with the one you love, love the one you're with," they sang. This longing for community, coupled with the counterculture's Peter Pan wish never to grow up, expanded into something like a wish to return to childhood, this time to be brought up communally under controlled conditions designed to eliminate completely the experiences of fear, frustration, and anxiety.

At Walden Two, such emotions as anger, jealousy, envy, and resentment are unknown, having been programmed out of the child early on through the gradual introduction of obstacles and annoyances into the child's environment so that he learns how to cope with disappointments gradually at his own level. Throughout this process, all those disciplining devices like force, threat, and punishment that young children hate, older children resent, and young adults finally forgive the moment they have children of their own, are expressly rejected. In place of punishment, Frazier has discovered the power of "positive reinforcement." Through experimental application of this power he is able to increase the probability of certain kinds of behavior and eliminate others. Unlike punishment, which breeds resentment and anxiety, positive reinforcement allows for the kind of control that allows the controlled to feel free, even though their behavior is completely manipulated.

To understand the counterculture's willing acceptance of conditioning, a position that would seem antithetical to their avowed faith in unfettered freedom, one has to understand the side of them that needed desperately to proselytize. Sixties-style rebels were not satisfied just to go their own way and mind their own business, despite all their talk about "doing your own thing." Like the "born agains" so many of them became, they felt compelled to recruit converts, and would argue relentlessly with anyone they could buttonhole in the hope of either winning a convert or justifying a position.

This impulse argues a mentality susceptible to conditioning and, therefore, fully capable of brainwashing others. It is all part of the egomania of people who feel they have got hold of the truth and are prepared to force that truth onto others, whatever it takes. The syndrome flourished throughout the seventies in encounter groups from "est" to "rolfing" to "primal scream." And all it takes to convert to the philosophy of conditioning is to equate conditioning with education. This is precisely what Skinner did, and once he had helped cult followers over this hurdle, the rest was easy.

In the view of Frazier, the founder of Walden Two whose arrogance seems calculated deliberately to throw us off guard, there is no valid distinction between conditioning and education. All education is simply a form of conditioning that aims at inculcating the values of a society into the individual. Every individual is ultimately manipulated by the contingencies of reinforcement to behave in a certain way. For Frazier, conditioning *is* education, but it is a form of education that implies greater knowledge, awareness, and control of the contingencies of reinforcement; it is education, in short, that leaves nothing to chance. Conditioning means planning the environment as well as planning the schedules of reinforcement aimed at increasing the probability of the kind of behavior desired.

Frazier assumes the truth of determinism, and in order to accept his utopian philosophy, his followers must accept it, too. In their naivete, of course, they feel that by opening themselves up to conditioning, they are simply fulfilling what has been determined already—what, they are convinced, is really themselves and not the robot they were becoming in the hands of their sadly misguided parents. It makes perfect sense for them to think that it would be more humane if people wanted to be good, wanted to do the socially accepted thing, automatically and not because they were forced to. Goodness should be painless, they think, and although Skinner frowned on the use of drugs, the flower children who followed him knew that even he did not know everything.

Another thing cult readers liked about *Walden Two* was Frazier's dismissal of democracy as a "pious fraud." This attitude went along with their doubts about the great virtues of democracy that their boring parents had rammed down their throats when they boasted of surviving with honor a depression and a war. Instead, cult followers looked upon a commune as a place where all would share power equally, only dimly aware that, in the end, somebody has to take charge. They did not worry, however, because they knew they could trust to someone like Frazier to take charge merely as an act of benevolence. Since a commune offers no temptation to power, anyone willing to assume leadership would be motivated entirely by love.

Every age needs its dreamers. In the sixties and seventies these dreamers were called gurus, a word taken from Hinduism and informally applied to any charismatic leader or guide. Richard Brautigan and Jack Kerouac were attributed this status, along with poets Allen Ginsberg and Lawrence Ferlinghetti, all of them on the "wrong side of thirty" at the time but "young at heart." But the term was bestowed on a few members of an even older generation, men whose vision squared with the new revolutionary mood, among them such venerables as Benjamin Spock, Timothy Leary, Daniel Berrigan, And B. F. Skinner. The first three paved the way for the dream. Skinner tried to make the dream a reality. He is no longer with us, but his disciples are still trying.

FOR FURTHER READING

Elms, Alan C. "Skinner's Dark Year and *Walden Two*" *American Psychologist* (May 1981): 470–79.

Howard, Mary K. "Orwell and the Futurists." *Cuyahoga Review* (Spring-Summer 1984): 17–21.

Jehmlich, Reimer. "Cog-Work: The Organization of Labor in Edward Bellamy's *Looking Backward* and in Later Utopian Fiction." In *Clockwork Worlds: Mechanized Environments in SF*. Westport, Conn.: Greenwood, 1983, 27–46.

Plank, Robert. "The Modern Shrunken Utopia." In *America as Utopia*. New York: Franklin, 1981, 206–30.

Roemer, Kenneth M. "Mixing Behaviorism and Utopia: The Transformations of *Walden Two*." In *No Place Else: Explorations in Utopian and Dystopian Fiction*. Carbondale: Southern Illinois University Press, 1983, 125–46.

Sullivan, E. D. S. "Place in No Place: Examples of the Ordered Society in Literature." In *The Utopian Vision: Seven Essays on the Quincentennial of Sir Thomas More*. San Diego, Calif.: San Diego State University Press, 1983: 29–49.

Warlock

Oakley Hall
(1958)

Oakley Hall's offbeat western, *Warlock*, could be called a cult author's cult book. Thomas Pynchon, in his introduction to Richard Fariña's *Been Down So Long It Looks Like Up to Me*, notes that while he and Fariña were classmates at Cornell, they came across *Warlock*, a book that Pynchon considered to be one of the best American novels ever written. "We set about getting others to read it too," he says, "and for a while had a micro-cult going. Soon a number of us were talking in *Warlock* dialogue, a kind of thoughtful, stylized, Victorian Wild West diction" (x-xi). When the Edward Dmytryk movie appeared in 1959, the cult grew, and today the film continues to do well in video rentals and rivals the popularity of such film cult classics as *Shane* and *The Searchers*.

As the story opens, the town of Warlock, a territorial mining settlement, is in a virtual state of siege at the hands of a gang of cattle rustlers led by a wanton killer named Abe McQuown. With no means of law enforcement other than a deputy sheriff (currently a man named John Gannon), a Citizens Committee takes over and hires a "peace" officer, Clay Blaisedell, a renowned gunman who has been known to take the law into his own hands when necessary.

The novel's action spans the year during which Blaisedell is Warlock's marshal, a year that begins in fear and desperation and ends in violence and destruction. Blaisedell, fearless and self-righteous, ignites the tragic chain of events that leads to this bitter resolution when he kills John Gannon's younger brother, Billy, in a tragic and pointless showdown. This incident unleashes a succession of treacheries, attempted lynchings, murders, and walks down the main street of Warlock at high noon.

Blaisedell is clearly the monomythical hero cult readers admire—

superior, mysterious, intimidating to both friend and foe. While his enemies are wise enough to fear for their lives, some of those he is out to protect harbor fears of another sort. They wonder if his protection does not come at too high a risk. Although Blaisedell always claims to act on behalf of the concerned citizenry, the fact that he often acts as if he is above the law bothers people who feel that the only way to respect the law is to work within it regardless of the risks involved.

One of the skeptics is John Gannon, the tragic center—and in some ways the tragic hero—of this curious tale. Another doubter is old Judge Holloway who, like the blind prophet Tiresias of classic Greek drama, knows the danger in believing that violation of the law can bring about respect for the law. He sees in this attitude the sort of overweening pride that spelled the downfall of men like Oedipus and Creon. What attracts cult readers about Blaisedell is the fact that his destiny refutes the myth of the tragic flaw, that inherent weakness (e.g., pride) that destroys even the noblest heroes. If there is a tragic flaw, it is not in Blaisedell but in the town of Warlock itself, for once Blaisedell departs, the town dies, as if in punishment for rejecting its savior.

Cult readers read *Warlock* as a parable. The people are being menaced, and they call in a leader to save them. The leader requires more authority than they are willing to grant. The leader does what he can, but his hands are tied. The result is a Pyrrhic victory: the town is saved but at the expense of its own livelihood. The leader is driven out, and the town sinks into oblivion.

Thus, cult readers understand Blaisedell's predicament when he boasts to Judge Holloway that he knows what to do in a situation like this and that he works best by himself. The judge accuses Blaisedell of setting himself above the rest, calls him a one-man lynch mob, and reminds him that to abuse one's authority is to court disaster. Above all, he accuses Blaisedell of the sin of pride, but Blaisedell only scoffs, arguing that a man's pride is the most important thing he has, the one thing that sets him apart from the pack.

Although what the judge says may make sense to the cautious reader, it is not the message that Blaisedell or his admirers want to hear. To them Judge Holloway sounds too much like Ellsworth M. Toohey, the art critic in Ayn Rand's *The Fountainhead,* whose envy of genius is so great that he does everything in his power to destroy it. That what the judge says could be interpreted as envy can be detected in the way he chides Blaisedell for always insisting on being right. You have to be accountable, he tells Blaisedell, to which Blaisedell asks, "To you, you mean, Judge?" People only say they are responsible to someone, he says, when they are afraid to face up to something alone. To him, being accountable to someone is passing the buck. A man who thinks like that is crippled.

To Judge Holloway's accusation that he sets himself above the law, Blaisedell says that under certain circumstances he cannot do otherwise until he has done what he has been hired to do. When the judge argues that Blaisedell will not know when that time comes, Blaisedell replies that others will tell him. And when the judge suggests that maybe they'll be afraid to, Blaisedell insists that he'll know intuitively.

Soothsayers like Judge Holloway know all about leaders who listen only to flatterers or who kill messengers who bring them bad news. A reader who identifies with Blaisedell, however, will prefer the romantic illusion that true leaders (like Howard Roark in *The Fountainhead*) need no outsiders to draw the line for them. The true leader relies only on himself. To do less would be to admit uncertainty, surely a weakness more fatal than pride.

Henry Holmes Goodpasture, a town father whose journal entries are interspersed within the narrative of the novel, writes that he thinks Blaisedell must enjoy his role as angel with a sword or he would not undertake it, but he wonders if Blaisedell can endure to be called devil. The answer is obviously yes. Blaisedell is not a knight in shining armor; he is a rebel angel who is on the side of justice only because he has more to gain from those he protects than from those who threaten them. By defending the citizens of Warlock against McQuown and his gang, Blaisedell has the excuse he needs to rid himself of not just an enemy but a rival.

Goodpasture thinks that it takes a warlock to be marshall of Warlock and that Blaisedell fills the bill, but Blaisedell is not evil in the satanic sense. He is not an allegory of what is bad. His mentality is closer to that of Hesse's Max Demian, who worships Abraxas, the god of both good and evil. In this respect, he symbolizes the hope that the age-old conflict between good and evil can be resolved by incorporating them in one figure. The ideal he represents is of the figure who balances good and evil, who knows how to deal effectively with both so that they do not get confused, the leader who truly can be depended on to take the law into his own hands only in order to serve a higher law.

If Judge Holloway acts as the prophet Tiresias in this western Greek drama, Henry Holmes Goodpasture acts as the chorus, echoing the shifting moods and apprehensions of the townspeople. In one of his journal entries, Goodpasture comments on the way in which the populace has become divided into two camps over Blaisedell: those soberly inclined and those wildly inclined, those responsible and those irresponsible, those peace-loving and those outlaw and riotous by nature. Ultimately, he says, the people are divided into the camps of respect and of fear, and Blaisedell has only emphasized the distance between them. Those who fear themselves and hate their neighbors, fear and hate Blaisedell, he says, while those who respect themselves and their neighbors, respect him.

Tom Morgan, Blaisedell's inseparable partner, plays Iago to Blaisedell's Othello. Morgan connives and conspires, lies and even murders, but unlike Iago's scheme to ruin Othello, his machinations are meant to rescue Blaisedell from his enemies. The result, however, is strangely the same, for in the end they insulate their masters from the world around them and thus precipitate their downfall. Listening to only one voice, regardless of whose side it is on, means riding for a fall. But even here, Blaisedell escapes the fate of men like Julius Caesar or Othello, who fall prey to flatterers and suffer at their hands. In *Warlock*, Tom Morgan goads Blaisedell into shooting him, leaving Blaisedell free to seek out another town to rescue.

If there is anything tragic about Blaisedell it is the impression one gets at the end of the book that there may not be any more towns to rescue. Heroes like Blaisedell are no longer needed in towns that have surrendered to the rule of law, regardless of how inimical to their own survival. And once such men are no longer needed, their breed will disappear. In the debate over whether history makes heroes or heroes make history, Hall favors the view that the times create the climate in which heroes thrive. Provide sufficient challenge, and men will arise to meet that challenge. The irony of the rule of law is that it restricts the enforcer as well as the criminal. Thus, when enforcers exceed the law, they become outlaws, not super-heroes.

Cult readers see Blaisedell as a super-hero and as a dying breed, especially in a democracy where fear of power exceeds fear of crime. To them, a man like Blaisedell would know instinctively where to draw the line, would never abuse his power in any way detrimental to those he was sworn to protect. Their trust in him is exemplified in the casting of Henry Fonda as Blaisedell in the movie version of *Warlock*. Henry Fonda had a reputation as the man no one could dislike. Even when he shot a child in the face at close range in one of his movies, audiences could not hate him. "He must have had a good reason," they thought. Regardless of whatever part he later played, he would always be Tom Joad in *The Grapes of Wrath*, alienated, persecuted, bloody but unbowed, suffering in the name of righteousness—a good guy in a nasty world. If Henry Fonda is Blaisedell, then Blaisedell could do no wrong.

If there is a cartoon quality to all of this, it is a shadow of the same cartoon quality that haunts so much of cult fiction. Unfortunately, westerns have an extra hard time of it because they have long since become parodies of themselves. Thus, it is impossible for a story like *Warlock* not to suffer comparison with others in its genre. Alas, what redeems it for cult readers is precisely what puts mainstream readers off: it takes itself too seriously. But then all cult fiction does, and this is why it inspires such a passionate response. *Warlock*'s has waned, but only because its admirers have gone on to take something else just as seriously.

FOR FURTHER READING

Dmytryk, Edward. "Warlock." *South Dakota Review* (Autumn 1985): 102–11.
Garfield, Brian. "*Warlock* Revisited: The Vanishing Western." *South Dakota Review* (Autumn 1985): 72–101.
Work, James C. "The Violent God in Oakley Hall's Novel *Warlock*." *South Dakota Review* (Autumn 1985): 112–34.

Zen and the Art of Motorcycle Maintenance

Robert M. Pirsig
(1974)

"A lot of people are listening better these days. Particularly the kids. They're really listening . . . and not just *at* you—*to* you . . . to *you*. It makes all the difference" (167). Thus spake Robert Pirsig in *Zen and the Art of Motorcycle Maintenance*, and he was absolutely right. The kids *were* listening, particularly to him, and they made his book the ultimate cult book of the age. In the aftermath of Kent State, as the youth movement was beginning to lose momentum, what it needed was a manifesto, an apologia, a rationale for where it had been, what it stood for, and where it was going—a statement of sufficient caliber to command the respect of the movement's detractors and the acquiescence of its participants.

"The place to improve the world is first in one's own heart and head and hands, and then work outward from there," Pirsig wrote. "Other people can talk about how to expand the destiny of mankind. I just want to talk about how to fix a motorcycle. I think that what I have to say has more lasting value" (291).

Such a sentiment had enormous influence on the young people of the early seventies who felt frustrated by the failure of the activist sixties to effect the changes they so desperately wanted to see in the social and political structures of their day. By itself this statement may sound cloying and banal, echoing, it would seem, the syrupy "power of positive thinking" of the fifties; but such an assessment is a deceptive oversimplification. In context, the statement concludes a hundred pages of closely reasoned philosophical debate and emerges as a valiant, if not quite successful, attempt to resolve the conflict of the divided mind. To Pirsig's way of thinking, this conflict, described variously as the "schism in the soul" (Arnold Toynbee), the "dissociation of sensibility" (T. S.

Eliot), and "the breakdown of the bicameral mind" (Julian Jaynes), and known familiarly as the split between Classic and Romantic, is responsible for the increasing ugliness of so much of modern life. William Butler Yeats sums it up succinctly in "The Second Coming" when he says that the forces of good lack the conviction to do what is best while the forces of evil make headway with passionate intensity.

Pirsig appealed to those who were eager to show the world that you could be "full of passionate intensity" and still be "the best." The "hippies" of the sixties fancied themselves throwbacks to the pure Romanticism of Rousseau and his back-to-nature disciples. Long hair, communal living, naked romps in the forests, folk singing—all were attempts to shake off the cheap veneer of modern life and get back to basics. Pirsig understood this impulse, but he also saw it as restrictive, as only being half alive and thus a source of endless frustration, like trying to dance on one foot only.

His goal in *Zen and the Art of Motorcycle Maintenance*, therefore, was reconciliation. He wanted to reconcile Romanticism and Classicism by awakening Romantics, who thrive on chaos and abandon, to an appreciation of the classical notion of structure and discipline. He wanted both sides to see that Romantic aesthetics and Classical principles share the same coin, each side containing the key to the other. Ultimately, he hoped to reconcile Romanticism and Classicism by proving that both drink from the same fountainhead. He labels this source Quality and takes considerable pains—and most of the book—to define and explain what he means by it.

Put simply (perhaps too simply) Quality is a respect for excellence, and excellence can only be achieved when beauty and function are harmoniously blended. The pursuit of one without the other is doomed to end in failure, meaning ugliness. Ugly art is art that ignores the necessity of structure, and ugly structures are those that ignore the necessity of art. Quality, then, is expressed in the *attitude* that is taken toward a task, and that attitude must reflect harmony between the objective understanding of the task's underlying principles and a subjective appreciation of its surface aesthetics.

Pirsig believes that if conflict over the concept of Quality can split the world into hip and square, Classic and Romantic, technological and humanistic, then resolution of that conflict can unite that world. "A real understanding of Quality doesn't just serve the System," he says, "or even beat it or even escape it. A real understanding of Quality *captures* the System, tames it, and puts it to work for one's own personal use, while leaving one completely free to fulfill his inner destiny" (217).

Quality is neither a part of mind, nor is it a part of matter. Quality is the parent of mind and matter, the event that gives birth to mind and matter. It is a third entity, independent of the two. The world is composed of mind, matter, and Quality, he says. "Blessed Trinity!" (232)

At this point we are getting closer to the book's appeal to cult readers. Squareness is seen as a uniquely intellectual disease, the instant processing of experience through reason instead of letting the moment of apprehension enter our consciousness uninhibited by preconceived notions. By substituting "hip–square" for "Romantic–Classic," Pirsig was making an analogy that was immediately relevant to his readers. He was then able to charm the hip into making concessions to the square by assuring them that the square would make equal concessions in return. The hip doubted this very much and thus were frankly surprised when the book gained a following on both sides of the hip–square split.

There were, in fact, a sizable number of squares who picked up the book prepared to dislike it, only to find themselves turned into cult followers by its sweet reasonableness. As for its appeal to both sides of the schism, it did not hurt the book's reception that its title contained the words "Zen" and "motorcycle," two provocative buzzwords of the day. "Zen" was a word on every hippie's lips at the time, and although few understood its underlying principles, many succumbed to its Oriental appeal, especially those who had become disciples of Hermann Hesse's *Siddhartha*. The "motorcycle" of the title was loaded with what cult readers would have called "heavy" symbolic significance. At one level it was an instrument by which the bourgeois could be further annoyed, for it conjured up visions of gangs of unwashed bikers roaring down quiet suburban streets, tearing up towns, abducting willing daughters, and generally hastening the decline of the American Way of Life.

At a more Romantic level was the image of the motorcycle as liberator, the vehicle that brought one closest to nature and to the feel of the road. Rather than cross the country in an air-conditioned cocoon of glass and steel, true children of nature preferred to let the wind ruffle their hair, the smell of pine needles fill their nostrils, the feel of the roadbed vibrate through their bodies. Of course, readers who came to *Zen and the Art of Motorcycle Maintenance* expecting a lot of groovy paeans to the holiness of the Harley-Davidson were surprised at first at what they found: the motorcycle as teaching tool to demonstrate the necessity of reuniting Classical reason with Romantic emotion. Even greater was the surprise of those who came to complain and stayed to praise, for they found their disdain for motorcycles dissolving in their respect for Pirsig's vast learning and impressive reasoning. The motorcycle as the perfect metaphorical intersection of these divergent attitudes took on such authority that no substitute seemed possible—even though Pirsig admitted that any substitute would do.

The problem, as Pirsig explains it, is in the way one looks at a motorcycle. Either one sees it for what it is or for what it means. He calls this a conflict of *visions of reality*, arguing that the world as we see it right here, right now, is reality regardless of what scientists say it might be, but that the world as revealed by its scientific discoveries is also reality, regardless of how it might appear. Those who ignore either side do so at their peril, he warns. His concern, however, is not so much with the stereotyped whipping boy, the scientist with no sense of aesthetics. He is concerned about the counterculturist who cannot be bothered with underlying principles. Pirsig says that people who think this way are in the "groovy dimension," that they approach mechanical things without really thinking about them. On the surface they care about technology, but since they botch it every time they try to get it to work for them, they have turned against it. They are fine as long as their motorcycle is functioning properly and they can zoom down the highway, but they are devastated if their points burn out.

Unlike the multitude of Romantics who are disturbed about the chaotic changes science and technology force upon the human spirit, Pirsig, with his scientifically trained Classic mind, is able to do more than just wring his hands in dismay or blanketly condemn the whole situation without offering any solution. He identifies the cause of our current social crises as a genetic defect within the nature of reason itself. And until this genetic defect is cleared, he says, the crises will continue. Our current modes of rationality are not moving society forward into a better world. They are taking it further and further from that better world.

Pirsig uses the Renaissance to illustrate what he means. It was a revolutionary period in all respects, yet for the most part few had any inkling of what was going on beneath the turmoil on the surface. Here was a society convinced the Earth was flat with the sun the center of the universe. Columbus's journey, then, becomes a symbol of the boldness that is required to depart from conventional wisdom and bring about a fundamental restructuring of the way we view the world. The only way people could adopt post-Columbian thinking was to abandon the entire medieval outlook and enter into a new expansion of reason. Columbus voyaged into a land about which absolutely nothing was known and all assumptions were dreadful. After Columbus, thinking changed drastically, but it has remained relatively unchanged since, says Pirsig, and thus is not capable of coping with modern crises.

The whole structure of reason that we have inherited, some of it from as long ago as ancient times, is no longer adequate. Pirsig labels it emotionally hollow, aesthetically meaningless, and spiritually empty. This is the sort of sweeping attack on tradition that post-sixties counterculturists welcomed, for they saw it not as the spiteful rejection of the past that had characterized the childish iconoclasm of the sixties.

Instead, Pirsig's attack came with scholarly credentials, and rather than criticizing the past as the history of folly, it simply said that the rules that once had worked were now out of date and had to be changed.

Pirsig argued that existing crises could not be solved by rational means because rationality itself was the source of the problem. However, attempts to solve the problem by abandoning "square" rationality altogether and going by feelings alone also seemed to be going in the wrong direction. The solution Pirsig offered was not to abandon rationality but to expand the nature of rationality so that it was capable of coming up with a solution.

When expansion is needed at the roots, Pirsig argued, it has to cut itself off from ingrained modes of rationality and drift laterally until a new solution presents itself. It is at this point that Pirsig becomes just vague enough to spare his intellectually involved readers the worry of having to get personally involved in anything. Whereas "getting involved" had been a mandate in the sixties, by the middle seventies disillusionment had set in, and the prevailing mood was one of concerned detachment. One could change the world only by changing oneself. The place to improve the world is first in one's own heart and head and hands, and then work outward from there, said Pirsig. Thus, it was about this time that society began to witness the rise of a number of groups and methods guaranteed to put one in touch with oneself: transcendental meditation, est, rolfing, primal scream, and others. Pirsig's emphasis on restructuring one's thinking fit in perfectly with this new mood. His approach sounded a bit like brainstorming and a bit like mind-altering, and enough like both to make it easy to accommodate his ideas to the new sensibility.

The way to solve the conflict between human values and technological needs is not to run away from technology, says Pirsig, but to break down the barriers of dualistic thought that prevent a real understanding of what technology is. This will result not in an exploitation of nature but in a fusion of nature and the human spirit into a new kind of creation that transcends both. When this transcendence occurs, as it has already in such events as the first airplane flight across the ocean or the first footstep on the moon, a kind of public recognition of this transcendent nature of technology occurs. But this transcendence should also occur, albeit in a less dramatic way, at the individual level, on a personal basis, in one's own life.

The message that this novel ultimately transmits to its readers is the contention that Classic understanding should not be overlaid with Romantic prettiness. Rather, Classic and Romantic understanding should be united at a basic level. In the past our common universe of reason has been in the process of escaping, rejecting the romantic, irrational world of prehistoric man. It has been necessary since before the time of Socrates to reject the passions, the emotions, in order to free the rational mind for an understanding of nature's order which was as yet unknown. Now it is time to further an understanding of nature's order by reassimilating those passions that were originally renounced. The passions, the emotions, the affective domain of man's consciousness, are a part of nature's order too, maybe the central part.

"The real [motor]cycle you're working on is a cycle called yourself," says Pirsig. "The machine that appears to be 'out there' and the person that appears to be 'in here' are not two separate things. They grow toward Quality or fall away from Quality altogether" (319).

"You've got to live right too," he says, echoing Johann Wolfgang von Goethe's precept that to be a good writer you must first be a good person. "It's the way you live," says Pirsig, "that predisposes you to avoid the traps and see the right facts" (318).

There is an irony implicit in this philosophy that helps explain Pirsig's own decline into madness [as depicted in the story of Phaedrus in the novel] the first time he tries to deal with the concept of Quality and the problem of reconciling the hip with the square. Quality, like belief in God, requires a leap of faith that is beyond either reason or emotion. Philosophy, regardless of how hard it tries to incorporate feeling, is forced to do it logically, and logic is inimical to spontaneity, which is what it takes to make that fateful leap. Thus, at the end of this disturbing book, there is still the sense of something illusory, of something inconclusive, of something seductive waiting to lure Pirsig and the reader into the snake pit of philosophical inquiry.

St. Augustine says that we are restless hearts because Earth is not our true home. Human unhappiness, he reminds us, is evidence of our immortality. Intuition tells us we are meant for some other city. Pirsig's motorcycle journey is ultimately as frustrating as his philosophical one. Once he reaches California, like Kerouac before him, he can only turn around and head back. And the same is true of his pursuit of the mystery of Quality. When he gets to its core, he knows that the solution he offers is made null and void by its very utterance, and he is left with that restlessness of soul that tells us we are meant for some other city.

FOR FURTHER READING

Burnham, Christopher C. "Heroes Obscured: *Zen and the Art of Motorcycle Maintenance*" *South Dakota Review* (Summer 1986): 151–60.

Ellwood, Robert S. "Conservative and Radical Themes in American Zen: Three Writers." In *Zen in American Life and Letters*, ed. by Robert S. Ellwood. Malibu, CA: Undena Publications, 1987, 147–60.

Harpham, Geoffrey Galt. "Rhetoric and the Madness of Philosophy in Plato and Pirsig." *Contemporary Literature* (Spring 1988): 64–81.

Raymond, Michael W. "Generic Schizophrenia in *Zen and the Art of Motorcycle Maintenance*." *CEA Critic: An Official Journal of the College English Association* (March 1981): 18–25.

Rodino, Richard H. "The Matrix of Journeys in *Zen and the Art of Motorcycle Maintenance*." *Journal of Narrative Technique* (Winter 1981): 53–63.

Shearon, Forrest B. "Visual Imagery and Internal Awareness in Pirsig's *Zen and the Art of Motorcycle Maintenance*." *Kentucky Philological Association Bulletin* (1983): 53–62.

Chronological Listing of Cult Fiction

An asterisk (*) indicates additional classic cult fiction titles not among the top fifty discussed at length in this volume.

Goethe, Johann Wolfgang von. *The Sorrows of Young Werther*. 1774.

*Chateaubriand, François-René de. *Atala*. 1801.

Chateaubriand, François-René de. *René*. 1802.

Shelley, Mary. *Frankenstein, or the Modern Prometheus*. 1818.

*Pater, Walter. *Studies in the History of the Renaissance*. 1873.

Huysmans, Joris-Karl. *Against Nature*. 1884.

*Pater, Walter. *Marius, the Epicurean*. 1885.

Villiers de l'Isle-Adam, Philippe Auguste. *Axel*. 1890.

*Stoker, Bram. *Dracula*. 1897.

Joyce, James. *A Portrait of the Artist as a Young Man*. 1916.

Hesse, Hermann. *Demian*. 1919.

Fitzgerald, F. Scott. *This Side of Paradise*. 1920.

Hesse, Hermann. *Siddhartha*. 1922.

*Gibran, Kahlil. *The Prophet*. 1923.

Fitzgerald, F. Scott. *The Great Gatsby*. 1925.

Hemingway, Ernest. *The Sun Also Rises*. 1926.

*Valle-Inclán, Ramon del. *Tirano Banderas*. 1926.

Hesse, Hermann. *Steppenwolf*. 1927.

Lawrence, D. H. *Lady Chatterley's Lover*. 1928.

Wolfe, Thomas. *Look Homeward, Angel*. 1929.

Huxley, Aldous. *Brave New World*. 1932.
Hilton, James. *Lost Horizon*. 1933.
*Dinesen, Isak. *Out of Africa*. 1937.
*Steinbeck, John. *The Grapes of Wrath*. 1939.
West, Nathanael. *The Day of the Locust*. 1939.
Camus, Albert. *The Stranger*. 1942.
*Wright, Austin Tappan. *Islandia*. 1942.
*Wylie, Philip. *Generation of Vipers*. 1942.
Rand, Ayn. *The Fountainhead*. 1943.
Orwell, George. *Animal Farm*. 1945.
*Burns, John Horne. *The Gallery*. 1947.
Skinner, B. F. *Walden Two*. 1948.
*Bowles, Paul. *The Sheltering Sky*. 1949.
*Orwell, George. *1984*. 1949.
*Jones, James. *From Here to Eternity*. 1951.
Salinger, J. D. *The Catcher in the Rye*. 1951.
Thompson, Jim. *The Killer Inside Me*. 1952.
Amis, Kingsley. *Lucky Jim*. 1954.
Golding, William. *Lord of the Flies*. 1954.
Tolkien, J.R.R. *The Lord of the Rings*. 1954–55.
Wilson, Colin. *The Outsider*. 1956.
Kerouac, Jack. *On the Road*. 1957.
*Seeberg, Peter. *The Impostor*. 1957.
*Connell, Evan S. *Mrs. Bridge*. 1958.
Hall, Oakley. *Warlock*. 1958.
Nabokov, Vladimir. *Lolita*. 1958.
*Southern, Terry, and Mason Hoffenberg. *Candy*. 1958.
*Burroughs, William S. *Naked Lunch*. 1959.
Knowles, John. *A Separate Peace*. 1959.
Miller, Walter M., Jr. *A Canticle for Leibowitz*. 1959.
*Roth, Philip. *Goodbye, Columbus*. 1959.
*Barth, John. *The Sot-weed Factor*. 1960; rev 1967.
*Bataille, George. *Guilty*. 1961.
Heinlein, Robert. *Stranger in a Strange Land*. 1961.
Heller, Joseph. *Catch–22*. 1961.
Burgess, Anthony. *A Clockwork Orange*. 1962.
*Huxley, Aldous. *Island*. 1962.
Kesey, Ken. *One Flew Over the Cuckoo's Nest*. 1962.

*Cortázar, Julio. *Rayuela*. 1963.
Plath, Sylvia. *The Bell Jar*. 1963.
Herbert, Frank. *Dune*. 1965.
*Cortázar, Julio. *Hopscotch*. 1966.
Fariña, Richard. *Been Down So Long It Looks Like Up to Me*. 1966.
Brautigan, Richard. *Trout Fishing in America*. 1967.
Hinton, S. E. *The Outsiders*. 1967.
*Carrier, Roch. *La Guerre, Yes Sir!* 1968.
Castaneda, Carlos. *The Teachings of Don Juan*. 1968.
Clarke, Arthur. *2001: A Space Odyssey*. 1968.
*Wolfe, Tom. *The Electric Kool-Aid Acid Test*. 1968.
*Connell, Evan S. *Mr. Bridge*. 1969.
Vonnegut, Kurt. *Slaughterhouse-Five*. 1969.
*Bach, Richard. *Jonathan Livingston Seagull*. 1970.
Finney, Jack. *Time and Again*. 1970.
*Segal, Eric. *Love Story*. 1970.
*Michener, James. *The Drifters*. 1971.
Robbins, Tom. *Another Roadside Attraction*. 1971.
Thompson, Hunter S. *Fear and Loathing in Las Vegas*. 1971.
*Adams, Richard. *Watership Down*. 1972.
*Goldman, William. *The Princess Bride*. 1973.
*Pynchon, Thomas. *Gravity's Rainbow*. 1973.
Pirsig, Robert M. *Zen and the Art of Motorcycle Maintenance*. 1974.
King, Stephen. *The Stand*. 1978. Expanded edition: 1990.
Adams, Douglas. *The Hitchhiker's Guide to the Galaxy*. 1979.

Works Cited

Adams, Douglas. *The Hitchhiker's Guide to the Galaxy*. New York: Pocket Books, 1981.

Aldiss, Brian. *Frankenstein Unbound*. Greenwich, Conn.: Fawcett Crest, 1973.

Amis, Kingsley. *Lucky Jim*. New York: Penguin, 1976.

Beckson, Karl, ed. *Aesthetes and Decadents*. New York: Vintage, 1966.

Brautigan, Richard. *Trout Fishing in America*. New York: Delacorte, 1979.

Burgess, Anthony. *A Clockwork Orange*. New York: Norton, 1962.

Camus, Albert. *The Stranger*. New York: Vintage, 1954.

Castaneda, Carlos. *The Teachings of Don Juan*. New York: Ballantine, 1969.

Chateaubriand, François-René de. *René*. In *Continental Edition of World Masterpieces*, ed., Mack et al. New York: Norton, 1962 (1336–58).

Clarke, Arthur. *2001: A Space Odyssey*. New York: NAL, 1968.

Fariña, Richard. *Been Down So Long It Looks Like Up to Me*. New York: Penguin, 1983.

Finney, Jack. *Time and Again*. New York: Simon & Schuster. 1970.

Fitzgerald, F. Scott. *The Great Gatsby*. New York: Scribner's, 1925.

———. *This Side of Paradise*. New York: Scribner's, 1960.

Goethe, Johann Wolfgang von. *The Sorrows of Young Werther*. New York: Vintage, 1973.

Golding, William. *Lord of the Flies*. New York: Coward-McCann, 1962.

Hall, Oakley. *Warlock*. New York: Bantam, 1988.

Heinlein, Robert. *Stranger in a Strange Land*. New York: Berkley, 1968.

Heller, Joseph. *Catch–22*. New York: Simon & Schuster, 1961.

Hemingway, Ernest. *The Sun Also Rises*. New York: Scribner's, 1920.

Herbert, Frank. *Dune*. New York: Ace, 1990.

Hesse, Hermann. *Briefe*. Frankfurt: Suhrkamp Verlag, 1965.

———. *Demian*. New York: Bantam, 1965.

———. *Siddhartha*. New York: New Directions, 1951.

———. *Steppenwolf*. New York: Modern Library, 1963.

Hilton, James. *Lost Horizon*. New York: Pocket Books, 1939.
Hinton, S. E. *The Outsiders*. New York: Dell, 1967.
Huxley, Aldous. *Brave New World*. New York: Harper & Row, 1946.
Huysmans, Joris-Karl. *Against Nature*. Tr. Robert Baldick. New York: Penguin, 1959.
Johnson, Paul. *Intellectuals*. New York: Harper & Row, 1988.
Joyce, James. *A Portrait of the Artist as a Young Man*. New York: Viking, 1964.
Kerouac, Jack. *On the Road*. New York: NAL, 1959.
Kesey, Ken. *One Flew Over the Cuckoo's Nest*. New York: Viking, 1971.
King, Stephen. *The Stand*. New York: Doubleday, 1990.
Knowles, John. *A Separate Peace*. New York: Macmillan, 1959.
Lawrence, D. H. *Lady Chatterley's Lover*. New York: Caedmon, 1959.
Miller, Walter M., Jr. *A Canticle for Leibowitz*. New York: Harper & Row, 1986.
Muggeridge, Malcolm. *Jesus: The Man Who Lives*. New York: Harper & Row, 1975.
Nabokov, Vladimir. *Lolita*. New York: Berkley, 1977.
Orwell, George. *Animal Farm*. New York: NAL, 1986.
Otten, Anna, ed. *Hesse Companion*. Albuquerque: University of New Mexico Press, 1977.
Pirsig, Robert M. *Zen and the Art of Motorcycle Maintenance*. New York: Bantam, 1975.
Plath, Sylvia. *The Bell Jar*. New York: Harper & Row, 1971.
Rand, Ayn. *The Fountainhead*. New York: Bobbs-Merrill, 1943.
Robbins, Tom. *Another Roadside Attraction*. New York: Ballantine, 1989.
Salinger, J. D. *The Catcher in the Rye*. New York: Signet, 1953.
Schorer, Mark. *D. H. Lawrence*. New York: Dell, 1968.
Shelley, Mary. *Frankenstein, or the Modern Prometheus*. New York: Bantam, 1967.
Skillion, Anne, ed. *Introducing the Great American Novel*. New York: Stonesong, 1988.
Skinner, B. F. *Walden Two*. New York: Macmillan, 1976.
Stone, Robert. Introduction to *The Day of the Locust*. New York: Random, 1989.
Theroux, Paul. *My Secret History*. New York: Putnam's, 1989.
Thompson, Hunter S. *Fear and Loathing in Las Vegas*. New York: Warner, 1982.
Thompson, Jim. *After Dark, My Sweet*. Berkeley, Calif.: Creative Arts, 1986.
———. *The Killer Inside Me*. New York: Quill, 1983.
Tolkien, J.R.R. *The Lord of the Rings*. Ballantine, 1986–88.
Villiers de l'Isle-Adam, Philippe Auguste. *Axel*. Englewood Cliffs, N.J.: Prentice-Hall. 1970.
Vonnegut, Kurt, Jr. *Slaughterhouse-Five*. New York: Delta, 1969.
West, Nathanael. *The Day of the Locust*. New York: Random House, 1939.
Wilde, Oscar. *The Picture of Dorian Gray*. New York: Penguin, 1985.
Wilson, Colin. *The Outsider*. Los Angeles: Jeremy P. Tarcher, 1982.
Wilson, Edmund. *Axel's Castle*. New York: Scribner's, 1931.
Wolfe, Thomas. *Look Homeward, Angel*. New York: Macmillan, 1982.

Bibliography of Primary Works: First and Current Editions

Current editions appear in brackets.

Adams, Douglas. *The Hitchhiker's Guide to the Galaxy*. New York: Crown, 1979. [Pocket Books, 1990]

Amis, Kingsley. *Lucky Jim*. New York: Doubleday, 1954. [Penguin, 1976]

Brautigan, Richard. *Trout Fishing in America*. New York: Dell, 1967. [Delacorte, 1979]

Burgess, Anthony. *A Clockwork Orange*. New York: Norton, 1962. [Ballantine, 1988]

Camus, Albert. *The Stranger*. Paris: 1942; New York: Knopf, 1946. [Random House, 1989]

Castaneda, Carlos. *The Teachings of Don Juan*. Berkley: University of California Press, 1968. [still in print]

Chateaubriand, François-René de. *René*. Paris: 1802. [University of California Press, 1952]

Clarke, Arthur. *2001: A Space Odyssey*. New York: NAL, 1968. [NAL, 1986]

Fariña, Richard. *Been Down So Long It Looks Like Up to Me*. New York: Random House, 1966. [Penguin, 1983]

Finney, Jack. *Time and Again*. New York: Simon & Schuster, 1970. [Simon & Schuster, 1980]

Fitzgerald, F. Scott. *The Great Gatsby*. New York: Scribner's, 1925. [Macmillan, 1981]

Fitzgerald, F. Scott. *This Side of Paradise*. New York: Scribner's, 1920. [Macmillan, 1988]

Goethe, Johann Wolfgang von. *The Sorrows of Young Werther*. Frankfurt-am-Main: 1774. [Penguin, 1989]

Golding, William. *Lord of the Flies*. London: Faber, 1954. [Putnam, 1964]

Hall, Oakley. *Warlock*. New York: Viking, 1958. [Bantam, 1988]

Heinlein, Robert. *Stranger in a Strange Land*. New York: Putnam, 1961. [Berkley, 1968]

Heller, Joseph. *Catch-22*. New York: Simon & Schuster, 1961. [Dell, 1985]

Hemingway, Ernest. *The Sun Also Rises*. New York: Scribner's, 1926. [Macmillan, 1987]

Herbert, Frank. *Dune*. New York: Chilton, 1965. [Ace, 1990]

Hesse, Hermann. *Demian*. Frankfurt-am-Main: S. Fischer Verlag, 1919. [Harper & Row, 1990]

———. *Siddhartha*. Berlin: Suhrkamp, 1922. [Bantam, 1982]

———. *Steppenwolf*. Berlin: Suhrkamp, 1927. [Holt, 1990]

Hilton, James. *Lost Horizon*. New York: Morrow, 1933. [Pocket Books, 1981]

Hinton, S. E. *The Outsiders*. New York: Viking, 1967. [New York: Dell, 1968]

Huxley, Aldous. *Brave New World*. London: Chatto & Windus, 1932. [Harper & Row, 1989]

Huysmans, Joris-Karl. *Against Nature*. Paris: 1884. [Penguin, 1959]

Joyce, James. *A Portrait of the Artist as a Young Man*. New York: Huebsch. 1916. [Penguin, 1964]

Kerouac, Jack. *On the Road*. New York: Viking, 1957. [Penguin, 1976]

Kesey, Ken. *One Flew Over the Cuckoo's Nest*. New York: Viking, 1962. [Penguin, 1977]

King, Stephen. *The Stand*. New York: Doubleday, 1978. Complete edition, 1990. [in print]

Knowles, John. *A Separate Peace*. New York: Macmillan, 1959. [Bantam, 1985]

Lawrence, D. H. *Lady Chatterley's Lover*. Florence: 1928. [Grove-Weidenfeld, 1987]

Miller, Walter M., Jr. *A Canticle for Leibowitz*. New York: Lippincott. 1959. [Harper & Row, 1986]

Nabokov, Vladimir. *Lolita*. New York: Putnam, 1958. [Random House, 1989]

Orwell, George. *Animal Farm*. New York: Harcourt Brace, 1945. [NAL, 1986]

Pirsig, Robert M. *Zen and the Art of Motorcycle Maintenance*. New York: Morrow, 1974. [Bantam, 1984]

Plath, Sylvia. *The Bell Jar*. London: 1963, under the name of Victoria Lucas; New York: Harper & Row, 1971, under the name of Sylvia Plath. [Bantam, 1983]

Rand, Ayn. *The Fountainhead*. New York: Bobbs-Merrill, 1943. [NAL, 1952]

Robbins, Tom. *Another Roadside Attraction*. New York: Doubleday, 1971. [Bantam, 1990]

Salinger, J. D. *The Catcher in the Rye*. Boston: Little, Brown, 1951. [Bantam, 1984]

Shelley, Mary. *Frankenstein, or the Modern Prometheus*. London: 1818. [University of Chicago Press, 1982]

Skinner, B. F. *Walden Two*. New York: Macmillan, 1948. [Macmillan, 1976]

Thompson, Hunter S. *Fear and Loathing in Las Vegas*. (First appeared in *Rolling Stone* magazine, issue 95, November 11, 1971, and 96, November 25, 1971, under the name of "Raoul Duke.") [Vintage, 1989]

Thompson, Jim. *The Killer Inside Me*. New York: Morrow, 1952. [Morrow, 1984]

Tolkien, J.R.R. *The Lord of the Rings*. 3 vols. London: G. Allen and Unwin, 1954–55. [Ballantine, 1986–88]

Villiers de l'Isle-Adam, Philippe Auguste. *Axel*. Paris: 1890. [Dufour, 1986]

Vonnegut, Kurt, Jr. *Slaughterhouse-Five*. New York: Seymour Lawrence/Delacorte, 1969. [Dell, 1978]

West, Nathanael. *The Day of the Locust*. New York: Random House, 1939. [NAL, 1983]

Wilson, Colin. *The Outsider*. London: Victor Gollanz, 1956. [Jeremy P. Tarcher, 1982]

Wolfe, Thomas. *Look Homeward, Angel*. New York: Scribner's, 1929. [Macmillan, 1982]

Books for Further Reading

Elson, Ruth Miller. *Myths and Mores in American Best Sellers, 1865–1965*. New York: Garland, 1985. A fascinating look at the enduring myths and shifting moral imperatives that underlay fiction popular from the end of the Civil War to the early days of the Vietnam conflict. This analysis of the phenomenon of the bestseller reveals those shifts in tastes and values that not only realign public opinion but also help explain its often surprising consensus.

Fiedler, Leslie A. *What Was Literature? Class Culture and Mass Society*. New York: Simon and Schuster, 1982. A predictably provocative look at the literature people really buy and really like and what their choices say about them, about society, about culture, and ultimately about literature itself.

Gitlin, Todd. *The Sixties: Years of Hope, Days of Rage*. New York: Bantam, 1987. In addition to a bracing mix of history, sociology, and behavioral science, this exciting book is a compelling overview of the whole cultural scene of the sixties, including the relevant literature. Written with energy and originality, it comes as close as anything to capturing the rogue spirit of that watershed decade.

Hinckley, Karen. *American Best Sellers: a Reader's Guide to Popular Fiction*. Bloomington: Indiana University Press, 1989. Less an explanation than an illumination of the world of the bestseller, this thorough addition to the growing scholarship of popular culture offers fresh insight into the tension between popular taste and popular prejudice.

Inge, M. Thomas, ed. *Handbook of American Popular Literature*. New York: Greenwood Press, 1988. A thorough and highly informative companion to works that owe their success more to the public than to the critics. Here, works that define the predilections of a society and the preoccupations of a culture finally get the serious treatment they deserve.

Marcus, Greil. *Lipstick Traces: A Secret History of the 20th Century.* Cambridge, Mass.: Harvard University Press, 1989. A bizarre but compelling view of modern times as seen through the prism of the Sex Pistols, the short-lived punk group that left "invisible traces" on society, those imperceptible influences that both underpin and undercut the prevailing attitudes and behavior of an entire culture. This is a literate, informed, and highly readable book that stubbornly refuses to pander to any reader's expectations.

Pringle, David. *Science Fiction: the 100 Best Novels.* New York: Carroll & Graf, 1985. A subjective but defensible list of the best of the genre that includes a few surprises among the predictable sci-fi chestnuts.

Skillion, Anne. *Introducing the Great American Novel.* Introduction by George Plimpton. New York: Stonesong Press, 1988. A unique collection of stimulating introductions by outstanding critics and writers, many of whom belong among the "greats" themselves. Unstuffy and eclectic.

Smith, Curtis C., ed. *Twentieth Century Science-Fiction Writers.* New York: St. Martin's, 1981. A comprehensive but generally uncritical survey of just about every sci-fi writer in the business. Uneven because of multiple authorship but balanced by thorough biographical and bibliographical material.

Tanner, Tony. *City of Words: American Fiction, 1950–1970.* New York: Harper & Row, 1971. A definitive study by an astute critic of the books that appealed to the young readers of the post–WW II generation. Many of these books achieved cult status, and Tanner is quick to recognize and account for much of their immediate, if often transient, appeal.

Index

About the Author

THOMAS REED WHISSEN is Professor of English at Wright State University. Among his academic interests are the topics of decadence in literature, cult literature, and writing and editing. His most recent books reflect these interests, including *A Way with Words* and *The Devil's Advocates: Decadence in Modern Literature* (Greenwood Press, 1989). His own "way with words" has led him into fiction, poetry, and lyrics as well as scholarship, and he is presently developing a study tentatively titled "Wretched Writing and Why It Works."